This
for J
alise

Ag
viola
Enro
tion
in w
trans
bility
(here
relati
to ac
most
most
the ab
most
regiona
ing requ

Global Governance and the Quest for Justice

Volume I: International and Regional Organisations
Edited by Douglas Lewis

Volume II: Corporate Governance
Edited by Sorcha Macleod

Volume III: Civil Society
Edited by Peter Odell and Chris Willett

Volume IV: Human Rights
Edited by Roger Brownsword

Global Governance and the Quest for Justice

Volume II: Corporate Governance

Edited by

SORCHA MACLEOD

·HART·
PUBLISHING

OXFORD AND PORTLAND, OREGON
2006

Published in North America (US and Canada) by
Hart Publishing
c/o International Specialized Book Services
920 NE 58th Avenue, Suite 300
Portland, OR 97213-3786
USA
Tel: +1 503 287 3093 or toll-free: (1) 800 944 6190
Fax: +1 503 280 8832
E-mail: orders@isbs.com
Website: www.isbs.com

Hart Publishing, 16C Worcester Place, Oxford, OX1 2JW
Telephone: +44 (0)1865 517530 Fax: +44 (0) 1865 510710
E-mail: mail@hartpub.co.uk
Website: http://www.hartpub.co.uk

British Library Cataloguing in Publication Data
Data Available

ISBN-13: 978-1-84113-406-2 (paperback)
ISBN-10: 1-84113-406-6 (paperback)

Typeset by Compuscript Ltd, Shannon
Printed and bound in Great Britain by
Biddles Ltd, King's Lynn, Norfolk

Tribute to John Parkinson

PROFESSOR JOHN PARKINSON

John Parkinson's untimely death in February 2004 was a great loss to the world of academia and to those who knew him. A practitioner at city firm Freshfields in his early career, John moved to Bristol University as a lecturer in law in 1980 and was appointed to a Chair in 1995. More recently, he was appointed as the chair of the government's Company Law Review, a measure of the esteem in which he was held. His contribution to the field of company law is undisputed, in particular, his text *Corporate Power and Responsibility* laid the foundations for a stakeholder approach to corporate governance. As Professor Keith Stanton put it, '[t]his put his work at the centre of the ongoing debate on corporate social responsibility and governance.' As such, it made John the ideal person to approach to assist with organising the corporate governance stream at the conference on Global Governance and the Search for Justice held at the University of Sheffield in April 2003. He brought an infectious enthusiasm to the endeavour and he admitted to me that he was very much looking forward to editing the resultant book as it was something he had never attempted before. Everyone who came into contact with him via the conference enjoyed his *quiet joi de vivre* as well as appreciating his insightful comments regarding corporate governance. As his co-editor I valued his help and his constructive criticism despite some fundamental theoretical disagreements! Many of the contributors also received substantial supportive advice and there is no doubt that the volume is better for it. It has been a difficult task to complete this book in John's absence and I hope that he would have been pleased with the result. His dry sense of humour, generosity of spirit and not least his intellectual contribution is sorely missed.

Sorcha MacLeod
Sheffield, January 2006

Preface

Law, as Lon Fuller famously remarked, orders social life by 'subjecting human conduct to the governance of rules';[1] but, as he also remarked, law is not just about *order*, it is about the establishment of a *just* order.[2] Law, formal as well as informal, hard or soft, high or low, purports to set (just) standards and to provide the framework for the (fair) resolution of disputes. Legal rules, of course, are not the only mechanisms for channeling behaviour—market prices, for example, may be as prohibitive as the rules of the criminal code—but it is a truism that it is society's need for effective and legitimate governance that offers the raison d'etre for law.

Fifty years ago, the legal imagination centred on governance within and by the nation state. The municipal legal system was the paradigm; its architecture (especially its division of the public from the private) clean-lined; its organization hierarchical; its modus operandi (even if Austin had over-stated the coercive character of law) largely one of command and control; and its authority unquestioned.[3] Beyond the boundaries of local legal systems, the first seeds of regional and globl governance had been sown but it was to be some time before they would begin to flower. If anyone ruled the world, it was the governments of nation states.

Fifty years on, the landscape of legal governance looks very different. To be sure, the municipal legal system remains an important landmark. However, governance within the nation state no longer respects a simple division of the public and the private; in many cases, hierarchical organization has given way to more complex regulatory networks; each particular regulatory space is characterised by its own distinctive regime of governance and stakeholding; command and control is no longer viewed as the principal regulatory response; and, confronted with various crises of legitimacy, nation states have sought to retain public confidence by aspiring to more responsive forms of governance.[4]

---

[1] Lon L Fuller, *The Morality of* law (New Haven: Yale University press, 1969) at 96.
[2] Lon L Fuller, 'Positivism and Fidelity to Law—A Reply to Professor Hart (1957–58) 71 *Harvard Law Review* 630.
[3] Cf HLA Hart, *The Concept of Law* (Oxford: Clarendon Press, 1961).
[4] See, eg, Juila Black, 'De-centring Regulation: Understanding the Role of Regulation and Self-Regulation in a 'Post-Regulatory' word' (2001) 54 *Current legal Problems* 103; Norman Douglas Lewis, *Choice and the Legal Order: Rising Above Politics* (London: Butterworths, 1996); Philippe

At the same time that local governance has grown more complex and difficult to map, the world beyond the nation state has moved on. Not only has regional governance developed rapidly (in Europe, to the point at which a Constitution for the enlarged Union is under debate), but manifold international agencies whose brief is global governance are now operating to regulate fields that are, in some cases, narrow and specialised but, in other cases, broad and general. If mapping municipal law has become more challenging, this applies *a fortiori* to governance at the regional or global level where the regulatory players and processes may be considerably less transparent. Moreover, these zones of governance—the local, the regional, and the global—do not operate independently of one another. Accordingly, any account of governance in the Twenty-First Century must be in some sense an account of global governance because the activities of global regulators impinge on the activities of those who purport to govern in both local and regional zones.

To a considerable extent, global governance has grown alongside the activities of organisations whose predominant concerns have been international security and the promotion of respect for human rights. However, it has been the push towards a globalised economy that has perhaps exerted the greater influence—that is to say, 'globalisation' has served to accelerate both the actuality, and our perception, of global governance. With the lowering of barriers to trade and the making of new markets (traditional as well as electronic), the processes of integration and harmonisation have been set in motion and the governance activities of bodies such as the IMF, the World Bank and the WTO have assumed a much higher profile.[5] If nation states still rule the world, their grip on the reins of governance seems much less secure.[6]

Against this background, *Global Governance and the Quest for Justice* is a four-volume set addressing the legal and ethical deficits associated with the current round of 'globalisation' and discussing the building blocks for modes of global governance that respect the demands of legality and justice. To put this another way, this set explores the tension between the order that is being instated by the governance that comes with globalisation (the

Nonet and Philip Selznick, *Law and Society in Transition: Toward Responsive Law* (New York: Harper & Row, 1978); and Gunther Teubner, 'Substantive and Reflexive Elements in Modern Law' (1983) 17 *Law and Society Review* 239, and 'After Legal Instrumentalism? Strategic Models of Post-Regulatory Law' in Gunther Teubner (ed), *Dilemmas of law in the welfare state* (Berlin: Walter de Gruyter, 1986) 299.

[5] See eg, Joseph Stiglitz, *Globalization and its Discontents* (London: Penguin, Allen Lane, 2002). For an account that is less focused on the economy, see Boaventura de Sousa Santos, *Toward a New Legal Common Sense* (2nd ed) (London: Butterworths, 2002).

[6] Compare the analysis in Brendan Edgeworth, *Law, Modernity, Postmodernity* (Aldershot: Ashgte, 2003). According to Edgeworth, governance in the 'postmodernized' environment is characterised by the decline of the monocentric national legal system.

reality, as it were, of globalised governance) and the aspiration of a just world order represented by the ideal of global governance.[7]

Each volume focuses on one of four key concerns arising from globalised governance, namely: whether the leading internationl and regional organisations are sufficiently constitutionalised, [8] whether transnational corporations are sufficiently accountable,[9] whether the distinctive interests of civil society are sufficiently represented and respected[10] and whether human rights are given due weight and protection.[11] If the pathology of globalised governance involves a lack of institutional transparency and accountability, the ability of the more powerful players to act outside the rules and to immunise themselves against responsibility, a yawning democratic deficit, and a neglect of human rights, environmental integrity and cultural identity, then this might be a new world order but it falls a long way short of the ideal of global governance.

In the opening years of the Twenty-First Century, the prospects for legitimate and effective governance—that is to say, for lawful governance—are not overwhelmingly good. Local governance, even in the best-run regimes, has its own problems with regard to the effectiveness and legitimacy of its regulatory measure; regionalisation does not always ease these difficulties; and globalised governance accentuates the contrast between the power of those who are unaccountable and the relative powerlessness of those who are accountable. Yet, in every sense, global governance surely is *the* project for the coming generation of lawyers.[12] If the papers in these volumes set in train a sustained, focused and forward-looking debate about the co-ordination of governance in pursuit of our best conception of an ordered and just global community, then they will have served their purpose—and, if law plays its part in setting the framework for the elaboration and application of such global governance, then its purpose, too, will have been fulfilled.

Roger Brownsword and Douglas Lewis
Sheffield, February 2004

---

[7] Compare the central themes of George Monbiot, *The Age of Consent* (London: Flamingo, 2003).

[8] Douglas Lewis (ed), *International and Regional Organisations*.

[9] Sorcha Macleod and John Parkinson (eds), *Corporate Governance*.

[10] Peter Odell and Chris Willett (eds), *Civil Society*.

[11] Roger Brownsword (ed), *Human Rigihts*.

[12] Cf Douglas Lewis, 'Law and Globalisation: An Opportunity for Europe and its Partners and Their Legal Scholars (2002) 8 *European Public Law 219*.

Contents

List of Contributors

Gavin Anderson is Senior Lecturer in the School of Law, University of Glasgow.

Jane Ball is a solicitor and lecturer in Law at the University of Sheffield.

Patrick Birkinshaw is a Professor of Law at the University of Hull and a barrister. He is Director of the Institute of European Public Law.

Clare Campbell teaches and researches in Company Law and Corporate Insolvency Law as well as European Community Law at the University of Sheffield.

David Campbell is Head of the Department of Law, Durham University, UK.

Professor Janet Dine is Director, Centre for Commercial Law Studies, Queen Mary College, London University.

Juanita Elias is a Lecturer in International Politics at the University of Adelaide.

Nicholas HD Foster is a Lecturer in Commercial Law at the School of Oriental and African Studies, University of London.

Carola Glinski is a lawyer and Research Fellow at the Centre for European Environmental Law, University of Bremen, Germany.

Stephen Griffin is a Professor of Law at the University of Wolverhampton.

Robert Lee is Co-Director of the ESRC Centre on Business Relationships, Accountability, Sustainability and Society (BRASS).

Yiannis Sakkas is undertaking doctoral research in International Corporate Insolvency Law, supervised by Clare Campbell

Rory Sullivan is Head of Investor Responsibility at Insight Investment.

Charlotte Villiers is a Professor of Company Law at the University of Bristol.

Aurora Voiculescu is Lecturer in Law at Open University and an Associate Research Fellow at the Centre for Socio-Legal Studies, Oxford University.

1

Corporate Governance and the Regulation of Business Behaviour

JOHN PARKINSON

INTRODUCTION

T HE TERM 'CORPORATE governance' has a range of meanings. For present purposes two stand out. The first refers to the various ways in which society attempts to control company behaviour in the public interest.[1] Here what is being 'governed' is the company itself, the most obvious modality being regulation by the state 'external' to the company, for example, the requirements of employment law, consumer law, or environmental law. The second meaning is the one more familiar to company lawyers, of 'company-level' governance: in the words of the Higgs review, the 'architecture of accountability' or 'structures and processes' that ensure that those responsible for managing companies do so in accordance with the legitimate objectives of the business.[2] Directors' duties, boards that contain members with a 'monitoring' role, and disclosure of financial and other information are examples of mechanisms of governance so understood. While some would argue otherwise,[3] corporate governance in the second sense can be regarded as a sub-set of governance in the first. That is, company-level controls reflect at least in part a state determination of what corporate objectives should be and of corresponding accountability arrangements. In the Anglo-American corporate world the purpose of such controls is generally viewed as being to enforce a goal of shareholder wealth

---

[1] See, eg A Demb and F-F Neubauer, The Corporate Board: Confronting the Paradoxes (New York, Oxford University Press, 1992) 2-4; ND Lewis, Law and Governance (London, Cavendish, 2001) 172.

[2] See D Higgs, Review of the Role and Effectiveness of Non-Executive Directors (London, DTI, 2003) 11.

[3] Eg, exponents of the nexus of contracts theory of the company, who emphasise the 'private', contractual origins of governance arrangements. For a critical overview, see WW Bratton, 'The Economic Structure of the Post-Contractual Corporation' (1992) 87 Northwestern University Law Review 180.

maximisation, justified as the best means of maximising the wealth of society as a whole.[4] The aims of governance need not, however, be so narrowly defined. It is with using company-level governance (from now on, just 'corporate governance') for the wider purpose of influencing the social and environmental performance of companies that this chapter is concerned.

While policy makers normally look to 'external' regulation as the means of controlling the social and environmental impacts of business, corporate governance is important as well, for two reasons. First, governance arrangements are likely to affect a company's propensity to comply with regulation. Companies are complex organisations and internal accountability structures that can cope with this complexity are needed to secure conformity with law down the lines of command.[5] At a more general level, the *commitment* to compliance is likely to be affected by the incentives that governance frameworks create. Where, for instance, the culture of the organisation is 'short-termist' because of pressures or inducements to maximise current share price, obeying the law may not be regarded as an issue of overriding importance.[6] The second reason for a concern with governance is the well-known limitations of regulation as a means of prescribing socially desired outcomes. These limitations result in part from problems inherent in the use of general rules.[7] For example, regulation has a tendency to be under- (or over-) inclusive, to set only base-line standards when many companies without undue cost could perform to a higher level, and to offer few incentives for continuous improvement. Of particular relevance to this volume's theme of globalisation, there may also be gaps in regulatory coverage. The standards imposed on multinationals by host jurisdictions are often non-existent or inadequate, and there is an absence of binding norms of international law to compensate.[8]

---

[4] See M Jensen, 'Value Maximization, Stakeholder Theory, and the Corporate Objective Function' (2001) 14 *Journal of Applied Corporate Finance* 8.

[5] See generally, F Haines, *Corporate Regulation: Beyond 'Punish or Persuade'* (Oxford, Clarendon Press, 1997); C Parker, *The Open Corporation: Effective Self-Regulation and Democracy* (Cambridge, Cambridge University Press, 2002).

[6] See S Wilks, 'Regulatory Compliance and Capitalist Diversity in Europe' (1996) 3 *Journal of European Public Policy* 536, contrasting the amenability to regulation of the 'social democratic' European company with the Anglo-American-type company.

[7] See CD Stone, *Where The Law Ends: The Social Control of Corporate Behaviour* (New York, Harper & Row, 1975) ch 18; I Ayres and J Braithwaite, *Responsive Regulation: Transcending the Deregulation Debate* (New York, Oxford University Press, 1992) 110–16; J Black, *Rules and Regulators* (Oxford, Clarendon Press, 1997) ch 1. Alternative regulatory techniques, such as fiscal or economic instruments may overcome some of the problems of 'command and control' regulation, but also have problems of their own. See N Gunningham and P Grabosky, *Smart Regulation: Designing Environmental Policy* (Oxford, Oxford University Press, 1998) 69–83; E Orts, 'Reflexive Environmental Law' (1995) 89 *Northwestern University Law Review* 1227, 1241–46.

[8] See generally, International Council on Human Rights Policy, *Beyond Voluntarism: Human Rights and the Developing International Legal Obligations of Companies* (Versoix, 2002). See also Sullivan in this volume.

The main emphasis of this chapter will be on how corporate governance might be used to overcome some of the limitations of external regulation, by making it an explicit function of governance to encourage 'socially responsible' conduct that includes going beyond what regulation demands. Such an approach might, but does not necessarily, involve departing from the principle of shareholder primacy, on which UK company law has hitherto been based. As far as corporate social responsibility (CSR) that is consistent with the traditional management goal of shareholder wealth maximisation is concerned, there are two types of reason why adopting higher standards of social or environmental performance might also be in the interests of shareholders, or at least not detrimental to them. First, higher standards may bring direct commercial benefits, for example,, where they result in reduced energy costs or better employee relations. Secondly, companies need to be responsive to market and civil society pressures for improved performance, exerted by groups such as consumers, employees, NGOs, and the media, since how the company reacts to these pressures and manages the related risks and opportunities can have significant financial implications.[9] These considerations suggest an approach to corporate governance reform that aims to ensure that companies take full advantage of those situations in which there is a natural convergence of business and societal interests, and also to secure a better alignment of company behaviour with market and civil society pressures.

While reforms with the objective of promoting CSR in this limited sense are likely to be an advance on governance arrangements that encourage a narrow preoccupation with 'shareholder value,' not all problems will be overcome: conflicts between the (long-, as well as short-term) interests of shareholders on the one hand, and those of other groups and the demands of ethical principle and social policy objectives on the other, will undoubtedly remain. Overlaps between public and private interests and the harmonising effect of market and civil society pressures take us only so far. The belief that these conflicts should not always be resolved in favour of shareholders, but rather in accordance with some conception of the requirements of the pubic interest, prompts a more radical approach to CSR and a search for appropriate governance mechanisms to institutionalise it.

Although this wider version of CSR involves a departure from shareholder primacy, it is useful for analytical purposes to distinguish it from 'stakeholder' approaches to the company. While stakeholder models also have that characteristic, they tend to have different focal concerns. CSR, in both the versions identified here, can be seen as an essentially regulatory concept,

---

[9] These processes, which serve to harmonise corporate and societal interests, might also be strengthened by various forms of 'soft' governmental intervention, separate from corporate governance reform. They include the creation of product labelling schemes or the brokering or endorsement of voluntary codes of standards.

as about the acceptance or imposition of constraints on the pursuit of the profit goal in the wider public interest. Stakeholder models involve replacing that goal with a more open-ended one of balancing the interests of a (defined) set of stakeholder groups.[10] A variety of arguments are relied on in support of stakeholder approaches, for example, that they may be more conducive to economic efficiency or enable effect to be given to the moral imperative of employee participation in enterprise decision-making.[11] While regulatory and stakeholder positions are not always easy to distinguish, it is with CSR as a form of regulation that this chapter is concerned.

The chapter proceeds as follows. The next section will look in more detail at the first version of CSR identified above ('modest CSR'). The following section will then examine some of the ways in which corporate governance arrangements are being, and might be, modified in the UK to give greater effect to it. Bearing in mind the limitations of modest CSR, the final section will consider the feasibility of governance reforms aimed at implementing an approach that goes further and envisages that shareholder interests should be overridden where some interpretation of ethical principle or the public interest demands it ('radical CSR').

MODEST CSR

A brief discussion of the European Commission's definition of CSR in its recent *Communication* is a useful way of clarifying how the term 'modest CSR' will be used in this chapter and the reasons for attempting to promote it. It says CSR is 'a concept whereby companies integrate social and environmental concerns in their business operations and in their interaction with stakeholders on a voluntary basis.' It is 'behaviour by businesses over and above legal requirements, voluntarily adopted because businesses deem it to be in their long-term interest.'[12] A number of elements in this definition warrant examination.

---

[10] An analogy with the conduct of an individual might make this distinction clearer. A person otherwise committed to pursuing self-interest might decide that it is wrong to tell lies in the course of so doing. The norm requiring truth-telling acts as a constraint on the pursuit of self-interest; its adoption does not signify a transformation of the individual's goal to one of a selfless concern for others. Similarly CSR, even when it consciously involves accepting lower profits, does not, as discussed here, involve a transformation of the purpose of the organisation. As used in the text, 'CSR' is also not intended to embrace 'philanthropic' activity, in the sense of a company's efforts to address social problems that are not of its own making, as distinct from conducting its core activities in a more responsible manner.

[11] On the former, see eg G Kelly and J Parkinson, 'The Conceptual Foundations of the Company: A Pluralist Approach' in J Parkinson, A Gamble and G Kelly (eds), *The Political Economy of the Company* (Oxford, Hart Publishing, 2000) 113, and the latter, R Archer, *Economic Democracy: The Politics of Feasible Socialism* (Oxford, Clarendon Press, 1995).

[12] Commission of the European Communities, *Communication from the Commission concerning Corporate Social Responsibility: A Business Contribution to Sustainable Development* COM (2002) 347 final.

First, while the idea of acting 'over and above legal requirements' has long been a concern of company law scholars in the literature on CSR, the tendency has been to regard achieving mere compliance with law as unproblematic, or at best an issue in the study of regulation rather than corporate law. For their part, regulatory theorists have not always paid much attention to the characteristics of the targets of regulation, as distinct from the regulatory framework within which they are required to operate.[13] Such an approach puts too heavy an emphasis on the design of regulation and the enforcement capabilities of regulators, however, at the expense of a concern with the disposition of the company to comply. A similar issue arises in relation to 'creative compliance,' the phenomenon of companies being technically in compliance, but exploiting or inventing loopholes in the law to evade its purpose. This problem too may not be capable of solution merely by the adoption of more elaborate regulatory techniques.[14] While moves to improve compliance and 'substantive' compliance will not be considered directly here, governance reforms aimed at encouraging companies to be socially responsible in the sense of going beyond the law may also have the effect of strengthening the factors that cause them to act within it, and should be evaluated on that basis.

Secondly, as the EC definition makes clear, voluntariness is integral to CSR, but acceptance that it has a role to play should not be equated with support for deregulation. The case for CSR sketched in the introduction is that it is desirable to encourage 'voluntary' behaviour that satisfies higher standards than those required by law, because there are limits to what regulation can achieve in securing the fulfilment of public policy objectives. That there are such limits is not an argument for reducing regulatory coverage, lowering the thresholds at which mandatory standards are set, or avoiding regulatory solutions to new sources of harm. Particularly given the weaknesses to which modest CSR is itself subject, considered below, it is appropriate to regard it as a supplement or stop-gap, not as an alternative to state regulation.[15] This is not to deny the possible value of regulatory

---

[13] See Wilks, 'Regulatory Compliance', above n 6), at 550. There is, however, now a growing body of literature that does precisely this. See, eg Haines, *Corporate Regulation*, above n 5; Parker, *The Open Corporation*, above n 5; Ayres and Braithwaite, *Responsive Regulation*, above n7; N Gunningham and J Rees, 'Industry Self-Regulation: An Institutional Perspective' (1997) 19 *Law & Policy* 363.

[14] See, eg D McBarnet and C Whelan, *Creative Accountancy and the Cross-Eyed Javelin Thrower* (London, John Wiley, 1999); D McBarnet, 'When Compliance is not the Solution but the Problem: from Changes in Law to Changes in Attitude' in V Braithwaite (ed), *Taxing Democracy: Understanding Tax Avoidance and Evasion* (Aldershot, Ashgate, 2004).

[15] This would appear to be the Commission's position too. See Commission of the European Communities, Green Paper, *Promoting a European Framework for Corporate Social Responsibility*, COM (2001) 366 final, para 22: '[c]orporate social responsibility should... not be seen as a substitute to regulation or legislation concerning social rights or environmental standards, including the development of new appropriate legislation'. See also *Communication*, above n 12, para 5.1.

flexibility, as where corporate or industry self-regulation substitutes for detailed 'command and control,' but within a public regulatory framework that underwrites minimally acceptable standards.[16]

Thirdly, while CSR refers to conduct that is voluntary, the techniques relied on to promote it might themselves involve the imposition of binding obligations. An example is social and environmental disclosure. There are arguments for leaving disclosure to voluntary initiative, such as that compulsion might stifle development in what is a dynamic area or result in uninformative, formulaic reporting. There are also strong counter-arguments, however, for instance that in the absence of legal requirements, reporting will mainly be confined to companies with a high public profile or niche 'ethical' businesses, or that reports will contain serious omissions or be otherwise misleading.[17] As will be discussed below, the effective promotion of CSR may therefore require mandatory reporting, and there is a range of other possible governance reforms that to a greater or lesser extent rely on the imposition of binding obligations.

Fourthly, as discussed below, commercial self-interest is an important driver of CSR, but this emphasis should not obscure the role of moral responsibility. Rather, ethics and corporate self-interest have a complex interconnection in CSR. For a start, there is no reason to suppose that those who work in companies are inevitably immoral or amoral.[18] They may choose to do the 'right thing' for its own sake. And public pressure for improved standards of responsibility might induce more than a narrow, instrumental reaction directed at alleviating short-term threats to profitability, instead triggering an authentically moral response and a process of organisational reflection. Further, somewhat paradoxically, managements might recognise that a commitment to certain non-instrumental values is in the company's long-term interests, and hence seek to institutionalise such a commitment: areas in which a business may become vulnerable to public criticism are liable to be unpredictable, and securing compliance throughout the organisation with the company's social, ethical, and environmental policies is likely to be easier if there is a widely diffused acceptance of the values that underlie them.[19] On the other hand, countervailing pressures to maximise profits may have a corrosive effect on ethical standards,[20] indicating a role for policy interventions designed to

---

[16] See, eg the concept of 'enforced self-regulation': Ayres and Braithwaite, *Responsive Regulation*, above n 7, especially ch 4.

[17] See text following fn 88, below.

[18] See Parker, *The Open Corporation*, above n 5, especially at 203–12, 294–95.

[19] On the debate about whether such an approach should be regarded as a truly ethical one, see K Gibson, 'The Moral Basis of Stakeholder Theory' (2000) 26 *Journal of Business Ethics* 245, 246–47.

[20] See L Mitchell and T Gabaldon, 'If I Only had a Heart: or, How can we Identify a Corporate Morality' (2002) 76 *Tulane Law Review* 1645, 1652–54.

protect and expand the 'fragile processes essential to an institution's moral competence.'[21]

Fifthly, while modest CSR is not then purely a market phenomenon, it is nevertheless the case that harnessing commercial self-interest plays a crucial part in driving forward improved standards of conduct. As already mentioned, there are two reasons why socially responsible behaviour may also be in the company's interests. The first is that there is to an extent a natural overlap between what is good for the company and good for society, which overlap may not currently be fully exploited. Examples include reductions in the use of energy or production of waste, employee training and the promotion of gender equality and ethnic diversity in the workforce.[22] Secondly, in addition to this natural overlap, it will often be in the company's interests to respond positively to the preferences of market and civil society actors regarding social responsibility issues, since these may have the capacity to reward or punish companies accordingly. The second of these factors may also reinforce the first, ie, the company may be pressured into taking actions that turn out to be independently profitable. The effect of market and civil pressure may also extend beyond ad hoc responses, encouraging companies to self-regulate, on an individual or industry basis, or to participate in co-regulatory or other voluntary standard-setting schemes. This trend towards 'codification' can serve as a useful means of making more specific the otherwise amorphous content of CSR, and providing a sharper focus for the efforts of campaigners to raise standards.[23]

The two factors in the previous paragraph are often referred to as the 'business case' for CSR.[24] Mention of the business case sometimes provokes scepticism about the likely social benefits of CSR, on the ground that the term suggests that CSR is simply the product of a business agenda, ie, that the real aim of companies and groups representing business in embracing it is to protect profits rather than to effect genuine improvements in social and environmental performance. The inference is that the gains to society will be small and that companies are just as likely to engage in obfuscation or distracting, image-building 'philanthropy' as to make a serious attempt to address the adverse effects of their core activities. This may be an accurate interpretation of the approach to CSR of many in the corporate sector, but it misstates the role that profits play in CSR viewed as an objective of public

---

[21] Gunningham and Rees, 'Industry Self-Regulation', above n13, at 382.

[22] Eg, D Kingsmill, *Review of Women's Employment and Pay* (London, Cabinet Office, 2001) 7, points to the 'rewards for organizations that find ways to overcome the barriers and constraints that currently limit the role and contribution of women.'

[23] See J Parkinson, 'Disclosure and Corporate Social and Environmental Performance: Competitiveness and Enterprise in a Broader Social Frame' (2003) 3 *Journal of Corporate Law Studies* 3, 11–27.

[24] For a fuller account of the ingredients of the business case, see Arthur D Little, *The Business Case for Corporate Citizenship* (Cambridge, undated).

policy. From the latter perspective the concern is not with profitability as an end in itself (though there is certainly a desire to avoid unnecessary damage to economic performance), but with making use of the profit motive in order to steer company behaviour in a socially approved direction.

To the extent that there is a coincidence of public and private benefit, this is sometimes expressed in terms of 'win-win' strategies, but such language too can be misleading. While popular for obvious reasons among business advocates of CSR, it understates its true potential, in implying that current corporate self-interest sets a limit to socially beneficial changes in behaviour. While its potential is certainly not unlimited, this fails to recognise the dynamic quality of social pressure, which by rewarding socially approved, and more relevantly here, penalising undesirable behaviour, changes the profit-maximising course of action for a business. That market and civil society pressure, or 'civil regulation,' can alter companies' cost structures and sometimes adversely affect profitability, is a point emphasised by the market-liberal critics of CSR, who argue, among other things, that it has a tendency to increase business, and putatively social costs.[25]

Having said this, there certainly are limits to the business case, and hence to the effect that modest CSR is likely to have in improving corporate standards.[26] As to the 'natural' overlap between private and public interests, although the idea that there are substantial untapped opportunities for the realisation of corporate and societal benefits is intuitively plausible, and there are documented cases of such outcomes being achieved,[27] it is obvious that there will be many cases in which the costs of reducing adverse social effects will exceed the private benefits. A company in a 'dirty' industry, for example, is unlikely to find that eliminating pollution pays for itself. With regard to the second, 'social pressure' component of the business case, this suffers from several major limitations. The first is that only a narrow range of the social or ethical issues that arise in business attract a significant level of interest on the part of those who are in a position to put pressure on companies. Consumer interest in corporate responsibility issues, for example, has been described as 'uneven and fickle.'[28]

[25] See D Henderson, *Misguided Virtue: False Notions of Corporate Social Responsibility* (London, IEA, 2001); M Wolf, 'Response to Confronting the Critics' (2002) 1 *New Academy Review* 62.

[26] There is a substantial body of research on the business benefits of social responsibility. For a review of a number of the studies, see J Cook and S Deakin, 'Stakeholding and Corporate Governance: Theory and Evidence on Economic Performance' (1999): http://www.dti.gov.uk/cld/review.htm. No very consistent picture emerges. The studies tend to focus on different aspects of social responsibility, and have difficulties determining the direction of causation (are responsible companies more profitable, or vice versa)?

[27] See, eg M Porter and C van der Linde, 'Green and Competitive: Ending the Stalemate' (1995) Sept/Oct *Harvard Business Review* 120, describing cost reduction and product improvements from better environmental management.

[28] Performance and Innovation Unit, *Rights of Exchange: Social, Health, Environmental and Trade Objectives on the Global Stage* (London, Cabinet Office, 2000).

While many consumers are concerned about child labour and certain aspects of environmental performance, other issues such as respect for employees' rights to collective bargaining in developing countries, or damage to the interests of indigenous communities, attract scant attention. Secondly, even where an activity is the subject of significant public concern, it may be sufficiently profitable for the company to decide that it is in its financial interests to 'manage' the attendant publicity or simply to tough it out. The protracted campaign against Nestlé and its marketing of infant formula milk in developing countries is an example.[29] Finally, businesses vary considerably in the extent to which they are exposed to market and civil society pressures. Large companies with a high public profile and which trade directly in consumer markets are the most susceptible, while others that deal in unbranded goods or operate in intermediate markets may be relatively immune.[30]

Aside from limitations in the business case itself, the commercial benefits that result to companies from socially responsible practices usually accrue over the long term. In the short term, the cost of investing in cleaner technologies, for example, may exceed the savings. Similarly, behaviour that is likely to damage the company's reputation might nevertheless be very profitable in the current accounting period. It has been argued that 'the single largest impediment to improved [occupational health and safety] performance is probably the emphasis of corporations on short-term profitability,'[31] and a similar point has been made with regard to environmental performance.[32] So in organisations that are financially marginal, are under pressure from the stock market to improve profitability, or employ managerial incentive pay schemes that reward short-term financial performance, the business case may have little purchase.

Given these limitations to the ability of modest CSR to raise business standards, that there is a case for going further and implementing some form of radical CSR remains a live issue. Some of the possibilities will be outlined in the final section. The potential of modest CSR should not, however, be undervalued and this chapter now turns to an examination of how corporate governance reform might improve its effectiveness.

---

[29] See R De George, *Competing with Integrity in International Business* (New York, Oxford University Press, 1993) 64–65.

[30] Though increased scrutiny of consumer companies' supply chains can cause them to impose higher standards on suppliers. See, eg P Grabosky, 'Green Markets: Environmental Regulation by the Private Sector' (1994) 16 *Law & Policy* 419, 429; DTI, *Engaging SMEs in Community and Social Issues* (London, DTI, 2002) 16.

[31] N Gunningham and R Johnstone, *Regulating Workplace Safety: Systems and Sanctions* (Oxford, Oxford University Press, 1999) 69.

[32] Gunningham and Grabosky, *Smart Regulation*, above n 7, at 164.

REFORMING CORPORATE GOVERNANCE

This section will look at a number of recent and proposed reforms to corporate governance in the UK designed to support modest CSR. It will also consider how these reforms might be improved or extended.

Directors' Duties and Board Composition

It is currently the duty of directors to act in the interests of the shareholders.[33] The duty is not clearly defined, however, and apparently its requirements are often misunderstood, with some directors believing that they are under an obligation to maximise current profits, even though this may prejudice the total returns to shareholders over the longer term.[34] Partly in order to correct such misconceptions, the recent company law White Paper has recommended that directors' duties be put into statutory form.[35] It will remain the duty of directors ultimately to serve the interests of the shareholders, but the duty will be stated in 'inclusive' terms, making explicit their obligation to take account of the long-as well as the short-term consequences of their decisions, the need to foster the company's business relationships, and to have regard to the community and environmental effects of the company's behaviour and to protect its reputation. This formulation has the effect of embedding a modest CSR philosophy in company law, in that it highlights the contribution to business success of the way the company manages social and environmental and related reputational issues, and hence the directors' responsibilities with regard to these issues. It is unlikely that the duty will have a major impact on behaviour in itself (it is not intended that directors' judgments should be routinely challenged in the courts), but it should be viewed alongside the proposals for wider disclosure, discussed below. These will make more transparent the ways in which companies integrate into their decision making the factors set out in the duty, and will facilitate external evaluation of performance under the relevant heads.

Statistics compiled for the Higgs review of the role of non-executive directors show that non-executives are 'typically white males nearing retirement age with previous PLC director experience.' A mere six per cent of non-executive posts are held by women, and only one per cent from black

---

[33] Companies Act 1985, s 309 requires directors also to have regard to the interests of employees. The effect of the section is unclear, though it was not intended to allow directors to subordinate shareholder interests to those of employees. See Company Law Review Steering Group, *The Strategic Framework*, para 5.1.21.

[34] See Institute of Directors, *Good Boardroom Practice* (London, IOD, 1999).

[35] See DTI, *Modernising Company Law* (London, DTI, 2002) paras 3.2–3.7 and draft clause 19 and schedule 2. The White Paper follows the recommendations of the Company Law Review Steering Group. See *Developing The Framework*, ch 2 and paras 3.9–3.58; *Completing The Structure* ch 3; and *Final Report* paras 3.5–3.11 and Annex C.

or ethnic minority groups.[36] The review calls for non-executives to be drawn from a wider pool, from both within the business sector and also more broadly, including from charitable and public sector bodies. It points out that the 'composition of a board sends important signals about the values of the company. A commitment to equal opportunities which can be of motivational as well as reputational importance is inevitably undermined if the board itself does not follow the same guiding principles.'[37] As far as modest CSR is concerned, a board with a diverse composition is also likely to have a better appreciation of the social and environmental context in which the company operates. A diverse board will have a broader knowledge base and may be more sensitive to stakeholder concerns.[38]

While there is a recognition by policy makers of the value of increased board diversity, actually bringing this about is more problematic. The Tyson report, commissioned following the Higgs review to explore ways of broadening recruitment, notes that 'the current lack of diversity on UK boards reflects more a lack of company demand for diversity... than a lack of supply' of appropriate candidates.[39] This suggests that a major change in attitudes on the part of current board members (and shareholders) is required. The present approach to recruitment seems to be based on the 'old boys' network,' with almost half the directors surveyed for the Higgs review being appointed through personal contacts or friendships.[40] Changes to the Combined Code instituted by Higgs to formalise the appointment procedure, for example, by requiring companies to evaluate the existing balance of skills on the board, to prepare a description of the capabilities required to supplement them, and to make use of advertising are likely to help.[41] There is also value in the Tyson report's proposal for conducting and publicising an annual census of boards, 'reporting measures of board diversity along several dimensions, including the gender, nationality, ethnicity, age and prior experience' of non-executives.[42] For this information to make a difference, however, there will need to be an audience with influence that takes an active interest in diversity of board composition. There is an obvious role here for trade unions, civil society groups and enlightened investors.[43]

---

[36] Higgs, *Review of the Role and Effectiveness of Non-Executive Directors*, above n 2, paras 10.21–22.

[37] *Ibid*, para 10.16.

[38] See L Tyson, *The Tyson Report on the Recruitment and Development of Non-Executive Directors* (London, London Business School, 2003) 6–7.

[39] *Ibid* 9.

[40] *Ibid* para 10.05.

[41] Higgs, *Review of the Role and Effectiveness of Non-Executive Directors*, above n 2, paras 10.09 and 10.11.

[42] Tyson. *The Tyson Report*, above n 38, at 20.

[43] As to the latter, see Henderson Global Investors, *Governance for Corporate Responsibility: The Role of Non-Executive Directors in Environmental, Social and Ethical Issues. A Discussion Paper* (London, 2003).

Aside from the question of diversity, the presence of a significant non-executive element on the board may in itself affect how well companies manage their social and environmental impacts. Non-executives have a role in strategy formation and in monitoring the performance of strategy. A crucial factor in their effectiveness is their independence of management, but their relative detachment from the pressures that executive management face for short-term financial performance is also an important feature of their position. Non-executives do not have the same personal stake in share-price performance as executives.[44] They are therefore more likely to pay greater attention to the determinants of the company's long-term success, including the management of risk and reputation and its responsiveness to stakeholder concerns.[45] Similarly, with only a limited financial interest in the company, the protection of personal reputation, and even the avoidance of legal liability, may for them be relatively more important considerations than for the executives. This may cause them to place added emphasis on regulatory compliance and the maintenance of high standards of social, ethical and environmental performance, failures in which might generate unwelcome negative publicity and damage their standing in the business and wider community.

It follows that measures to strengthen the position of non-executives as against executive management may have positive effects from a CSR perspective. Notwithstanding the significant improvements in board structure and functioning that began with the Cadbury report,[46] fundamental problems have remained, namely that non-executives have been in the minority on many boards, and that despite the presence of nomination committees, appointments have effectively been made by the chief executive, thereby undermining independence.[47] The revisions to the Combined Code following the Higgs review go some way to addressing these problems, in that they recommend that boards should contain a majority of independent non-executives, and they strengthen the role of the nomination committee, formalising its procedures and requiring a majority of its members to be independents. If complied with,[48] these provisions have the potential to enhance significantly the influence of the non-executive element on the board.

---

[44] The Higgs review, following its predecessors, recommends that non-executives should not be paid in share options: above n 2, para 12.27.

[45] There is evidence in the United States that 'outside' directors recognise that 'their responsibility encompasses more than shareholders and are very conscious about the needs and expectations of the various constituencies of their firms': see J Wang and H Dewhirst, 'Boards of Directors and Stakeholder Orientation' (1992) 11 *Journal of Business Ethics* 115, 120.

[46] Committee on the Financial Aspects of Corporate Governance, *Final Report* (London, Gee Publishing, 1992). In fact, the process began before Cadbury: see J Parkinson, 'Evolution and Policy in Company Law: The Non-Executive Director; in J Parkinson, A Gamble, and G Kelly (eds), *The Political Economy of the Company*, above n 11, at 233.

[47] For a discussion of these problems, see Company Law Review Steering Group, *Developing the Framework*, above n 33, paras 3.112–3.153.

[48] Boards must 'comply or explain.' There is a danger that there will be an increased level of non-compliance with provisions that present a significant threat to managerial autonomy.

The Role of Shareholders

The position of shareholders with regard to CSR is open to more than one interpretation. While the matter is not uncontroversial, pressure from the stock market to maximise short-term financial performance appears to be an important contributor to managerial short-termism. This, as noted above, is destructive of socially responsible business practices. There is accordingly an argument for weakening the ties between management and shareholders, for example, by impeding the operation of the market for corporate control, or prohibiting remuneration schemes that link pay to movements in share price. More in keeping with a modest CSR agenda, however, are attempts to encourage shareholders to play a role in strengthening corporate responsibility. The assumption is that within the bounds of the business case,[49] shareholders have the capacity and the incentive to act as a source of pressure for improved performance, reinforcing that from other market and civil actors.

As to the reality of this, on the positive side, there is now in the UK a substantial socially responsible investment (SRI) industry, ie, there is a body of investors who take a direct interest in the social, ethical and environmental performance of the companies in which they hold shares. UK-based institutional investors own around 50 per cent of the shares in listed companies, and in 2001 approximately a third of these were held in funds managed with some regard to SRI principles.[50] As the SRI market has grown, investment management firms have begun to provide dedicated SRI funds, and research organisations, analysts and rating agencies to offer related support services.[51] Ethical indices, notably the FTSE4Good and the Dow Jones Sustainability Group Index have also been created to facilitate SRI. Approaches take the form either or both of stock selection in accordance with social, ethical, and environmental criteria (not necessarily involving a rigid policy of excluding shares from disfavoured sectors),[52] and active engagement with managements to improve performance. With regard to the latter, some institutions have adopted a campaigning stance on issues such as climate change and human rights.[53]

---

[49] Given their fiduciary obligations, institutional investors must not act to the detriment of their beneficiaries.

[50] UK Social Investment Forum, *SRI Data*: www.uksif.org.

[51] See A Simpson, 'Money Talks: The Rise of Socially Responsible Investors' in R Cowe (ed), *No Scruples?* (London, Spiro Press, 2002) 21, 22; Arthur D Little, *Speaking the Same Language:Improving Communications between Companies and Investors on Corporate Responsibility* (London, Arthur D Little, 2003) 6–7.

[52] 'Negative screening', eg excluding shares in tobacco and armaments companies, is commonly a practice of consumer SRI funds, but is unlikely to have a major impact on corporate behaviour, given the relatively small scale of this activity (see UK Social Investment Forum, *SRI Data*, above n50) and the willingness of other investors to hold shares which may be performing well in financial terms.

[53] See R Cowe, 'Rules of Engagement' *Financial Times* (London) 4 April 2002.

While there has been a rapid increase in the adoption of SRI, it is never-theless apparent from the figures above that there is still a majority of investment institutions that take little or no account of social and environ-mental issues in the management of their assets. And where funds have SRI policies they are not necessarily being put into practice. There is evi-dence of a widespread scepticism on the part of fund managers, to whom the implementation of SRI policies is delegated by the bulk of pension schemes and which also manage other institutional assets, about their rel-evance to financial performance.[54] Many fund managers have a prefer-ence for investment appraisals based on financial ratios and are reluctant to factor 'soft' information into investment decisions.[55] In a major survey of fund managers and analysts fewer than five per cent volunteered that they took social and environmental factors into account.[56] Nor should the practical significance of the adoption of SRI engagement policies be over-estimated, against the background of the perennial concern that the institutions are in practice typically passive, even in the face of serious under-performance by investee companies assessed in purely conventional financial terms.[57]

These considerations suggest that there is a case for regulatory interven-tion in the investment industry, and not just at the corporate level, to pro-mote CSR. A rationale for intervention, consistent with the interests of the beneficiaries of investment schemes, is that through their apparent indiffer-ence to the social and environmental performance of the companies in which they invest, many funds may be failing to maximise the value of their assets, and at the same time disregarding the preferences of their ultimate beneficiaries. The amendments in 1999 to the Pensions Act, requiring pen-sion fund trustees to disclose the extent to which they take account of social, environmental or ethical considerations in portfolio composition and their policy on engagement, can be viewed in these terms.[58] There is evidence that pension scheme members support, for example, the use of the fund's voting rights to put pressure on companies to improve their social

---

[54] See C Gribben and A Wilson, *That's One Small Step... Socially Responsible Investment and Pension Funds* (Berkhamsted, Ashridge, 2000). Cf Deloitte and Touche, *Socially Responsible Investment Survey 2002* (London, Deloitte and Touche, 2002) 13–14.

[55] See Arthur D Little, *Speaking The Same Language*, above n 51, at 11.

[56] Business in the Community, *Investing in the Future: City Attitudes to Social and Environmental Issues* (London, BITC, 2001).

[57] See P Myners, *Institutional Investment in the United Kingdom: A Review* (London, HM Treasury, 2001) para 5.74.

[58] Pensions Act 1995, s 11A, added by the Occupational Pension Schemes (Investment, and Assignment, Forfeiture, Bankruptcy etc) Amendment Regulations 1999, SI 1999/1849. A pro-posal to apply a similar provision to large charities has been made: see Cabinet Office Strategy Unit, *Private Action, Public Benefit: A Review of Charities and the Wider Not-For-Profit Sector* (London, 2002). See also Charity Commission, *CC14: Investment of Charitable Funds* (London, 2003), clarifying the position of charitable trustees with regard to SRI.

and environmental performance, at least so long as this is not to their financial detriment.[59] By increasing transparency, the aim is to bring fund policy into line with member preferences. While trustees are not subject to formal control by the members,[60] the substantial increase in the assets managed in accordance with SRI principles appears to indicate a significant measure of success.[61]

As already suggested, however, that many funds may have adopted SRI policies does not necessarily mean that those policies are actually being implemented. For one thing, many policies are vague and hence difficult to operationalise; this may indicate a lack of seriousness of purpose on the part of trustees.[62] For another, policies are often unsupported by monitoring or other accountability mechanisms for ensuring that external fund managers engaged by the trustees are in compliance with them, nor are manager reward systems that are geared to compliance common.[63] It is presumably as a result of this that only very limited resources are devoted by the majority of fund management firms to SRI activity.[64]

A desirable response to these shortcomings would be to require trustees to disclose to members the steps they have taken to put their SRI policies into effect.[65] This might lead to a clarification of policies and more concerted action to implement them. To address the problem of inactivity at the level of fund managers, the latter should be obliged to disclose to their institutional clients how they have attempted to fulfil their mandates on SRI. It has been suggested with regard to engagement that among other things fund

---

[59] See Simpson, 'Money Talks', above n 51, at 22.

[60] Scheme members have the right to nominate one third of the trustees: Pensions Act 1995, s 16(6). It is not common for trustees to consult the members on SRI issues: see C Gribben and L Olsen, *Will UK Pension Funds Become More Responsible?: A Survey of Member Nominated Trustees* (London, Just Pensions, 2003) 10.

[61] A survey conducted shortly after the implementation of the disclosure requirements indicates that 48% of the funds questioned had requested their fund manager to take account of SRI considerations: E Mathieu, *Response of UK Pension Funds to the SRI Disclosure Regulation* (London, UK Social Investment Forum, 2000). Note also the Association of British Insurers' *Disclosure Guidelines on Social Responsibility* (London, ABI, 2001), introduced voluntarily by the insurance industry, but presumably to show a willingness to respond to the CSR agenda in order to avoid regulation. The *Guidelines* expect disclosure by companies, rather than insurers, but seem to have played a part in the large increase in the application of SRI criteria to their equity assets: see UK Social Investment Forum, *SRI Data*, above n 50.

[62] B Pearce and J Ganzi, *Engaging the Mainstream with Sustainability: A Survey of Investor Engagement on Corporate Social, Environmental and Ethical Performance* (London, Forum for The Future, 2002) reports little in the way of specific demand on the part of trustees for engagement.

[63] See Friends of the Earth, *Top Ten UK Pension Funds–How Ethical Are They?* (London, FoE, 2001) 7–8; D Coles and D Green, *Do UK Pension Funds Invest Responsibly? A Survey of Current Practice on Socially Responsible Investment* (London, Just Pensions, 2002), 9–10.

[64] See Deloitte and Touche, *Socially Responsible Investment Survey*, above n 54, at 18–19.

[65] Only a minority of funds currently do this: see Gribben and Olsen, *Will UK Pension Funds Become More Responsible?*, above n 60, at 12. Recent non-statutory initiatives aimed at combating institutional passivity may lead to an increase in disclosures about SRI (as well as in SRI

managers might be required to state 'whether engagement is by question-
naire, letter or meeting; how many meetings were held on which issues; why
those issues were chosen and prioritised; how many AGMs were attended
and how many votes were cast.'[66] Since trustees would need this kind of
information to discharge the disclosure obligation to members suggested
above, the matter could be left to contract, but in view of the centrality of
agency problems in the investor-manager relationship to the wider issue of
institutional passivity, there is a case for imposing by statute a duty on fund
managers to disclose publicly their records on engagement in respect of all
aspects of company performance.[67]

The Pensions Act disclosure requirements apply, of course, to pension
funds and not other institutional investors. Given the size of the holdings of
these bodies, particularly insurance companies,[68] there is a case for greater
transparency here too. Disclosure of policies with regard to social responsibility by providers of insurance and retail investment products would be
likely to stimulate a market in SRI funds in these sectors.

So far there is little evidence about the extent to which SRI is actually
having an effect on company behaviour. The impact of stock selection policies is particularly difficult to assess. Approaching the matter indirectly,
evidence that investors are willing to pay more for shares in 'socially
responsible' companies should rationally cause managements to respond.
The research findings regarding such price effects are as yet inconclusive,

---

engagement more directly), but they are probably insufficiently prescriptive to achieve the level
of transparency advocated above. Thus, the principles for investment decision-making that followed the Myners review, with which pension funds are expected voluntarily to comply, provide for the agreement with fund managers of an explicit strategy for engagement, together
with reporting to members of the results of monitoring of fund manager performance, though
they do not make specific reference to SRI. See the revised principles in HM Treasury and the
Department for Work and Pensions, *Myners Review: Institutional Investment in the UK: The
Government's Response* (London, 2002). The operation of the principles is currently under
review. Principles on shareholder activism introduced by the Institutional Shareholders'
Committee envisage disclosure by fund managers to clients of activism and its impact and
effectiveness, but leave the detail of the information to be provided to agreement between the
parties. See Shareholders' Committee, *The Responsibilities of Institutional Shareholders and
Agents–Statement of Principles* (Institutional London, 2002).

[66] www.justpensions.org/myners-subm-2002-04.shtml (response of Just Pensions to the
Government's consultation on the Myners report).

[67] Among other things, fund managers may be subject to conflicts of interest (they may be
reluctant to intervene in companies whose pension funds they manage or with whom they have
other commercial links). See Company Law Review Steering Group, *Final Report*, above n 33,
paras 6.34–36, recommending public disclosure of the exercise of voting rights, and not viewing the issue 'as purely a private law contractual matter.' See also DTI, *Modernising Company
Law*, above n 35, para 2.47, expressing the view that it is 'in the public interest for institutional investors to be required to disclose publicly how they have voted in respect of their share-
holdings in British quoted companies.'

[68] Holding around 20% of the stock market, to the pension funds 16%. See National
Statistics, *Share Ownership A Report on Ownership of Shares as at 31 December 2001*:
www.statistics.gov.uk/downloads/theme_economy/ShareOwnership2001.pdf.

however.[69] Also, the criteria that the market expects companies to meet are not well defined, ie, managements may have difficulty in interpreting exactly what forms of behaviour will command a premium and this may mute the impact of stock selection. With regard to shareholder activism, in a survey of the views of fund managers there was general agreement that only a few companies demonstrated any significant change following engagement. This may underestimate the effects, however, in that as the survey notes, improvements in social and environmental performance may be gradual and investor engagement is one of a number of cumulative sources of pressure that put these issues onto the strategic agenda.[70] A problem nevertheless is that even when acting collaboratively, the funds involved are likely to command only a small proportion of the votes in a company. This emphasises the importance of funds with a strong commitment to SRI attaining critical mass if it is to be an effective force. Efforts by investors to clarify and consolidate the different standards with which they expect companies to comply are also likely to increase the influence on managements both of engagement activity and investors' market behaviour.[71]

If shareholders (and other market and civil actors) are to be a significant force in improving the social and environmental performance of companies then transparency of corporate policies and outcomes is an essential prerequisite. There are indications that institutional investors consider the information currently provided by companies in this regard to be seriously inadequate.[72] Disclosure and its role in strengthening modest CSR are considered next.

Disclosure

Disclosure as a technique for increasing the accountability of companies for their social and environmental performance might in principle take two forms: reporting that is designed to meet the information needs of shareholders and that directed at the broader range of groups affected by or interested in the company's activities.[73] Disclosure of the first kind attempts to capitalise on the 'business case.' In other words, it is assumed that shareholders

---

[69] See n 52, above. There are, however, recent figures that show that shares on ethical indices have significantly outperformed the market as a whole: see J Fuller, *Financial Times, FTfm supplement*, 21 July 2003, 6.

[70] See Dresner, *Assessing Engagement* section II, 6–7.

[71] For efforts in this direction, see C Mackenzie/Insight Investment, *Defining Global Business Principles: Towards A New Role for Investors in Promoting International Corporate Responsibility* (London, Insight Investment, undated).

[72] See Gribben and Olsen, *Will UK Pension Funds Become More Responsible?*, above n 60, at 9.

[73] For a fuller account of this distinction, see Parkinson, 'Disclosure and Corporate Social and Environmental Performance', above n 23, at 6–11. As well as strengthening accountability, social and environmental disclosure might be justified by reference to the beneficial effect

have incentives to monitor the social responsibility of the companies in which they invest to the extent that the latter impacts on financial performance, and that increased access to information will improve the effectiveness of this process.

Reporting requirements that strengthen accountability to shareholders are intended, among other things, to increase the alignment of company behaviour with public pressure, where disregarding that pressure would have adverse financial effects. It is not part of their purpose to stimulate or strengthen the pressures themselves. This is, however, the objective of disclosure requirements of the second kind.[74] They aim to increase the flow of information to the parties affected by corporate activity, other market actors, and civil society groups, who may then rely on this information, for example, in deciding whether to buy the company's products or to mount a media campaign against it. The regulatory strategy involved here is thus one of attempting, by indirect means, to raise the cost to companies of 'irresponsible' behaviour (and of rewarding companies for 'responsible' conduct). Although it does not alter the duty of directors to maximise shareholder returns, and so in that sense is consistent with the principle of shareholder primacy, it involves an active intervention in the commercial environment in which the company operates that is intended to rebalance the interests of shareholders and others in favour of the latter.[75]

The Government's proposals for a mandatory operating and financial review (OFR) are for a disclosure regime of the first kind.[76] The OFR requirements, which will apply to large, 'economically significant' companies,[77] provide for reporting of a more qualitative and forward-looking character than is currently demanded. The overarching purpose of the OFR is to 'provide a discussion and analysis of the business and the main trends

---

on decision-making of the increased information available to management (resulting from the obligation to collect it for the purpose of disclosure). See, eg Stone, *Where the Law Ends*, above n 7, ch 18. Disclosure obligations imposed by company law are not the only means of making information about corporate impacts public. Other methods include disclosure of environmental information on public registers and product labelling schemes.

[74] A celebrated example is the US Toxics Release Inventory. The community pressure which has resulted from the obligation of manufacturers to report annual emissions of specified chemicals has apparently led to a substantial reduction in emissions. See A Fung and D O'Rourke, 'Reinventing Environmental Regulation from the Grassroots Up: Explaining and Expanding the Success of the Toxics Release Inventory' (2000) 25 *Environmental Management* 115.

[75] The second kind of disclosure can thus be viewed as part of a radical CSR agenda. Since it does not involve altering corporate objectives, however, it will be considered here under the 'modest CSR' heading.

[76] See DTI, *Modernising Company Law*, above n 35, para 4.28–4.46 and Annex D; *Draft Clauses* cls 73–80. See also, Company Law Review Steering Group, *Final Report*, paras 3.28–3.48 and 8.29–8.71.

[77] These are currently defined as public companies meeting two of the following three criteria: turnover exceeding £50 million, balance sheet total exceeding £25 million, employees exceeding 500, and for private companies £500 million, £250 million, and 5,000, respectively: DTI, *Modernising Company Law, ibid*, para 4.36.

and factors underlying the results and financial position and likely to affect performance in the future, so as to enable users to assess the strategies adopted by the business and the potential for successfully achieving them.'[78] It is intended that disclosures should cover such matters as business opportunities and risks and strategies for dealing with them, intangible assets, including the skills and knowledge of the workforce, and the company's policies and performance in relation to social and environmental issues.

Although the primary intended audience of the OFR is the shareholders, the company law White Paper also accepts that the information it contains will be a 'major benefit for a wider cross-section of a company's stakeholders.'[79] As this suggests, the two approaches to social and environmental reporting mentioned above are not entirely discrete, in that information provided to make more transparent how well the company is managing the social and environmental issues affecting it, for the benefit of shareholders, will inevitably also be of value to third parties, who might use the disclosures to increase pressure on the company to improve performance. The distinction is nevertheless important in determining exactly what information should be disclosed. The OFR is concerned with reporting social and environmental factors that have significant implications for the company and its shareholders. It is likely to contain much less information therefore than fully-fledged social or environmental reports, which have the different aim of providing a comprehensive account of a company's social and environmental impacts and are designed to address the information needs of affected parties and others with an interest in the issues at stake.

A separate point with regard to the OFR proposals is the distinction they draw between matters that must always be reported on, and others that must appear only when the directors consider them to be material to an assessment of the company's business. Disclosures that are central to CSR, namely those concerning workforce, social, community, and environmental issues fall into the latter category. This is not to say that whether to report in these areas is at the directors' discretion. The board is under a duty to consider in good faith what information is material, and the process through which it reaches a decision, though not the decision itself, is subject to auditor review. A failure to give proper consideration to relevant issues may thus result in the company being forced to produce a revised OFR.[80] It is unlikely that boards will consider it acceptable not to report at

---

[78] See Company Law Review Steering Group, *Developing the Framework*, above n 35, para 5.79.

[79] DTI, *Modernising Company Law*, above n 35, para 4.32.

[80] Following enforcement proceedings instigated by the Financial Reporting Review Panel. In the case of defective accounts, the court may order the cost of the proceedings and the expense incurred by the company in preparing revised accounts to be borne by the directors: Companies Act 1985, s 245B(4). See also Companies Act, s 233(5), which imposes a criminal penalty on directors who knowingly or recklessly sign accounts that are not in compliance with the Act.

all under the 'non-mandatory' headings, at least those that relate to the workforce and the environment,[81] but it is has been argued that structuring the OFR provisions in this way will result in directors taking the reporting of non-mandatory items less seriously or reporting in a superficial manner.[82]

The justification for the very flexible approach that has been adopted is that the quality and quantity of information disclosed are likely to be higher if the directors are given a broad freedom to show in their own terms 'what matters about the business as regards performance and direction.'[83] If the OFR reflects 'the company's priorities: its own vision as to the purpose and values of the business; and the way it analyses the business, sets strategy, and measures success,'[84] it will provide users with more tailored information and hence a better basis for evaluation than might emerge from a more prescriptive framework. The process of deciding what is material should also increase board-level discussion and scrutiny of the issues that are of particular significance for the company concerned.[85] Taking account too of the very different circumstances of individual companies, the proposals look to pressure from shareholders and other interest groups, rather than formal legal rules, to ensure meaningful reporting.[86]

The extent to which this approach will succeed is hard to judge. The experience with current, voluntary disclosure on social and environmental issues is not encouraging. The minority of firms that do report[87] often produce a selective, flattering account of the company's activities, and wide variations in the extent and type of information revealed, and in the formats in which it is presented, obstruct the crucial process of comparing performance within industrial sectors.[88] Putting reporting on a statutory footing should, however, lead to a substantial increase in the level of non-financial reporting. How useful the disclosures actually turn out to be will partly be

---

[81] See Operating and Financial Review Working Group on Materiality, *A Consultation Document* (London, DTI, 2003) 25.

[82] See J Williamson, 'A Trade Union Congress Perspective on the Company Law Review and Corporate Governance Reform' (2003) 41 *British Journal of Industrial Relations* 511, 521–24; House of Commons Trade and Industry Committee, *The White Paper on Modernising Company Law* Sixth Report of Session 2002(03 (London, Stationery Office, 2003) para 61.

[83] Company Law Review Steering Group, *Final Report*, above n 80, para 8.33.

[84] The Operating and Financial Review Working Group on Materiality, *A Consultation Document*, above n 81, at 12.

[85] DTI, *Modernising Company Law*, above n 35, para 4.33.

[86] See House of Commons Trade and Industry Committee, *The White Paper on Modernising Company Law*, above n 82, para 70.

[87] Less than one third of FTSE 350 companies produced an environmental report in 2001, and in 2000 only 35 companies published any kind of social report: D Doane, *Market Failure: The Case for Mandatory Social and Environmental Reporting* (2002): http://www.ippr.org/research/index.php?current=28&detail=events. The most recent figures for the top 100 companies are a little more encouraging. See KPMG, *KPMG International Survey of Corporate Sustainability Reporting 2002* (Amsterdam, KPMG, 2002).

[88] See D Doane, *Corporate Spin: The Troubled Years of Social Reporting* (London, New Economics Foundation, 2000).

determined by the reporting standards for the compilation of OFRs that are to be drawn up by the proposed new standards board. What these will contain is as yet unclear, but it is important that they should require that where disclosures are made, they are reasonably complete and not misleading, and that information is presented in a way that facilitates comparison of year-on-year performance and with that of other companies in the same sector. The rigour of these standards will also be a factor in the usefulness of the proposed system of auditor review. As well as considering the adequacy of the process for the compilation of the OFR, auditors will be required to review disclosures for compliance with reporting standards. They will also need to examine them for consistency with the accounts and information obtained during the course of the financial audit. This level of review, however, which falls short of a full audit, is likely to be of limited effectiveness in controlling the accuracy of information and preventing the material presented from being misleading through incompleteness.

The above reservations aside, the significance of the OFR should not be underestimated. For the first time, companies will be expected to reveal publicly their policies on social, including workforce, and environmental issues. Those that have no, or inadequate policies in these areas will be exposed to scrutiny and adverse comment. Further, a serious criticism of many companies is that while they purport to have adopted policies relevant to social responsibility, they fail to monitor performance, or seemingly to make any significant effort to implement them. The Kingsmill review of women's employment and pay, for example, drew attention to the fact that while a large number of companies have progressive human capital and diversity policies, 'few have done the necessary analysis as to how such policies relate to their key corporate objectives and whether the policies in question are actually delivering the desired results.'[89] A requirement that disclosure of the content of policies should be accompanied by information on performance under them,[90] will give companies an incentive to take seriously the policies they purport to have adopted. Another effect of the OFR requirements should be to expand companies' 'information nets,', ie, their systems for gathering information about social and environmental impacts, including through stakeholder dialogue,[91] that are a pre-condition for responsible behaviour.[92] In order to demonstrate that a proper process has

---

[89] Kingsmill, *Review of Women's Employment and Pay*, above n 22, para 5.36. See also E Joseph, *What's on the Agenda? How UK Directors Contribute to Social and Environmental Objectives* (London, IPPR, 2002) 29–30.

[90] The draft clauses (see DTI, *Modernising Company Law: Draft Clauses*, above n 35, cl 75) currently provide for separate decisions on the materiality of policies and performance of them, but it is understood that this feature of the illustrative draft will not be repeated in the final version.

[91] See Operating and Financial Review Working Group on Materiality, *A Consultation Document*, above n 81, at 26.

[92] See Stone, *Where The Law Ends*, above n 7, ch 18.

been followed in making judgments on materiality, companies will need to be able to show that they have appropriate management systems to monitor the risks and opportunities arising from the social and environmental performance of the business, and also to value the company's relationships.[93] While there will not necessarily be a reporting outcome, given the materiality test, these requirements should have a broader effect in leading to increased fulfilment of the cognitive prerequisites of responsibility.

Even if the OFR is successful in its own terms, however, it is highly unlikely that the material disclosed will fully satisfy the information needs of civil regulation. There is accordingly a case for supplementing it, as reporting techniques develop, with disclosure obligations that are designed specifically with that purpose in mind and which aim to reveal a more complete picture of corporate social and environmental impacts. DEFRA already issues voluntary guidelines for reporting on greenhouse gas emissions, waste, and water use. These could be extended and made mandatory. A more ambitious attempt to capture the full range of corporate impacts is the Global Reporting Initiative's (GRI) Sustainability Reporting Guidelines.[94] Approximately 300 organisations around the world are now reporting using the guidelines.[95] A number of countries have imposed more limited social and environmental disclosure requirements, and for companies listed on the South African stock exchange compliance with the GRI guidelines has been made mandatory.[96] It is conceivable that initiatives at a European level may eventually lead to similarly comprehensive reporting obligations.[97]

RADICAL CSR

As discussed earlier, modest CSR does not rely only on a natural overlap between the public interest and the interests of shareholders. Rather, pressures for the adoption of higher standards of social and environmental performance located in the market and civil society can alter what is the

[93] See Operating and Financial Review Working Group on Materiality, *A Consultation Document*, above n 81, para 9. For additional proposals for the reporting of human capital, see *Accounting for People: Report of the Task Force on Human Capital Management* (London, DTI, 2003).

[94] Amsterdam, 2002.

[95] See News Update July 2002: http://www.globalreporting.org.

[96] See H Ward, *Legal Issues in Corporate Citizenship* (London, IIEG, 2003) 4.

[97] See R Howitt, 'Europe Promotes Best Practice' (Autumn, 2002) *Ethical Performance Best Practice* 6, 6–7. The Commission is currently taking steps to develop commonly agreed guidelines and criteria for measurement, reporting, and assurance for (voluntary) triple bottom line reporting by mid- 2004: Commission of the European Communities, *Communication from the Commission concerning Corporate Social Responsibility: A Business Contribution to Sustainable Development* COM (2002) para 5.3, and see also para 7.3. See also, *Commission Recommendation on The Recognition Measurement and Disclosure of Environmental Issues in the Annual Accounts and Annual Reports of Companies* 2002/453/EC.

profit-maximising course of action for a company. The limitations of this form of social control have also been touched on: the pressures are often too weak and the range of issues encompassed too narrow to produce outcomes that strike an acceptable balance between the generation of wealth and respect for widely held ethical and social values. Governance reforms of the kind outlined in the previous section can help, but are unlikely to eliminate these problems. The question inevitably arises therefore of whether we should turn to more radical forms of CSR, that depend not on responses to external preferences largely mediated through the market, but on a more fundamental reshaping of corporate objectives. A detailed examination of the changes to governance arrangements that would be necessary to institutionalise radical CSR will not be attempted here,[98] but what follows is a brief overview of the main approaches and the problems that they are likely to face in practice.

The available techniques might broadly be described as judicial and political. Those of the first kind involve altering directors' duties to introduce new behavioural norms, ultimately enforceable by the courts. One option, that the revised duties should take the form of detailed prescriptions, defining in advance the requirements of socially responsible conduct, does not look feasible. If the desired behaviour could be identified with reasonable precision it would be possible, and preferable (because of the greater certainty of outcomes) to mandate it in external regulation. It is precisely where this cannot be done that CSR becomes relevant. A more feasible approach would be to impose a duty in general terms requiring directors to take account of the welfare of the various groups or interests affected by their decisions, in addition to the shareholders, the latter not to be overriding. It would be unrealistic to expect a court to be able to review the outcomes of such a decision-making processes, however. Determining the 'right' course of action requires managers to make trade-offs, but there are no obvious standards by which a court could evaluate whether an appropriate resolution of interests had been achieved.

Even if expressed in mandatory terms, therefore, 'pluralist' duties would be likely to function in practice as conferring a *discretion* to depart from profit maximisation where ethical or social policy considerations so dictate, given the need to frame the duty as a subjective one (a duty to act in accordance with what the directors consider in good faith to be an appropriate resolution of interests).[99] This presents a difficulty because there is no guarantee that such a discretion, if granted, would be exercised. After all, given the subjective nature of the current duty, it does little in practice to constrain the

---

[98] For a more detailed discussion, see J Parkinson, *Corporate Power and Responsibility: Issues in The Theory of Company Law* (Oxford, Clarendon Press, 1993) ch 11.

[99] For a discussion of pluralist duties, see Company Law Review Steering Group, *The Strategic Framework*, above, n 33, paras 5.1.24–5.1.33.

freedom of a board to adopt whatever standards of social responsibility it considers appropriate. The reality is that stock market-related pressures and incentives have a much greater impact on behaviour than fiduciary duties. The effectiveness of a change in the core duty could, however, be increased by imposing collateral duties on directors to be properly informed about the social and environmental effects of the company's policies and/or to consult with relevant interested parties.[100] Such duties, unlike the core duty, are capable of being enforced and could expand the factors taken into account in the decision-making process. The drawback is that even if complied with, they do not ultimately oblige managements to depart from their preferred course of action, and so whether they would in practice achieve much more than a duty expressed in 'inclusive' terms is debatable.

Although of limited value in themselves, changes in directors' duties would be necessary to provide an appropriate context for political mechanisms for instituting radical CSR. Rather than relying on the threat of judicial enforcement, such mechanisms effect change by broadening the range of participants and perspectives in company decision-making, and crucially altering the balance of power and hence decisional outcomes. There are numerous possibilities.[101] Directors might be appointed to represent various non-shareholder interests, either to a unitary board or a supervisory board within a two-tier structure. Such directors might be in a minority or majority position. 'Non-shareholder' directors might have a general public interest mandate, or be appointed by, and representative of particular groups or interests. Alternatively, the constituencies to which the directors as a whole are accountable could be expanded beyond the shareholders, through the appointment, for example, of some kind of 'stakeholder council.'[102]

Increasing the range of groups that have a say in decision making clearly has the capacity to alter corporate priorities. A number of difficulties in devising workable arrangements would have to be faced, however. One is ensuring that all relevant interests have a voice, and another that those who speak for them have a legitimate right to do so. Self-evident distortions might result from failure to meet these requirements. It is also possible to call into question the rationality of the outcomes of decision-making processes that involve multiple participants with conflicting interests. Decisions may be determined by relative bargaining power and the shifting composition of temporary coalitions rather than a good faith assessment of

---

[100] Proposals of this kind are, among others, contained in the Corporate Responsibility Bill 2002, supported by the Corporate Responsibility Coalition (CORE), made up of a number of NGOs.

[101] For a consideration of some of the proposals, see Parkinson, *Corporate Power and Responsibility*, above n 98, at 386–93.

[102] See R Cowe, *Stakes Not Shares: Curbing the Power of Corporations* (London, New Economics Foundation, 2001).

the merits. There is therefore a danger that the gains from a social responsibility perspective will to a degree be arbitrary, and at the same time a risk that the efficient operation of the enterprise will be compromised. These criticisms are clearly pertinent to a decision-making model embodying 'low politics,' ie, one characterised by interest group bargaining and compromise, or the 'raw play of power.'[103] A more optimistic view might be taken of a rather different model that aims to encapsulate 'high politics.' Here obligations are defined 'by a public philosophy, by a theory of the enterprise and of its place in the community.'[104] Outcomes are determined by consensus or 'rational agreement'[105] rather than by inter-group trade-offs. But the challenge is to design institutional arrangements that are capable of putting such ideals of deliberative democracy into effect.

The uncertainties attaching to how radical CSR might be successfully implemented, together with the possible risks to national competitiveness that it creates, have unsurprisingly made it unattractive to governments. Measures supportive of modest CSR, on the other hand, have found favour in the UK, and a number of ways in which they might be strengthened have been suggested above. An agenda that aims to maximise transparency and to increase the sensitivity of companies to outside opinion offers a promising way of supplementing more conventional forms of regulation and establishing normative frameworks where the imposition of mandatory standards is currently not feasible. Nevertheless, for reasons that have been considered, the results are bound to be patchy, both in terms of the regulatory objectives that can be fulfilled in this way, and the companies that are likely to be affected. Accordingly, modest CSR must not be a distraction from the need, where appropriate, to establish binding controls and to shape markets through the use of fiscal and economic instruments in ways that are equal to the social and environmental challenges created by global business activity.[106]

---

[103] See P Selznick, *The Moral Commonwealth: Social Theory and the Promise of Community* (Berkeley, University of California Press, 1992) 351.

[104] *Ibid.* See also G Teubner, 'Corporate Fiduciary Duties and Their Beneficiaries: A Functional Approach to The Legal Institutionalization of Corporate Responsibility' in K Hopt and G Teubner (eds), *Corporate Governance and Directors' Liabilities: Legal, Economic and Sociological Analyses of Corporate Social Responsibility* (Berlin, de Gruyter, 1985) 149.

[105] See H Steinmann, 'The Enterprise as a Political System' in Hopt and Teubner, *ibid*, 401.

[106] See generally, R Cowe and J Porritt, *Government's Business: Enabling Corporate Sustainability* (London, Forum for the Future, 2002).

2

Corporate Governance and Constitutional Law: A Legal Pluralist Perspective

GAVIN W ANDERSON

INTRODUCTION

IN THIS CHAPTER, I address issues of corporate governance from the perspective of constitutional law. To many, this will appear counterintuitive. Constitutional law, as students learn in their first week at law school, is concerned with the institutions of the state. If constitutional law is quintessentially public law, company law is generally regarded as a private law subject, often taught as part of commercial or business law–indeed, the influential law and economics school tells us a corporation is simply a nexus of contracts.[1] The separation of these discourses is deeply embedded in the legal imagination, and limits the sorts of questions deemed suitable for inquiry. For example, constitutional lawyers may inquire into electoral systems for legislatures, but not for directorships of companies, and devote much energy to analysing the accountability of decisions taken around the cabinet table, but not in the boardroom. My argument is that this disciplinary divergence increasingly ill serves those interested in constitutional law and corporate governance, and that if we are to take seriously the former's concern with the accountability of political power, and the latter's aim of subjecting corporate activity to greater scrutiny in the wider public interest, then there is much to gain from opening a dialogue between the discourses

I have two objectives in this chapter. The first is to highlight the constitutional relevance of the modern corporation. In that regard, I argue that questions about the exercise and accountability of corporate power engage central issues of constitutional law, and so should feature more prominently

---

[1] See WW Bratton Jr, 'The New Economic Theory of the Firm: Critical Perspectives from History' (1989) 41 *StanLRev* 1471, 1478–80.

on the radar of constitutional scholarship. (By corporation, I refer here to large multinational corporations–enterprises like Wal-Mart, Royal Dutch Shell and News International). The second is to elaborate how a fuller engagement with the role of corporations casts doubt on the adequacy of our prevailing assumptions about constitutional law in the age of the global economy, and to demonstrate that these assumptions impede the goal of holding power (whatever its provenance) to account. This latter point is important in light of recent developments to apply public law ideas and mechanisms, in particular human rights, in the field of corporate governance.

Addressing these points attains some urgency when placed in the context of the global economy, which for many represents an aggrandisement of multinational corporations' (MNCs) power, at the expense of nation states.[2] There has been voluble and growing opposition to these developments, and concern about the democratic implications of the corporate agenda. However, one of the paradoxes of the present age is that while at the grass-roots level, political activism appears to be on the up,[3] in official terms, we have seen a 'shrivell[ing of] the range of the politically contestable.'[4] Many political parties in advanced democracies have signed up to the Washington consensus, based in ideas of free trade, fiscal restraint, low taxes, deregulation and privatisation.[5] MNCs are major beneficiaries of this consensus, which takes the pursuit of redistributive macroeconomic measures off the political agenda, and promotes the organisation of economic activity on a global scale. The contrast between the New International Economic Order of the 1970s, when developing countries sought to impose tighter controls on corporate profit-making,[6] with the present New World Order in which the same countries clamber over each other to offer incentives for Foreign Direct Investment[7] is palpable.

It is against this backdrop I argue that broadening the scope of constitutional discourse clarifies the fault lines for closing down (and potentially opening up) political debate on corporate power. The chapter consists of three parts. In the first part, I argue that the actions of MNCs raise issues of considerable constitutional import, and show the difficulty of ignoring

---

[2] See, eg DC Korten, *When Corporations Rule the World* (San Francisco, Berrett-Koehler, 1995).

[3] See, eg M Barlow and T Clarke, *Global Showdown: How the New Activists are Fighting Global Corporate Rule* (Toronto, Stoddart, 2002).

[4] D Kennedy, 'The Forgotten Politics of International Governance' [2001] *European Human Rights Law Review* 117, 120.

[5] R Falk, *Predatory Globalization: A Critique* (Oxford, Polity Press, 1999) 2.

[6] See SR Ratner, 'Corporations and Human Rights: A Theory of Legal Responsibility' (2001) 111 *Yale L J*, 443, 454–58.

[7] D Held, & A McGrew, D Goldblatt and J Perraton, *Global Transformations: Politics, Economics and Culture* (Cambridge, Polity Press, 1999) 259.

MNCs for both traditional and contemporary objects of constitutional scholarship. In the second part, I consider the implications of this argument for our dominant state-centred paradigm of constitutional law. I contrast this with the alternative paradigm of legal pluralism, rooted in critically informed empirical sociology, to show that the question of which paradigm prevails has important consequences for our interrogation of (all forms of) political power. In the third part, I demonstrate the practical benefits of a (critical) legal pluralist approach by highlighting the limits of reworking existing conceptions of human rights law as a means of democratising corporate power. Here I argue that to the extent these conceptions retain, rather than disturb, traditional understandings of law, they are unlikely, in the long term, to move political discourse to a point where it seriously undermines present consolidations of corporate power. I conclude that the state-centred approach to constitutional law needs to be displaced from the legal imagination in order to move beyond the current confinements of political debate.

THE CONSTITUTIONAL RELEVANCE OF THE CORPORATION

Study of constitutional law remains within the state-centred paradigm. Open any major text on the subject, and we see the familiar litany that constitutional law is concerned with establishing and regulating the institutions of the nation-state.[8] More recently, the meaning of constitutional law appears to have narrowed, as witnessed by the global spread of judicially administered charters of rights[9]—as higher law limits on what the *state* may do. In this section, I highlight three strands of recent scholarship which doubt the utility of this primary focus on the state if our concern is with outlining a system of government, or with directing the exercise of political power.[10] The first emphasises the close relations between states and corporations, and the

---

[8] See, eg AW Bradley and KD Ewing, *Constitutional and Administrative Law* (13th edn (Harlow, Pearson, 2003) 3: '[C]onstitutional law concerns the relationship between the individual and the state, seen from a particular viewpoint, namely the notion of law.'

[9] See R Hirschl, 'The Political Origins of Judicial Empowerment through Constitutionalization: Lessons from Four Constitutional Revolutions' (2000) 25 *Law & Soc Inq'y* 91 at 92, fn 1.

[10] I should be clear that I am not suggesting that we reify our understandings of constitutional law according to either of these understandings, or indeed that there always exists something called 'the constitution' (or 'The Constitution') which, with better cartographic devices, we might be able to map more fully— such an approach would be inconsistent with the legal pluralist perspective I later adopt. Rather, my point is that to the extent constitutional lawyers in their scholarship suggest that these are the main concerns of their subject, we might legitimately ask whether this can be achieved by omitting, or significantly downgrading, the role of corporations. The accompanying passage should accordingly be read in rhetorical terms, as a means of opening up the issue of how our dominant assumptions about constitutional law impact upon broader issues of political accountability.

extent to which the latter are implicated in policy-making and execution. The second speaks to how, at the national level, corporations are bypassing states as the direct provider of legislative and executive functions. The third links burgeoning corporate influence to the emergence of new forms of constitutionalism, grounded in global economic processes, which provide further protection for corporations against regulation unfavourable to their interests.

The State-Corporate Nexus

It is a commonplace that the state has been significantly reconfigured over the past twenty or so years.[11] Extensive programmes of privatisation, beginning with state-owned utilities,[12] but now extending to, for example, social security[13] air traffic control,[14] and even law and order,[15] have led to a 'shrinking [of] the state'[16] with the result that private corporations have been established or warranted by the state as the immediate means of delivering services to the public. This has resulted not just in a change of personnel, but in different ways of carrying out the state's former functions, with accounting norms such as effectiveness, efficiency and value for money becoming the guiding criteria.[17] These processes are well-documented, and there is much scholarly interest in the issues of the accountability of public power thrown up by these changes–for example, in terms of its regulation of privatised industries.[18] However, what receives considerably less attention, but which is at least arguably of greater constitutional importance, is not just how corporations now execute a significant range of public services, but how they are involved in the policy process which has led to the reconfiguration of the state in their interests.

A growing body of social science literature highlights the institutional links between corporations and government. Given the recent direction of

[11] See S Strange, *The Retreat of the State* (Cambridge, Cambridge University Press, 1997).

[12] See C Graham and T Prosser, '"Rolling Back the Frontiers"? The Privatisation of State Enterprises' in C Graham and T. Prosser (eds), *Waiving the Rules: The Constitution Under Thatcherism* (Milton Keynes, Open University Press, 1988) ch 5.

[13] See N Harris, 'The Welfare State, Social Security, and Social Citizenship Rights' in N Harris, *Social Security Law in Context* (Oxford, Oxford University Press, 2000) 3, 9.

[14] See Department of Transport, *Transport Act 2000: Public/Private Partnership for National Air Traffic Services Ltd.* (Report to Parliament, March 2001):
http://www.aviation.dft.gov.uk/nats/pr0103/index.htm.

[15] One report states that as of September 2001, there were '142,521 beds in 181 facilities under contract or construction as private secure adult facilities in U.S., U.K., and Australia': http://www.ucc.uconn.edu/~logan/

[16] H Feigenbaum, J Henig and C Hamett, *Shrinking the State: The Political Underpinnings of Privatization* (Cambridge, Cambridge University Press, 1998) 2.

[17] See D Slater and F Tonkiss, *Market Society: Markets and Modern Social Theory* (Oxford, Polity Press, 2001) 138–43.

[18] See T Prosser, *Law and the Regulators* (Oxford, Clarendon Press, 1997).

economic policy, it would be surprising if the views and decisions of the CEOs of multinationals did not have a significance beyond the board-room.[19] However, it is equally important to emphasise the more formal ways in which corporations are 'increasingly international political actors.'[20] For example, it is now commonplace for transnational firms to have their own 'embassies', and representatives prosecuting their interests, in major centres of political power, such as Washington[21] or Brussels.[22] Also, corporations are mobilising as a political group. David Korten recounts how since the early 1970s, US-based transnational corporations have formed organisations such as the Business Roundtable,[23] which consists of business leaders, including the CEOs of an important cross-section of the Fortune 500,[24] and which conduct 'aggressive campaigns' to promote their interests in the political process.[25] Similar organisations exist in Canada,[26] and the United Kingdom.[27]

The most visible link between states and corporations is probably the practice of business donations to political parties. In the US, it is estimated that in the 2000 US elections, corporate donations to campaigns through official political action committees totalled some $US259.8 million, before including the 'soft money,' which is given overwhelmingly from the corporate sector.[28] Constitutional law tends to deal with this issue in terms of

---

[19] See, eg T Clarke, *Silent Coup: Confronting the Big Business Takeover of Canada* (Toronto, James Lorimer & Co, 1997) 113.

[20] W Grant, *Business and Politics in Britain* (rev edn, Basingstoke, Macmillan, 1993) 85.

[21] Korten, *When Corporations Rule the World*, above n 2, at 143.

[22] Grant, above n 20, at 85.

[23] Korten, above n 2, 142–45. Korten quotes the Business Roundtable's self-description of itself (144) as 'an association of chief executive officers who examine public issues that affect the economy and develop positions which seek to reflect sound economic and social principles. Established in 1972, the Roundtable was founded in the belief that business executives should take an increased role in the continuing debates about public policy.'

[24] *Ibid*, 144.

[25] *Ibid*, 145.

[26] See Clarke, above n 19, who discusses (20) the Business Council on National Issues: 'From the outset the BCNI was designed to be a powerful alliance. Its membership list included the presidents or CEOs of the country's leading chartered banks, the top 10 insurance companies, and no less than 18 oil and pipeline corporations. Brand name oil and gas companies like Shell, Imperial Oil, Gulf and Texaco were represented by their CEOs on the BCNI, along with their counterparts from big manufacturing firms such as Ford, Kodak and CIL. Canadian transnational enterprises like Inco, Alcan, Stelco, and Trizec worked side by side with U.S. giants like IBM, Xerox, Bechtel and ITT. Indeed, the BCNI was largely composed of corporations that followed the dictates of international capital.' For Clarke, what gives the BCNI coherence as a political grouping is 'a common political commitment to a free market economy, dominated by a dynamic private sector and very limited (if any) forms of government intervention and regulation': *ibid*, 21.

[27] See J Boswell and J Peters, *Capitalism in Contention: Business leaders and Political Economy in Modern Britain* (Cambridge, Cambridge University Press, 1997) 179.

[28] http://www.fec.gov/press/press2001/053101pacfund/053101pacfund.html. See T Ferguson, *The Golden Rule: The Investment Theory of Party Competition and the Logic of Money-Driven Political Systems* (Chicago and London, University of Chicago Press, 1995)

capping expenditure in the aim of securing greater electoral equality. However, there is little in the constitutional literature about how corporate donations do impact on the policy-making process. In this regard, research such as Thomas Ferguson's into the dollars-votes nexus in the US adds to our practical knowledge of constitutional law. Ferguson suggests that all this activity is not just public-spiritedness on the part of CEOs, but that there is a link between corporate financial support and the direction of public policy. In an extensive analysis of US electoral history, he argues that 'political changes are usually–but not always–intimately involved with shifts in the balance of power among ... large investors.'[29] One of the consequences of this increasingly close relationship is the blurring of business and governmental personnel.[30] While the cash-politics nexus may historically have been associated primarily with the US–not an insignificant phenomenon given the scale of US capital and political power–concerns over the link between big money and politics have grown in other G8 countries, including Italy, Japan, France, Germany and the UK.[31]

The Corporate-State Nexus

The state-corporate nexus suggests an empirical gap in orthodox constitutional accounts. However, while earlier calls to fill this gap by admitting the constitutional importance of corporations have gone largely unheeded,[32] the present globalising context means theory can no longer avoid

351. Ferguson estimates that just over a third of monies donated in Senate races, and a quarter to House campaigns, come from PACs; as far as Presidential elections are concerned, Ferguson argues that the role of PACs is 'insignificant', as the vast majority of campaign finance comes directly from individual and corporate donations.

[29] *Ibid*, 87. Ferguson discusses the 1992 election of Bill Clinton in this context, noting (297) that from the start, the Clinton campaign had strong business support in his own state of Arkansas, including Tyson Foods, Murphy Oil, Wal-Mart, Beverley Enterprises, 'and the investment banking and oil interests associated with the Stephens family.' Other businesses also lent their support, including the investment house, Goldman, Sachs. Ferguson suggests (298) that the interests of the businesses for Clinton differed only marginally from those which had supported the previous Bush administration: 'Together with the myriad of Washington lobbyists for U.S. and foreign multinationals who contributed heavily to the campaign...these interests virtually guaranteed what in any case rapidly became obvious: that the Clinton campaign accepted free trade and an open world economy as its fundamental strategic premise.' For Ferguson (275), the success of business in securing their agenda in the Clinton presidency was revealed in the economic plan announced in February 1993, which saw 'President Clinton reverse candidate Clinton's priority of economic growth over deficit reduction.'

[30] Ferguson, for example, refers (*ibid*, 275–76) to Bill Clinton's appointment of Robert Rudin, an executive with Goldman, Sachs, to head his National Economic Council, and Lawrence Summers as treasury undersecretary for international affairs, as symptomatic of 'an economic team that looked like Wall Street.'

[31] *Ibid*, 352.

[32] AS Miller, *The Modern Corporate State: Private Government and the American Constitution* (Westport, CT, Greenwood Press, 1976) 37–49.

confronting practice. The Washington consensus has not so much led to the state's disappearance, as its reconfiguration,[33] and so while it is important to highlight ways in which governments act like, and often through businesses, we should also include in our analysis ways in which businesses act like and through governments. In other words, while the contemporary political understandings of the 'weak state'[34] may have significantly changed expectations as to who should perform the state's traditional functions and how, nonetheless these functions are still performed. Increasingly, in the contemporary world, governmental functions are performed by corporations.[35] Indeed, it has been observed that the 'dismantling' of state mediating institutions has helped reorient attention to alternative structures of political authority such as corporations.[36]

The argument that corporations exhibit state-like characteristics has been made historically, for example, by highlighting how entities like the British East India Company circulated its own currency and possessed a distinct military capability.[37] We can update this to the present age by showing that in many areas of social life, decisions of multinational companies are the direct source of political decisions affecting citizens' daily lives, and not their national governments.[38] In some cases, this takes a more direct form: in the former Soviet bloc, for example, we have witnessed 'state capture' by MNCs, whereby the latter buy laws and policies to secure greater market liberalisation.[39] Others document that where the state no longer does or can act as functionary, corporations have acquired 'quasi-governmental'[40] or 'quasi-state'[41] roles. For example, in Nigeria Royal Dutch-Shell now acts as a surrogate state, spending $52 million in 1999 providing infrastructure and services such as roads and bridges, hospitals and schools.[42] While state failure in the developing world may make the phenomenon of corporate rule more

---

[33] L Panitch, 'Rethinking the Role of the State' in JH Mittelman (ed), *Globalization: Critical Reflections* (Boulder, Co., Lynne Rienner, 1996) 83, 85.

[34] J Jenson and B de Sousa Santos, 'Introduction: Case Studies and Common Trends in Globalizations' in J Jenson and B de Sousa Santos (eds), *Globalizing Institutions: Case Studies in Social Regulation and Innovation* (Aldershot, Ashgate, 2000) 9 at 17–19.

[35] See A Claire Cutler, 'Private international regimes and interfirm cooperation' in R Bruce Hall and TJ Biersteker (eds), *The Emergence of Private Authority in Global Governance* (Cambridge, Cambridge University Press, 2002) 23 at 33.

[36] S Deakin and A Hughes, 'Comparative Corporate Governance: An Interdisciplinary Agenda' (1997) 24 *JLS* 1, 1.

[37] Held et al, *Global Transformations: Politics, Economics and Culture*, above n 7, at 239.

[38] L Sklair, *The Transnational Capitalist Class* (Oxford, Blackwell, 2001) 48.

[39] JS Hellman, G Jones, D Kaufman and M Schankerman, *Measuring Governance, Corruption, and State Capture: How Firms and Bureaucrats Shape the Business Environment in Transition Economies* (Washington, EDRB and the World Bank Institute, 2000).

[40] D Litvin, *Empires of Profit: Commerce, Conquest and Corporate Responsibility* (New York, Texere, 2003) 269.

[41] N Hertz, *The Silent Takeover: Global Capitalism and the Death of Democracy* (London, Heinemann, 2001) 186.

[42] *Ibid*, 173.

obvious there, it can be found in more subtle ways in developed states. For example, the financial markets have proved to be an effective instrument of corporate will through the practice of assigning credit ratings to states which promote disciplines of low tax and fiscal restraint.[43] As has been observed, these ratings not only constrain states with regard to macroeconomic policy, confirming the extent to which national fiscal policy does not lie in the hands of national finance ministers,[44] but also affect a broad range of policy areas.[45]

The idea that corporations are major political actors is being accepted within the corporate world through the discourse of corporate social responsibility (CSR). Sometimes framed as corporate citizenship,[46] this goes beyond the 'minimal' requirements of corporate citizenship, ie, compliance with state company law, and also focuses on 'a complex relationship of interlocking rights and responsibilities [between a corporation and its communities].'[47] Instead of purely economic concerns, this discourse speaks in terms of human rights and environmental standards which have generally been seen as applicable solely to states.[48] While some doubt the motives behind CSR,[49] these developments are emblematic of how, when corporations effectively act like states, this will raise questions over their political accountability. It is perhaps one of the ironies of the global economy that it may politicise what has tended to be perceived as non-political in the form of the activities of privately owned corporations.

Corporations and the 'New Constitutionalism'

The previous two sections addressed the constitutional relevance of MNCs in terms of the traditional objects of constitutional study–whether focusing on the exercise of power by state institutions, or the legislative and executive

---

[43] C Leys, *Market-Driven Politics: Neoliberal Democracy and the Public Interest* (London, Verso, 2001) 23.

[44] For example, Leys *(ibid)* suggests that Gordon Brown's public statements leading up to the 1997 general election in the United Kingdom were designed to avoid the 'risk premium of 1 or 2 per cent' generally assigned to 'left-labour' governments in the 'north'.

[45] Leys, *(ibid, 22)*: 'Even matters that might once have seemed purely the province of politics, such as professional training and qualifications, or the protection of the national language, can turn out to be of concern to "the market", not to mention matters as vital to investors as proposals to tighten the regulation of money markets or to impose new obligations on the managers of pension funds.'

[46] See M McIntosh, D Leipziger, K Jones and G Coleman, 'Corporate Citizenship: Successful strategies for responsible companies' (London, Financial Times, 1998).

[47] *Ibid*, xxi.

[48] This thinking is reflected, eg, in the preamble to the OECD Principles of Corporate Governance, which explains that part of their rationale is that 'factors such as business ethics and corporate awareness of environmental and societal interests of the communities in which they operate can also have an impact on the reputation and long-term success of a company.': OECD Directorate for Financial, Fiscal and Enterprise Affairs (Ad Hoc Task Force on Corporate Governance), *OECD Principles of Corporate Governance* (Paris, OECD, 1999).

[49] See, eg Hertz, above n 41, at 176–84.

functions associated with the nation-state. However, as a result of the worldwide spread of charters of rights,[50] constitutional law increasingly takes the form of higher law, judicially administered limits on state institutions, generally in the form of fundamental rights.[51] In this section, I question whether we can understand fully the present nature of constitutional limits on the state without again bringing corporations into the picture. In this regard, I discuss some recent scholarship under the heading of the 'new constitutionalism' which challenges the orthodox conception of constitutions as creations of state law which organise formal legal normativity within the bounds of state sovereignty. Instead, new constitutionalism stresses the need for a constitutional perspective grounded in analyses of the global economic processes (of which MNCs are the main engines).

New constitutionalism has been described as 'the quasi-legal restructuring of the state and internationalization of international political forms' which confer 'privileged rights of citizenship and representation on corporate capital.'[52] Stephen Gill places three sets of processes at the heart of the new constitutionalism: 'measures to reconfigure state apparatuses, measures to construct and extend liberal capitalist markets, [and] measures for dealing with the dislocations and contradictions.'[53] These measures should be regarded as constitutional as their object is to pre-commit states to neoliberal political economy, and so remove discussion of alternative models from political debate.[54] On this account, corporations once again emerge as major constitutional actors, now on a global scale, as the new constitutionalism not only enhances their capacity to exercise political power, but also provides them with the means to sustain this power in the face of democratic challenges. This is achieved by a combination of institutional and ideological factors.

The watchword of the new constitutionalism is 'discipline', and one way this is manifested is where international structures discipline national constitutions to accept the constraints of the Washington consensus. David Schneiderman has outlined how membership of NAFTA resulted in formal and informal changes in the constitutions of Canada[55] and Mexico,[56] designed to ease restrictions on foreign investment (for example by neutralising Clause 27

---

[50] See R Hirschl, *Towards Juristocracy: The Origins and Consequences of the New Constitutionalism* (Cambridge, Mass, Harvard University Press, 2004).

[51] See H Klug, 'Universal Values and the Politics of Constitutional Understanding' in C Sampford and T Round (eds), *Beyond the Republic: Meeting the Global Challenges to Constitutionalism* (Sydney, Federation Press, 2001) 191.

[52] D Schneiderman, 'Investment Rules and the New Constitutionalism' (2000) 25 *Law & Soc Inq'y* 757, 758.

[53] S Gill, 'The Constitution of Global Capitalism' (2000): www.theglobalsite.ac.uk, 11, 13 and 15.

[54] See Schneiderman, above n 52, at 758.

[55] D Schneiderman, 'NAFTA's Takings Rule: American Constitutionalism Comes to Canada' (1996) 46 *UTLJ* 499.

[56] Above, n 52, at 764–67.

of the Mexican Constitution which subjected foreign investment to domestic laws). Discipline is also now exercised at the global level, principally through the establishment of the World Trade Organization (WTO) in 1995, which some regard as the '"constitutional structure" of the contemporary world trading system.'[57] The WTO differs from previous trade agreements in two important respects. First, its scope, as its policing of least trade-restrictive practices by states goes beyond trade in goods[58] and includes also public health, culture and environmental protection.[59] Secondly, its Dispute Settlement Body (DSB) goes further than GATT arrangements,[60] and can order states which act inconsistently with WTO agreements, to bring national law into compliance,[61] or face having to pay compensation,[62] or withdrawal of WTO concessions.[63] Although initiated by states, claims under this process are in practice brought on behalf of MNCs,[64] which have so far won some important concessions.[65] In this way, the WTO and its mechanisms effectively open themselves to act as a proxy for the exercise of corporate power.[66]

---

[57] JH Jackson, *The World Trading System: Law and Policy of International Economic Relations* (2nd edn, Cambridge, Mass, MIT Press, 1997) 11.

[58] These now include trade in services, trade related intellectual property measures, trade related investment measures and trade in agricultural goods: *ibid*, 305–17.

[59] L Wallach, 'The World Trade Organization's Five Year Record: Seattle in Context' in E Goldsmith and J Mander (eds), *The Case Against the Global Economy & For a Turn Towards Localization* (London, Earthscan, 2001) 175, 177.

[60] Jackson, above n 57, at 125.

[61] Art 22, para 1 of the *Understanding on Rules and Procedures Governing the Settlement of Disputes* (being Annex 2 to the *Agreement Establishing the World Trade Organization*): http://ww.wto.org/english/docs_e/legal_e/28-dsu.wpf.

[62] *Ibid*, Art 3, para 7.

[63] *Ibid*, Art 22, para 2.

[64] Many actions are raised by the US, where, given its leading role in forging the global economy, symbiosis between state and corporate interests are most pronounced. For example, the challenge to the EU ban on beef which had been treated with artificial hormones (WT/DS 26 and 28), Wallach argues, was brought 'by the US at the behest of its agribusiness and pharmaceutical interests (supra note 61 at 179).' Also, the Banana case, (WT/DS 31), where the US successfully argued that the EU had been giving preferential treatment to bananas produced by former colonies of Member States in the Caribbean, was brought by the US at the behest of the Chiquita corporation (based in the US): J Mander and D Baker, *The World Trade Organization: Processes and Rulings*: (http://www.ifg.org/wto.html).

[65] The DSB has not been shy to use these powers: for example, it has ruled that an EU decision to ban US beef injected with (potential carcinogenic) artificial hormones (WT/DS 26), Canadian attempts to give tax advantages to domestically produced magazines (WT/DS 31), and the US federal law that required imported shrimp to be caught by methods which protected sea turtles (WT/DS 58) all illegally restricted free trade as set down in the WTO agreements, and ordered the parties concerned to amend their laws or face further sanctions. (See Wallach, above n 59, at 180).

[66] Eg, in the shrimp-turtle case, the main losers under the US *Endangered Species Act* were the large industrial fishing concerns, who had to bear the cost of adapting boats to meet these standards (small fishing vessels themselves pose relatively little threat to ocean life such as turtles). As Mander and Baker point out (above n 64), the DSB's ruling, 'means that many financial and administrative costs (hiring more border inspection personnel, training for officials to inspect boats) become the burden of countries that wish to protect environmental standards. Previously, the burden of proof was on the exporting commercial interests.'

The net effect of the new constitutionalism is to 'lock-in' the policies of the Washington consensus.[67] This serves corporate interests by freeing up foreign direct investment, which by the late 1990s had reached record levels,[68] and which, when allied to technological advances,[69] facilitates the establishment of global corporate networks[70] thus intensifying the reach of MNCs.[71] This globalisation of market principles also reinforces the new constitutionalism through 'mechanisms connected with consumerism,'[72] leading some to speak of the 'constitutionalization of the culture-ideology of consumerism.'[73] The extent to which states willingly subscribe to the Washington consensus, often making it unnecessary to invoke the institutional mechanisms, is evidence of the ideological hold of its ideas.[74]

This last point is important, as it emphasises that the state does not disappear when we focus on the constitutional relevance of corporations in the context of the global economy–indeed, it is the author of many of the reforms discussed. Rather, following David Held et al, we can point to 'a complex interrelationship between corporate and state power' which 'enhances the global power of corporate capital.'[75] My argument is that the nature of this relationship has ramifications for constitutional study. Take, for example, public health. If we want to understand how government policy is formulated, we must have regard to the intense lobbying by the private sector,[76] and its contribution to the widespread opening of health services to market forces.[77] Secondly, if we want to locate the execution of health policy, we must take account of corporations becoming the direct source of health care for many people, particularly in developing countries whether in the setting up of clinics, or running AIDS education campaigns.[78] Thirdly, if we wish to chart the limitations on state health policies

---

[67] Gill, above n 53, at 10.

[68] Held et al, above n 7, at 243.

[69] JH Mittelman, 'The Dynamics of Globalization' in Mittelman (ed), *Globalization: Critical Reflections*, above n 33, at 1, 6–7.

[70] See Held et al, above n 7, at 259–70.

[71] *Ibid*, 244.

[72] Gill, above n 53, at 10. Gill gives the examples of 'market ideas in education [and] leisure activity (for example private sponsorship of amateur sports and social clubs).'

[73] D Schneiderman, 'Constitutionalizing the Culture-Ideology of Consumerism' (1998) 7 *Soc & Leg St* 213.

[74] R Falk, *Predatory Globalization: A Critique*, above n 5, at 2.

[75] Held et al, above n 7, at 281.

[76] Leys, *Market-Driven Politics: Neoliberal Democracy and the Public Interest*, above n 43, at 207–08.

[77] V George and P Wilding, *Globalization and Human Welfare* (Basingstoke, Palgrave, 2002) 63.

[78] Hertz, *The Silent Takeover: Global Capitalism and the Death of* Democracy, above n 41, at 171. As Hertz observes, companies' activities here are not necessarily motivated by compassion, but by how rampant disease in the relatively inexpensive labour markets can affect their profit: '[e]ach employee infected by HIV costs a mining company approximately £10,000 a year once AIDS develops.'

deviating from neoliberal norms, then we have to include the WTO framework in our analysis: for example, the attempts of the WTO secretariat to extend (in effect on behalf of US health care companies) GATS to health services.[79] Thus, the (by no means isolated[80]) example of health care attests to the constitutional relevance of multinational corporations, and suggests that there be a more prominent engagement between constitutional law and corporate power: we now consider what form that engagement should take.

CONSTITUTIONAL LAW AND LEGAL PLURALISM

In the previous part, I argued that the activities of MNCs are now central to the key concerns of constitutional lawyers, whether in terms of describing the exercise of political power within a polity, or analysing the (de jure and de facto) legal limits on state power. In this section, I consider how positing this empirical gap aids constitutional law's implicit normative agenda of holding political power to account. (Or, from the perspective of corporate governance, how does this attempt to link the latter discourse with constitutional law advance the greater democratic scrutiny of corporate power?) My claim is that the constitutional relevance of the corporation does *not* lie in dealing with corporate power through an extension of existing constitutional thought and practice; rather, it is in questioning the adequacy for present times of our dominant assumptions of constitutional law. More specifically, it highlights the importance of which knowledge of constitutional law prevails in framing public discourse's engagement with issues of corporate power. In the following section, I illustrate this point by outlining how adopting a different knowledge of law, based in the alternative paradigm of legal pluralism, shifts the agenda of inquiry from that entailed by the traditional state-centred approach.

Critics often argue that while hegemonic forms of globalisation appear to herald the ultimate triumph of liberal ideas (whether in political or economic terms), their contradictions in fact make globalisation inherently unstable.[81] Here, I develop this critique to problematise two of the central assumptions of liberal theory with regard to constitutional law. I take as my point of

---

[79] Leys, above n 43, at 209. The issue arises through the Secretariat's argument that, notwithstanding the exemption provided in GATS in those areas designated by states as government services, that health care should be subject to its liberalising regime as it was a mix of private and public provision in the UK.

[80] Similar arguments can be advanced for example with regard to agriculture (see V Shiva, 'The World Trade Organization and Developing World Agriculture' in Goldsmith and Mander (eds), *The Case Against the Global Economy & For a Turn Towards Localization*, above n 59, at 203) and genetically modified organisms (see F Macmillan & M Blakeney, 'Regulating GMOs: Is the WTO Agreement on Sanitary and Phytosanitary Measures Hormonally Challenged? (Part 2)' (2000) 6 *Int Tr L & Reg.* 161).

[81] See Gill, 'The Constitution of Global Capitalism', above n 53, at 5.

departure, Wojciech Sadurski's observation that 'if there is one central thought in liberal thinking, it is that the organized authority of the state must be confined within clearly defined borders,' which, he contends, 'is also a central insight in modern thinking about constitutions.'[82] This captures two core elements of the dominant constitutional paradigm, namely that constitutional law operates within a bounded geographical territory, and is the formal emanation of state legal processes. This picture may be adapted when states form themselves into new official structures,[83] but the basic organisational points of territoriality and formality hold. The descriptive accuracy of this picture is increasingly undercut in the context of globalisation: the new constitutionalism outlined above highlights both the possibility of speaking of a global constitution, and that constitutional norms issue not only from official state or supra-state processes, but also, for example, from the decisions of MNCs.

Legal pluralism addresses these points in two important ways. First, it seeks to ground any understanding of law in empirically informed social theory, and secondly, and consequently, it seeks to give a fuller account of the range and nature of normative activity in the social world. By highlighting the main strands of some recent scholarship that promotes these ideas, we can begin to see the implications for constitutional accounts of corporate power. Perhaps the most well-known, and certainly the most ambitious, legal pluralist social theory is that of Boaventura de Sousa Santos.[84] Santos presents a highly complex 'structure-agency map'[85] of modern capitalist society. This posits six basic forms of power, law and knowledge respectively, which, though interrelated, are structurally autonomous.[86] To flesh out these different forms of power, law and knowledge, Santos distinguishes between six structural places–the householdplace, the workplace, the marketplace, the communityplace, the citizenplace, and the worldplace – which are 'the most consolidated clusters of social relations in contemporary capitalist societies.'[87]

Santos's objective here is to counter the dominant state-centred epistemology of law, with an account of the plurality of law. This is revealed by showing how six basic forms of law[88] are 'anchored in, constituted by, and

---

[82] W Sadurski, 'Liberalism and Constitutionalism' in M Wyrzkowski (ed), *Constitutional Cultures* (Warsaw, Institute of Public Affairs, 2000) 137, 137.

[83] See, eg S Douglas-Scott, *Constitutional Law in the European Union* (Harlow, Longman, 2002).

[84] B de Sousa Santos, *Toward a New Legal Common Sense: Law, Globalization and Emancipation,* (2nd edn, London, Butterworths, 2002).

[85] *Ibid,* 371.

[86] *Ibid,* 370.

[87] *Ibid,* 374

[88] Santos defines law as 'a body of regularized procedures and normative standards that is considered justiciable–ie, susceptible of being enforced by a judicial authority—in a given group and contributes to the creation and prevention of disputes, as well as to their settlement through an argumentative discourse coupled with the threat of force (*ibid,* 86).'

constitutive of' the six structural places.[89] One of these forms is the state law of the citizenplace, produced by the institutions of the nation-state. However, other forms include: the domestic law of the householdplace; the production law of the workplace; the exchange law of the marketplace; the community law of the communityplace, and the systemic law of the world-place.[90] For example, the highly informal domestic law is 'the set of rules, normative standards and dispute settlement mechanisms both resulting from and in the sedimentation of social relations in the householdplace.'[91] The structural places not only explain the nature of different types of law, but also their relation to each other, as the legal regime within any of the structural places is an articulation between different forms of law. Thus, the law of the householdplace, such as provisions of family law with regard to childcare, is constituted by both domestic and state law which 'engage in a constant process of interaction, negotiation, compromise, conflict, mutual reinforcement, mutual neutralization.'[92]

Santos's primary objective here is to uncouple law from the state, and (re)couple it with social power.[93] If we turn now to the legal regimes affecting MNCs, we would include state company law in our analysis. To this, we should also add the systemic law of the worldplace,[94] such as the WTO processes discussed above. However, the law many commentators identify as most important in MNCs' practical operations is a global *lex mercatoria*, which consists of 'worldwide commercial practices, ... standardized contracts [and] activities of global economic associations.'[95]

The key point is that this *lex mercatoria*, which has no provenance in the state, and does not require to be sanctioned by the state in order to exist,[96] can only be explained by a pluralist understanding of law (in Santos's terms, as part of the exchange law of the marketplace). This changes our view of the relationship between states and corporations: state law no longer has a privileged position, but is one of a number of overlapping, interpenetrating legal

---

[89] *Ibid*, 384. Santos seems to imply that this is not an exclusive list of 'the great variety of legal orders circulating in society.'

[90] *Ibid*, 384–95.

[91] *Ibid*, 385.

[92] *Ibid*, 386.

[93] *Ibid*, 356. Thus, for example, while the householdplace in western states has historically witnessed a high degree of isomorphism between domestic law and state family law, this is now becoming much looser in light of developments such as the reduced reach and provision of state welfare services. For Santos, although the general perception is that this has created a '*tabula rasa*', the more accurate reading is that 'we can see that what are changing are the boundaries and the combination between the state law of the household and domestic law' (*ibid*, 386–87).

[94] *Ibid*, 392–93.

[95] G Teubner, '"Global Bukowina": Legal Pluralism in the World Society' in G Teubner (ed), *Global Law Without a State* (Gateshead, Athenaeum Press, 1997) 3, 9.

[96] J-P Robé, 'Multinational Enterprises: The Constitution of a Pluralistic Legal Order' in *Global Law Without a State* 45, 63.

orders. Moreover, it need not be the most important legal order–as evidenced by the success of *lex mercatoria* 'regulating market exchanges with great autonomy *vis-à-vis* the nation states.' [97] Thus, a legal pluralist account of constitutional law would accord a prominent place to the analysis of the operations of MNCs. If the concern of constitutional law is how that political power is exercised, then legal pluralism underscores the artificiality of confining our analysis to one locus of power, and one form of law, that of the state.

This account of legal pluralism, if more broadly accepted, would significantly change the face of constitutional scholarship. However, I want to make a stronger point as legal pluralism has far-reaching consequences for the issue of corporate accountability. The critical point of legal pluralism is that our knowledge of law is socially contested and constructed, and that the reduction of law to positive state law is a result of successful strategies in the nineteenth century to advance a scientific and professional view of law.[98] Its widespread acceptance today does not represent some essential truth, but rather reflects the extent to which the statist view of law is accepted as commonsense in the minds of legal subjects. In this way, legal pluralism emphasises how 'it is knowledge that maintains and creates realities.'[99] This leads to two points: First, if the propagation of certain forms of legal knowledge is the key, this places the legal subject more at the centre of analysis than in positivist accounts of law where sovereignty is still regarded as an external object of inquiry.[100] Rather, while existing legal knowledge structures subjects' thoughts and actions, this should not be exaggerated because, as the primary creative source of legal knowledge, subjects are also a site of transformative agency when they constitute their legal subjectivity in counterhegemonic ways. Secondly, any supposed definition of law is a mix of analytical and political claims which seeks to shape reality by embedding itself in the imagination of legal subjects. Accordingly, we should ask what picture of reality the dominant paradigm seeks to portray, and whether this closes down the creation of alternative worlds.

A (CRITICAL) LEGAL PLURALIST ANALYSIS OF RIGHTS CONSTITUTIONALISM

If our conceptions of law are socially contested and created, so are our conceptions of constitutional law. Those who speak of the model of entrenched, judicially administered, fundamental rights as representing

---

[97] Santos, above n 84, at 390.

[98] *Ibid*, 40–44. See also HW Arthurs, *Without the Law: Administrative Justice and Legal Pluralism in Nineteenth-Century England* (Toronto and Buffalo, University of Toronto Press, 1985) ch 1.

[99] M-M Kleinhans and RA Macdonald, 'What is a Critical Legal Pluralism?' (1997) *12 Can J of Law & Soc'y* 25, 38.

[100] *Ibid*, 39.

some constitutional 'essence'[101] forget the hand of powerful agencies such as the World Bank and USAID in actively promoting this apparent truth in central and eastern Europe, Latin America, and Africa.[102] To regard rights constitutionalism as the only possible model can thus be rightly criticised as 'mistakenly tak[ing] the part for the whole.'[103] Rights constitutionalism is partial though in another sense, namely that its increasingly global adoption serves important ideological purposes. Our dominant understandings of constitutional law put in place a set of beliefs about law and power which resists attempts to subject corporations to greater democratic accountability. This is a point of general importance, but also contemporary relevance, given recent moves to adapt rights discourse to promote corporate accountability. Indeed, the success of corporate governance strategies, whether based in extending constitutional mechanisms or otherwise, can be measured to the extent they reinforce or disturb the state-centred paradigm in individuals' perception of their normative worlds.

Normative Downgrading of Corporate Power

The first way in which state-centred accounts of constitutional law support the corporate agenda is through its uncoupling of law from social power. Santos argues that this should be seen as part of the central dichotomies in liberal theory, at the heart of which is the divide between the state and civil society. Thus, the state is the exclusive site of politics, and only its official commands should be designated as law. In contrast to this coercive exercise of social power is civil society, seen as 'the realm of economic life, of spontaneous social relations.'[104] Thus, only the social power exercised by the state is singled out for systematic restraint through constitutional forms. This separation of politics from economics serves well the social power found in the marketplace, as its norms are not seen in political terms, and so do not raise the same sorts of normative inquiry–such as their legitimacy[105]–as those of the state. This thinking reaches its zenith in the classical liberal dualism of the naturally free individual and the coercive state; however, it also underpins modern forms of liberalism that acknowledges the

---

[101] See AE Dick Howard, 'The Essence of Constitutionalism' in KW Thompson and RR Ludwokowski (eds), *Constitutionalism and Human Rights: America, Poland and France* (Lanham, MD, University Press of America, 1991) 3.

[102] See B de Sousa Santos, 'Law and Democracy: (Mis)trusting the Global Reform of Courts' in Jenson and Santos (eds), *Globalizing Institutions: Case Studies in Social Regulation and Innovation*, above n 34, ch 10, 259–65.

[103] D Castiglione, 'The Political Theory of the Constitution' (1996) 44 *Pol Studies* 417, 417.

[104] Santos, *Toward a New Legal Common Sense: Law, Globalization and Emancipation*, above n 84, at 363.

[105] RA Macdonald, 'Metaphors of Multiplicity: Civil Society, Regimes and Legal Pluralism' (1998) 15 *Ariz J Int'l & Comp L* 69, 79

state may not be the only threat to freedom in two important ways. First, while civil society can be a source of coercion, when this is manifested, it is seen as pathological, and so is a lower order threat than the state–the main default is still the need to limit the state's political power. Secondly, this pathology is dealt with by extending state politics–democratic deliberation remains exclusively in the state, buttressing the notion that politics does not occur in other spheres of social life.[106]

Recently, some writers have suggested that public law processes protecting human rights against states should be extended to corporations.[107] This takes seriously the extent of corporate power in the modern world, and sees human rights law as a means of promoting its accountability where company law regimes have implicitly failed. While motivated by seeking to remedy all abuses of power, expanding current human rights instruments may in fact reinforce the dominant paradigm; it may result in some short-term reverses for MNCs, but ultimately is unlikely to disturb existing power relations. This is so for three reasons. First, it provides normative support for not regarding corporate power as raising the same political concerns as that of the state. Corporations have been major beneficiaries of rights adjudication, as courts in a number of jurisdictions have equated them with individual persons whose rights require to be vindicated. This should not just be seen as perverse thinking, but rather reflects the deep hold of the idea that rights exist to protect civil society from the state. It therefore requires a considerable conceptual leap for courts to apply rights directly against civil society. Moreover, where courts do reach corporate action, this is through the filter of the state, for example, under the European Convention system where states may be liable if their positive law permits one non-state entity, possibly a corporation, to victimise the rights of another non-state entity.[108] States are still seen here as the ultimate violator of rights, and so the state-civil society divide remains in place. This point is further underscored if we look at how courts might apply rights to corporations, for example, by requiring national public order laws to be amended that enable corporations to curtail freedom of association. While this may impinge on some corporate activity, the underlying rationale is still to prevent the violation

---

[106] See A Fraser, *Reinventing Aristocracy: The Constitutional Reformation of Corporate Governance* (Aldershot, Dartmouth, 1998) 56.

[107] See, eg MK Addo (ed), *Human Rights Standards and the Responsibility of Transnational Corporations* (The Hague, Kluwer, 1999); MT Kamminga, 'Holding Multinational Corporations Accountable for Human Rights Abuses: A Challenge for the EC' in P Alston (ed), *The EU and Human Rights* (Oxford, Oxford University Press, 1999) 353; Ratner, 'Corporations and Human Rights: A Theory of Legal Responsibility' above n 6, and C Scott, 'Translating Torture into Transnational Tort: Conceptual Divides in the Debate on Corporate Accountability for Human Rights Harms' in C Scott (ed), *Torture as Tort: Comparative Perspectives on the Development of Transnational Human Rights Litigation* (Oxford and Portland, OR, Hart Publishing, 2001) ch 2.

[108] See, eg *Plattform 'Ärtze für das Leben,'* Series A, vol 139.

of individual liberty in the free realm of civil society, and so leaves in place, and tacitly legitimates, the state-civil society framework that serves corporate interests well.

Methodological Downgrading of Corporate Power

The second way in which rights discourse reinforces corporate power is at the methodological level. The call to apply human rights to corporations is part of a general change in the way we view politics; where constitutionalism has been adopted, political campaigners increasingly prosecute their case not through legislative politics, but litigation over rights, whether regarding abortion, equality, or industrial relations. This results in a normative method where arguments are directed to the standards that courts ought to apply, eg, that social and economic, and civil and political, rights be treated on a par. It is assumed, in terms of the command model of law, that if the argument is won, these rights will be delivered. However, there is now considerable empirical evidence that the impact of constitutional litigation is exaggerated, that it frequently fails to engineer social change, and that where this does occur, it is better attributed to social forces beyond courts and constitutions.[109] However, to criticise liberalism for misdescribing law's relation to society slightly misses the point as the command model is not interested in getting its sociology right, but rather plays an ideological role.[110] First, it encourages activists to see the constitution's commands as the primary route to justice ('the constitution as the "object of all longing"'[111]) and so privileges the liberal worldview, where the state-civil society divide thrives. Secondly, and crucially, it directs our inquiry away from a more empirical focus on questions such as what forms of social power have a greater effect on freedom and equality, and whether they impede the operation of constitutional norms, questions which might undermine rights constitutionalism's legitimacy as the principal means for processing political disputes. In these ways, the normative method further can restrict public discourse from critically scrutinising the activities of corporations.

These points are underlined when we place them in the context of the global spread of charters of rights. For some, the dominant characteristic of constitutional globalisation is the enhancement of formal equality rights

---

[109] See G Rosenberg, 'Constitutional Cants' in Sampford and Round, *Beyond the Republic: Meeting the Global Challenges to Constitutionalism*, above n 51, ch 18.

[110] S Veitch, 'Ronald Dworkin and the Power of Ideas' (2004) *Acta Juridica* 44.

[111] UK Preuss (trans DL Schneider), *Constitutional Revolution: The Link Between Constitutionalism and Progress* (Atlantic Highlands, NJ, Humanities Press, 1995) ch 2. This captures the view of a constitution as 'both historically unique and sacred because it creates a lasting possibility for human progress' (*ibid*, 37).

through guaranteeing procedural rights of participation.[112] This can be seen to be at the expense of other conceptions of democracy, which might emphasise substantive equality through material redistribution. In this way, the increasing tendency to conceive of politics in terms of constitutional politics, and to see constitutional politics as raising questions of fair procedure, potentially forecloses the range of political debate, again to the advantage of the political power exercised by corporations. Thus, while bodies enforcing human rights might protect shareholders' voting rights against interference,[113] it is more difficult to imagine them making corporations uphold the right to basic subsistence by turning profits to the alleviation of poverty in developing countries–especially as they have not enforced the same standards on states.[114] To the extent that this account of constitutionalism is accepted as commonsensical, it puts beyond inquiry the political consequences of working within the state-centred paradigm of constitutional law.

CONCLUSION

In this chapter, I have sought to demonstrate the insights that a constitutional perspective can bring to debates over the democratic accountability of corporations. In particular, highlighting the need for constitutional lawyers to take seriously the activities of large corporations challenges the most deep-rooted assumptions of the dominant constitutional paradigm–that concern with the exercise of political power is best prosecuted by focusing on state institutions. Subjecting such assumptions to the scrutiny of legal pluralism, which posits multiple interacting sites of normative power in the social world, questions their theoretical adequacy in the age of the global economy, and, to the extent they are found empirically wanting, asks what purpose they serve. This, in turn, directs us to the critical legal pluralist point that our knowledge of law helps shape the material world, for better or for worse. In this regard, I have argued that the implicit state-centred patterns of thought that dominate the legal academy and practice contribute to the systematic discounting of the democratic implications of corporate power. To the extent that our existing conceptual structures of constitutional law impede the goal of holding power to account, this leads to the conclusion that they need to be unthought. The

---

[112] Santos, 'Law and Democracy: (Mis)trusting the Global Reform of Courts', above n 102, at 272–73.

[113] MK Addo, 'The Applicability of the Human Rights Act to Private Corporations' in L Betten (ed), *The Human Rights Act 1998: What it Means* (The Hague, Kluwer, 1999) 191, 194.

[114] See J Bakan, *Just Words: Constitutional Rights and Social Wrongs* (Toronto, University of Toronto Press, 1997) 51–55.

critical constitutional challenge for the future is how to transcend this entrenched way of thinking, to create a reality that problematises rather than protects private power. The task of rethinking constitutional law is beyond the scope of this chapter. However, I close with three thoughts on how this paradigm shift may be effected.

The first is that significant changes in how we conceptualise law are unlikely to occur in the absence of major reforms in legal education. The idea that only state law is properly 'law' is instilled in lawyers from the very outset of their training–it is legal pluralists who continue to bear the burden of the qualifying adjective, be it 'indigenous', 'industrial' or 'household' law. An important first step would be for more members of the academy to be conscious of the qualifying adjective of 'state' which always should be placed before 'law.' Secondly, there is much of interest in the relative success of a myriad of pressure groups and organisations associated with the World Social Forum in galvanising popular and non-violent resistance to corporate power.[115] These groups are simply regarding corporations as sources of political authority, and devising means of holding that power to account, unconcerned with whether or not the official narrative catches up. If we are to take legal pluralism seriously, for many the paradigm shift is already under way. Thirdly, while legal pluralism points out the deficiencies of exclusively state-centred approaches, this does not mean that the state as a site of political struggle is unimportant–indeed, the rise of the Washington consensus can be attributed in part to its harnessing state forms to its goals.[116] It also remains the case that for many, the state has been the best hope of achieving some measure of progressive social change. Here, opponents of the corporate agenda might learn from the strategy of the latter's proponents in agitating for new state forms[117] which seek to constrain the market according to the needs of social justice. The prize in each case is to instil in the legal and political mindset a new way of thinking which reclaims all forms of political power for democratic deliberation and scrutiny.

---

[115] See P Kingsnorth, *One No, Many Yeses: A Journey to the Heart of the Global Resistance Movement* (London, Free Press, 2003).

[116] See J Gray, *False Dawn: The Delusions of Global Capitalism* (London, Granta, 1998) chs 1 and 2.

[117] See, eg D Held and M Koenig-Archibugi (eds), *Taming Globalization: Frontiers of Governance* (Oxford, Polity, 2003).

3

Enron and the End of Corporate Governance

DAVID CAMPBELL AND STEPHEN GRIFFIN

[A] theory of markets need not be a *Loblied* to private enterprise, and in the case of Adam Smith most assuredly was not.

D Reisman, *State and Welfare* (1982) at 225

INTRODUCTION

THE SARBANES-OXLEY Act of 2002[1] (SOA) is the US Congress' principal response to the failures of corporate governance dramatically evidenced by the collapse of Enron. As it introduces stringent disclosure, transparency and reporting requirements supported by severe criminal sanctions levelled at corporate executives, SOA appears to be a very serious attempt to protect investors and so strengthen the US corporate system.

However, for those familiar with the literature of corporate governance the suspicion immediately arises that measures of this sort targeted at corporate executives may be fruitless and, therefore, that no matter how fierce its formal provisions, SOA may prove to be merely the latest in a long line of corporate governance initiatives which have failed to remedy the serious defects which we have known since at least Adam Smith are inherent in the joint stock form.

Fearing this to be the case, we will argue that, as an alternative to the extension of the accepted models of corporate governance, consideration should be given to reducing or eliminating the ability of executives to pursue

---

* We should like to thank Kevin Dowd, Paddy Ireland, the late John Parkinson and Charlotte Villiers for their comments.

[1] Sarbanes-Oxley Act 2002 (Public Company Accounting Reform and Investor Protection Act) Pub L 107–204, 30 July 2002, 116 Stat 745.

the advantages of limited liability.[2] Limited liability does not provide rational encouragement to business initiative but rather, by eliminating the fear of incurring personal liability should risk-taking result even in disastrous loss, gives an unbalanced incentive to such risk-taking. Enron is merely the latest disaster which should lead us to consider whether limited liability should be maintained as the foundation of company law.

Such questioning obviously has implications for all approaches to company law. However, we wish to focus on what we call 'left-wing corporate governance,' the identifying characteristics of which are antipathy to the 'market' and a consequent anxiety to rein in the market's pernicious 'economic' influences upon the corporation. The Left has had acceptance of markets thrust upon it by the failure of Marxism, for the communist economy is accepted not only to be unworkable but despicable, and planning in the social democratic countries is rightly criticised the more it approximates to a general plan. No sensible contributor to debates on economic organisation now wishes to do away with markets completely, for this is acknowledged to be impossible. But merely grudging acceptance of markets is not enough. Markets can and must be given a positive place in left-wing corporate governance. We will show that: (1) the public company is a non-market institution; (2) limited liability is a state intervention which ousts the market in order to improve upon the consequences that it is feared market governance of firms would produce; (3) these market consequences are broadly ones which left-wing corporate governance itself seeks to produce through public regulation; and consequently, (4) left-wing antipathy to the market as a way of regulating corporations should be replaced by a commitment to institutionalising welfare-enhancing markets. As corporate governance really is identified by its opposition to markets, it may be best to call this the end of corporate governance.

The Collapse of Enron

In December 2001, the Enron Corporation suffered what was, at the time, the largest bankruptcy the US had seen. The proximate cause of this collapse was the exposure of the gross manipulation of basic rules of corporate financial governance by Enron's senior management in continued pursuit of the rapid growth for which the company had become noted. Enron had pursued an ambitious growth policy involving the incursion of very large debt as it turned itself from a power utility of a more ordinary sort into a gigantic dealer in energy derivatives by taking out positions at gearing

---

[2] We will confine ourselves to discussing the public company, but our remarks would apply to the private company, with the additional point that a company which does not intend to raise equity finance lacks the principal justification given for the availability of incorporation.

ratios so enormous that Enron's strategy was termed 'asset-lite' growth. Enron sought to avoid full disclosure of its debt in order to maintain confidence in its stock and ease pressure on its credit ratings.

Enron's Chief Financial Officer (CFO), Andrew Fastow, created a number of 'Special Purpose Entity' (SPE) 'investment partnerships' as a way of concealing the company's debt. As distinct legal entities, albeit effectively subsidiaries of Enron, these partnerships had their own legal capacity to borrow funds, and debt thereby incurred could be kept off Enron's balance sheet. Many of the most significant transactions involving SPEs were entered into not in pursuit of bona fide objectives but so that favourable financial statements could be made about Enron itself.

The Financial Accounting Standards Board stipulated that an SPE could be created where its independent owner(s) made a substantial capital investment in the entity (a minimum of 3 per cent of total capital) and took a substantial part in the risks and rewards of ownership, exercising ultimate control over the SPE. However, in Enron's case these requirements were never met. For example, in 1997 an SPE was created to take over a previously legitimate energy project known as JEDI. The project was in debt and Enron wished to wipe that debt from its balance sheet. To recreate JEDI as an SPE, Enron assisted one of its senior employees, Michael J Kopper, a close associate of Fastow, to form a new partnership company named Chewco. However, this partnership company had no financial capacity to acquire 3 per cent of JEDI, and, in effect, Enron financed Chewco's purchase of the JEDI interest almost entirely with its own debt. Notwithstanding the shortfall in the 3 per cent requirement, Enron maintained the pretence of Chewco's independent status and failed to consolidate Chewco, and so JEDI, into its overall financial statements.

Other improper transactions included the hedging agreements by which Enron purported to insure itself against potential losses from its derivatives dealings. Instead of entering into these agreements with independent third parties, Enron's agreements were with related SPEs, namely the LJM1 and LJM2 partnerships controlled and managed by Fastow and other Enron employees. The SPEs were given Enron stock in return for covering losses sustained in the course of hedging operations. The losses were in this way set off against the SPEs, but in reality they remained Enron debt as the SPEs were effectively integral parts of the Enron Corporation. The hedging agreements thereby involved no substantive transfer of economic risk, and so not merely lacked transparency but contained a very serious inherent flaw, for if Enron's stock fell substantially, the hedges would likely fail; as indeed they eventually did.

Despite the Enron management's manipulation of the company's true financial position, the company's accounting returns for the third quarter of 2001 showed an after tax loss of US$544 million. Following this announcement, the Securities and Exchange Commission (SEC) required Enron to provide better information about its related party transactions. Enron's revised, more properly consolidated financial statements reduced the company's reported net income between 1997 and 2000 by US$500 million, reduced shareholders' equity by US$3.2 billion, and increased reported debt by US$2.5 billion. Such statements destroyed market confidence in the company. In December 2001, Enron filed for Chapter 11 bankruptcy relief. At the height of the company's success, its stock had peaked at US$90 per share. At the time of its bankruptcy petition, its stock was valued at just 26 cents per share.

Though it is incidental to our argument here, any account of Enron's collapse would be misleading if it did not mention that as the situation worsened for Enron, the senior management sought to protect themselves by insider dealing, a prohibited fraud in the US. Large-scale stock sales took place at times which can only be viewed as indicating the management's knowledge that the company would soon be plunged into grave difficulty; clear cases of the officers jumping the sinking ship. In a gross example of manipulation, management even sold stock at the same time as Enron forbade other employees from doing so. Of course, these sales of stock could themselves have nothing but a prejudicial effect on the company as a whole, however valuable they were for the individuals concerned.

The Responsibility of the Enron Board

Responsibility for Enron's collapse must be apportioned between all of the company's various internal and external corporate watchdogs; namely the board of directors, individual executives, the company's auditors, the company's lawyers, investment banks, credit rating agencies, and SEC. However, the most culpable parties were the directors, executives and auditors. Enron was an example of 'crony capitalism,' in which the ties between the company's management and auditors were so close that little attention was paid to Enron's real financial position, which was hidden by collusive accounting. Although Enron's auditors, the now defunct accountancy firm Arthur Andersen, certainly merit extensive criticism, and though we have seen the conduct of the company's executive directors was a mixture of recklessness and fraud, we shall say a little more only about the company's board.

In the US, the ultimate responsibility for the internal governance of a public company rests with its board of directors, comprised of a majority of directors who are devoid of day-to-day managerial responsibilities. Both state and federal law impose duties of loyalty and care on these directors, although favourable presumptions are made about their diligence under the business judgement rule, and their personal liability for a breach of duty may be limited or even eliminated by the company's constitution other than where the breach involved bad faith or intentional misconduct, a knowing violation of the law, or where the director gained an improper personal benefit at the expense of the company. The US corporate economy institutionalises an enterprise culture in which risk-taking is encouraged by directors being able to escape the imposition of any form of liability other than for acting in bad faith.

After Enron's collapse, a special committee of the company's board was set up under William Powers Jr, a former law school dean appointed a director of Enron in the wake of the collapse, to investigate that collapse.[3] The Powers report concluded that the board had failed to act with sufficient diligence when approving the partnership transactions. Although the board had put various controls in place and had directed its audit and compliance committee to conduct annual reviews of the partnership transactions, these reviews were seriously inadequate. This inadequacy was not addressed by the company's management nor brought to the board's attention. The Powers report found that the board had failed to take adequate care to protect the interests of shareholders and that it had overreached itself in a number of respects. The board had failed to adequately monitor the activities of senior management, having only five meetings a year and spending under an hour reviewing even the most complicated transactions. Yet, despite this lack of diligence, members of the Enron board enjoyed remuneration packages of twice the national average for a public corporation. In 2000, directors received an annual fee of US$350,000, which raises the apprehension that their objectivity and independence were compromised.

Corporate Governance and SOA

On 30 July 2002, SOA was passed in direct response to the Enron scandal, the legislation being further justified as WorldCom Corporation filed for bankruptcy in the preceding week, and in so doing replaced Enron as the largest ever US corporate failure. In tandem with corporate governance rules adopted by the New York Stock Exchange (NYSE), SAO aims to protect investors by increasing the accuracy and reliability of corporate disclosure and reporting.

In relation to disclosure provisions, SOA requires the Chief Executive Officer (CEO) and CFO of public companies to certify that they evaluated the effectiveness of the company's internal controls, that disclosure to the company's auditors and audit committee took place, and that an attempt had made to identify all significant deficiencies in the design or operation

---

[3] Special Investigative Committee of the Board of Directors of the Enron Corporation, *Report* (1 February 2002) (the Powers Report).

of the company's financial reporting. Under SOA, s 906, any officer who knowingly makes a false return is liable to a fine of US$1million and imprisonment for up to 10 years or both. If the violation is deemed wilful, then the fine increases to US$5m and the potential term of imprisonment increases to up to 20 years. However, while SOA criminalises misconduct which is of a 'knowing or wilful nature,' it is silent in respect of negligent conduct.

In respect of transparency provisions, SOA seeks to strengthen the role and independence of the audit committee. Audit committees are to have sole responsibility for hiring and firing the company's independent auditors and for approving any significant non-audit work by the auditors. SOA precludes any person who is affiliated with a major shareholder from being on the audit committee and further requires that an audit committee member must not receive any remuneration from the company other than that received in his capacity as a director, and that a member of the committee must not be an affiliated person of the issuer or any of its subsidiaries.

SOA further requires SEC to direct that securities exchanges require listed companies to maintain audit committees comprised only of independent directors. Recent NYSE reforms extend SOA transparency rules by obliging listed companies to have audit, compensation and governance committees comprised only of independent directors. The boards of NYSE listed companies are required to have a majority of directors who satisfy a test of independence (previously only three independent directors were required).[4] A director will be classed as independent where he has no material relationship with the company either directly or as a partner, shareholder or officer of an organisation which has a relationship with the company.

SOA also contains several new reporting requirements for public companies. Significantly given the facts of the Enron case, SEC, in compliance with SOA, has enacted rules seeking disclosure of all off-balance sheet transactions, arrangements obligations and other relationships of the issuer with unconsolidated entities or other persons that have, or are reasonably likely to have, a current or future effect on a company's financial condition. In an attempt to prevent insider dealing, SOA amends the Securities Exchange Act 1934 to provide that directors, executive officers and shareholders holding 10 per cent of issued capital must quickly disclose any change in their ownership of shares to SEC. Further, SOA, s 306 prohibits executives and directors from trading personal holdings of company securities at any time when the company forbids at least half of its other employees from doing so. Any executive officer or director who violates this provision may, irrespective of the individual's motives, be liable to disgorge his profits from the sale of such securities.

---

[4] Corporate Accountability and Listing Standards Committee of the New York Stock Exchange, *Report*: http:/www.nyse.com.

Criminal Law Penalties

SOA creates new federal offences in an attempt to prevent the obstruction of justice (s 802), fraud (s 807), and retaliation against whistleblowers (s 1107). These offences attract severe sanctions, including imprisonment of up to 25 years. SOA also increases the penalties for existing federal crimes; for example, criminal penalties for violations of existing federal mail or wire fraud statutes are increased from a maximum of five to a maximum of 20 years' imprisonment. The maximum penalty for a wilful violation of the Securities Exchange Act is increased from a fine of US$1m to a fine of up to US$5m, and/or imprisonment up from 10 to 20 years.

In addition to the criminal provisions, SOA has also sought to increase the ease by which directors may be disqualified from holding office in public companies. SEC now has the authority to conditionally or permanently disqualify where the conduct of a person demonstrates 'unfitness' to serve as an officer or director. Previously 'substantial unfitness' was required, and SOA addresses the obvious concern that this standard was too high. Furthermore, SOA amends the Bankruptcy Code to make it more difficult for a security law violator to file for bankruptcy in order to protect his personal assets from a disgorgement penalty. SOA provides that an individual debtor who files for bankruptcy will not be discharged from any debt associated with a violation of the federal securities laws or any law or regulation connected to a fraudulent act.

Having hopefully shown the basic character of SOA as a response to Enron, we do not wish to put forward a detailed evaluation of that response, for reasons which we trust will become clear. What we hope to have shown is that SOA has a familiar quality. It is huge and the penalties it provides, should they ever be applied, are draconian. But this is merely an exaggeration of the familiar stuff of corporate governance, and it is to the feeling of déjà vu that overcomes one as one reads SOA to which we want to draw attention. Rather like the blockbuster movie that, in the absence of real novelty in its script or direction, tries to create sensation by being merely louder and cruder than its predecessors, SOA is merely exaggerating the tired and familiar. But so, we want to argue, we should have expected, for Enron itself is merely an exaggerated version of the commonplace.

Enron: Déjà Vu All Over Again

The central feature of corporate failures even including Enron is their normality. Innovation is stimulated by the greater than normal profit that successful investment in a novel business strategy will yield over established alternatives. Such investment obviously involves risk. If the investment is successful, then those responsible for the novel strategy are lauded as

Schumpeterian innovators; if it is a failure, they may be criticised for 'misdeeds'.[5] If SOA has any effect, it will be to make the pains of being found guilty of a misdeed more severe in an attempt to discourage those investments that fail.[6] But SOA cannot seek to prevent all failures, because failure is of course as indispensable a part of the market economy as success. The only way to prevent the failure of investment is to prevent investment.

The language of 'misdeed', 'fraud', 'crime' etc can have only limited relevance to the type of corporate failure which Enron exemplifies. Leaving aside their insider dealing, Enron's executives *did* use SPEs to facilitate wash and roundtrip trades and mark-to-market accounting in ways which were improper and illegal by the standards of existing corporate governance law and practice, and we can allow that it is right to seek to prevent these actions. (*A fortiori* we can seek to prevent the destruction of the evidence of these actions by Enron and Arthur Andersen). But it would not be right to seek to prevent the 'asset-lite' business strategy that was the cause of all the trouble, for this was just the sort of novel business strategy that brings rewards to the Schumpeterian innovator, and did bring credit to Enron, which had been *Fortune's* favourite company for years prior to the crash. Even if it was clear *ex post* that asset-lite was an outright mistake (though this is not the case), this does not speak to whether one should prevent it *ex ante*, and no regulator who is not blessed with omnicognisance could hope to do so in a way consistent with market principles (which omnicognisance in any case makes redundant). The language of moral blame does not help very much. Fastow is now excoriated for using SPEs in the way he did; but if he had thought SPEs were outright bad things, he would hardly have used the initials of his wife and children to name the LJM companies.[7]

The difficult theoretical problem is not, then, to prevent misdeeds; it analytically is the case that misdeeds should be prevented and the problem such prevention poses is one of regulatory technique. But recognising this merely means that it becomes very important to identify which behaviour is to count as a misdeed, and if doing so is to help in cases like Enron, this requires us accurately to draw the boundaries between legitimate and illegitimate risk-taking by companies. Enron makes it clear that we have not been entirely successful in doing this even though almost 150 years have passed since the birth of general limited liability. For example, in his still

---

[5] Report of the Staff to the Senate Committee on Governmental Affairs, *Financial Oversight of Enron: The SEC and Private-sector Watchdogs* (8 October 2002) 1.

[6] As this paper was in proof, Kenneth Lay and Jeffrey Skilling were, on 25 May 2006, convicted of offences which, though subject to appeal, are predicted to lead to them serving more than 12 years in prison: D Litterick, 'Enron Pair Braced for Jail as "Guilty" Verdict Rings Out' *Daily Telegraph* (26 May 2006). The issue of the *Daily Telegraph* that reported this verdict also carried a 'Business Comment', the title of which conveys the gist of the Comment: A Osborne, 'The Post-Enron Protection Risks Penalising Everybody'. At a later point in the proof stage, beneath lay died of heart failure before sentence was passed.

[7] D Mackenzie, 'Ethnoaccountancy' (22 May 2003) *London Review of Books* 6 at 9.

indispensable work on the Victorian companies acts,[8] Hunt describes the reaction to the first crash after the institutionalisation of general limited liability in terms that could have been directly taken from the coverage of Enron.[9] No single bankruptcy had ever caused 'so great a shock to credit' wrote *The Times*. Trading in shares was 'almost exterminated' by an episode of 'extravagance and folly' wrote *The Economist*.[10] As we say, the point about Enron is its normality, for the Enron crash is different only in quantity rather than quality from the history of failures since the Victorian era; and indeed all that is different are the nominal values, for severe crashes have always been described in apocalyptic terms.

Risk, Planning and the Market

In order to move forward, let us consider the following:

> There is a surplus of capital on the market and it is looking everywhere for a profitable home; bogus companies, set up for the happiness of mankind and the enrichment of the entrepreneurs, are shooting up out of the ground like mushrooms … The sole aim of these joint-stock companies is, of course, briefly to raise the value of the stock so the entrepreneurs can rid themselves of their share at a profit; what then becomes of the stockholders does not bother them: 'After us the deluge!' In three or four years, five-sixths of these companies will have gone the way of all flesh and with them the money of the ensnared stockholders. As always, it will be mainly small people who put their savings into these 'most reliable and profitable' enterprises and always, when the swindle has forced the stock up to its peak on the market–and it serves them right.[11]

Although in substance it could be, the language gives it away that this is not a criticism of the promoters of dotcom companies who got out in time, or the management of Enron if their fortunes remain intact. It was actually directed against promotion during the boom of the early 1870s. Its author was Engels, and we focus on this example to turn to Engels' and Marx's solution to such episodes, which was of course to eliminate the 'anarchy' of capitalist production completely. In an early work[12] written before he had

---

[8] BC Hunt, *The Development of the Business Corporation in England 1800–67* (Cambridge, MA, Harvard University Press, 1936).

[9] The crash in question concerned the 1866 collapse of Overend, Gurney Ltd. In response to this crash, a proposal was put forward very like the sort we argue should be considered now: J Howell, *Partnership Law Legislation and Limited Liability Reviewed in Relation to the Panic of 1866* (London, Effingham Wilson,1869).

[10] Hunt, above n 8, at 153–55.

[11] F Engels, 'On the Company Swindle in England' in K Marx and F Engels, *Collected Works*, vol 23 (London, Lawrence and Wishart, 1988) 35 at 35.

[12] F Engels, 'Outlines of a Critique of Political Economy', in K Marx and F Engels, *Collected Works*, vol 3 (1975) 418.

met Marx which was to have a great influence on Marx's thinking,[13] Engels was highly critical of the market because in it the ends of production are not set by a central authority and, in this sense, are not known in advance of production; indeed, there are no overall ends. Engels and later Marx traced many of the shortcomings of capitalist production to this central characteristic of the market, which they thought represented anarchy. As a solution, they conceived of a planned economy in which ends (and means) would be completely known and this anarchy removed.[14] In such an economy, misallocations of resources would not take place and so communist investment under a plan would not be attended by risk in the way capitalist investment, by taking an equity position or otherwise, is.[15]

We now regard Engels' and Marx's views as Utopian in part because we do not think risk is entirely a product of the weaknesses of the capitalist mode of production but also stems from bounds on rationality which are ineliminable so long as human beings are not omnicognisant. Appreciation of the transaction costs of planning alerts us to the inevitable weaknesses of such planning, which experience of command and control empirically confirms. This being so, Engels' and Marx's solution cannot be effective in the way they wished because the replacement of the capitalist mode of production cannot eliminate risk.[16] We therefore must compare alternative economic institutions in terms of the way they handle ineliminable risk, and once we do this we can see a further weakness of Engels' and Marx's criticism of capitalism, one of great relevance to left-wing corporate governance.

Engels and Marx had a much more sympathetic view of joint stock than might be expected. Recognising the division between ownership and control in the joint stock company, and seeing that the capitalist *qua* provider of finance had no necessary role in decision-making within such a company,[17] they welcomed joint stock as a harbinger of communist production.[18] Joint stock makes it plain that management as a function is separate from the provision of investment funds, and this lesson could be quickly carried over to socialised production if investment was made a planned rather than a private decision and the capitalist *qua* capitalist therefore really rendered superfluous. Given their views of the anarchy of the market, this is a natural

---

[13] K Marx, *A Contribution to the Critique of Political Economy*, in K Marx and F Engels, *Collected Works*, vol 29 (1987) 257 at 264.

[14] K Marx, *Capital*, vol 1, in K Marx and F Engels, *Collected Works*, vol 35 (1996) 807.

[15] Indeed, engaging in this sort of talk about resource allocation at all seems highly inappropriate to the communist economy, which is conceived as a realm of unconstrained freedom: D Campbell, 'The Critique of Bourgeois Justice after the Failure of Marxism', in A Kerner, J Priban and J Young (eds), *Current Legal Issues in the Czech Republic and the United Kingdom* (Prague, Czech Republic, Charles University Press, 2003) 9.

[16] *Cf* AC Pigou, *Socialism Versus Capitalism* (London, Macmillan, 1937) 42–44.

[17] The finance capitalist may, in fact, use his role of investor to secure a decision-making role or may have such a role for other reasons, but this does not disturb the basic point.

[18] K Marx, *Capital*, vol 3, in K Marx and F Engels, *Collected Works*, vol 37 (1998) 434–39.

step. Engels and Marx were acute in seeing that the joint stock company has as its core characteristic the expansion of the planned part of the economy at the expense of the unplanned, for in the joint stock company allocations are carried out under the hierarchical authority of management rather than by the market.[19] It is, in Engels' and Marx's view, a historical irony that the process by which joint stock allows the speculation which magnifies capitalist anarchy is the very process by which the socialisation of the capitalist economy as a whole proceeds.[20]

If, however, one gives up the idea of complete planning, one has to give up the idea of expanding hierarchy to cover 100 per cent of economic allocation, and one therefore must ask where the optimal boundary between market and hierarchy should be drawn.[21] This is an inevitably difficult matter to which Coase has shown there can be no, as it were, final answer, for the optimal amount of competition must itself be continuously determined by competition.[22] All theories of concentration and centralisation of capital recognise that firms which fail to integrate functions which incur avoidable transactions costs when carried out by the market will suffer a competitive disadvantage. But Coase argued that, in an overall competitive economy, the obverse is also the case: firms which integrate functions which could be carried out at smaller transactions costs by the market will suffer the opposite competitive disadvantage. In an overall competitive economy, firms should reach their optimal size in response towards these centralising *and* decentralising incentives, and in this way the overall amount of planning in the economy as a whole (the aggregate of firm sizes) will be optimised. Understanding this requires a grasp of the comparative transaction costs of hierarchy and market, and here, we believe, a serious mistake is made by Engels and Marx and by left-wing corporate governance.

Engels and Marx could see planning as a panacea, and postulate a single cartel as the end point of centralisation in the capitalist economies based on joint-stock[23] (at which point then, as we have seen, capitalism is easily socialised as it had already become effectively planned), only because they had no appreciation of the transactions costs of non-market organisation. There are many, extremely important reasons for this relating to Engels'

---

[19] This point holds even though Engels and Marx of course believed that the direction of labour-process under communism would be a very different thing to what it was under capitalism (K Marx, 'Economic and Philosophical Manuscripts of 1844', in K Marx and F Engels, *Collected Works*, vol 3 (1975) 229 at 270–83, though it is fair to say that their attempts to show how in any concrete way were very weak (Campbell, above n 15).

[20] Marx, above n 18, at 439.

[21] RH Coase, 'The Nature of the Firm', in RH Coase, *The Firm, the Market and the Law* (Chicago, University of Chicago Press, 1986) 33.

[22] D Campbell and M Klaes, 'The Principle of Institutional Direction: Coase's Regulatory Critique of Intervention' (2005) 29 *Cambridge Journal of Economics* 263.

[23] K Marx, *Capital*, vol 1 (Penguin edn, 1976) at 779. This passage, interpolated by Engels into the fourth German edition, is omitted from the *Collected Works* edition, which gives only what Marx had put in the previous editions.

and Marx's background social philosophy into which we cannot go here.[24] But one reason which we would like to discuss is that in a strong sense the joint stock company simply was not acknowledged to be a non-market organisation. The specific character of left-wing criticisms of the corporation influenced by Engels and Marx is that in them the actions of management are regarded essentially as the product of market influences. In the capitalist economy, 'market' or 'economic' forces are dominant, and the giant corporation is as much a simple part of this as the private company analysed by Marx himself.[25] In the light of our awareness of managerialism after Berle and Means,[26] this stance perforce is now taken up subject to various caveats,[27] but the pernicious influence of the market always determines in the last instance.[28] From this perspective, public regulation such as the work of the factory inspectors Marx himself eulogised in volume one of *Capital*,[29] which we would now regard as part of corporate governance, is intended to oust or limit market influences. Corporate governance is an attempt to extend such regulation over the economic incentives driving management behaviour which draws on the greater sophistication of our knowledge of managerialism after Berle and Means.

In previous work, one of the present authors has argued that treating public companies as directly market institutions, particularly as this is done in the currently fashionable 'nexus of contracts' approach, is indefensible,[30] and we do not wish to repeat the general argument here. Rather, we wish to bring that argument to bear on left-wing corporate governance, focusing on that aspect of it which is especially relevant to the Enron and dotcom crashes: the limited liability of public companies.

[24] A Walicki, *Marxism and the Leap to the Kingdom of Freedom* (Stanford, CA, Stanford University Press, 1995) chs 1–2.

[25] Marx treated the share only as an exception to his general account of the capitalist economy, and one of the present authors has argued that this is the principal shortcoming of his economics (and of the politics built upon it): D Campbell, *The Failure of Marxism* (Aldersot, Dartmouth, 1996) ch 10.

[26] AA Berle and G Means, *The Modern Corporation and Private Property* (New Brunswick, New Jersey, Transaction Publishers, 1991).

[27] PA Baran and PM Sweezy, *Monopoly Capital* (New York, Monthly Review Press, 1966) ch 2.

[28] A variant traceable to Burnham places great weight on the, as it were, political power of bureaucracy rather than on economic influences as more usually understood in the Marxist tradition, and commits itself to regulation in an attempt to give this power a more benign character, though Burnham's characteristic mood was to be fatalistic about the possibility of doing this: J Burnham, *The Managerial Revolution* (New York, John Day, 1941). Following C Wright Mills ('A Marx for the Managers' (1942) 52 *Ethics* 200), it is our opinion that views such as Burnham's are based on nothing more than an extreme emotional pessimism about the iron cage of bureaucracy, and we will ignore this political variant of managerialism.

[29] Marx, *Capital*, vol 1, above n 14, at 234 n 1.

[30] D Campbell, 'Adam Smith, *Farrar on Company Law* and the Economics of the Corporation' (1990) 19 *Anglo-American Law Review* 185 and D Campbell, 'The Role of Monitoring and Morality in Company Law: A Criticism of the Direction of Present Regulation' (1997) 7 *Australian Journal of Corporate Law* 343.

Limited Liability and its Critics

Though a common shortcoming, it requires a certain ignorance of the history of one's discipline for company lawyers to regard the public company as part of the system of natural liberty turning on the invisible hand which we identify with Adam Smith, for Smith was a profound critic of joint stock companies. One of the reasons for this was that:

> The directors of such companies ... being the managers of other people's money than their own, it cannot well be expected that they should watch over it with the same anxious vigilance ... Negligence and profusion must always prevail, more or less, in the management of such a company ... The joint stock companies ... over and above managing their own affairs ill, to the diminution of the general stock of society, can in other respects scarce ever fail to do more harm than good [for their method of operation] necessarily breaks, more or less, that natural proportion which would otherwise establish itself between judicious industry and profit, and which, to the general industry of the country, is of all encouragements the greatest and most effectual.[31]

The granting by the state of general limited liability makes public companies attractive to capitalists and no doubt played an enormous part in the growth of such companies and with them the advanced capitalist economy as a whole. It is essential to note, as Smith did, that it does this by isolating investors from the full range of market influences. The most common and vulgar strophe of the economic and business literature in which the apologists of the advanced capitalist economy seek to legitimate the extraordinary remuneration of the business elite is that that elite is composed of risk-taking entrepreneurs. But the legislative 'partitioning' of investors' and executives' personal assets from those of the firm is the central feature of the public company.[32] With limited liability, investors may reap the full benefit of success, but they are exposed to the risks of failure only to the extent of their (fully paid up) shareholding. The normal employment contract of directors of a public company makes them bear no personal responsibility for other than wrongful conduct; if they are equity holders, their liabilities are limited in the same way as are those of other investors. In the light of the remuneration packages of Enron's executives, which are not different in kind from similar packages throughout the corporate economy, one has to stretch the point to say that the executives of large public companies are exposed to the economic risks of failure in any significant way, and certainly they are more or less completely cocooned from the most fundamental market pressure, fear of personal bankruptcy. By in this way distancing directors from the down-side of their decisions, the public company based

---

[31] Adam Smith, *The Wealth of Nations* (Glasgow edn, 1976) 741, 758.
[32] H Hansmann and R Kraakman, 'The Essential Role of Organisational Law' (2000) 110 *Yale L Jl* 387.

on incorporation and limited liability severely handicaps or even eliminates the core function of the market. As Eucken put it:

> The purpose of the unlimited liability of the entrepreneur in a competitive econ-
> omy is to make him careful in the disposition of his resource, and in investing and
> producing, and automatically to eliminate him if unsuccessful. Unlimited liabili-
> ty is part of a competitive system, and its destruction by legal policy endangers
> the functioning of this system.[33]

All this was perceived by those who, in the name of the market, opposed the Victorian companies legislation which granted general limited liability after a vexed debate. We cannot here discuss this debate thoroughly but must merely pick out certain contributions. We have been directed by a leading historian of this debate, Mr Paddy Ireland of the Kent Law School,[34] to one representative legal[35] contributor, Edward William Cox,[36] whose views we shall quote at length. Cox was a barrister who did not enjoy great success at the Bar but turned his energies to legal (and other) publishing and was, inter alia, the founder of *The Law Times*.[37] Among his numerous treatises, he wrote a company law textbook which enjoyed the success of running to numerous editions.[38] The first edition of 1855 was written when the law of public companies was that stated in the Joint Stock Companies Act 1844, which of course did not exempt the members of such companies from the *ceteris paribus* unlimited liability borne by partners. Faced with the passage of the Limited Liability Act 1855 and the Joint Stock Companies Act 1856[39] which granted general[40] limited liability,

---

[33] W Eucken, *The Foundations of Economics* (Hoboken, NJ, John Wiley and Sons, 1992) 316.

[34] At the time this was drafted, Mr Ireland's most recent statement of his own views on the implications of the Victorian companies legislation for current thinking about corporate governance was 'Property and Contract in Contemporary Corporate Theory' (2003) 23 *Legal Studies* 453.

[35] An excellent example of the thinking we are trying to describe on the part of an economist was given by one of Marx's *betes noire*, JR McCulloch, below n 48.

[36] DNB, vol 4 at 1334–35.

[37] *The Law Times*' 'hostility' to limited liability noted in *Gower's Principles of Modern Company Law* (6th edn, 1997) at 43 n 49 reflects Cox's views. (The most recent edition of *Gower* (7th edn, 2003) no longer covers this debate.)

[38] DNB, vol 4 at 1335 tells us that there were six editions. In this paper we quote from EW Cox, *New Law and Practice of Joint Stock Companies* (4th edn, 1857), the latest edition known to the British Library catalogue and held by the library.

[39] Supplemented by the Companies Winding Up (Amendment) Act 1857. The position was consolidated under the Companies Act 1862.

[40] Cox had to deal with the position under the 1856 Act, which granted limited liability to companies with seven members (it had been 25 members under the 1855 Act). Of course, this itself constituted a peculiar distortion of competition, for it is hard to defend giving limited liability to any number and not to smaller numbers or to an individual. Cox was clear-minded enough to acknowledge this and sought to advise individual traders how to avail themselves of the privilege of limited liability: above n 38 at xviii–xix. After the 12th Company Law Directive (89/667/EEC) implemented by SI 1992/1699, our company law now extends incorporation to more or less any individual who wants it under the Companies Act 1985, s 1.

Cox was obliged to completely revise the second edition of his book,[41] and when doing so he did not stint in his complete disapproval of 'new law' which will lead to 'enormous evils'[42]:

> The Law of Partnership hitherto has been ... that he who acts through an agent should be responsible for his agent's acts, and that he who shares the profits of an enterprise ought also to be subject to its losses; that there is a moral obligation, which it is the duty of the laws of a civilised nation to enforce, to pay debts, perform contracts and make reparation for wrongs. Limited Liability is founded on the opposite principle and permits a man to avail himself of acts if advantageous to him, and not to be responsible for them if they should be disadvantageous; to speculate for profits without being liable for losses; to make contracts, incur debts, and commit wrongs, the law depriving the creditor, the contractor, and the injured, of remedy against the property or the person of the wrongdoer, beyond the limit, however small, at which it may please him to determine his own liability. Thus it practically enable a trader to speculate for the chances of indefinite gain, without being liable for more than a small definite loss ... This is effected by depriving the persons so dealing with [such a trader] of their common law right to recover their debts, enforce their contracts, or obtain redress for injuries done to them.[43]

We do not wish to enter into questions about the nature of the corporation which revolve around the 'concession theory' when we say that limited liability under the Companies Acts *was* and *is* not the product of private negotiation in a market but of a public intervention.[44] That the state created limited liability is, of course, allowed by all, but that by doing so it ousted the market is by no means realised by all; indeed in our leading company law textbooks the introduction of limited liability is often described as the result of laissez faire,[45] which is precisely what it was not.[46] As Cox noted, it was

---

[41] Cox, *New Law and Practice of Joint Stock Companies*, above n 38, at preface to 2nd edn.
[42] *Ibid.*
[43] *Ibid*, at i(ii.
[44] Though we do not want to make much of this, the history of the Victorian legislation shows this to be true in a particularly direct way. The initial impetus for the debate in the 1850s which culminated in the 1855–56 legislation was provided not by capitalists seeking limited liability protection for their entrepreneurial zeal but by Christian socialists who sought to make it easier to invest in 'socially useful projects': J Saville, 'Sleeping Partnership and Limited Liability' (1956) 8 *Economic History Review* 418. Smith, for whom the joint stock company was an exceptional form requiring a charter, was clear that the argument for granting such a charter had to lie in 'the publick spirited purpose of promoting some particular manufacture': above n 31 at 758.
[45] *Farrar's Company Law* (4th edn, 1998) at 21 and *Gower, Gower's Principles of Company Law*, above n 37, at 42.
[46] As *Gower, ibid* at 46 argues, it was wrong of Maitland to run together the possibility of obtaining limited liability by private negotiation and the introduction of general limited liability by fiat: FW Maitland, 'Trust and Corporation', in FW Maitland, *Collected Papers*, vol 3 (1911) 321 at 391–92. See further HN Butler, 'General Incorporation in Nineteenth Century England: Interaction of Common Law and Legislative Processes' (1986) 6 *International Review of Law and Economics* 169.

and is perfectly possible for those *ceteris paribus* exposed to unlimited liability to contract with others to limit their liability as one of the terms on which they deal.[47] This would be limited liability established through negotiation on the market. But the Companies Acts generally imposed limited liability, and it is a very different matter to negotiate to a position of limited liability than to negotiate away from unlimited liability (even when this is allowed), for the competitive setting is completely changed by this intervention: '[t]he law ... steps in and forces a risk shifting not created in the market place.'[48] In sum: limited liability is not a creature of the market but rather a public intervention in the market. As McCulloch put it at the time of the 1855–56 legislation:

> In the scheme laid down by Providence for the government of the world, there is no shifting or narrowing of responsibilities, every man being personally responsible for his actions. But the advocates of limited liability proclaim in their superior wisdom that the scheme of Providence may be advantageously modified, and that debts and obligations which the debtors, though they have the means, shall not be bound to discharge.[49]

Limited liability works by reducing the risk of investing in or running a company in which liability is limited. The point is to stimulate economic growth by increasing the incentive to engage in business activity, or rather to decrease the disincentive to do so.[50] When serving on the 1854 Royal Commission whose Report was the occasion of the 1855–56 legislation,[51] GW Bramwell, later Baron Bramwell, advocated limited liability in order to allow those forming companies to enjoy 'the unrestricted and unfettered exercise of their own talents and industry,'[52] and in doing so he was both giving voice to a strong theme in the contemporaneous economic literature[53] and anticipating innumerable subsequent statements to similar effect. Bramwell had some warrant for posing the issues in terms of escaping regulatory constraint, for his views were formed against the background of the

---

[47] Cox, *New Law and Practice of Joint Stock Companies*, above n 38, at ii.

[48] KJ Arrow, 'Insurance, Risk and Resource Allocation', in KJ Arrow, *Collected Papers*, vol 4 (Cambridge, MA, Belknap Press, 1984) 77 at 83.

[49] JR McCulloch, 'Partnerships, Limited and Unlimited Liability', *Encyclopaedia Britannica*, vol 17 (8th edn, 1859) 321. See also JR McCulloch, *Considerations on Partnerships with Limited Liability* (1856) 10–11.

[50] FH Easterbrook and DR Fischel, *The Economic Structure of Corporate Law* (Cambridge, MA, Harvard University Press, 1991) ch 2.

[51] We use this careful phrasing because the report was by no means unanimous in its recommendation of limited liability, and, indeed, it is not really easy to say exactly what policy would follow from an attempt to implement its conclusions.

[52] Royal Commission on Assimilation of Mercantile Laws in the UK and Amendments in the Law of Partnership as Regards Questions of Limited or Unlimited Responsibility, *First Report* (1854) (Cd 1791; BPP, 27, 445) 29.

[53] CE Amsler R Bartlett and C Bolton, 'Thoughts of Some British Economists on Early Limited Liability and Corporate Legislation' (1981) 13 *History of Political Economy* 774.

Joint Stock Companies Act 1844's response to earlier scandals, which did include a paternalistic general obstruction of limitation of liability.[54] The position is now entirely reversed, though one would hardly recognise this from the language of the majority of those who express views on this matter now, who either assume that general limited liability is inevitable or that it inevitably is a good thing.

If we recognise that limited liability is a public intervention rather than the outcome of a market process, then it must be the case that the implicit welfare claim behind this intervention is that the rate of investment and growth produced by the intervention is superior to that which would be produced by the market operating with unlimited liability. Of course, if untrammelled economic growth and increased welfare are simply identified, then limited liability is justified (accepting that it does effectively promote growth).[55] But if they are not, then surely the public intervention of limited liability must be called into question, for the possibility must be considered that the slower rate of growth which would be produced by the more extensive competition promoted by unlimited liability might optimise welfare.

Limited Liability and the Left-wing Case for Corporate Governance

If one approaches the question of limited liability from a right-wing position broadly sympathetic to capitalist accumulation, then the defence of it as stimulating growth noted above takes its place within a general preparedness to reward the business elite extremely generously because this is taken to be essential to the capitalist dynamic.[56] Although this thinking to some extent legitimates the remuneration of Enron's management, Enron and other crashes nevertheless give pause to it because they raise the question whether the costs of such dislocations actually outweigh the benefits of the rate of growth made possible by limited liability. If one accepts this might be the case, it is difficult to continue with one's overall approving attitude towards giving every possible encouragement to capitalist accumulation, and the acuteness of this dilemma goes a long way towards explaining the agonised character of many of the right-wing responses to Enron, which both can see that something is going wrong and yet are extremely loathe to reduce the rate of growth by increasing the disincentive to speculate.[57]

---

[54] 7 and 8 Victoria c 110, s 25. See further M Rix, 'Company Law: 1844 and Today' (1945) 55 *Economic Journal* 242.

[55] There are very interesting reflections on the difficulties of drawing clear conclusions about this in DH MacGregor, 'Joint Stock Companies and the Risk Factor' (1929) 39 *Economic Journal* 491.

[56] J Schumpeter, *Capitalism, Socialism and Democracy* (1942) 73–74.

[57] CL Culp and WA Niskanen (eds), *Corporate Aftershock* (Hoboken, NJ, John Wiley, 2003).

We do not wish to pursue the welfare discussion from this right-wing perspective, for this requires an entirely different argument from the one we wish to address to the left-wing perspective broadly influenced by Engels and Marx. Even eschewing the attempt to do away with the anarchy of capitalist production completely, left-wing corporate governance still rightly regards the assumption that unlimited economic growth is good as more the product of the alienation of economic life than a defensible welfare judgement. If this is so, it is foolish to defend general limited liability as an intervention to encourage growth, for the results of the intervention are unwelcome; and, of course, it is disgust with many environmental and social consequences of the actions of corporations that motivates left-wing corporate governance.[58]

In respect of narrowly, as it were, financial matters, Enron shows the 'dark side' of running corporations with an intense focus on enhancement of shareholder value.[59] Powerful advocates of corporate governance have rightly been quick to point out that shortly after shareholder primacy had been claimed to have obtained such hegemony as to make debate about the basic nature of company law redundant,[60] the Enron crash set the historical clock running again.[61] This observation is entirely correct in so far as it goes.[62] The fanatical emphasis Enron placed on shareholder value does not optimise welfare and, inter alia, excessively increases the damage caused by a crash. But the analysis of how this emphasis could get such a hold is inadequate, and writings on corporate governance of this nature seem to us to miss their main target.

In cases like Enron, corporate management is criticised for pursuing economic advantage to excess, and this excess is traced to untrammelled domination by the 'economic'. LE Mitchell has been a powerful advocate of a more 'patient' and 'responsible' capitalism which will mitigate this excess,[63]

---

[58] In the relatively technical terms of company law, this is often represented as reducing or removing the insulation limited liability gives against criminal actions or torts: R Paehlke, 'Environmental Harm and Corporate Crime' in F Pearce and L Snider, *Corporate Crime: Contemporary Debates* (Toronto, Toronto University Press, 1995) 305 and T Gabaldon, 'Experiencing Limited Liability: On Insularity and Inbreeding on Company Law' in LE Mitchell (ed), *Progressive Company Law* (Boulder, CO, Westview Press, 1995) 111.

[59] W Bratton, 'Enron and the Dark Side of Shareholder Value' (2003) 76 *Tulane Law Review* 1275.

[60] H Hansman and R Kraakman, 'The End of History for Corporate Law' (2001) 89 *Georgetown L J* 439.

[61] S Deakin, 'The Return of History to Corporate Law', inaugural lecture on appointment to the Robert Monks Chair of Corporate Governance, Judge Institute of Management, University of Cambridge (2003). We are grateful to Professor Deakin for allowing us to see the text of this lecture in advance of publication. See also J Armour, S Deakin and S Konzelmann, 'Shareholder Primacy and the Trajectory of UK Corporate Governance' (2003) 41 *British Journal of Industrial Relations* 531.

[62] In particular, in his inaugural lecture, Professor Deakin raises serious questions about the value of SOA on which we have relied heavily.

[63] LE Mitchell, *Corporate Irresponsibility: America's Newest Export* (New Haven, CT, Yale University Press, 2001).

and he and TA Gabaldon now give the following prescription in the light of Enron:

> Now one thing we could do is alleviate the practical constraint managers feel requires them to maximise short-term corporate profits and/or (viewed more-or-less interchangeably) short-term shareholder value. This is not to say that we advocate turning corporations into nonprofits ... All of us like to profit. After all, all of us like to eat ... We would have no objection to keeping the profit motive for the corporation if we believed it left managers to function in [a] moral way ... But there is a problem ... our shareholders, our capital markets, do not like short-term costs ... capital market behaviour suggests that the devil will indeed take the hindmost [If] we alleviated the profit pressure [we] would take away [the] excuse ... for bad behaviour by allowing managers to defend it on the grounds of profit maximisation.[64]

The remedy for excessive concentration on profit maximisation proposed by left-wing corporate governance is to destroy shareholder primacy by balancing other stakeholder interests against the shareholder. We do not wish to argue against this policy in a direct way, and certainly not to defend the claim that it is a legitimate general goal to maximise profit under the conditions in which the modern corporation does business. But we do want to redirect the stakeholder policy, establishing the necessary constraint not by legal and political intervention against what is perceived to be the market but by institutionalising a market which, as Smith and Eucken saw, will itself constrain profit maximisation.

It is not the 'economic' or the 'market' that leads reckless executives to act as they do, but the public intervention which limits their liability, thus distorting the market. Furthermore, this intervention thereby makes such action *rational* and *legitimate*. For the point missed in the left-wing corporate governance literature is that excessive concentration on profit maximisation has been given public endorsement. It is not the mysterious economic which leads to this excessive concentration, but rather the law of limited liability, for if the law intervenes to gives capitalists incentives to accumulate beyond those they would enjoy under the market, they will naturally respond to those incentives. Pointing to the 'legislative sanction given to ... lax notions already but too prevalent with respect to the obligation to pay debts and perform contracts,' Cox made a point the importance of which cannot be overestimated:

> When the law itself has discarded this duty [to pay debts and perform contracts], it can scarcely be expected that it will be respected by the community. The promotion of fraud, by the removal of every prohibition against it, and of all punishment for it, as also by the positive facilities provided for it, is [a] lamentable feature of the new law.[65]

---

[64] LE Mitchell and TA Gabaldon, 'If I Only Had a Heart: Or, How Can We Identify a Corporate Morality?' (2002) 76 *Tulane L Rev* 1645 at 1666–67.
[65] Cox, *New Law and Practice of Joint Stock Companies*, above n 38, at preface to 2nd edn.

It is to Bratton that we owe the striking idea that Enron illustrates the 'dark side' of shareholder value. His argument is both acute and unusually well-balanced, for it aims to 'de-emphasise the rogue and to focus on the regular'[66] to show that much of what Enron's management did was quite normal and that, given the ineluctability of risk, there is a limit to what we can do about this. He nevertheless draws attention to the inadequacy of market self-regulation as it is preached by the business elite, rightly showing that the Enron crash would make self-regulation a joke had it not already been one prior to that crash:

> That the firm with the seventh largest market capitalisation and also the firm that preached market discipline the loudest turned out to be the shabbiest of shops with the Cupertino of outside directors, outside auditors, and institutional investors, highlights the limits of what self-regulation and market incentives can achieve.[67]

Who can doubt that Enron's management behaved much as Bratton says and that self-regulation is inadequate? But we hope to have shown that equating self-regulation with market incentives is quite wrong. This equation is, in fact, particularly hard to sustain when reflecting on Enron. Enron's growth was possible only because of the tremendous effort it put into manipulating the regulatory structures which allowed it to do what it wanted, and the size both of its political expenditures and the closeness of its business and political networks are, like almost everything else about the Enron crash, both striking and yet, in the end, merely an exaggerated version of the commonplace. That Senator Phil Gramm, who was principally responsible for ensuring that the Commodity Futures Modernisation Act of 2000 was extremely sympathetic to Enron, was married to Ms Wendy Gramm, an outside director and audit committee member of Enron who has so far been in receipt of between US$1m-$2m from the company (with, as this is first drafted, power to add),[68] is an obvious disgrace. But surely it is a disgrace for the political process at least as much as for 'the market,' for the senator's value to Enron was not, of course, his business acumen but his political influence. The political process which created Enron is being subjected to searching criticism; but it is to consideration of limited liability as the basic link between politics and capitalist enterprise that we should turn.

The basic lesson Bratton draws from Enron is this:

> [A] century and a half ago, conservatives steeped in the classical economic model of Adam Smith voiced suspicions about the accumulation of significant assets within corporate organisations. Only when human beings owned property, they said, could individual interest and moral responsibility work together to keep the

---

[66] Bratton, 'Enron and the Dark Side of Shareholder Value', above n 59, at 1283.
[67] *Ibid*, at 1360.
[68] *Ibid*, at 1275, 1279–80.

use of the property consonant with the interests of society as a whole. Corporate ownership subverted market control of private economic power and diluted responsibility among the members of a group. We still hear many voices advocating market control. But we hear it in a fundamentally different context in which corporations, rather than individuals, own the producing assets. For that reason, market controls taken alone cannot possibly assure responsible use of economic power. For the same reason, we should treat with utmost scepticism actors who preach market discipline from positions of safety behind the shields of corporate entities.[69]

This does, we think, express the left-wing case for corporate governance at its most sophisticated and its basic thrust must be accepted. But for such acceptance to be productive, it is important that Bratton's view be modified. Bratton is right not to accept the views of those who shelter behind the market. But he is wrong to think their views represent the position which would in fact be established by a market. Their views represent the position established by ousting the market through public intervention. It should be to the intervention that generalises limited liability rather than to the market which would *ceteris paribus* impose unlimited liability that he should aim his fire. We wish to draw our argument to a close with a few remarks on the reason that left-wing corporate governance makes the debilitating mistake of effectively agreeing with the business elite's alienated view of its relationship to the market.

The Left and the 'Economic'

Left-wing corporate governance is undermined by a specific instance of a general confusion about the nature of the capitalist economy that, though it runs counter to the basic thrust of Engels' and Marx's work, has generally undermined the politics based on that work. Left-wing corporate governance criticises the public company for articulating only too well the 'economic' forces of capitalism, and wishes to ameliorate those forces by public regulation which will balance those forces against other stakeholder interests which do not have an economic grasp on the control of the corporation in the way that the shareholders and/or management do but need special legal recognition.

It may be sought in this way to deny shareholder primacy over control of the company, but it is clear that the shareholder has theoretical primacy. Why is the shareholder's place in the company assured, indeed simply assumed, and other interests brought in only subsequently? It is, in our opinion, because the control of the 'economic' is simply assumed, and the

---

[69] *Ibid*, at 1361.

analysis proceeds from this. As the broad origins of the left-wing approach to these matters lies in Marx's critique of the fetishism of commodities as an alienated understanding of the nature of social life,[70] the left-wing's typical acceptance of the capitalist's alienated view of the ineluctability of the economic must be one of the most amazing paradoxes in social theory, but it nevertheless is the case.

When one does not simply accept the category of 'the economic' but examines how it is that these economic forces take the shape they do, then, in respect of our concern with company law, one is brought sharply up against the crucial role of the legal system. It is not surprising that the Left finds itself struggling against 'the economic.' This is a mysterious force which cannot be understood, and the core theme of Engels and Marx's entire work was to stress that humankind grapples against such alienated forces in vain.[71] But if this mysterious force is replaced with a clear understanding of the set of political and legal arrangements that produces specific economic institutions, one can make progress. This requires difficult, close analysis rather than airy theorising about global economic forces and the like,[72] but it is the only way forward. The crucial thing is that the Left must turn the critique of alienation against the Left's own concept of the 'economic.'[73]

The Market and Limited Liability

In order to do this, the Left will have to develop a more serious and positive view of markets. When grudgingly accepting markets, the Left makes little of their positive aspects. It is not, in fact, markets as such but the fact that they cannot be got rid of that is accepted, and this is because there is little penetration of why it is that markets are in fact so (relatively) attractive that the attempt to do away with them has rightly been a failure.

We strongly suspect that a market in the personal liabilities of (investors and) managers would be more attractive than statutory general limited liability. It would of its nature provide economic incentives which would balance the currently overwhelming incentive towards profit maximisation provided by limited liability. To begin to devise the necessary governance structures, a great deal of intellectual lumber must be cleared away, the largest piece of which is the belief that limited liability is a product of the market rather than a drastic statutory intervention in it. Like all the economic

---

[70] Marx, *Capital*, above n 14, at ch 1, sec 4.

[71] K Marx and F Engels, *The German Ideology* in K Marx and F Engels, *Collected Works*, vol 5 (1976) 19 at 51.

[72] D Campbell, 'The Limits of Concept Formation in Legal Science' (2000) 9 *Social and Legal Studies* 439.

[73] G Leff, *The Tyranny of Concepts* (London, Merlin Press, 1961).

institutions of advanced capitalism, general limited liability did not spring fully formed into economic life but was the product of legal arrangements which, in this case, were the subject of vexed debate. The result of this debate was the limitation or prevention of the working of the market in what formerly was thought a crucial way in order to accelerate capitalist accumulation. The Left simply has not been sophisticated enough to deal with this properly. Identifying advocacy of capitalist accumulation with the market, it has sought to work against the market through corporate governance. The result has been a very weak mimicking of the consequences of the *ceteris paribus* unlimited liability which the market requires. If the Left is to make progress here, it must in a sense draw the corporate governance movement to an end. It must grasp the value of unlimited liability and ask for the restoration of the market.

This is not to ask for deregulation. The market, like any other allocative structure, can, in modern conditions, be created only by regulation. The Left must now seek regulation which will promote a market based on unlimited liability, and the enormous, detailed effort that will be required will show soon enough that we are not dealing with the mysterious, ineluctable 'economic' but with the concrete economic processes of concrete economic institutions created by concrete political and legal debate. While our ambition in this paper is to make the Left take a different general attitude to the market rather than to advance detailed proposals for a welfare enhancing market, we must say one or two things about the positions of executives and (other) shareholders.

As we have mentioned, there currently is nothing in the role of executives *qua* executives that exposes them to the liability we believe should be considered, or would do so even if our broad proposals were adopted. It may, of course, be the case that executives are also shareholders, in which case they would de facto be so exposed, but this is merely a coincidence which they may seek to avoid by being paid in anything other than the equity of the company they manage. How executives should be exposed to liability is the most important issue, and we do not, we repeat, want to enter into detail here, though certainly would welcome the opportunity to do so if the debate took the direction we would wish. Some suggestions can, however, briefly be made. It might be statutorily implied into executives' employment contracts that they receive part of their remuneration in the form of shares in the company and that these shares are of a class that creates personal liability to the degree thought fit. One possibility is unlimited liability of the holder, but there are ways of placing a limit on that liability, such as having executives' shares only part-paid with the unpaid margin representing a very substantial personal liability. It might, alternatively, be implied that executives accept liability in a way which approximates to the liability of a partner, or by giving a personal guarantee which can be part of the pooled assets of the company in liquidation. This need not entirely or even mainly be a matter of statutory compulsion. Once general limited liability was removed, that executives have personal liability might prove to be a competitive advantage in the obtaining of credit and the negotiation of its terms. An analogy to the personal guarantees typically required of the directors of small incorporated companies might be drawn.

One could go on, but one other point must be made. Whatever, as it were, positive provision is made to expose executives to personal liability, there will have to be extensive negative regulation of the way they might arrange to have the company effectively indemnify themselves against this liability, or certainly to make any such indemnification arrangements transparent to creditors.

The natural way in which unlimited liability would impact on executives is, however, not by immediately exposing them to liability, but by exposing shareholders, cause those shareholders to increase the diligence of their monitoring of the management of the company. We have reservations about this broadly related to the transaction costs of monitoring such huge organisations which are not touched by the arrangements for liability. The most commonly accepted argument for limited liability is that it allows relatively small investors who would be adverse to the risk of shouldering a corporation's huge liabilities, about which they realistically can know almost nothing, to invest. Recognised by Smith,[74] certainly influential in the debate that led to the 1855–56 legislation,[75] and apparently effective in encouraging investment from this source,[76] this argument has been used to approve the historical record of limited liability[77] and is still put to use today in the leading defences of the share and stock dealing.[78] There is, however, counter-evidence to this argument,[79] and of course it is a much more difficult argument to make now when corporations are much less reliant on outside equity at all and when institutional investors dwarf small investors as sources of equity finance.[80]

---

[74] Smith, *The Wealth of Nations*, above n 31, at 741.

[75] C Fane, *Limited Liability: Its Necessity as a Means of Promoting Enterprise* (1845).

[76] HA Shannon, 'The Limited Companies of 1866–83' (1933) 4 *Economic History Review* 290.

[77] G Todd, 'Some Aspects of Joint Stock Companies 1844–1900' (1932) 4 *Economic History Review* 46.

[78] HG Manne, 'Our Two Corporation Systems: Law and Economics' (1967) 53 *Virginia Law Review* 259 at 262–63. See further H Demsetz, 'Towards a Theory of Property Rights' (1967) 57 *American Economic Review* 347 at 358–59.

[79] PZ Grossman, 'The Market for Shares of Companies with Unlimited Liability: The Case of American Express' (1995) 25 *Journal of Legal Studies* 63.

[80] Indeed, as the typical criticism of institutional investors in the corporate governance literature is that they are somnolent, exposing them to greater liability for the failures of companies in which they hold equity and which they are supposed to be monitoring is a policy worth considering: K Dowd, *Competition and Finance* (Basingstoke, Macmillan, 1996) ch 3. One way of doing this would be to reinstitute the use of the partly paid share, and indeed this was used as a way of encouraging belief in the creditworthiness of limited liability

But even if one accepts this argument,[81] it is by no means an insuperable obstacle to our proposal, for once one sees the issues in terms of constructing the appropriate legal framework, there is no necessity to think that the abandonment of limited liability has to apply equally to all the involved parties.[82] In the UK it is, for example, perfectly possible to limit the liability of shareholders who play no part in the management of the corporation under the Companies Act 1985, s 2, whilse exposing those that do play such a part to a greater liability, or even unlimited liability, under s 306. This specific possibility reflects the continuance in the English law[83] of setting up companies along the line of the French partnership *en commandite*, which was extensively discussed as an alternative to general limited liability during the debate leading to the 1855–56 companies legislation.[84] That general limited liability has more or less destroyed the necessity of even considering business organisations of this nature should not, we submit, prevent a fresh appraisal of their value now.[85]

companies in the period immediately after the 1855–56 legislation, with individuals who were in both senses creditworthy holding such shares (sometimes of great nominal value) as earnests of companies' soundness: JB Jefferys, 'The Denomination and Character of Shares 1855–85' (1946) 16 *Economic History Review* 45. Under the negotiating framework created by general limited liability, this practice has so fallen into desuetude that the Company Law Review Steering Group now proposes not only the abolition of the possibility of creating 'reserve funds' but even the concept of authorised share capital itself: *Modern Company Law for a Competitive Economy: Company Formation and Capital Maintenance* (1999) paras 3.16, 2.21.

[81] Though now less certain about the position, one of the present authors has argued that capitalist investment on a simple profit maximisation basis, without the flexibility introduced by the share and discretion over the payment of dividends, became impossible for largescale undertakings in the later part of the nineteenth century. This certainly was the belief of highly influential critics and defenders of capitalism at the time: Campbell, *The Failure of Marxism*, above n 25, at ch 10.

[82] A very interesting consideration of the welfare implications of unlimited liability, P Halpern, M Treblicock and S Turnbull, 'An Economic Analysis of Limited Liability in Corporation Law' (1980) 30 *University of Toronto L Jl* 117, makes this assumption, and this plays a very large role in this important paper's conclusion that public companies should enjoy general limited liability.

[83] Since the Companies Act 1867, 30 and 31 Victoria c 131, ss 4–8.

[84] MB Begbie, *Partnership 'en Commandite', or Partnership with Limited Liabilities* (1848) and MB Begbie, *Partnership en Commandite, or Limited Liability Recognised and Permitted by the Existing Law of England* (1852). See also Howell, *Partnership Law Legislation and Limited Liability Reviewed in Relation to the Panic of 1866*, above n 9. See further M Lobban, 'Corporate Identity and Limited Liability in France and England 1825–67' (1996) 25 *Anglo-American L Rev* 397.

[85] There are, of course, other possible ways of achieving the same broad effect, eg a partnership limited under the Limited Partnerships Act 1907. There is no impulse to exploring the possibilities of extending liability under any of these forms, and, of course, the Limited Liability Partnerships Act 2000 goes in just the wrong way. One does not have to be at all sympathetic to our argument here to see that this baneful statute is a preposterous interference with the responsibilities it is right that those who will avail themselves of it should bear, and we can look forward to it smoothing the path of those who wish to behave like Enron's management and auditors.

CONCLUSION

Despite the obvious difficulties of devising the regulation necessary to get any of this to work, we believe there may be very important gains of regulatory economy and effectiveness to be made. For among the possible benefits of the reform we are suggesting may be an ability to reduce the preposterous growth in the volume of companies law and corporate governance soft law, to which SAO makes its own contribution; and to increase the effectiveness of the controls on executives' actions, replacing the uncertain effectiveness of interventionist regulation with what everybody agrees are highly effective economic incentives. The howls of protest by the business elite amplified in the business literature which we predict would greet *any* argument for the rebirth of unlimited liability companies, will show the Left it is heading in the right direction. Had it not developed such an antipathy to the system of natural philosophy and the market when pursuing the failed Utopia of complete abolition of capitalist anarchy, embarking on this promising line of argument would not involve such a complete rethinking of the Left's position as it now does. As this rethinking will involve refocusing our company law towards the promotion of welfare enhancing markets rather than working against what are taken to be the ineluctably bad outcomes of markets, and, as we have said at the outset, corporate governance really is identified by its opposition to markets, it may be best to call this the end of corporate governance.

4

European Integration and Globalisation: The Experience of Financial Reporting Regulation

CHARLOTTE VILLIERS

INTRODUCTION

MUCH OF THE debate on European integration centres on the relationship between 'globalisation' and 'europeanisation'. Whereas the two processes have in the past been viewed separately, there is now a broad recognition that a relationship exists between them.[1] International relations and politics circles have observed this, but controversy exists over whether the two processes are antagonistic to each other or whether they are in fact 'working in combination.'[2] Professor Francis Snyder, in the legal field, asked in his seminal paper are they friends or rivals–'is the EU part of the problem or part of the solution in relation to globalisation?'[3]

Many EU policies are justified as reactions to globalisation. European integration–in both its negative and positive integration forms–is frequently explained by reference to the context of globalisation. The consequences, however, are potentially far reaching. European integration in the face of globalisation has implications for the institutional and political structure of the EU and affects the ability of European citizens to participate in the

Thanks are due to participants for their feedback when I presented an earlier version of this paper at a seminar in the Centre for European Legal Studies, University of Cambridge, 5 March 2003. Accepted for publication in 2003.

[1] See for a discussion of the debate, Morten Kelstrup, 'The European Union and Globalisation: Reflections on Strategies of Individual States' available at: http://www.copri.dk/publications/WP/WP%202001/38-2001.doc.

[2] See, eg Paolo Graziano, 'Europeanisation or Globalisation? A Framework for Empirical Research' available at: http://www.isaf.no/nova/nyheter/kalender/COSTa15/Papers/Graziano.pdf.

[3] Francis Snyder, 'Globalisation and Europeanisation as Friends and Rivals: European Union Law in Global Economic Networks' EUI Working Paper LAW No 99/8, available at http://www.ive.it/LAW/WP-Texts/law99_8.pdf.

decision-making processes.[4] This in turn leads us to question how legitimate are the decisions that are eventually reached.

One area of activity which allows us to consider the debate in a contextual framework is financial reporting. In this area the European Commission has displayed a willingness to participate in the international harmonisation of accounting standards, reflecting the globalised nature of capital markets. For example, the Commission accepted in 1990 an invitation to become a member of the Consultative Group of the International Accounting Standards Committee and to sit on the Committee's board in an observer capacity.[5] At the same time, the Commission is anxious to protect the achievements of the European Union in the regulation of financial reporting.[6]

This chapter will explore the regulatory activity directed at financial reporting and will offer some broader observations about how this reflects upon the relationship between EU integration and globalisation. The first part will describe EU policy towards financial reporting and how it is shaped by the reality of a globalised capital market. The second part will examine the legislative results of the EU's financial reporting policy. The third part will consider how this shapes the EU's overall accounting regulation. The final part will suggest what this might signify more generally in the EU's political and institutional context.

EU FINANCIAL REPORTING POLICY IN A GLOBALISED CONTEXT

Financial reporting has traditionally been regulated within the framework of the EU's company law harmonisation programme and has been dealt with by the Accounting Directives of 1978[7] and 1983.[8] A key characteristic of those Directives was their flexibility, particularly in the broad range of options they afford to Member States and to companies in the way accounts are regulated and presented. Increasingly in the company law programme Member States have been granted greater freedom and in part that is the very essence of Directives as a legal instrument, since they leave to Member States discretion in the manner in which their provisions will be implemented. The

---

[4] See, eg Jan Aart Scholte, 'Civil Society and Democracy in Global Governance' CSGR Working Paper No 65/01, available at: http://www.warwick.ac.uk/fac/soc/CSGR/wpapers/wp6501.pdf.

[5] See Commission Communication, *Accounting Harmonisation: A New Strategy Vis-a-vis International Harmonisation* COM (1995) 508 (14.11.95).

[6] COM (1995) 508 para 1.

[7] Council Directive 78/660/EEC of 25 July 1978 on the annual accounts of certain types of companies OJ L222, 14.8.78, 11 (amended by Directive 2001/65/EC, OJ L283, 27.10.01, 28).

[8] Council Directive 83/349/EEC of 13 June 1983 on consolidated accounts, OJ L193, 18.7.83, 1 (amended by Directive 2001/65/EC, OJ L283, 27.10.01, 28). See also Council Directive 86/635/EEC of 8 December 1986 on the annual accounts and consolidated accounts of banks and other financial institutions, OJ L372, 31.12.86, 1 (amended by Directive 2001/65/EC, OJ L283, 27.10.01, 28) and Council Directive 91/674/EEC on the annual accounts and consolidated accounts of insurance companies OJ L374, 31.12.91, 7.

Accounting Directives have indeed been described as 'second generation Directives' that marked a move away from the more prescriptive 'first generation Directives' within the company law programme at least.[9]

However, at the same time, alongside these developments within the EU, internationally a process of convergence has been emerging. The International Accounting Standards Committee (hereinafter 'IASC') was founded in 1973 and today, as the International Accounting Standards Board (hereinafter 'IASB'), one of its stated objectives is,

> to develop, in the public interest, a single set of high quality, understandable and enforceable global accounting standards that require high quality, transparent and comparable information in financial statements and other financial reporting to help participants in the world's capital markets and other users make economic decisions.[10]

These measures are considered essential to the increasing importance of the international activities of those businesses which look beyond their own national markets for capital investment. Yet the capacity for international trade and investment is limited if financial reporting is substantially different across trading borders. Such differences make comparisons between the financial statements of different businesses more difficult. The existence of such differences increases costs of producing and analysing financial statements. Ernst and Young describe the position in the following way:

> A deep, accessible and liquid capital market in Europe is important for the development of new businesses in Europe. The growth and entrepreneurial culture essential to development will thrive better with a clear route to market for equity. This is particularly important to an enlarged community as new businesses will grow more strongly with the help of equity capital. Conversely, without an integrated capital market these potential macro-economic benefits will not be realised, economic growth will be lower and the opportunity of achieving competitive advantage in the global capital markets will be lost.... Without high quality, reliable, comparable and transparent financial information, even if all other barriers are removed, investors will remain skeptical and demand a premium for their capital.[11]

---

[9] See, eg Rafael Guasch Martorell, 'La Armonización en el Marco del Derecho Europeo de Sociedades: La Obligación de Resultado Exigida por las Directivas Societarias a los Estados Miembros' (1994) 596 *Revista General De Derecho* 5651 at 5663. See also L Woods and C Villiers, 'The Legislative Process and the Institutions of the European Union: A Case Study of the Development of European Company Law' in P Craig and C Harlow (eds), *Lawmaking in the European Union–Proceedings of W G Hart Legal Workshop 1996* (London, Sweet & Maxwell, 1998).

[10] IASC Foundation Constitution, Part A, para 2, last revised on 8 July 2002, available at: http://www.iasc.org.uk.

[11] See http://www.ey.com/GLOBAL/content.nsf/International/Assurance_-_IAS_-_Case_for_ Single_Financial_Reporting_Framework. 'The Case for a Single Financial Reporting Framework'.

In 1990 a conference took place within the EU organised by the Commission. It was concluded there that the EU needed to take into account the harmonisation efforts at a broader international level and to co-operate with the international accounting standard setters.[12] In 1995 the Commission published a Communication indicating its recognition of a need to alter and modernise its accounting regime.[13] Its own Directives were not as demanding as the rules of the Securities and Exchange Commission in the US with the consequence that European companies would have to prepare a second set of accounts if they were seeking capital on international markets.[14] Such a situation can be confusing. The same information presented in different ways could lead to different interpretations and comparability would become difficult to achieve and expensive.[15] The Commission also recognised that the options within the Directives caused a lack of a common position on accounts in Europe with the consequence of weakening the EU's role on the international accounting standards setting scene.[16] The Commission therefore decided to seek a more positive role and at the same time preserve its own accounting regulation achievements.[17]

In 2000 another Communication was published focusing on financial reporting strategy.[18] This Communication stated that 'globalisation and information technology developments have created a unique momentum to realise a single, efficient and competitive EU securities market.'[19] Member States' securities markets were consolidated by new technologies, globalisation, the introduction of the Euro and information and communication technologies as well as electronic trading platforms.[20] In the 2000 Communication document the Commission also noted that there had been strong pressure towards convergence of accounting standards.[21] The Commission saw the need for a single set of comparable financial statements by a European company. Thus the Commission stated:

> Relevant, timely, reliable and comparable information about the performance and financial position of an enterprise continues to be of central importance in safeguarding the interests of investors, creditors and other stakeholders to ensure a level playing field between competitors.[22]

---

[12] See COM (1995) 508 para 2.6.

[13] COM (1995) 508, above n 5.

[14] COM (1995) 508 paras 1.2, 1.3 and 3.3.

[15] COM (1995) 508 para 3.3.

[16] COM (1995) 508 para 3.4.

[17] COM (1995) 508 paras 1.4 and 1.5.

[18] Communication from the Commission: *EU Financial Reporting Strategy: the way forward*, COM (2000) 359 final, Brussels 13.6.2000.

[19] COM (2000) 359 Executive Summary.

[20] COM (2000) 359 para 3.

[21] COM (2000) 359 para 5.

[22] COM (2000) 359 para 8.

The European Commission adopted the strategy of supporting the core set of standards created by the International Organization of Securities Commission and the IASC and the 2000 Communication document proposed the endorsement of the international standards by the EU. The plan was that they would become effective by 2005 in order to comply with the conclusions of the Lisbon European Council which set the goal of a fully integrated financial services market by then.[23]

THE NEW ACCOUNTING LEGISLATION

The result of the Commission's policy in legislative terms is a Regulation for the endorsement and enforcement of the international accounting standards created by the IASB[24] together with a proposed Directive to modernise the existing Fourth and Seventh Directives to enable them to be compatible with the international accounting standards that are to be endorsed.[25]

The Regulation

The Regulation states the need to supplement the legal framework applicable to publicly traded companies in their financial reporting activities. Thus Article 3 provides for the Commission to decide, under the Committee procedure set out in Decision 1999/468/EC,[26] on the applicability within the Community of international standards provided they: are not contrary to the true and fair view principle, are conducive to the European public good, and they meet the criteria of understandability, relevance, reliability and comparability required of the financial information needed for making economic decisions and assessing the stewardship of management. Adopted international standards shall be published in the Official Journal as a Commission Regulation and from January 2005 companies will have been required to prepare consolidated accounts in conformity with those international standards if at their balance sheet date their securities are admitted to trading on a regulated market of any

---

[23] COM (2000) 359 para 13.

[24] Reg (EC) No 1606/2002 of the European Parliament and of the Council of 19 July 2002 on the application of international accounting standards OJ L243, 11.09.02, 1.

[25] Proposed Directive of the European Parliament and of the Council amending Council Directives 78/660/EEC, 83/349/EEC and 91/674/EEC on the annual and consolidated accounts of certain types of companies and insurance undertakings COM (2002) 259/2 final, Brussels (9.7.02). The European Parliament voted to approve the proposal on 14 January 2003 and the proposal is expected to be adopted by the Council of Ministers: see IP/03/47.

[26] Art 6 refers to Decision 1999/468/EC as laying down the relevant procedure.

Member State.[27] The enforcement of such international standards is currently being negotiated.[28]

The Proposed Directive

The existing Directives still have a role since they apply to non-publicly traded companies and to those areas not touched by the international accounting standards and they continue to apply to the annual accounts of all companies. Yet to some extent the Directives have been superseded by modern accounting theory and practice so they are not entirely compatible with international standards.[29] The proposed Directive seeks to modernise them and to bring them into line with the international standards[30] with added requirements also of financial reports containing analyses of environmental, social and other aspects relevant to an understanding of the company's development and position.

THE NEW ACCOUNTING REGIME

The new legislation and the European Commission's commitment to the adoption of the international accounting standards have significantly altered the accounting regime in the EU. A number of observations can be made:

A Two-tier Accounting System

A two-tier accounting regime has possibly been created. One level will apply to publicly traded companies for whose consolidated accounts the international accounting standards will be applicable. Another level will apply to other businesses and to the annual accounts of all limited companies. It should be noted, however, that Member States have been given the options of extending the application of the international standards to annual accounts and to non-publicly traded companies.[31] If the Member

---

[27] Art 4.
[28] Para 16 of the preamble states that 'a proper and rigorous enforcement regime is key to underpinning investors' confidence in financial markets. Member States, by virtue of Article 10 of the EU Treaty, are required to take appropriate measures to ensure compliance with international accounting standards. The Commission intends to liaise with Member States, notably through the Committee of European Securities Regulators (CESR), to develop a common approach to enforcement.'
[29] See the explanatory memorandum to the proposed Directive.
[30] See IP/02/799.
[31] Art 5 of the Reg.

States take up these options that would reduce the extent of the two-tier system. The potential impact is further reduced (at least in the short term prior to any revision of the international accounting standards) by the Directive's attempt to modernise the existing Directives so that they operate in a broadly similar way to the international accounting standards.

Priority to International Accounting Standards

If, despite modernising the Directives, any incompatibility between an adopted international accounting standard and the Directives should arise, the Regulation has the effect of the international accounting standards taking precedence. This is acknowledged specifically by the Commission in its 1995 Communication document.[32] The IASB has also adopted a co-operative stance and expressed a willingness in such circumstances to re-examine any international accounting standards which are found not to be in conformity with the Directives.[33]

Mandatory Standards

The Regulation has the effect of making the international accounting standards mandatory. This is an interesting result since the IASB itself does not endow the standards with this status because it would not have authority to enforce them. The IASB acknowledges that Member States have the option of giving them legally binding status. The Regulation itself is, of course, directly applicable and any endorsed international standard would become directly applicable as it would be given effect by way of a Regulation. Currently, however, it is not clear how that direct applicability would be given effect in practice since the enforcement mechanism has not been clarified. As is known, under Article 249 EU Treaty, a Regulation, being directly applicable, becomes part of the domestic law of the Member States without needing transposition, with the effect that, so long as their provisions are sufficiently clear, precise, relevant to the situation of an individual litigant, are capable of being relied upon and enforced by individuals in their national courts.

Enforcement Negotiations

The Regulation's preamble states that the Commission intends to liaise with Member States through the Committee of European Securities Regulators

---

[32] See para 5.3 of the 1995 Document, COM (1995) 508.
[33] *Ibid.*

to develop a common approach to enforcement,[34] so it leaves to speculation the penalties that may be applied for non-compliance. Prior to the entry into force of the Regulation, those countries which have already made use of the International Accounting Standards and International Financial Reporting Standards require companies to give particulars of material departures from those standards and the reasons for such departures. It is often left to the professional bodies to regulate the issue. The Institute of Chartered Accountants in England and Wales advocates a global enforcement system, but in the short term it suggests a uniform enforcement of international standards across Europe.[35] In the view of the Institute, the effectiveness of international accounting standards 'depends on uniform enforcement, so as to prevent companies seeking to benefit from arbitrage where national enforcement systems or rulings differ.'[36] The Institute's preference is for a referrals procedure rather than a system of pre-clearance on the acceptability of a proposed accounting treatment.

The Committee of European Securities Regulators published a proposed statement of principles in October 2002,[37] suggesting the establishment by Member States of Competent Independent Administrative Authorities that would have ultimate responsibility for enforcement of compliance and such enforcement would be predominantly risk based combined with rotation and/or sampling of the financial information of selected companies. It would comprise of a range of formal checks to in-depth substantive checking of the information provided by the selected companies. In the case of a material misstatement enforcers should take appropriate action to achieve disclosure and if relevant a correction of the misstatement. What is apparent is that the proposal suggests a degree of discretion to the Member States. Thus, the global and uniform enforcement system advocated by the Institute of Chartered Accountants in England and Wales is unlikely to be achieved.

Importance of Committees in the Endorsement Process

The endorsement process, like the Commission's proposed enforcement negotiations, makes heavy use of committees. As has already been noted above, the Regulation refers to Decision 1999/468/EC which sets out the

---

[34] Preamble, para 16.

[35] See Institute of Chartered Accountants in England and Wales, *Policy Statement on EU Endorsement and Enforcement of International Accounting Standards*, Tech 23/00, available at: http://www.icaew.co.uk /index.cfm?AUB=TB21_4069.

[36] *Ibid.*

[37] Committee of European Securities Regulators, Proposed Statement of Principles of Enforcement of Accounting Standards in Europe, Consultation Paper, October 2002, CESR/02–188b, available at http://www.europefesco.org.

Committee Procedure. The Communication documents also refer to the comitology procedure, justified on the basis of the subsidiarity and proportionality principles for the purpose of amending the Directives. Yet what exists in reality is an extremely complex arrangement with the involvement of several committees whose precise roles and status are not entirely clear. As was proposed in the 2000 Communication document, the endorsement mechanism requires a two-tiered structure comprising a technical level and a political level.

The Technical Level

The technical level consists of the European Financial Reporting Advisory Group (hereinafter 'EFRAG'), a committee of independent experts from the private sector,[38] to advise the Commission on the suitability of international accounting standards and their compatibility with the Directives. A supervisory board ascertains that individual members of the technical group work in the European interest.

The Political Level

Following advice from EFRAG the Commission then puts forward its proposal to the Accounting Regulatory Committee consisting of official representatives from the Member States and chaired by the Commission. The Accounting Regulatory Committee votes by qualified majority voting whether to accept the proposal to adopt the international accounting standards. If the Committee votes against the proposal the Commission may submit it to the Council of Ministers. The Council of Ministers is then given three months to adopt or block the proposal, also by qualified majority voting. If it blocks the proposal the Commission can resubmit it. The European Parliament also has a right to comment but not to veto.[39]

Alongside these committees, the Contact Committee, which was set up under the Fourth Directive, is to check the compatibility of the international accounting standards and the Directives and any changes to the Directives which are necessary will be effected by the Committee. The aim is to achieve a common position internationally and between Europe and the relevant international bodies, in particular the IASB. Thus, a technical subcommittee of the Contact Committee has a role of 'meeting regularly to

---

[38] For further information about EFRAG, see http://www.iasplus.com/efrag/efrag.htm.

[39] This interpretation of the procedure is offered in the Consultation Document issued by the Department of Trade and Industry: *International Accounting Standards: A Consultation Document on the Possible Extension of the European Regulation on International Accounting Standards*, URN 02/1158, 30 August 2002, at 35–36, paras 7–11.

discuss matters particularly relating to international accounting standards' and also seeks common positions on exposure drafts.[40] It appears that EFRAG plays this role as the Contact Committee's technical subcommittee. Through this arrangement the Commission seeks effective participation in the IASB's standard setting process. [41]

The Accounting Advisory Forum, which represents users and preparers of accounts also exists[42] and meets with the Contact Committee but it is not clear at which stage this is consulted. Indeed, the Commission, in 1995, noted the weakness of this Forum since 'in the absence of a clear mandate, the results of its work do not carry enough weight to exercise a real influence on accounting developments.'[43]

What it is possible to conclude is that the endorsement process comprises of a rather messy arrangement. There are several committees involved, some more official than others, and with overlapping roles. It is not clear precisely who makes up the committees. For example, what is meant by the term 'official' when we refer to the official representatives of the Member States in the Accounting Regulatory Committee?[44] The EFRAG members come from the private sector from bodies such as the Union des Confederations de l'Industries et des Employeurs d'Europe (UNICE) and the Federation des Experts Comptables Europeens (FEE) but there is no indication that they must come from specified bodies and it claims also to operate independently of each of the European organisations involved.

The justification for the use of committees is acceptable when reference is made to the principles of subsidiarity and proportionality, but the usual criticisms of the committee process can also be levelled against the arrangements that are apparent in the field of financial reporting. Gráinne de Búrca set out the better-known criticisms in her essay in the edited collection *The Evolution of EU Law.*[45] She included lack of transparency; the complexity and opaque nature of the system; the marginalisation of the European

---

[40] See http://www.europa.eu.int/comm/internal_market/en/company/account/committ/contact/index.htm.

[41] See COM (1995) 508, at para 5.4 in which the Commission states: 'In order to ensure an appropriate European input into the continuing work of the IASC, the Contact Committee will examine and seek to establish an agreed position on future Exposure Drafts (or draft standards) published by the IASC. An agreed Union position on Exposure Drafts can thus be conveyed to the IASC.'

[42] This was set up by the Commission after the 1990 Conference in order to open up the debate on accounting issues at European level and to influence the work of national standard setting bodies: see COM (1995) 508 para 2.7.

[43] *Ibid.*

[44] This is a common question raised about the so-called official representatives within the committee process: see, eg De Búrca below.

[45] Gráinne de Búrca, 'The Institutional Development of the EU: A Constitutional Analysis' in P Craig and Gráinne de Búrca (eds), *The Evolution of EU Law* (Oxford, Oxford University Press, 1999) 55–81, esp at 71–75.

Parliament leading to claims of democratic deficit and the haphazard nature of the process. All these criticisms are valid in the example of committee usage within the field of financial reporting. Indeed, with so many committees involved the arrangement arguably distances the European Parliament even further as well as the companies and investors which are directly affected by the regulations that emerge from the process.

Role of the IASB

The role of the IASB is relevant to the arrangement. Yet this body is also open to criticism. First there is evidence that the IASB is open to lobbying which can stand in the way of a democratic result.[46] This problem is exacerbated by the fact that, as Scholte observes, the IASB has no provisions for public participation or consultation.[47] Currently the European Commission has an observer role with the IASB and EFRAG seeks to influence its decisions by submitting opinions on exposure drafts and consultations, but none of this gives a clear formal role to the EU in the decision-making process leading to the eventual standards created. The membership of the IASB is based on technical expertise[48] and its own Constitution states specifically that selection of members shall not be based on geographical representation.[49] The role of the IASB's members is 'to act in the public interest and to have regard to the IASB framework.'[50] There is nothing in the Constitution that refers to the EU or any role of the EU. Yet geographical domination of the IASB is also apparent and is considered by some to be problematic. For example, Feng notes the dominance of seven countries in what purports to be an international body.[51] One might correct Feng on her number but generally it is fair to say that a small(albeit geographically wide–number of jurisdictions has dominated the IASB since its beginnings. In 1973 the IASC was founded as a result of an agreement by the accounting bodies in Australia, Canada, France, Germany, Japan, Mexico, the Netherlands, the United Kingdom and Ireland and the United States. Today,

---

[46] See Stephen A Zeff, '"Political" Lobbying of Proposed Standards: A Challenge to the IASB, *Accounting Horizons*, vol 16, March 2002. Zeff notes a campaign by US industry to oppose any attempt by the IASB to develop a standard on employee stock options that goes further than the disclosure requirement in the FASB statement No 123.

[47] See Scholte, 'Civil Society and Democracy in Global Governance', above n 4, at 16.

[48] IASC Constitution, para 20.

[49] IASC Constitution, para 21.

[50] IASC Constitution, para 24.

[51] Madame Feng Shuping, *Strengthen Co-operation to promote International Convergence of Accounting Standards*, Speech at the IASB National Standards Setters' Meeting, 18 November 2002, at http://www.iasplus.com/china/0211iasbfeng1.pdf.

based in London, the board members come from nine countries.[52] This leaves out the majority of the EU's Member States from the important process of setting standards that will most likely eventually apply in their jurisdictions as a result of EU endorsement of those standards. One might argue that this development by which the international standards are likely to become mandatory across the EU, would justify an examination of the possibility of changing the membership rules of the IASB to widen or ease the possibility of access to participants from states where it is likely that the standards will apply.

Change in Direction from the Company Law Programme

One notable feature of the Commission's stance on financial reporting is that it demonstrates a potentially different approach from that which has developed previously in the company law programme. That programme, encompassing the Accounting Directives, has become increasingly more flexible and has bowed more and more to the demands of the Member States. It has been possible, as was noted above, to identify 'generations' of Directives which, by and large, coincided with successive EC/EU enlargements as well as the introduction of new legislative processes. Thus, the First and Second Directives are rather prescriptive with broadly mandatory provisions. The second generation Directives, which include the Accounting Directives, offer more options to the Member States and to the companies being regulated. The Eleventh and Twelfth Directives suggest a third generation in which they consist mainly of principles with the details to be made up by the Member States. The proposed Thirteenth Directive may well fall within the 'new approach' Directives and the fact that it has still not been adopted and has altered dramatically in character from its earlier drafts also highlights the power of negotiations among the Member States.[53]

The generosity of the Accounting Directives in the options they provide to the Member States and to companies, was concluded ultimately by the Commission to have created a fragmented EU financial reporting which has hindered the EU's position in the establishment of deep and liquid capital markets.[54] This has led the Commission to use the device of a Regulation to impose on Member States an obligation to adopt the international financial reporting standards created by a body outwith the EU's regulatory

[52] See http://www.iasc.org.uk/cmt.
[53] For a full account of this pattern of development in the company law programme, see C Villiers, *European Company Law: Towards Democracy?* (Aldershot, Ashgate, 1998).
[54] See COM (2000) 359 para 4.

structure. Indeed, the financial reporting strategy, which falls within the new approach policy, is more similar to that seen in the capital markets regulation which comprises very little detail but has the effect of adopting wholesale provisions created by an outside, expert, private body.

This new approach may demonstrate a recognition that the increasingly flexible approach within the programme of company law Directives went too far and eventually failed to achieve the required level of harmonisation. One might interpret the adoption of the international standards as a sign that the Member States have given up their role in the standards creating process, leaving that task to technical experts from the private sector and later also relying on expert opinion about the appropriateness of turning such standards into legally effective norms that will become applicable in the Member States throughout the EU.

US Standards Come Closer

The European Commission made a positive choice of the IASB's standards in preference to the Generally Accepted Accounting Principles in the US (hereinafter 'US GAAP'). Primarily this was because the international accounting standards of the IASB are drawn up with an international perspective rather than being tailored to the US environment. Additionally, the US GAAP are very detailed and technically demanding. Furthermore, the EU has no influence on the elaboration of US GAAP. Yet, the recent Memorandum of Agreement between the IASB and the US Financial Accounting Standards Board to achieve real convergence between their respective accounting standards[55] will bring the US GAAP closer to the EU and its Member States and the companies operating within the EU. In addition, the recent Sarbanes-Oxley Act, introduced in the wake of the Enron scandal, threatens to impose a requirement to comply with its standards. The Act gives the US regulator power to inspect and punish EU accounting firms involved in auditing companies with US share listings.[56] Thus, the Commission's stated attempt to reduce the costs of requiring to produce multiple versions of financial statements might be lost as a result of the potential for double regulation arising from the Sarbanes-Oxley Act. Needless to say, attempts are now being made to avoid this double regulation potential.

---

[55] See the announcement at http://www.iasc.org.uk/cmt/0001.asp. 29 October 2002.
[56] For commentary on the Act, see A Parker, 'Britain to Press US for Easing of Audit Plans' *Financial Times*, 24 February 2002 and A Parker, 'Accountants Urge Cap on Claims' *Financial Times*, 24 February 2002.

COMING BACK TO GLOBALISATION–
THE GENERAL IMPLICATIONS

Clearly, globalisation has influenced the European Commission's policy. However, the Commission appears to view globalisation in a particular way, even though arguably globalisation has occurred in many different guises since the Middle Ages. The Commission has treated globalisation as an exclusively economic phenomenon[57] and in the context of financial reporting this includes reference to trade flows, information technology and communications.[58] As globalisation tends to focus on market making, the response to the process has been mainly a negative integration response; a neoliberal project aspiring towards intensified trade and financial flows and investments. No more than lip service is paid to positive integration. One might argue that the proposed requirement of environmental and social reports contributes to the development of positive integration. However, the emphasis on negative integration arguably reflects the nature of financial reporting itself.

It is possible to see Europeanisation as both a conduit for global forces and a shield against them[59] which reflects doubt on the ability of national governance to deliver appropriate policies to meet the external conditions.[60] Indeed the activity observed reveals a hope for the EU to exert political influence on the international developments. It shows Europeanisation not only as a response to globalisation, but as an acceptance of and furtherance of globalisation with attempts to strengthen the European economy. Thus according to Rosamond, globalisation is used as an exogenous referent by actors seeking to argue for the further Europeanisation of governance capacity and deeper European economic integration. He adds that much of this is bound up with the discursive elaboration of a European economy or of European firms which seek a European level regulatory framework to assure competitiveness globally.[61]

---

[57] B Rosamond, 'Europeanisation and Discourses of Globalisation: Narratives of External Structural Context in the European Commission' (Working Paper, 2000) available at: http://www.warwick.ac.uk/fac/soc/csgr/wpapers/wp5100.pdf2000, at 16.

[58] See COM (2000) 359 final para 3.

[59] See VA Schmidt, 'Convergent Pressures, Divergent Responses: France, Great Britain and Germany Between Globalisation and Europeanisation' in DA Smith, DJ Solinger and SV Topik, *States and Sovereignty in the Global Economy* (London-New York, Routledge, 1999) 172–92.

[60] B Rosamond, above n 57.

[61] B Rosamond, 'Globalisation and the European Union' Paper presented to a conference on The European Union in International Affairs, National Europe Centre, Australian National University, 3–4 July 2002 available at: http://www.anu.edu.au/NEC/rosamond.pdf at 10 and B Rosamond, 'Imagining the European Economy: "Competitiveness" and the Social Construction of Europe as an Economic Space' (2002) *New Political Economy* vol 7, issue 2 at 157.

He suggests that globalisation may be used as a strategic exercise designed to enhance Europeanisation, the position of the Commission and the pursuit of neoliberal modes of economic governance. Stated another way, globalisation tends to be seen as a form of liberalisation which must be met with furtherance of liberalisation.[62]

Article B of the EU Treaty has the objective for the EU of being able to assert its identity on the international scene. It is still, however, for the Member States to create international agreements. In the area of financial reporting it has been possible to observe some genuine attempts by the EU to assert its identity on the international stage. As was noted above, the Commission has claimed a co-operative approach with the IASB to adopt international accounting and financial reporting standards but it seeks to align these with the true and fair view principle as well as to ensure that such standards support European policy and in order to be adopted they must be relevant, reliable and comparable. The European Commission has also sought to have a participatory influence on the creation of the standards via the Contact Committee and EFRAG but how sufficient and how well co-ordinated is this manner of participation is unclear. Kelstrup argues that the lack of internal coherence makes the EU a weak international actor.[63] The complicated arrangement that has emerged in the financial reporting field may well exacerbate the problem.

A greater role has been carved out for the European Commission at least regarding the endorsement process relating to the international accounting standards. The adoption of the committee process certainly appears, within this arena, to have further marginalised the European Parliament and the Council of Ministers. This trend corresponds with observations made by the critics of the committee process[64] and by those in the international relations and politics circles. For example, Rosamond notes the Commission as being at the heart of a supranational coalition involving experts and corporate actors.[65]

The financial reporting experience also highlights the increasing emphasis on a multi-level approach to governance within the European Union in which national governments no longer have a monopoly of control. This

---

[62] See, eg the views expressed by two consecutive trade Commissioners: L. Brittan 'The Challenges of the Global Economy for Europe' speech to the Vlerick Annual Alumni Meeting, Ghent 1998, and P Lamy 'Globalisation: a win-win process', Brussels, 15 September 1999, available at: http://www.europa.eu.int/trade/speeches_articles/spla01en.htm both of these references are made by Rosamond (2000), above n 60, at 17.

[63] Kelstrup, 'The European Union and Globalisation: Reflections on Strategies of Individual States' available at: http://www.copri.dk/publications/WP/WP%202001/38-2001.doc

[64] See, eg K Bradley, 'The European Parliament and Comitology: On the Road to Nowhere?' (1997) 3 *ELJ* 230.

[65] Rosamond (2000), above n 57, at 14.

theoretical model of multilevel governance was developed by Marks, Hooghe and Blank and as part of their theory they suggested that:

> States do not monopolize links between domestic and European actors, but are among a variety of actors contesting decisions that are made at a variety of levels. ...States are an integral and powerful part of the EU, but they no longer provide the sole interface between supranational and subnational arenas, and they share, rather than monopolize, control over many activities that take place in their respective territories.[66]

This multi-level governance appears also to be operated at the point of creating implementing norms where such norms result 'from the interaction of the Commission, state technocrats, and interest groups.'[67] Indeed, the picture is ultimately one of a very complex structural arrangement. Thus as Jørgensen and Rosamond describe, 'the EU has become recently more "multi-actor", multi-level and multi-process. Formal mechanisms have been colonised by an array of governmental and non-state actors and patterns of informal interaction have become institutionalised.'[68]

Part of this structure entails a stronger reliance on the private sector, although in the financial reporting field this is arguably nothing new. In the UK at least, most accounting regulation has been within the jurisdiction of bodies such as the Accounting Standards Board. Moreover, the private bodies may well be best equipped to create standards since they have expertise and are likely to be among those who are specifically affected. Nevertheless, within the EU regulatory and legislative processes such a strong reliance on the private sector might be problematic from the perspective of political and democratic legitimacy. There is often a lack of formality within private organisational activities, and indeed we have witnessed no clear sign of a formal role for the EU in the decision-making process of the IASB. As noted above, the IASB is also dominated by a small handful of states. This means that potentially interested parties from a large number of Member States within the EU are given no genuine opportunity for involvement or influence in the eventual standards created. This is a common problem within the global setting. For example, commentators have noted that in institutions such as the World Trade Organisation, the International Monetary

---

[66] G Marks, L Hooghe and K Blank, 'European Integration from the 1980s: State-Centric *v.* Multiple-Level Governance' (1996) 34 *JCMS* 341 at 346–47.

[67] P Craig, 'The Nature of the Community' in P Craig and Gráinne de Búrca, above n 45, 1, at 19, referring to Marks, Hooghe and Blank, above n 66, at 367–69.

[68] KE Jørgensen and Ben Rosamond, 'Europe: Regional Laboratory for a Global Polity?' CSGR Working Paper No 71/01, May 2001, available at: http://www.warwick.ac.uk/fac/soc/CSGR/wpapers/wp7101a.pdf at 6.

Fund and the World Bank, decision making is strongly influenced by few countries representing specific interests involving free trade issues.[69] The problem is deepened by the fact that democratic representation is generally flimsy since many international organisations are formed by representatives of national governments which have quite uneven statuses and are not directly elected.[70]

The increased emphasis on private organisations in the financial reporting field also reflects a more universal effect of globalisation processes. For example, Wallace notices in EU policy making generally an accumulation of technical expertise to produce agreed standards and policy norms.[71] Wallace considers this trend to be an OECD import.[72] Further, networks of technocrats are often in the driver's seat in global governance, and as Scholte observes, a significant regulation of global relations has come to reside in the private sector.[73] Indeed, the very nature of globalisation is shaped by private actions since the process is largely driven by the activities of multinational firms. Additionally, private bodies such as the IASB and the FASB are deepening the globalisation processes, for example, by their recent agreement on convergence of their respective accounting standards, noted above.

What might be suggested overall is that the traditional institutional structure, and the so called classic Monnet method, the Community method, has not been adequately equipped to deal with the challenges presented by globalisation. There is a greater need for 'regulation through expertise.' It could be argued that the financial reporting arena shows that European acceptance of globalisation in turn requires reference to global rules and deference to global actors by inserting rules created by those global actors into the legislative programme of the EU. The highly technical nature of the standards being created together with the continuing enlargement of the EU, give reason to the Commission for delegating the negotiations regarding the creation of the standards to an outside body with the intention of later embedding such standards into the EU's own legislative framework. The realistic alternative seems to be probable failure to create any common rules at all. The constitutional and institutional arrangements would certainly

---

[69] See Graziano, Europeanisation or Globalisation? A Framework for Empirical Research', above n 2, at 9, and Scholte, 'Civil Society and Democracy in Global Governance', above n 4, at 14.

[70] Graziano, above n 2, at 8.

[71] H Wallace, 'The Institutional Setting: Five Variations on a Theme' in H Wallace and W Wallace (eds), *Policy Making in the European Union* (4th edn, Oxford, Oxford University Press, 2000).

[72] *Ibid.* See also, OECD (n.d.) International Benchmarking Network, at: http://www.oecd.org/puma/mgmtres/pac/Benchmarking/links.

[73] Scholte, 'Civil Society and Democracy in Global Governance', above n 4, at 12.

make the achievement of any body of standards difficult. Ultimately, it could be argued, as Snyder suggests, that globalisation sustains and creates interests and relationships which undercut traditional constitutionalism as a mode of EU governance.[74]

CONCLUSION

There is undoubtedly a symbiosis between globalisation and Europeanisation. The two phenomena do appear to be operating in parallel and in tandem. In the words of Professor Snyder: 'globalization and Europeanization are complementary, partly overlapping, mutually reinforcing, but also competing processes.'[75] There is still a long way to go in the field of financial reporting. Clearly the push towards greater convergence of standards internationally is strong. The effect from a legislative perspective seems to be more delegated legislation which is at the same time more prescriptive. Both such trends are justified as practically necessary. The legislative process is too slow and cumbersome to operate without access to delegated legislation and a more prescriptive approach seems necessary to achieve a coherent and common European framework. In the short term at least a two-tier accounting system is likely to emerge, though this could eventually disappear or at least diminish as steps are taken to achieve compatibility between the Directives and the standards.

The financial reporting field has also confirmed suggestions that globalisation requires changes to the constitutional, institutional and regulatory arrangements of the EU. Thus, as Scholte notes, globalisation has gone hand in hand with a reconfiguration of regulation; from government to governance, a supra-territorial, multi-layered governance.[76] This, in turn has meant stronger roles for the Commission and for the private sector with serious implications for democracy. Such a development presents a challenge for creating a legitimate process. What is required is clear evidence that the process fits within the five principles of good governance set out in the Commission's White Paper on European Governance: openness, participation, accountability, effectiveness and coherence.[77] At the moment any claim that these principles has been satisfied would not be convincing. As Scholte argues, in each area of global policy, popular

---

[74] Snyder, 'Globalisation and Europeanisation as Friends and Rivals: European Union Law in Global Economic, above n 3.

[75] *Ibid*, at 1.

[76] Scholte, 'Civil Society and Democracy in Global Governance', above n 4, at 10.

[77] European Commission: 'European Governance: A White Paper' COM (2001) 428. See also Scholte, 'Civil Society and Democracy in Global Governance', above n 4, at 12.

participation, consultation, transparency and accountability are generally weak.[78]

The constitutional challenges that globalisation brings to the EU are considerable indeed. These affect the procedural aspects, of course, but ultimately it will be the substantive results that count. In the field of financial reporting at least, that judgement will become necessary after 2005.

---

[78] Scholte, 'Civil Society and Democracy in Global Governance'.

5

Imperialism and Accountability in Corporate Law: The Limitations of Incorporation Law as a Regulatory Mechanism

NICHOLAS HD FOSTER
JANE BALL

INTRODUCTION[1]

THE MOST POWERFUL type of group of modern times is the nation-state. However, since its inglorious heyday in the late nineteenth and early twentieth century, its highly autonomous nature has been curbed, externally through the role played by numerous international organisations, internally through the decline in popularity of insular protectionism and the socialist/communist need to centralise control in the state apparatus, as well as by the growth of other centres of power. One such centre of power is the corporation. According to the title of one book, they are 'imperial',[2] according to another, they might rule the world.[3] Shell Nigeria acts in some ways like a government, spending over US$50 million per year in infrastructure projects, consulting those affected by its activity in order to ensure, if not its popularity, its acceptance.[4] Total sales of the

---

[1] The literature regarding the accountability of corporations is large and growing larger. References have been kept to a minimum. More can be found in DM Branson 'The Social Responsibility of Large Multinational Corporations' (2002) 16 *Transnational Lawyer* 121.

[2] RJ Barnet and J Cavanagh, *Global Dreams: Imperial Corporations and the New World Order* (New York, Touchstone, 1995).

[3] DC Korten, *When Corporations Rule the World* (2nd edn, San Francisco, Berrett-Koehler Publishers, 2001).

[4] Shell, Social Investment Overview, available at: http://www.shell.com (visited 13 May 2003); Shell SPDC 2002 Integrated Environment & Community Development Stakeholders' Workshop Action Close–Out Report (Shell, 2003).

top twenty corporations are more than US$1,600 billion and they employ more than five million people.[5]

This power should not be exaggerated. Contrary to what some commentators seem to imply, particularly when they draw up tables showing corporations as having more economic weight than many countries: 'States remain sovereign. They wield legal powers that no individual or corporation can possess.'[6] Shell Nigeria's activities are exceptional. They are only undertaken because of the particular capacity problems of the Nigerian state. Shell cannot possibly take over all state functions, nor would its management wish to do so.

It remains true, though, that corporations can exercise great power. In accordance with the general principle of checks and balances in society, that power needs to be kept within bounds. One type of law which states use for the purpose of such control is the law which gives the corporation legal life, its 'incorporation law'. It is a reasonably obvious choice, since it is the law which determines the parameters of the corporation's existence.[7] However, in a globalised world, states may find their ability to use this type of law seriously curtailed, with many corporations able to evade it with relative ease.

This chapter is mainly concerned with the extent to which corporations can practise such evasion and briefly considers the possibility of an alternative approach.

Facilitation and Control

For our purposes, incorporation law can be considered as having two aspects. The first is its facilitative capacity, giving the grouping its legal form and the legal mechanisms which enable it to function. The second is its ability to regulate the corporation.

Until the recent growth in the importance of the corporation, these aspects received relatively little attention outside the sphere of company law. Far more attention was paid to similar concepts in the context of the nation state, in which facilitative and regulatory concepts evolved slowly over time in well-known ways, varying from state to state, with much interchange of ideas between countries. Notably there emerged the idea of an entity distinct from the person of the monarch, 'the State' or 'the

---

[5] UNCTAD *World Investment Report 2001: Promoting Linkages* (New York, United Nations, 2001) cited in H Kovach, C Neligan, and S Burall, *Power without Accountability? The Global Accountability Report 1* (One World Trust, 2003) 15.

[6] G Soros, *The Crisis of Global Capitalism: Open Society Endangered* (London, Little, Brown and Company, 1998) 109.

[7] On the numerous other mechanisms which can be used for this purpose see, eg, H Ward, *Legal Issues in Corporate Citizenship* (London, Globalt Ansvar–Swedish Partnership for Global Responsibility, 2003).

Crown.'[8] Control evolved in tandem, also over long periods and with much difficulty, including violent upheavals such as the Wars of the Three Kingdoms, 1639–51[9] and the French Revolution, 1789. A greater role for assemblies led to the concept of different entities within the state, such as 'the King/Queen in Parliament,' 'the judiciary' and 'the executive,' as well as to the separation of those entities from each, with the executive being, in theory, supervised and controlled by the other two. Political control came to be exercised by the participants in the state through their representatives. Legal control came to be exercised by the judges.

The history of the corporation is quite different. Despite the fact that it has deep historical roots, with evidence of 'company' type contracts reaching back to the ancient near East, and some corporations such as the East India Company having state-like powers, its general significance did not match that of the state for centuries. For this reason, facilitative concepts were slow to develop beyond such ancient ideas as the commenda contract/company on the European mainland (a kind of limited partnership, in which one party contributed capital and the other commercial expertise, the investor's liability in the venture being limited to the capital contributed; it gave rise to statutory equivalents in civilian legal systems) and the more recent, if still venerable, trust in England.[10]

It was only after the Industrial Revolution, when advances in technology allowed and required the mass concentration and exploitation of resources, that the corporation became a major force. Without wishing to minimise the importance of the long history during which the component ideas were developed, it is not too inaccurate to point to this period as the turning point in facilitative ideas, because it was at this time that the most important idea of this type, incorporation, was made easily available to the general population by simple registration.[11]

---

[8] See, eg J-M Carbasse, *Manuel d'introduction historique au droit* (Paris, Presses universitaires de France, 2002) 153; EH Kantorowicz, *The King's Two Bodies: A Study in Mediaeval Political Theology* (Princeton, Princeton University Press, 1957).

[9] More commonly, if inaccurately, known as 'the English Civil War.' See N Davies, *The Isles: A History* (London, Macmillan, 1999) 490.

[10] For a history of the commenda and its relationship to other similar contracts, see JH Pryor 'The Origins of the Commenda Contract' (1977) 52 *Speculum* 5. On companies as contracts and in particular the French approach to this issue, see NHD Foster 'Company Law Theory–England and France' (2000) 48 *American Journal of Comparative Law* 573–621 at 585–86 and 596–600.

[11] The first significant enactment in the UK was the Joint Stock Companies Act 1844. Limited liability was introduced after many debates by the Limited Liability Act 1855. Much of what we think of as characteristic of the UK company was introduced later, by the Joint Stock Companies Act 1856. In France the Code Civil of 1804 and the Commercial Code of 1807 made very little provision for companies. The first extensive regulation was contained in the Law of 24 July 1867, Art 21 of which was the first provision allowing *sociétés anonymes* to be formed without specific authorisation of the Conseil d'Etat. Corporate legislation was passed by various states of the United States throughout the early to mid-nineteenth century, starting with New York in 1811.

On the regulatory side the nation-state was concerned to submit corporations to its control and prevent them from threatening the power of the state by becoming 'independent commonwealths within the kingdom.'[12] An important method used in the taming process was the assumption by the nation-state of the leading role in giving legal form to corporations. In the common law, one way of achieving this was the reservation to the state of the grant of legal personality (the 'concession theory'); in French law legal personality is granted by case law, but in practice registration is a prerequisite to this recognition as far as companies are concerned.[13] Whatever the theoretical method used, the state gave itself the power to impose restrictions on corporations by incorporating those restrictions into the very structure of their legal existence.

The Enterprise, the Legal Entity and the Mismatch

There are, however, fundamental problems with the approach to regulation just described. In order to understand them it is necessary to understand the nature of the corporation, the way in which it takes legal form, and the separation which took place between the real-world grouping (which will be called, from this point on, the 'enterprise') and the legal construct which was created in order to give it legal standing (the 'legal entity').

The Enterprise

The enterprise is what the lay person thinks of as the corporation, in other words (roughly speaking) a group of people acting with a common purpose for commercial gain. Examples of such groups are IBM, Microsoft and Shell. Space does not permit a detailed ontological analysis. Suffice it to say that it can be regarded as a unit for everyday purposes, despite being made up of various human and other components. This approach is justifiable because the group has a kind of reality, constituted by a difference between the outcomes possible with a co-ordinated group and those which are possible with an uncoordinated collection of individuals. The outcomes are of two types, internal and external. Internal outcomes are manifested by the changed behaviour of the participants in the enterprise. External outcomes are manifested by the effects which the group actions of the enterprise produce on the rest of the world.

---

[12] Sir Robert Sawyer, the Attorney-General, in proceedings in 1682 (8 ST 1039), cited in W Holdsworth, *A History of English Law* (3rd edn, London, Methuen, 1924) vol 9, at 46.

[13] Cass civ 2e 28 janv 1954: D1954, 2, 217, note Levasseur: 'la personnnalité civile n'est pas une création de la loi, qu'elle appartient, en principe, à tout groupement pourvu d'un possibilité d'expression collective pour la défense d'intérêts licites, dignes, par suite, d'être juridiquement reconnues et protégés.'

The Legal Entity

The legal entity has a different reality. Unlike the enterprise, which is composed of parts which have a physical existence, the legal entity is a pure abstraction with no physical parts, an invention of the law. It has a certain reality which, like that of the enterprise, derives from a difference in outcomes as between its 'existence' and 'non-existence.' With the legal entity, though, the difference is determined by the law. If the law determines that 'a company exists,' this in fact means that the participants in 'the company' have different rights and obligations from those which they would have had if 'the company did not exist.' In other words, going through the formalities of 'company formation' results in different legal outcomes for the participants from those which would have obtained if the formalities had not been observed. Examples of the legal entity include IBM United Kingdom Holdings Limited, Microsoft System Sales UK Limited and Shell & BP Services Limited.

In the legal entity the messiness of the enterprise is artificially tidied up. The roles of the participants are referred to in the language of the legal entity as if they were people ('shareholders', 'directors' and 'employees'). Different rights and obligations are assigned to those roles.

The difference between the reality of the enterprise and that of the legal entity resulted in a split between the two. The legal entity, originally designed to be the legal clothing of the enterprise, can be used simply to alter the legal relationships between individuals who 'form a company' as among themselves and as between them and other individuals in the complete absence of any underlying enterprise. To take the example of a company with limited liability, I can form a single shareholder company which borrows £100 from you. Effectively, I have borrowed the money, there is nobody else involved in the company and there is no enterprise behind it. However, so long as there are no circumstances present which might allow the 'veil of incorporation' to be lifted, if the company fails to pay you, I am not liable.[14]

The Mismatch

Once the distinct and separate nature of the legal entity was realised, it became possible to create the various types of legal entities which we have today, disconnected (either wholly or partially) from any real enterprise,

---

[14] It is this dichotomy between the reality of the enterprise and the reality of the legal entity which is at the heart of *Salomon v A Salomon & Company, Limited* [1897] AC 22, HL(E). See in particular the arguments of counsel at 27, where he refers to the desire of Aron Salomon: 'to convert his unlimited into a limited liability.'

entities which we call 'subsidiaries', 'dormant companies', 'off-the-shelf companies' and so on. This is not to say that there is no link between enterprises and legal entities. Most enterprises act through one or more legal entities and many legal entities are connected in some way to an enterprise.

A consequence of the difference in the natures of the two phenomena is the difference in their relationship to the nation-state.

The legal entity is a creation of the law, ie, of a jurisdiction, therefore its nature is inevitability jurisdictional, therefore national or sub-national.[15] As the European Court of Justice put it: 'unlike natural persons, companies exist only by virtue of the national legal system which governs their incorporation and operation.'[16]

The enterprise, though, is only artificially definable by reference to a nation-state. As the privatising governments of the Thatcher era discovered, in a globalised world without foreign exchange, ownership, or management restrictions, capital has neither nationality nor passport, and management can be of any nationality, as can employees. So enterprises are essentially non-national:

> For business purposes the boundaries that separate one nation from another are no more real than the equator. They are merely convenient demarcations of ethnic, linguistic and cultural entities.[17]

The fact that the enterprise is non-national, and the legal entity national, poses a regulatory problem. Enterprises can in theory choose their incorporation law, and therefore the degree of control exercised by it, so long as they can find a 'host' jurisdiction prepared to allow them to incorporate in that jurisdiction.

The ability of an enterprise to shop around in this way should not be exaggerated. If it wishes to incorporate, it must choose at least one jurisdiction in which to do so, and sometimes will be obliged, either by legal or commercial constraints, to be represented by a legal entity in a jurisdiction with a more onerous incorporation law than it would wish. However, the possible consequences of the evasion of incorporation law regulation by choice of incorporation jurisdiction do merit consideration.

---

[15] Although not strictly correct, the word 'national' has been used here in preference to 'municipal' to denote the law of a jurisdiction, since the impetus for corporate regulation comes from the nation-state, and 'municipal' could be construed as referring to a sub-division of the nation-state.

[16] *Überseering BV v Nordic Construction Company Baumanagement GmbH* C208/00, ECJ at §18, citing *The Queen v Treasury and Commissioners of Inland Revenue, ex parte Daily Mail and General Trust* [1988] ECR 5483, ECJ. A legal entity can, of course, have a link with another jurisdiction if its human actors conduct activities there.

[17] A former IBM executive, quoted in T Nairn, 'Internationalism and the Second Coming' (1993) 122 *Daedalus* 155 at 157, quoted in turn in L Cao, 'Corporate and Product Identity in the Postnational Economy: Rethinking U.S. Trade Laws' (2002) 90 *California L Rev* 401 at 403.

VARIETIES OF NATIONAL CONTROL

Since corporate regulation effected by incorporation law is still national, it can vary quite significantly from one jurisdiction to another. These variations derive from different conceptions of the role of groups in general and the role of enterprises in particular, and result in incorporation law regimes of two main types: the Civilians and the Commoners. The Civilians and the Commoners, tracing their ancestry respectively, in the first instance, to France and England, and at a later stage influenced by German and United States ideas, inhabit two different mental, cultural and ideological worlds.[18]

We must be careful not to exaggerate the differences between the two traditions, for both include a high degree of regulation. However, those differences are significant, it being fair to say, as a broad generalisation, that the common law conception of the enterprise is of an essentially private grouping while the civilians view it as quasi-public.[19] These divergent conceptions of the role of the enterprise in society give us different conceptions of the enterprise itself.

In the common law world, private interests should be allowed free rein unless there are pressing reasons to restrict them. In particular, primacy is given to the private interests of the investors/'owners'.

In the civilian tradition, it is more important to protect public than private interests. The enterprise is viewed as part of a regulated economy in which one of its functions is to provide social benefits, such as employment, for citizens.[20] Notably, many civilian systems will have some attempt to ensure that legal entities have an enterprise, or something resembling it,

---

[18] A few Neutrals, such as China, pick and choose. For an overview of company law worldwide, see C Jordan, *An International Survey of Companies Law in the Commonwealth, North America, Asia And Europe* (London, DTI, 1998). On its spread, see K Pistor, Y Keinan, J Kleinheisterkamp and MD West, 'The Evolution of Corporate Law: A Cross-Country Comparison' (2002) 23 *University of Pennsylvania Journal of International Economic Law* 791. The efficacy of transplanting company law is not discussed herein. On this issue, see, eg (on Russia) B Black and R Kraakman, 'A Self-Enforcing Model of Corporate Law' (1996) 109 *Harvard L Rev* 1911; O Berkowitz, K Pistor and JF Richard, 'Economic Development, Legality, and the Transplant Effect' 47 *European Economic Review* 165, especially pp 174ff (adoption by columbia of Spanish Corporate law); C Jordan, *Law Matters: Corporate Governance Law Reforms* (2000) available at:http://www.worldbank.org/wbi/corpgov/core_course/core_pdfs/jordan_lawmatters.ppt.

[19] The words 'public' and 'private' need some clarification. 'Private' means that the legal system considers the company to concern only the individuals who make it up, much as a contract is normally considered to concern the parties to it, and not others; 'public' means that the legal system considers the company as constituting a powerful body which can affect non-participants, and therefore has a responsibility to those non-participants and a need to be controlled. The words are not to be taken in their French technical legal sense, in which companies are private law institutions, as opposed to public law legal persons such as the state, hospitals and universities.

For the US literature, see A Wolfe, 'The Modern Corporation: Private Agent or Public Actor?' (1993) 50 *Washington and Lee L Rev* 1673 at 1673–74. On the different ideologies of public and private law, see JW Singer, 'The Legal Rights Debate in Analytical Jurisprudence from Bentham to Hohfeld' (1982) *Wisconsin L Rev* 975 at 982–83.

[20] On the different approaches of the common law and civilian traditions to economic freedom, see PG Mahoney, 'The Common Law and Economic Growth: Hayek Might Be Right' (2001) 30 *Journal of Legal Studies* 503.

underlying them, notably by imposing minimum capital requirements (intended to ensure that the underlying enterprise is properly capitalised, thereby protecting creditors from the risks of an insufficiently funded venture); a recognition criterion based on the place of activity rather than on the place of incorporation (the doctrine of the 'seat', based on the assumption that the attempt to ensure that there is an enterprise underlying the legal entity has worked)[21]; and extensive involvement and protection of employees.

The doctrine of the seat needs some more explanation.[22] There is considerable variation among those jurisdictions which have it. Only Germany and France will be examined here.

In France, Art 1837 Civil Code provides that companies which have their seat on French territory are subject to French law. The seat must be 'real', and this reality will be determined by the court. For example, if the French court comes to the conclusion that a seat abroad is a sham, and that the real seat is in France, it will apply French law. This is supposed to permit policing of companies by criminal penalties, since those penalties are only effective if the seat is in the jurisdiction in which the penalties are imposed. In Germany, the legal capacity of a company is determined by the law of the place where its administration is established, its seat. In order to enjoy legal capacity a company which transfers its administration to Germany must be reincorporated in Germany.[23] The doctrine,

> prevents the provisions of company law in the State in which the actual centre of administration is situated, which are intended to protect certain vital interests, from being circumvented by incorporating the company abroad.[24]

Other systems (notably those of the common law, but a few civilian systems have similar attitudes in some areas), take a different view. English law, for example, is not concerned to ensure that the legal entity has any significant 'reality' in the sense of there being a substantial enterprise underlying it, so long as the formal minimum requirements are met (one person who acts as a member/director and one person who acts as a secretary, the filing of accounts and other documents, etc).[25] Nor does it base any control mechanism on any requirements for, or assumptions about, such a reality. A prime example of

---

[21] For a discussion of the different recognition theories, see R Drury, 'The Regulation and Recognition of Foreign Corporations: Responses to the Delaware Syndrome' [1998] *CLJ* 165 at 168–75.

[22] See PJ Omar, 'Centros Revisited: Assessing the Impact on Corporate Organisation in Europe' (2000) 11 *ICCLR* 407 at 408; PJ Omar, 'Centros Redux: Conflict at the Heart of European Company Law' (2002) 13 *ICCLR* 448 at 449–50 and The High Level Group of Company Law Experts, *A Modern Regulatory Framework for Company Law in Europe: A Consultative Document of the High Level Group of Company Law Experts* (Brussels, European Union, 2002) 32–34.

[23] Per the ECJ in *Überseering BV v Nordic Construction Company Baumanagement GmbH* C208/00, ECJ at §5.

[24] *Ibid*, at §16.

[25] All of these can be corporate bodies, in which case the 'reality' underlying the legal entity is tenuous.

this attitude is the complete absence of any minimum capital requirement for private companies. Recognition of foreign legal entities is based on their place of incorporation and there is no concept of the seat, let alone any attempt to use such a concept to regulate the enterprise by ensuring that the legal entity is subject to the control of the incorporation law of the jurisdiction concerned. There is little, if any, employee participation or protection. These attitudes result in considerable advantages for the incorporator. In England and Wales, for example,

> the shares do not have to be fully paid up, formation is much quicker, no prior examination of the constitution is necessary and the conditions governing the amendment of the constitutive documents, the transfer of shares and publicity are less strict.[26]

Having reached this point, a qualification of what has just been said is necessary. The divide between common law and civilian law is very rough, for there is considerable variation. For example, of the civilian jurisdictions in the European Union, Denmark, Finland, the Netherlands and Sweden do not have the 'seat' doctrine.[27] Germany has a group liability concept which is useful for the protection of other stakeholders, but which is not found elsewhere.[28]

Racing to the Bottom? Centros, Überseering and Inspire Art[29]

The mismatch between (1) the non-national nature of the enterprise and (2) its local legal manifestation, combined with the new extension of the freedom of the enterprise to pick and choose jurisdictions, could eventually lead to the predominance of the attitudes of one model of incorporation law, or at least to a considerable conflict between those models.

---

[26] See Advocate-General Alper's opinion in *Kamer van Koophandel en Fabrieken voor Amsterdam v Inspire Art Ltd* C167/01, ECJ at III, 4.

[27] Those which do have it include Austria, France, Germany and Luxembourg: PJ Omar, 'Centros Revisited: Assessing the Impact on Corporate Organisation in Europe', above n 22, at 407.

[28] See J Peter, 'Parent Liability in German and British Law: Too Far Apart for EU Legislation?' (1999) *European Business L Rev* 440.

[29] *Centros Ltd v Erhvervs- og Selskabsstyrelsen* C212/97 [2000] Ch 446, ECJ; *Überseering BV v Nordic Construction Company Baumanagement GmbH* C208/00 [2002], ECJ; *Kamer van Koophandel en Fabrieken voor Amsterdam v Inspire Art Ltd* C167/01 [2003], ECJ. Numerous commentaries on the *Centros* case include P J Omar, 'Centros Revisited: Assessing the Impact on Corporate Organisation in Europe', (2000) 11 ICCLR 407; commentaries on the *Überseering* case include W H Roth, 'From Centros to Ueberseering: Free Movement of Companies, Private International Law, and Community Law', [2003] ICLQ 177 and E Micheler, 'Recognition of Companies Incorporated in Other EU Member States', [2003] ICLQ 521, in which the *Inspire Art* case is also discussed; a casenote on the *Inspire Art* case is H De Wulf and S Dejonghe, 'Netherlands Company Law - Corporate Seats' (2004) 15 ICCLR N29-30. See also *Commission of the European Communities v Portugal* Case C-171/02, ECJ, Apr 29, 2004, in which a minimum capital requirement for security firms wishing to set up business in Portugal was found to be in breach of Art 43 EC (§54 of the judgment); and *Sevic Systems AG v Amtsgericht Neuwied* (C411/03) [2006] All ER (EC) 363, [2006] 1 CMLR 45, ECJ and *Marks & Spencer plc v Halsey (Inspector of Taxes)* (C446/03), [2006] All ER (EC) 255, [2006] Ch 184, ECJ (these cases were decided after this article was completed, so a discussion of them could not be included).

In the US, the mismatch between states and enterprises famously led to a 'race to the bottom,' in which state legal systems competed for incorporation and other business by attempting to provide the corporate law regime which is most attractive to incorporators, a race won by Delaware.[30] The US model is interesting, but evolved as a result of competition among very similar common law systems. More pertinent, perhaps, are the *Centros*, *Überseering* and *Inspire Art* cases which provide, in the exaggerated setting of a legal right to establishment granted by EU law, examples of a direct confrontation between common law and civilian concepts.

All the cases concerned Articles 43 and 48 EC Treaty. Pursuant to these Articles, companies enjoy the same freedom of establishment within the European Economic Area as individuals, and Member States may not restrict that freedom (with limited exceptions). To qualify, companies must have one or more of their place of incorporation, principal place of administration, or principal place of business, in a Member State, and must be set up to make a profit.

In the *Centros* case, two Danish nationals and residents incorporated Centros Limited in England and Wales with a nominal capital of £100, which was not paid up. The company applied to set up a branch in Denmark. The Danish Trade and Companies Board refused the application on the grounds that the only reason for incorporating the company in England and Wales was to avoid the onerous minimum capital requirements of Danish law (DKK200,000 about €27,000 or £19,300 at the time of writing). On a reference by the Danish Supreme Court to the European Court of Justice (ECJ) for a preliminary ruling, the ECJ held that the motive did not remove the company's right to freedom of establishment.

The *Centros* case concerned capital requirements, not the seat, although it seemed to many that the demise of the doctrine was an inevitable consequence of the decision. The *Überseering* case did directly raise the question of the seat. Überseering BV ('Überseering'), incorporated in the Netherlands, owned buildings in Germany. In 1992 Überseering engaged a German company, Nordic Construction Company Baumanagement GmbH ('Baumanagement') to renovate the buildings. In 1994 two German nationals and residents acquired all the shares in Überseering. Überseering was dissatisfied with the standard of work and sued Baumanagement in 1996, alleging breach of contract.

The German courts reasoned as follows: the legal capacity of a company is determined by the law of the place where its administration is established; the acquisition of the shares by the German nationals meant that the administration of Überseering was transferred to Germany; hence its legal capacity was determined by German law; under German law, in order

---

[30] The principal issues are discussed in ME Eisenberg, 'The Structure of Corporation Law' (1989) 89 *Columbia L Rev* 1461 at 1505–14.

to enjoy legal capacity a company which transfers its administration to Germany must be reincorporated in Germany[31]; Überseering had not been reincorporated in Germany. Therefore it did not have legal capacity in Germany.

The ECJ, however, held that this conclusion was contrary to the principle of freedom of establishment, despite the German government's arguments that the seat doctrine protected creditors (by ensuring a minimum share capital), minority shareholders and employees, and prevented tax evasion. The Court did furnish a caveat:

> It is not inconceivable that overriding requirements relating to the general interest, such as the protection of the interests of creditors, minority shareholders, employees and even the taxation authorities, may, in certain circumstances and subject to certain conditions, justify restrictions on freedom of establishment.

But the Court went straight on to say:

> Such objectives cannot, however, justify denying the legal capacity and, consequently, the capacity to be a party to legal proceedings of a company properly incorporated in another Member State in which it has its registered office. Such a measure is tantamount to an outright negation of the freedom of establishment conferred on companies by Articles 43 EC and 48 EC.[32]

The *Inspire Art* case is of dual interest. Not only does it provide a further example of a common law legal entity being used in preference in a civilian type, it also furnishes us with an instance of possible civilian countermeasures. Inspire Art Limited was incorporated in England and Wales solely in order to benefit from the perceived advantages of English incorporation law over the incorporation law of the Netherlands. The Netherlands legislature had enacted the Pure Form Foreign Companies Act 1997 specifically in order to deal with the phenomenon of such Delaware and English 'pseudoforeign' companies.[33] The Act provided that companies with 'no real connection with [their state of incorporation]' (Article 1) had to register as a 'foreign pure form company' (Article 2), publicise this status (Article 3), and comply with the Dutch minimum capital requirements (Article 4). Non-compliance was punishable by the imposition of personal liability on the company directors (Article 4). The ECJ came to the conclusion that:

> It is contrary to Articles 43 EC and 48 EC for national legislation ... to impose on the exercise of freedom of secondary establishment in that State by a company formed in accordance with the law of another Member State certain conditions provided for in domestic company law in respect of company formation relating to

---

[31] Per the ECJ in *Überseering BV v Nordic Construction Company Baumanagement GmbH* C208/00, ECJ at §5.

[32] At §92.

[33] See §31 of the Opinion of Advocate General Alper.

minimum capital and directors' liability. The reasons for which the company was formed in that other Member State, and the fact that it carries on its activities exclusively or almost exclusively in the Member State of establishment, do not deprive it of the right to invoke the freedom of establishment guaranteed by the EC Treaty, save where the existence of an abuse is established on a case-by-case basis.[34]

In the EU, the ECJ's caveat to its decision in *Überseering*[35] may provide an escape route of sorts for the seat doctrine, but it is submitted that the caveat should be read restrictively, and that Paul Omar's description of the effect of the judgment as an 'earthquake in jurisprudential terms in the German-speaking world' will prove to be correct in terms of practice as well.[36] This seems to be confirmed by the *Inspire Art* case, since the Dutch court and the German, Dutch and Austrian governments argued specifically that the Dutch measures contested in *Inspire Art* were justified by the exception, and this argument was rejected.[37]

More generally, the cases can be interpreted as showing that, in a straight contest between common law and the more protective type of civilian law attitude, the common law has a distinct advantage. Add to this the predominance of US (and, to a lesser extent, English/UK) ideas in legal globalisation, and the existence of micro-states eager to cash in on any opportunity to gain registration income, legal-organisational biodiversity seems threatened, as does the long-term survival of a stricter corporate regulatory regime, for:

> the company's founding members are placed at an advantage, since they are able, when choosing the place of incorporation, to choose the legal system which suits them best.[38]

In other words, these examples seem to show that attempts to regulate the enterprise using incorporation law on a national level may founder in an environment where enterprises have the freedom to establish themselves

---

[34] *Kamer van Koophandel en Fabrieken voor Amsterdam v Inspire Art Ltd* C167/01, ECJ, Nov 15, 2003, §142.

[35] Above, n 29.

[36] PJ Omar, 'Centros Revisited: Assessing the Impact on Corporate Organisation in Europe', above n 22, at 407.

[37] See §63ff and §155(2) of Advocate-General Alper's Opinion, §82, §86 and §§95-99 of the judgment. See also The High Level Group of Company Law Experts, *Report of the High Level Group of Company Law Experts on a Modern Regulatory Framework for Company Law in Europe* (Brussels, European Union, 2002) 102: 'for a Member State to adopt a version of the real seat doctrine which automatically denies recognition to a company which has its "real seat" in a country than that of its incorporation was a disproportionate measure which can never be justified' (footnote omitted). Eva Micheler discusses even more wide-ranging possibilities: E Micheler, 'Recognition of Companies Incorporated in Other EU Member States', above n 29, at 529.

[38] *Überseering BV v Nordic Construction Company Baumanagement GmbH* C208/00, ECJ at §15.

elsewhere. In order to avoid any inconvenient regulation, all the enterprise has to do is incorporate in another jurisdiction with less restrictive incorporation law. Such a result is one that regulators in both the common law and civilian traditions, whatever their differences concerning the degree and manner of regulation which is appropriate, would presumably wish to avoid.

MATCHING THE REGULATION TO THE REGULATED

This conclusion may be alarmist, for the degree to which company law can be harmonised worldwide is controversial. In the closely related field of corporate governance, for example, many commentators see considerable cultural resistance to Anglo-Saxon pressures.[39] It must also be said that, to date, few large enterprises have taken advantage of the possibilities of regulatory evasion.[40] It is also important to note that once an enterprise is established in a given jurisdiction, it may be difficult, expensive or both to change (to 'migrate').[41] However, if it does turn out that common law ideas spread and dominate, which, it is submitted, is at least a distinct possibility, incorporation law may well have serious limitations as a means of corporate regulation in a globalised environment. Two questions then arise: (1) Can national non-incorporation law perform the necessary regulatory function? (2) What role is there for international regulation?

As regards the first possibility, similar problems arise to those encountered in incorporation law. The enterprise remains non-national in nature, whereas regulation is territorial. Once again, we must not exaggerate, for the vast majority of enterprises are obliged to operate within jurisdictions in which their activities are highly regulated. But there are many, particularly the largest, which can at least partially evade regulation, for example by moving some functions to low labour cost and low labour regulation jurisdictions.

Deficiencies of national regulation lead naturally to thoughts of international action. However, here too the mismatch between the non-national nature of the enterprise with national regulation causes problems. Even

---

[39] See AN Licht, 'International Diversity in Securities Regulation: Roadblocks on the Way to Convergence' (1998) 20 *Cardozo L Rev* 227 at 227 (comparing corporate governance to securities market law). But see DM Branson, 'The Very Uncertain Prospect of "Global" Convergence in Corporate Governance' (2001) 34 *Cornell Intl L J* 321.

[40] According to Branson: 'A vexing conundrum has been precisely why so few, if any multinationals have moved to an offshore incorporating state. Scholars have raised the possibility of a "bandit" multinational moving off shore but it seems not to have occurred.' DM Branson, 'The Very Uncertain Prospect of "Global" Convergence in Corporate Governance', above n 39, at 357. The cases that have come before the European Court of Justice seem to confirm this. However, this is not to say that the issue is irrelevant just because it concerns small enterprises, nor that it could not concern larger enterprises in the future.

[41] On migration within the European Union see J Bisacre, 'The Migration of Companies Within the European Union and the Proposed Fourteenth Company Law Directive' [2001] *ICLQ* 251.

though the term is often used, international regulation is not effective *supra* (above, or over) nations, and therefore at least arguably over everyone and every body/grouping in or across nations, including non-national enterprises.[42] It is made and enforced *inter* (among) nations, because the makers of international law, and the components of international organisations, are nation-states. Agreement must come from them and norms must be enforced by them. An international solution would therefore only work if there were to be a very broad, if not worldwide, consensus on the entire content of incorporation law and the conflict of law rules which deal with recognition of legal entities, otherwise an enterprise could simply avoid the regulatory net by incorporating in one of the states not party to the multilateral effort. However, the profound ideological divide between the two traditions constitutes a considerable obstacle to the formation of such a consensus. If decades of concerted efforts have failed to bridge the divide on employee participation in the relatively narrow forum of the European Union,[43] it is hard to see how agreement could be reached on a broader range of issues on a worldwide basis.[44]

None of this seems to bode very well for the prospects of the regulation of the enterprise through incorporation law. However, there may be an alternative solution, which can be found by reconsidering the fundamental problem underlying all the possibilities so far considered. The nineteenth century nation-state based method of using incorporation law to regulate enterprises has led us to a dead end because it attempts to regulate the non-national enterprise by regulating the national legal entity, failing to take into account the mismatch between the natures of the enterprise and the legal entity and the consequences of the mismatch for regulation. It would seem logical therefore to abandon vain attempts to regulate A by regulating B, and match the regulation to the regulated by controlling the enterprise directly.

This suggestion poses all sorts of difficulties, given the elusive nature of the enterprise. However, there are indications of a readiness to use this approach, such as the common use of the word 'undertaking' by the EU,[45]

---

[42] Some would argue that European Union law is an exception. Even in this case, however, the law is ultimately based on agreement between Member States.

[43] The main, and failed, document was the Draft Fifth Directive on Company Law. For a recent instalment of the saga, see the National Works Councils Directive (Dir 2002/14/EC of the European Parliament and of the Council of 11 March 2002 establishing a general framework for informing and consulting employees in the European Community), due to be implemented by March 2005, but which may not be fully implemented in the UK until 2008.

[44] A possible alternative to a binding multilateral agreement is a code of conduct. But reaching agreement could be just as difficult, and even if agreement were reached, it would suffer from an exaggerated form of one of the fundamental problems of regulation: the conscientious abide by regulations, while the ruthless and the sloppy ignore them.

[45] Defined for UK company law use by s 259(1) Companies Act 1985, and linked to the complex definition of a subsidiary in s 258. Other issues that might arise, such as the legitimacy of any international body regulating enterprises, are more problematic. Might corporations invoke a principle of 'no regulation without representation'?

and it is familiar to accountants, tax lawyers and tax authorities. It has the advantage of dealing with the reality of the situation and of side-stepping at least some of the problems created by the existence of two, conceptually different, models of incorporation law.[46] It is submitted that this method would at least constitute a sound base from which to tackle this admittedly difficult task. It would at least be preferable to relying on the fundamentally flawed idea of the enterprise and the legal entity being inevitably linked.

---

[46] Related thinking is to be found in the idea of the 'Centre of Main Interest' (COMI) contained in Art 3(1) Regulation on Cross-Border Insolvency (Reg 1346/2000) which relies to a considerable extent on the enterprise concept, even if it is in a sense the mirror image of what is proposed, since it determines the legal order applicable for the insolvent legal entity by reference to the activity of the enterprise underlying it.

6

*Creating a Globalised Insolvency Law**

CLARE CAMPBELL AND YIANNIS SAKKAS

INTRODUCTION

G LOBALISATION FIRST AND foremost describes the political and economic process in which, in the words of Alex Seita in his inspiring article on *Globalisation and the Convergence of Values*, increasing internationalism,

> is causing and being reinforced by a worldwide convergence of economic and political values that portend a possible, though distant, future world in which human beings will look upon themselves as part of a single humane civilization comprised of a single human race.[1]

In this venture, law and the legal regulation of commercial affairs have occupied a central position in the process of civilising economic interchange. One of the most important examples of legal regulation is that dealing with the consequences of commercial default. The absence of a globalised response to debt default can lead to costly parallel procedures, as witness the multiplicity of bankruptcies initiated as a result of the collapse of BCCI. Mostly, these procedures involve bankruptcy or liquidation with the attendant multinational industry-wide or commercial collapse. On the other hand, the presence of a coordinated approach to default enables cooperation and synchronisation which, at its best, can facilitate financial rescue, preserve wealth producing assets, assist in successful commercial transfers and preserve or renew employment.

Within the confines of the nation state, insolvency or bankruptcy laws have played a significant role in collectivising both the realisation of the debtor's assets and the distribution of the estate to creditors and, more

---

* The material contained in this chapter was up-to-date at the time of the conference on Global Governance and the Leach for Justice held at the University of Sheffield in April 2003.
[1] A Seita, 'Globalisation and Convergence of Values' (1997) 30 *Cornell Intl L J* 429.

recently, in collective reorganisation and rescue. National insolvency review bodies have consistently acknowledged that a coherent, collective insolvency law is essential to maximise creditor benefit and to prevent commercial anarchic action when there is terminal or near terminal financial default. Similarly, reorganisational insolvency proceedings or corporate turnaround is only possible and effective where there is a single binding procedure.[2]

In a world where multinational enterprises operate with ease across boundaries and continents, where banking and loan facilities are available without limitations of time and nationality and where securitisation instruments are common currency, the effect of global default, such as that rippling from the Enron and Worldcom defaults, affect creditors, secured and otherwise, employees and government and regional authorities throughout the world. In this context a global approach to insolvency law that provides a secure, transparent and overriding substantive regulation as well as effective procedural structures is essential to ensure the security of international commercial transactions. Many academics as well as professional and other institutions have responded to the challenge to devise an effective rule of law in this area.

The aim of this chapter is to give an overview of the theoretical work that has underpinned efforts to devise international solutions to global default. We shall examine the strong example of a modified universalist approach that is supplied by the EC Regulation on Cross Border Insolvency.[3] Thereafter, there is a consideration of the effect of the UNCITRAL Model Law on cross border insolvency which is designed to achieve pragmatic cooperation between courts and insolvency practitioners and to build a globalised approach from the 'grass roots.'[4] We shall briefly examine the reception of the Model Law into the legal systems of states such as Japan and South Africa and also the proposed acceptance of its terms by the US in the projected Chapter 15 of the US Bankruptcy Code.[5] Finally, we shall review the work being done by various international pressure groups such as INSOL International which has focused on the involvement of lending institutions in international corporate rescue.

---

[2] In this respect consider the poor track record of English CVAs under the Insolvency Act (IA) 1986 where there was no protective moratorium and the reorganisation of finances could be prevented at any time by the presentation of a winding up petition. This situation has been rectified by the Insolvency Act 2000 which imposes a moratorium on the presentation of a CVA petition.

[3] Council Reg (EC) 1346/2000 of 29 May 2000, OJ L160/1.

[4] The Model Law is available from the UNCITRAL website, and the English text is at: http://www.uncitral.org/english/texts/insolven/insolvency.htm.

[5] For details of the proposed Chapter 15 see: http://www.ianb.uscourts.gov/newcode/chapter15.pdf.

THEORETICAL BACKGROUND

In the first place, acknowledgement should be made of the very considerable efforts of two academics whose work has dominated the theoretical, as well as the practical, scene so far as the structures of a globalised response to insolvency are concerned. Professor Ian Fletcher[6] in the UK and Professor Jay Westbrook[7] in the US have, together with continental scholars whose work formed the background to the EC Regulation, contributed immense theoretical works illuminating the area of international commercial default.

It is evident from their work that three main approaches to global insolvency law have emerged. These are universalism, territorialism and contractualism.

Universalism

The universalist approach propounds a system of default management, whether it be based on liquidation or reorganisation, in which one court 'administers the insolvency of the debtor on a worldwide basis with the help of the courts in each affected country'[8] and which necessitates the pooling of the assets of the debtor wherever such assets are situated and the recognition of the jurisdiction of a designated court to adjudicate claims against the estate and to deal with the ultimate distribution of the realised assets.

The international pooling agreement that, in part, brought an end to the BCCI bankruptcy could serve as an exemplar of a universalist approach. Though the solution in that case was partly mediated through governments rather than through the courts, arrangements were made for the kingdom of Abu Dhabi to pay large compensatory sums into a pooling agreement to be distributed by the liquidator of BCCI, ensuring the globalised treatment of creditors and debtors (in the main).[9] This universalist treatment played

---

[6] See IF Fletcher, *Insolvency in Private International Law: National and International Approaches* (Oxford, Oxford University Press, 1999) and 'The Quest for Global Insolvency: A Challenge for our Time' [2002] *Current Legal Problems* 427

[7] See especially, 'Theory and Pragmatism in Global Insolvencies: Choice of Law and Choice of Forum' (1991) 65 *Am Bankr L J* 457; 'Creating International Insolvency Law' (1996) 70 *Am Bankr L J* 563; 'Multinational Enterprise in General Default: Chapter 15, the ALI Principles and the EU Insolvency Regulation' (2002) 76 *Am Bankr L J* 1 and 'A Global Solution to Multinational Default' (2000) 98 *Mich L Rev* 2276.

[8] JL Westbrook, 'Multinational Enterprises in General Default: Chapter 15, The ALI Principles, and the EU Insolvency Regulation' (2002) 76 *Am Bankr L J* 1, at 6.

[9] There were notable exceptions to this globalised treatment as in relation to the creditors in England and Wales who were permitted to use their set-off rights under English Insolvency Rules before claiming in the overall insolvency administered by the Luxembourg liquidator. For details of this exception, see *Re BCCI SA (in liq) (No 11)* [1997] Ch 213.

an important role in shielding the government of Abu Dhabi from extensive legal action, and ensured that there was some distribution to creditor banks and local and regional authorities and even, in some cases, to individual creditors.

Despite the attraction of the universalist approach and its modified implementation on a regional basis,[10] (if this is not a contradiction in terms), it is neither feasible nor possible as a solution to multinational insolvencies in the near future. The reasons for this are both political and commercial.

The politics of national self-determination would emphasise a perceived loss of sovereignty and economic autonomy should a universalist approach be adopted. There would be a perception that 'powerful' states might 'lose out' in failing to obtain control of the main proceedings in a global administration of default. There would be a danger that control might be ceded to legal and/or commercial systems not in tune with the commercial or economic values of the 'powerful'. Where rescue depends on the co-operation of powerful international and national banks, to countenance such a loss of control to a system not rich in a history of safe security laws or where administration is not entrusted to the well-honed hands of insolvency practitioners, would be an anathema. This concern will be echoed when we examine the EC Regulation and its central proposition that there should be universal recognition of the proceedings commenced in the state where the debtor has its 'centre of main interests.'

A second problem encountered in embracing a universalist approach is that commercial considerations delving deep into a state's system of rights and contractual and proprietary interests may well come into conflict with opposing systems in other states. As an example of this phenomenon we could take the complex system of security interests over corporate property that form the web of fixed and floating charges often accompanying bank lending in the UK. Similar, but by no means identical bank financing instruments exist in other common law jurisdictions and naturally civil law systems have developed complementary but distinct systems of debt guarantee or proprietary interests in moveable property. A truly universalist system would encounter mammoth problems of conflict of laws and priority determination in relation to the complex interests that subsist in the administration of an insolvency, especially where these rights and interests are protected by national and local contractual obligations. A globalised solution to the problems outlined here is not to be underestimated and is the reason for our pessimism as to the long-term goal of a single international law dealing with global default.

---

[10] See the EC Reg as an example of a universalist approach to insolvency administration.

Territorialism

A second approach to global insolvency is that of cooperative territorialism in which it is envisaged that each country would, either through its court system or its insolvency administration, take control of locally situated assets and utilise these in meeting the claims of local creditors. Naturally, in an economic world order in which there is dispersion of assets and creditors, narrow territorialism is both outmoded and inappropriate. However, as has been pointed out by at least one commentator who adopts a pragmatic approach to multinational default, it is important to recognise the immediate value and effectiveness of co-operative territorialism in which each state would respect judgments given in other states and would seek to co-operate with other jurisdictions insofar as such co-operation benefited or at least did not prejudice national or local creditors.[11]

An example of the way in which the judiciary have taken to heart the necessity for co-operation in matters of global insolvency is provided by the attitude of the UK courts to their powers under the insolvency legislation[12] to assist foreign insolvency proceedings following a letter of request from a court in another jurisdiction. The courts in the UK have proved that they are receptive to such requests especially where to do so would assist in a global reorganisation of corporate resources.[13]

A further development demonstrating judicial creativity at a time when national legislative efforts have been slow to keep pace with the results of multinational default, is the development of ad hoc Protocols to provide immediate pragmatic solutions utilising provisions of national law in a resourceful fashion. The Maxwell litigation in the US and England highlighted the developmental possibilities of such judicial co-operation. Maxwell Communications Corporation plc (MCC) was at one and the same time in Administration in England and its US subsidiaries, which accounted for nearly 75 per cent of the group's value, were in Chapter 11 proceedings in the US. In order to prevent these simultaneous primary proceedings descending into conflict, chaos and needless loss of value for creditors, the national judges involved, Judge Broznan in the US Bankruptcy Court and Hoffmann J, as he then was, in the Chancery Court, presided over the appointment of an examiner in the US proceedings and administrators in the English action. Their work was to be co-ordinated through a Protocol.

---

[11] See LM LoPucki, 'Cooperation in International Bankruptcy: a Post-Universalist Approach' (1999) 84 *Cornell L Rev* 696. See also commentary on territorial approaches in IF Fletcher, *Insolvency in Private International Law : National and International Approaches* (Oxford, Oxford University Press, 1999).

[12] S 426 Insolvency Act 1986.

[13] *Re Dallhold Estates (UK)* [1992] BCC 394; contra *Hughes v Hannover Ruckversicherungs AG* [1997] BCC 921 Also IF Fletcher, 'Section 426: the New Cross Border Insolvency Law' [1988] *Insolv Int* 41.

This document set out the terms for cross-border co-operation and, as a result of a harmonisation of effort, the Protocol proved to be a remarkably successful way of conducting concurrent reorganisation of the assets of the global enterprise.[14] Even though the final procedure involved separate reconstruction plans they were, in fact, mutually dependent. By means of co-operative territorialism, the insolvency practitioners managed to set up a single regime acceptable to creditors in both jurisdictions.[15]

This Protocol became the precursor to other cross-border court led co-operative Protocols, eg, concluding the proceedings in the Everfresh insolvency involving the courts of the US and Canada and the Nakash Protocol involving personal bankruptcy proceedings conducted in Israel and parallel proceedings under Chapter 11 in the US.[16]

However, the sequel to the Maxwell case clearly demonstrates the drawbacks associated with cooperative territorialism. In that case, during the period prior to the adoption to the Chapter 11 plan, various payments were made to banks in the US in the 'twilight period' so that these payments could potentially be challenged as preferences. These transactions might have been contestable according to US law but not under the similar anti-avoidance provisions of English law.[17] The upshot of this was that the UK administrators felt obliged to bring an action in the US courts to avoid the payments made to various banks. The response was an application by the banks for an injunction in the English courts to try and prevent action which would conflict with the Chapter 11 moratorium in the US.[18] The injunction was not granted, the English courts being of the view that the US courts were best placed to deal with the issue of preference avoidance. In the final result, the US court did not apply the anti-avoidance provisions and said that US law would not apply to the transfers.[19]

This excursion into the anti-avoidance provisions in US and English law serves to demonstrate that while cooperation between courts through Protocols works well as a matter of procedure and facilitates the adoption of a combined reorganisation plan, it is limited by the inability of national laws to deal in a globalised way with the conflicts generated by substantive

---

[14] B Leonard, 'Managing Default by Multinational Ventures: Co-operation in Cross-border Insolvencies' (1998) 33 *Tex Intl L J* 543.

[15] For examples of such Protocols, see the website of the International Insolvency Institute which carries the texts of Protocols dealing with cross border insolvencies: www.iiiglobal.org/international/protocols.html.

[16] *Ibid.*

[17] This is because of the 'generous' treatment of bank credit and security as a result of the interpretation of s 239 IA in that there must be a 'desire to prefer' and also that desire must influence the giving of the preference. This section has been subject to interpretation in *Re M C Bacon Ltd (No 1)* [1990] BCC 78.

[18] *Barclays Bank plc v Homan* [1992] BCC 757.

[19] *Re Maxwell Corporation* 170 B R 800 at 818.

insolvency, securitisation and proprietary laws. It also demonstrates the limitations in terms of time, expense and uncertainty inherent in a territorial approach to international insolvency, even where that approach is basically cooperative.

Contractualism

The third approach to multinational insolvency is that of the contractualists. The chief proponent of this method of resolving problems associated with multinational default is Professor Robert Rasmussen.[20] In common with other applications of the contractualist approach in the commercial arena, the aim is efficiency and the avoidance of transaction costs in redistributional bankruptcy. Rasmussen considers that this is best achieved by permitting the parties engaged in commerce to enter into contracts that govern, among other things, the choice of law and jurisdictional options available upon insolvency. This view is posited on the notion that private ordering of commercial decisions best reflects the needs and the conduct of the business community. In the context of default, it represents the best way of dealing with multinational insolvencies. According to Rasmussen, 'contractualism allows each independent corporate entity to specify in its corporate charter the jurisdiction that will handle any bankruptcy proceeding involving that entity.'[21]

The main justification for this approach rests upon the self-determination of the corporation and the desire of business people to have certainty as to the regime which will best fit their position on default.

There are both political and practical objections to the contractualist approach. There is clearly a danger that 'choice of bankruptcy jurisdiction' clauses in company documents may lead to some states being chosen as 'debtor havens' rather in the way that Delaware corporation law became notorious for its corporation friendly tax and corporate governance laws. This danger can be demonstrated by the choice that is sometimes made to put corporations into 'strategic bankruptcy' in the US to gain the advantage of the Chapter 11 moratorium which, while important for preserving going concern value, also can be damaging to the interests of involuntary creditors as witness the effect of Chapter 11 actions on tort damages claims.

---

[20] RA Rasmussen, 'Debtors' Choice: A Menu Approach to Corporate Bankruptcy' (1992) 71 *Texas L Rev* 51; 'New Approach to Transnational Insolvencies' (1997) 19 *Mich J Intl L* 1; and 'Resolving Transnational Insolvencies through Private Ordering' (2000) 98 *Mich L Rev* 2252.

[21] *Ibid*, 'Resolving Transnational Insolvencies through Private Ordering', at 2254.

A second objection to contractualism is the practical one of disclosure and transparency. Even where corporation charters and company articles of associations are registered, it will be difficult to make the enterprises' choice of law and jurisdiction clauses transparent to creditors, especially creditors whose interests are unprotected by securities. The problems of information and fairness are too intractable to be left to the vagaries of private contractual ordering. This practical matter is but an example of a wider objection to the contractualist approach, namely that the effects of bankruptcy are felt most profoundly by third parties and enabling a contractual choice to bind non-contracting parties to both a choice of law and a choice of forum could give rise to oppression and denial of third party rights.

In the light of this contextual awareness, we now turn to regional and global attempts to create an international insolvency law.

THE EC REGULATION 1346 ON CROSS-BORDER INSOLVENCY PROCEEDINGS

A legal framework to deal with international insolvencies is pivotal to economic harmonisation and nowhere is this more evident than in the European Union. The European Council has responded to this perceived need with Regulation 1346[22] which is a community legal instrument designed to introduce a compulsory regime to address issues of jurisdiction and coordination to intra-European insolvencies where more than one Member State wishes to initiate insolvency proceedings. However, this pan-European insolvency regime does not set out to establish a uniform European insolvency law and is only authoritative on procedural matters, prevailing over state principles of private international law.

For over three decades, the EU Commission and Council were engaged in formulating an insolvency Convention. The background work on an insolvency text began in 1963 but it was not until 1994 that a proposed model obtained substantial agreement in the Member States.[23] The suggested insolvency text was formulated as a Convention and had to be ratified by all the participating states. Following the British government's refusal to ratify it within the prescribed time, the European Insolvency Convention failed to receive the required unanimous support and subsequently lapse. Nonetheless, on 29 May 2000 following the combined initiative of Germany and Finland, the European Council adopted many of the 1995 insolvency Convention's provisions and this time endorsed it with the legal status of a Regulation.

---

[22] Council Reg (EC) 1346/2000 of 29 May` 2000, OJ L160/1.
[23] PJ Omar, 'The wider European Framework for Insolvency' (2001) 17 *Insol L & P* 135.

The Regulation became directly applicable and binding on all Member States[24] on 31 May 2002. By virtue of Article 249 of the European Community Treaty there is no need to implement the provisions of a Regulation into national legislation.[25] However, Member States wish to enact any consequential alterations in their national legislation that are required for the efficient operation of the Regulation to avoid commercial ostracism. The United Kingdom has responded to this challenge with the Enterprise Act 2002. Part X of that Act amends the Insolvency Act 1986 with a view to creating an insolvency regime more compatible with the collectivism promoted by the Regulation.

The theoretical pedestal that led to the adoption of this legal instrument is mirrored by its objectives. The Regulation aims to establish a legal framework for the efficient operation of intra-European insolvency proceedings. This is mainly achieved by promoting a degree of co-operation between the courts and insolvency practitioners in different jurisdictions and at the same time, aims to reduce formalities by implementing a simplified procedure for creditors to exercise their rights. Finally, the Regulation is partly characterised by a rescue ethos. It is important to note that the objectives of this legal instrument could be achieved only if one of the involved parties initiates cross border insolvency proceedings that fall under the remit of the Regulation

According to Article 1, 'the Regulation will only apply to collective insolvency proceedings, which entail the partial or total divestment of a debtor following the appointment of a liquidator.' These proceedings are listed in Annexes A and B for each country separately. The enlargement of the European Union with the introduction of new Member States will require the Annexes to be amended to include the insolvency proceedings of the ten new states. The Council reserves the right to amend these Annexes in order to take into account new developments[26]

Main Proceedings

The effective functioning of a cross-border insolvency entails the co-ordination of the proceedings in the different Member States. To this effect, the Regulation provides for a hierarchical structure of main and secondary proceedings with the main proceedings having a prominent role in the cross-border insolvency litigation. For this reason there can only be one set of

---

[24] Denmark, in accordance with Arts 1 and 2 of the Protocol on the position of Denmark annexed to the Treaty on European Union and the Treaty establishing the European Community is not participating in the adoption of Regulation 1346, and is not bound by it.
[25] EC Treaty Art 249 (ex Art 189).
[26] Art 45.

main proceedings, but there is no limitation to the number of secondary proceedings provided that the requirements of the Regulation are fulfilled.

The jurisdiction to initiate main proceedings will depend on the location of the debtor's centre of main interest. The law of the state of primary litigation, ie, where the centre of main interest is situated, will determine the conditions for the opening, conduct and closure of the insolvency litigation[27]. Article 4(2) sets out a comprehensive list of the matters covered by the main proceedings. Perhaps the importance and scope of this provision cannot be fully comprehended at this early stage of life of the Regulation. However, in practice the competence of Article 4 (2) is likely to reach to all legal areas that are associated with the efficient functioning and conclusion of insolvency litigation. Hence, the courts of the state of primary jurisdiction will apply national insolvency legislation to manage the debtor's assets whether they are located in that state or anywhere else within the EU.

Secondary Proceedings

However, the transnational effect of main proceedings should also afford recognition to the diversity of rights and interests being created and existing under different legal codes. Hence, the Regulation stipulates the conditions in which concurrent proceedings will take place.[28] To this effect, the universal competence of main proceedings will not reach out to states where secondary proceedings are in place and will not affect rights which are specifically excluded by the Regulation. Secondary proceedings may only be opened in Member States where the debtor possesses an establishment[29]. The effects of secondary proceedings are restricted to the assets of the debtor situated in the territory of that Member State and can only be winding up proceedings. Furthermore, secondary proceedings may not be challenged in another Member State[30]. In fact, great emphasis is laid on the co-operation between primary and secondary proceedings. To ensure that both primary and secondary proceedings contribute to the efficient realisation of the entirety of the debtor's estate the Regulation provides for the concurrent operation of the two schemes. A precondition for achieving sufficient co-ordination between the two operations is the duty placed upon insolvency practitioners to collaborate closely and to this effect Article 31 provides that the liquidators in the primary and ancillary litigation shall be duty bound to co-operate with each other.[31]

---

[27] Art 4(2).
[28] Recital 12.
[29] Art 3(2).
[30] Art 17(2).
[31] Art 31(3).

However, to guarantee the combined effect of co-ordination and to ensure the dominant role of the main proceedings, the liquidator in such proceedings has the power to intervene in the secondary jurisdiction.[32] The liquidator's powers include the competence to request the opening or even the suspension of the ancillary litigation for up to three months provided that such action will also be in the interests of creditors in the secondary proceedings. More importantly, secondary proceedings could be ended without liquidation when the law of the state, where the proceedings are taking place, allows for corporate turnaround or composition or a measure to that effect.[33] This is very significant if the Regulation is going to provide an environment for corporate turnaround. Otherwise, the liquidation of the assets in any secondary proceedings would impede a possible reorganisation of the corporation and subsequently hinder a rescue attempt.

Centre of Main Interests

The centre of main interest also has to be understood in the context of main and secondary proceedings. The jurisdiction in which to start main proceedings will depend on the location of the debtors Centre of Main Interest (usually abbreviated to COMI). However, COMI is not defined in the Regulation. In the case of a company or legal person, there is a rebuttable presumption that the place where the registered office is situated will be the centre of its main interests.[34] It is not clear however what evidence will be required to rebut the effect of Article 3(1). Perhaps guidance can be found in Recital 13 of the Preamble to the Regulation, which states that the centre of a debtor's main interest should correspond to the place where the debtor conducts his affairs and must be identifiable by third parties. As Omar has argued, the absence of a complete definition could be a deliberate omission aiming to reconcile the civil law test for jurisdiction based on the real seat rule with the common law presumption of incorporation or residence jurisdiction.[35] This means that the courts will have to define the COMI, which is the main pillar supporting the application of the Regulation and is likely to be the epicentre of disputes.[36]

One of the first opportunities for judicial consideration of the Regulation by the English courts was provided by the controversial international insolvency of the Enron Corporation. As anticipated in the unreported case of

---

[32] Recital 18.

[33] Art 34.

[34] Art 3(1).

[35] PJ Omar, 'New Initiatives on Cross Border Insolvency in Europe' 5 *Insolvency Lawyer* 211–18, 214.

[36] C Campbell and Y Sakkas, 'Transnational Insolvencies and the Impact of EC Regulation on Insolvency Proceedings' (2003) 19 *Insol L & P* 48.

Re Enron Directo SA, the court's attention was drawn to the pivotal point of COMI. In this case it was held that the COMI of the Spanish incorporated company Enron was not in Spain but in England. Lightman J was convinced that evidence indicating that all important management decisions were taken in England was enough to rebut the presumption that the COMI coincided with the place of an incorporation.

In the case of *BRAC Rent-A-Car International Inc*[37] the issue was whether the courts of a Member State had jurisdiction under the Regulation to initiate insolvency proceedings in relation to a company incorporated in Delaware US with a centre of main interest in England. Lloyd J, adopting a textual interpretation ruled that this was possible under the Regulation since its scope of application depended on the location of the COMI. The judge's reasoning was that a more limited interpretation of the Regulation would exclude from its ambit all companies incorporated outside the EU. Arguably, this could be manipulated by debtors to circumvent the application of the Regulation, which would subvert the intention of the drafters. Nevertheless, despite the fact that the judge attached so much importance to the COMI he did not provide a definition.

However, in the recent case of *Re Daisytek-ISA Ltd & Ors*[38] McGonigal J's inductive reasoning could prove useful in determining the state of the COMI. The case also deals with the issue of group insolvencies, for which there is no reference in the Regulation, a matter that has concerned many scholars. Daisytek was the holding company of an insolvent European group of companies. The group encompassed three German companies, one French and ten English companies registered in Germany, France and England respectively. McGonigal J was presented with petitions for administration orders in relation to the group's insolvency proceedings.

It was held that the court had jurisdiction to make administration orders in respect of the French and the German companies if there was sufficient evidence that their COMI was situated in England. To rebut the presumption in Article 3 (1) the judge referred again to Recital 13, which states that COMI should coincide with the place where the debtor regularly administers his affairs and is ascertainable by third parties. The court held that the identification of COMI requires a comparative evaluation of the interests administered in Germany and France and those administered in England. On the facts, the group's management and financial functions were operated from Bradford which was also the place that potential creditors would identify as the debtor's COMI[39]. Therefore, it was held that the English court had jurisdiction to make administration orders in respect of

---

[37] [2003] 2 All ER 201.
[38] *Re Daisytek-ISA Ltd & Ors* [2003] BCC 562.
[39] *Geveran Trading Co Ltd v Skjevesland* [2003] BCC 209.

the French, the German and the English companies of the Daisytek group. This is potentially a very important case, the impact of which should be carefully considered before it is applied in complex cases of pan-European group insolvencies. This is especially so since the legal effect of decisions made by national courts will not be restricted to that state but also be binding in other members of the European Union without any further formalities[40].

However, at the moment we can only comment on cases that come before the English courts. Nevertheless, there might be a decision, by the courts of other Member States, that deals with contingent areas arising from the operation of the Regulation. However, it is very difficult to be aware of such cases unless somewhere along the line there is an English creditor affected by these proceedings or the case finds its way to the European Court of Justice. This obstacle could be overhauled by the existence of a comprehensive reporting system.[41]

The combined effect of the European integration along with monetary unification provides fertile ground for a mobile business environment. Hence, the possibility that the location of a debtor's main interest may shift from one state to another is not a distant one. The European Court of Justice has the authority to rule on the interpretation and validity of Regulation 1346/2000 but only in cases where a national court of final instance requests such a ruling 'if it considers that a decision on the question is necessary to enable it to give judgement.' Hence, it is left to the discretion of the Member States to refer questions relating to the interpretation of the Regulation. In other words, seeking an ECJ ruling is optional, and such a ruling cannot be sought by a lower level court.

The restricted nature of the reference procedure means that some important issues of interpretation may not come to the ECJ for many years. Additionally, reference by higher courts will significantly increase the cost of legislation since the case has to progress from all the judicial levels prior to reaching the ECJ.[42] Hence, this development will adversely affect the rights of creditors, since this time- consuming process combined with an amplified cost of legal action, will reduce the remaining assets. Therefore, national courts should approach the task of interpretation in a spirit of commitment to the principle and objectives of this Regulation[43].

---

[40] Art 16.
[41] C Campbell and Y Sakkas, above n 36.
[42] I Fletcher, 'A New Age of International Insolvency 'The Countdown has Begun: Part 1' (2000) 13(8), *Insol Int* 57–61, at 58.
[43] *Ibid.*

Exclusions

Although the Regulation purports to be the authoritative text in cases of bankruptcies that cross national frontiers, certain business sectors have been expressly excluded from the ambit of this instrument, including insurance and collective investment undertakings. These will be specifically covered by the forthcoming Winding-up Directive for insurance undertakings[44] and the Winding-up Directive for credit institutions.[45] In addition, given the differences between national legislation on fundamental issues, selected rights are reserved to be dealt with in accordance with the *lex situs*. The Regulation declares that the opening of primary proceedings will not affect the rights *in rem*,[46] rights to set-off,[47] reservation of title clauses,[48] contracts relating to immovable property,[49] the law governing payment systems and financial markets[50] and finally contracts of employment.[51] These exclusions are promulgated to protect the position of creditors and third parties who relied on the applicability of a different legal code.[52]

Other Developments

Although, under European law a Regulation does not require implementation in national legislation, there are initiatives taken by states to facilitate its efficient operation. A recent example is the UK's Practice Note from the Chief Registrar designed to introduce procedural changes following the adoption of the Regulation.[53] The Practice Note, includes newly prescribed requirements for petitions for administration orders, winding up, bankruptcy, and administration orders in insolvent estates and petitions by contributories. The new forms require the petitioner to provide a statement indicating whether the Regulation applies, the location of the debtor's COMI as well as the nature of proceedings–main or secondary.

Arguably, the new practice favours English creditors who will undoubtedly want to benefit from the trans-European competence of main proceedings. In principle, other Member States could follow the same form of procedure.

---

[44] Directive 2001/17/EC.
[45] Directive 2001/24/EC.
[46] Art 5.
[47] Art 6.
[48] Art 7.
[49] Art 8.
[50] Art 9.
[51] Art 10.
[52] P Kennet , 'Current Developments in Private International Law' (2001) 50 *Intl & Comp L Q* 190.
[53] [2002] BCC 572.

However, this must be in conformity with the procedural rules of the highly codified civil law systems followed by the majority of the European countries. The practical implications of the new Practice Note combined with the UK's strong presence in the financial market, could create a propensity for the English Insolvency Act to be the *lex concursus* of many cross-border insolvencies. Perhaps this was not the intention of the Chief Registrar when issuing the note. Nevertheless, it is interesting to see whether the same logic will be adopted by the new insolvency rules that will follow after the enactment of the Enterprise Act 2002.

However, the Practice Note in its current form may create more anomalies than it purports to solve. The questions that arise are to what extent a creditor's statement would be enough and what evidence will be required in support. Furthermore, what will happen in the case where main proceedings are initiated, and subsequently recognised in all Member States,[54] based on a misleading statement as to the COMI in accordance with the form described in the practice note?

Conclusion

In practice, the operation of Regulation 1346 is impaired by the absence of clear definitions and lack of guidance. Although the Regulation is an instrument with international competence, the effectiveness of its enforcement could be restricted by the territorial view and interpretation of the national courts. This is true for Member States with a more Euro-sceptic approach and also for future Member States with no experience in dealing with European legislation. Perhaps the most important challenge for the Regulation is to successfully lay down the foundations for a fully integrated and unified European insolvency code.

THE MODEL LAW ON CROSS-BORDER INSOLVENCY

The EC Regulation is undoubtedly a major step forward in regulating both procedure and substance in cross-border insolvencies within, and to a limited extent beyond, the boundaries of the European Union. Given the absence of a binding international instrument of equivalence to an EC Regulation and a final court for interpretation, international efforts to forward the quest for a globalised approach to cross-border insolvency require a looser model of law making.

---

[54] Art 16.

Against the background of the strong feeling that there was a pressing need for an international instrument to deal with cross-border insolvency, a colloquium was organised at the initiative of UNCITRAL and INSOL International which met several times variously in Vienna and New York between 1995 and 1997 to draft a Model Law on Cross Border Insolvency.[55] In 1997, the UN General Assembly passed a resolution recommending that states reconsider their insolvency laws in the light of the adopted Model Law[56].

In considering the place of this device in the globalisation of insolvency law, the first issue worthy of comment is the choice of a Model Law as a legal instrument. From UNCITRAL's working papers it is possible to deduce that the prime reason for adopting this form was shrewdly pragmatic.[57] While Conventions suffer the fate that they only become operative once the required number of signatories have ratified and can be derailed by apathy or international political infighting, a Model Law can be adopted by states on a voluntary basis, and as the required terms of the Law are adopted, experience will be gained as to its practical effectiveness as a means of mediating co-operative territorialism.

The Model Law on Cross Border Insolvency is designed to achieve international co-operation in the field of cross-border insolvencies by establishing a coherent and integrated system of recognition and then ascribing some mandatory and some permissive results of that recognition. The ultimate objective of the Model Law is to facilitate the maximisation of the debtor's estate and, where possible, to co-ordinate the rescue of financially troubled companies.

Because the very nature of a Model Law is that its reception into national legal systems is voluntary and its terms may be modified or rejected in part, so that in effect it can be tailored to the needs of the incorporating state's laws and administrative practices, it was considered that it would be an ideal format for practical globalisation, avoiding the mandatory nature of traditional Conventions and regional binding instruments. As a further impetus for incorporation into local laws, the provisions of the 32 Article

---

[55] For background to the drafting of the Model Law, see A Berends, 'The Model Law on Cross-Border Insolvency: a comprehensive overview' (1998) 6 *Tu.J Int'L & Comp L* 309. The Model Law is but one of many Models drafted by UNCITRAL others being on International Commercial Arbitration (1995), International Credit Transfers (1992), Procurement of Goods and Services (1994), Electronic Commerce (1996) and Electronic Signatures (2001). The work of UNCITRAL is continuing with a Draft Legislative on Insolvency Law : see Doc A/CN.9/551 *Report of Working Group V (Insolvency Law) on the work of its thirtieth session March/April 2004.*

[56] General Assembly Res 52/158 of 15 December 1997.

[57] See Report of UNCITRAL–INSOL Colloquium, New York, 1994 at para 19: 'It could be foreseen that much work might be conducted in a form that would avoid the difficulties that would be raised by attempting global unification of the substantive law of insolvency.'

Model Law are succinct, direct and designed to require the minimum amount of interpretation.

The Model Law does not aim to achieve globalised results through unification of substantive insolvency laws which are indeed so diverse that such an objective would currently be unachievable; rather it addresses practical issues that are designed to preserve assets, facilitate reorganisation and establish mechanisms for the recognition of duly appointed foreign representatives in insolvency proceedings.

Scope

The scope of the Model Law is wide and is designed to cover collective proceedings where the control of the assets of the debtor passes to a court or to some other official body for the purposes of realisation or reorganisation.[58] It is envisaged that enacting states will exempt from the operation of the Model Law certain types of enterprise, generally those whose insolvency is dealt with under separate provisions in national law, such as insurance companies and banks and credit institutions.[59]

The Model Law contains a number of significant definitions that, in part, parallel those of the EU Regulation. The term 'foreign proceeding' describing the types of proceeding that may be subject to recognition by local courts, is defined to encompass any collective judicial or administrative proceeding (including interim proceedings) pursuant to insolvency law in which the assets and affairs of the debtor are subject to the control or supervision of a foreign court for the purposes of reorganisation or liquidation.[60]

Since co-operation between courts and insolvency practitioners lies at the heart of the Model Law's objectives, recognition of foreign proceedings is central to its operation. Such proceedings may be recognised as either 'foreign main proceedings' or 'foreign non-main proceedings.'[61] The definition of the former echoes the words of the EU Regulation in that foreign main proceedings take place where the debtor has its 'centre of main interests.' In this context, Article 16(3) creates a rebuttable presumption that the place where the debtor's registered office is situated or where an individual's habitual residence is located, is the centre of the debtor's main interests. Once more, it may be opined that the interpretation and application of this phrase in a practical context will be central to the success of the Model Law project as a facilitator of international co-operation.

---

[58] Art 2(a) Model Law.
[59] Art 1(2).
[60] Art 2(a).
[61] Art 2(b) and (c).

Access

The driving force behind recognition of proceedings will be the application by a foreign representative to local courts. In this respect, and building on the experience of ad hoc appointments of foreign representatives in the 'Protocol' cases, persons or bodies authorised to administer the reorganisation or liquidation of the debtor's estate, or to act as a representative in those proceedings, may apply directly to the courts in any state enacting the Model Law.[62] The adoption of this direct approach thus obviates the necessity for time-consuming and costly procedures such as letters rogatory or mutual registration of judgments.

Recognition of foreign representatives is to be achieved following straightforward presentation of either a certified copy of the decision of a foreign court or a certificate from such a court indicating the commencement of insolvency proceedings and the appointment of a foreign representative, or recognition may follow from 'any other evidence acceptable to the court' of the existence of foreign insolvency proceedings.[63] In order that the formalities of recognition are carried out in an expeditious fashion, the Model Law enjoins states to ensure that proceedings are decided at the earliest possible time.[64]

The Model Law also extends access to insolvency proceedings to foreign creditors[65] and confirms that they should receive equal treatment with local creditors for the purpose of commencing insolvency proceedings and ranking in the distribution of assets.[66]

As has been demonstrated by the circumstances of some international insolvencies, such as that of the Singer company, the ability to apply for immediate interim relief so as to prevent the initiation or continuance of local proceedings that might endanger an overall rescue plan, may be crucial to the success of a global workout.[67] To this end, the Model Law enjoins states to make available temporary relief pending the hearing of the application for recognition. Such relief may include staying execution against the debtor's assets in order to preserve them for consideration in the overall reorganisation or liquidation[68] and additionally, the local court is empowered to entrust the administration or realisation of all or part of the debtor's assets into the hands of the foreign representative or other person

---

[62] Arts 9 and 15(1).
[63] Art 15(2).
[64] Art 17(3).
[65] Art 13.
[66] Art 13(2).
[67] E D Flashen, and L Plank, 'The Foreign Representative : a New Approach to Coordinating the Bankruptcy of a Multinational Enterprise' (2002) *10 Am Bankr Inst L Rev* 111.
[68] Art 19.

designated by the court in order to protect or preserve the value of the assets that are perishable, susceptible to devaluation or that may otherwise be in jeopardy. The Model Law in this respect provides international legislative legitimacy for the arrangements that have hitherto been worked out in Protocols. The interim relief measures granted under the auspices of Article 19 are designed to be temporary in nature and to be superseded by the decisions taken in the final recognition proceedings.

The Effect of Recognition

The effect of recognition will depend on whether a local court recognises a foreign proceeding as a foreign main proceeding (FMP) or a foreign non-main proceeding (FNMP). In the event that recognition is given as a foreign main proceeding, Article 20 provides that there is a mandatory automatic stay on the commencement or continuation of actions in the local domain against the debtor's assets. Likewise, this moratorium extends to any transfer of or granting of security rights over the debtor's assets. Local creditors are still permitted to register their claims with a court or administrative agency in order to preserve their position in the insolvency. This mandatory stay of proceedings upon recognition of an FMP is designed to preserve the status quo and allow the foreign insolvency practitioner a breathing space in which to negotiate an orderly outcome to the international insolvency. This may involve co-ordination of several national insolvency proceedings. The moratorium on recognition of an FMP will undoubtedly be a sensitive area in the operation of the Model Law and thus Article 20(2) leaves scope for enacting states to provide for exceptions and limitations on the moratorium. For example, an adopting state may well wish to exempt enforcement of secured claims from the operation of the moratorium.

Where the proceeding is recognised as an FNMP, the local court may grant a stay of proceedings but the operation of this relief is permissive rather than mandatory.[69] In addition to granting a discretionary stay on proceedings and on already commenced executions against the debtor's estate, additional measures may be requested in any proceedings recognising foreign proceedings, main or non-main. A foreign representative may apply for the examination of witnesses, the taking of evidence or the delivery of information concerning the debtor's affairs or assets.[70] So far as FNMP are concerned, the Model Law indicates that the local court, in granting discretionary relief, must be satisfied the relief relates to assets that

---

[69] Art 21.
[70] Art 21 (a–g).

should, according to its local laws, be administered in the FNMP[71] or that a request for information concerns material required in that proceeding.[72] Furthermore, in granting or denying relief under the interim measures (Article 19) or under its discretionary powers (Article 21) the local court must be satisfied that the interests of creditors and other interested parties are protected.[73]

The distinctive treatment of FMP and FNMP is also important in connection with the commencement of anti-avoidance actions, such as actions for fraudulent transfers of corporate property or actions for recovery from those accorded undue preference in order to avoid the impact of insolvency ranking provisions. Upon recognition of a foreign proceeding, the representative has standing to initiate anti-avoidance actions in the local state and to take remedial action, for example, in the nature of tracing actions. However, where the proceeding is recognised as an FNMP, the local court must be satisfied that the action relates to assets that should be administered in the FNMP.[74]

Co-operation between Courts and Insolvency Practitioners

The central pillar of the Model Law is the facilitation of effective co-operation between courts and insolvency practitioners in different states. While in the national context, courts enjoy general jurisdictional competency, where international insolvency is concerned, they often require some specific legislative provision in order to exhibit competence.[75] Where states currently do not legislate for international competence, the Model Law, if adopted, will provide the mechanism by which national courts are empowered to co-operate with one another and with insolvency practitioners.

The distinctive nature of the Model Law as compared with traditional treaties or bi- or multi-national conventions, is that in-bound and out-bound co-operation does not depend on reciprocity. Incorporation of the Model Law into the state system of insolvency administration, particularly where there are procedural barriers to judicial co-operation, or where the judiciary do not possess wide discretionary powers (as may be the case in some civil law systems) will enable national courts to exercise flexibility in the extremely important arena of multinational default. To this end, Article 25 provides '(I)n matters referred to in Article 1, the court shall co-operate to the maximum extent possible with foreign courts or representatives...'.

---

[71] Art 21(2).
[72] Art 23(2).
[73] Art 22.
[74] Art 23(2).
[75] In the UK such competence is conferred by the Insolvency Act 1986 s 426 and in the US by US Bankruptcy Code s 304.

The modes of co-operation are specified in a non-exhaustive fashion in Article 27 and include the appointment of persons to act at the direction of the court,[76] the communication of information between courts and practitioners, the co-ordination of the administration and supervision of the debtor's assets and affairs or the co-ordination of concurrent proceedings regarding the same debtor.

Not only is co-operation between courts facilitated by the terms of the Model Law, but between insolvency practitioners.[77] It is noticeable that the drafting of Articles 25–27 gives courts and practitioners far-reaching powers to determine the extent and mechanics of co-operation.

Concurrent Proceedings

Chapter V of the Model Law deals with the complex issue of the co-ordination of simultaneous local and foreign proceedings. It is central to the success of the Model Law project that there are effective guidelines to deal with such parallel procedures in the absence of a universalist solution to global insolvency.

The Model Law does not seek to impose any limitation on the opening of concurrent proceedings. It regulates the results of such concurrence. First, Article 28 provides that local proceedings may only be commenced after the recognition of FMP, if the debtor has assets in the local state and the effects of such proceedings are restricted to locally situated assets. Additionally, such proceedings may only be put into operation to the extent necessary to implement co-ordination as required under Articles 25–27. Secondly, Article 29 deals with the situation where local proceedings have already been commenced and an application for recognition of a foreign proceeding is filed. In this case, any relief granted under Article 19 (urgent interim relief) or Article 21 (discretionary remedies granted upon recognition of a foreign proceeding) must be consistent with the local proceedings. If the local court recognises the proceeding as an FMP, then Article 29(a)(ii) is particularly significant in that it states that Article 20 (the automatic stay of proceedings) does not apply. Article 29 underlines the paramountcy of local proceedings in this context. The mechanics of operating the Model Law will mean that where a global insolvency is envisaged, the enterprise where the debtor has its centre of main interests should apply for recognition of

---

[76] See in this event the appointment of foreign representatives by the US Courts to protect the assets of US corporations with foreign subsidiaries.

[77] Art 26. Many international law and accountancy firms have developed expertise in cross-border insolvency work through appointments as foreign representatives and their past cooperative practices will be placed on a structured footing should the Model Law be adopted.

this proceeding as the FMP in all other states that have adopted the Model Law at the earliest date to avoid local proceedings taking precedence under Article 29(a)(ii) in order to ensure an effective reach for an automatic moratorium. The third alternative is the situation where local proceedings are commenced after the recognition or filing for recognition of foreign proceedings. If the foreign proceedings are recognised as FMP, Article 29 permits the local court to modify or terminate a stay of proceedings if it is inconsistent with local proceedings. In the context of creating a globalised approach to insolvency proceedings, Article 29 is particularly significant in maintaining 'a pre-eminence of the local proceedings over foreign proceedings.'[78] This approach prevents a clash of jurisdictional hierarchy and provides the secure psychology on which the Model Law is based in which co-operation is encouraged in a non-threatening framework.

There may, of course, be complex situations in which multiple simultaneous proceedings are pending before a local court in respect of the same debtor enterprise. Article 30 deals with this circumstance first, by invoking the principles of co-ordination and co-operation under Articles 25–27 and then specifying that any relief granted to a representative in an FNMP must be consistent with the FMP. This, therefore, establishes a workable hierarchy for the recognition and operation of multiple actions.

Reception

Ultimately, the effectiveness of the Model Law depends on its widespread adoption in a range of states, preferably states with differing legal traditions. Its influence will be enhanced if states that do not already have established formal bilateral or multilateral links, as do the EU or the NAFTA states, adopt the Model Law in order that it may be used in uncharted territory. The Model Law would then govern transnational insolvencies between countries where adoption of its terms has taken effect.

The most significant adoption to date is that of Japan, which enacted its Law on Recognition of and Assistance in Foreign Proceedings (LRAFP) in 2001 based upon the Model Law. The Japanese law enables a trustee, representative or debtor in possession in a foreign insolvency to file for recognition in the Japanese (Tokyo District) Court. That court may then order assistance to be given, including temporary suspension of compulsory execution proceedings, and make a prohibition order against the commencement of such proceedings. Japanese implementation law has additionally created the role of 'recognition trustee' enabling the appointee to this position to have exclusive authority to manage and dispose of the debtor's

---

[78] UNCITRAL, Guide to Enactment of the Model Law, para 190.

business in Japan.[79] It is noteworthy that Japan, that has seen so many international insolvencies, including the joint insolvency proceedings in the US and Japan of Maruko Inc.[80] was one of the first states to adopt the Model Law as the framework for co-ordinating international insolvency recognition.

The Model law has also been adopted in South Africa in its Cross-Border Insolvency Act 42 2000. However, this adoption is subject to the requirement that foreign countries for and against which it will be effective, must be designated by the Minister of State. Thus, South Africa has chosen to retain sovereign control over the reach of the legislation and could be expected to operate its state discretion on the basis of reciprocity. Additionally, the South African adoption of the Model Law has subjected its terms to some modification. This transformation into South African law has a particular significance because of the very distinct nature of the Roman-Dutch concepts being harmonised in the interests of globalisation.[81]

Other countries currently adopting the Model Law include Eritrea, Mexico and Montenegro.

The UK has made arrangements for the adoption of the Model Law by enabling legislation in s 14 Insolvency Act 2000. The process required to bring the law into effect requires the production of a statutory instrument and the alteration of the terms of s 426 Insolvency Act 1986.

US legal institutions and academics have shown considerable enthusiasm for the adoption of the Model Law and the preparative processes in the Senate and House of Representatives have culminated in a new Chapter 15 being proposed to the US Bankruptcy Code. This would incorporate the Model Law with a very close correlation between the two instruments. It is envisaged that adoption of the Model Law (in place of the current s 304 of the US Bankruptcy Code) would bring greater certainty to transnational insolvencies in which US courts have been asked to assist foreign insolvency proceedings or in which foreign representatives have been appointed in respect of outbound assistance.[82]

Chapter 15 is part of the Bankruptcy Reform Bill that is currently going through the House of Representatives and the Senate.[83] The Bill was not enacted in the 2002 Congressional session as it failed to obtain the Senate's

---

[79] S Abe, 'Recent Developments in Insolvency Laws and Cross-Border Practices in the United States and Japan' (2002) 10 *Am Bankr Inst L Rev* 47.

[80] A Quittner, 'Cross-Border Insolvencies–Ancillary and Full Cases: the Concurrent Japanese and United States Cases of Maruko Inc' (1995) 2 *Intl Insolvency Rev* 171.

[81] A Smith and A Boraine, 'Crossing borders into South African Insolvency Law: From the Roman-Dutch Jurist to the UNCITRAL Model Law' (2002) 10 *Am Bankr Inst L Rev* 135.

[82] For a detailed background of the adoption of the Model Law as Chapter 15 of the Bankruptcy Code, see House of Representatives Report No 3, 107th Cong, 1st session 2001 on *Bankruptcy Abuse Prevention and Consumer Protection Act 2001.*

[83] The Bankruptcy Abuse Prevention and Protection Act 2003 HR 975.

support. The provisions responsible for the disagreement mainly related to bankruptcy abuse prevention proposals and had little to do with Chapter 15. This time, the US is very close in adopting the Model Law. This development will arguably be a significant progress in the area of global insolvency law capable of influencing more states to consider a possible implementation of the Model Law in their national insolvency legislation. Chapter 15 aims to facilitate mechanisms to achieve the corporate turnaround of companies in financial hardship[84] and in cases where that is not possible, to provide the legislative framework for the fair and efficient administration of the debtor's estate that will protect the interests of creditors[85] and at the same time will maximise the return on the debtor's assets.[86] Paragraph 1501 excludes from the remit of Chapter 15 foreign insurance companies and entities that are regulated by the Securities Investor Protection Act 1979, stockbrokers and commodity brokers. Natural persons, who are citizens or permanent residents of the United States with a specified debt limit, are also excluded from this Chapter. Furthermore, the international obligations arising out of treaties and agreements that the US is party to will prevail over the requirements of this Chapter.[87] Also, the courts retain the power to deny authorisation to proceedings under this heading if they contravene the public policy of the US.[88]

On adoption, Chapter 15 will effectively be the US legal framework for dealing with global insolvencies. It will apply in cases where the assistance of the US courts is requested by a foreign court or a foreign representative in connection with the operation of foreign insolvency proceedings.[89] Subject to the pre-mentioned exclusions, the US courts can make an order recognising either the foreign main or non-main proceedings,[90] which will effectively trigger the application of Chapter 15, if it is satisfied that an authorised foreign person or entity has filed all the prescribed documents which are listed in paragraph 1515. Additionally, this Chapter will be used to provide authorisation to a US trustee or other entities to act in a foreign country according to the foreign applicable law.[91]

The drafters of Chapter 15 made a conscious effort to use the phraseology and structure of the Model Law.[92] With good reason, Westbrook

---

[84] Para 1501(a) Chapter 15.
[85] Para 1501(a) 3.
[86] Para 1501(a) 4.
[87] Para 1503.
[98] Para 1506.
[89] Para 1501(b).
[90] Para 1517.
[91] Paras 1501 and 1505.
[92] JL Westbrook, 'Multinational Enterprises in General Default: Chapter 15, The ALI Principles, and the EU Insolvency Regulation' (2002) 76 *Am Bankr L J* 1.

argues that some deviations in the wording were necessary. Some definitions adopted by the Model Law include phrases that judges across the Atlantic could find unusual. That could result in an unintended interpretation of the provisions. Subsequently, some departure from the original language was viewed as necessary to ensure that the purpose of the Model Law would be well served. Finally, paragraph 1508 states that in interpreting this Chapter, the courts should take into consideration its international origin and the need to promote an application in line with the application adopted in other countries.

OTHER CO-ORDINATION AND HARMONISATION MEASURES

The EU Regulation and the Model Law, once operational or adopted in national legal systems, legitimate the work of cross-border insolvency representatives and ensure that judicial decisions and appointments taken in the context of the legislation are inviolable.

There are other formalised, but non-legislative, efforts designed to facilitate international co-operation in insolvency proceedings and these play a significant part in the creation of a globalised law. On a regional basis, the American Law Institute (ALI) has been instrumental in devising a set of Principles applicable to cross-border insolvencies affecting Canada, the US and Mexico. The 'Principles of Co-operation' emanate from the work of the Transnational Insolvency Project (TIP) and they seek to provide the basis for judicial co-operation and reduce contentious proceedings in regional insolvency matters. The main thrust of the TIP project is that insolvency harmonisation is best achieved through court-to-court communication rather than through the more rigid constraints of legislation. The project represents the work of distinguished scholars and practitioners within the Americas and reflects the belief that in the fast moving world of insolvency, private sector initiatives such as those of the ALI are more likely to be a fruitful mode of dispute resolution and financial reconstruction than formal legislative initiatives.[93] Utilising 'soft law' in the sense of principles to be adopted in court practice, the ALI project is designed to inject flexibility into case proceedings. This would be a useful way of developing regional legal integration and legitimating regional workouts.

Underpinning the work of national legislatures as well as regional and international organisations is a substantial body of developmental research to which acknowledgement should be paid. Two agencies in particular have played a conspicuous role in the development of a globalised law. The first

---

[93] JL Westbrook, 'The Transnational Insolvency Project of the American Law Institute' (2001) 17 *Conn J Intl L* 99.

is the World Bank, and especially its Development Institute which has carried out research in comparative insolvency law and reorganisational economics. Its *Principles and Guidelines for Effective Insolvency and Creditor Rights Systems* has played an influential role in the recent legislative changes made to eastern European and east Asian internal insolvency laws. The *Principles* provide guidance to national legislatures and insolvency regulators as to the ideal structures necessary to establish predictable, transparent and affordable insolvency procedures. They emphasise the importance of reliable methods of debt recovery both for unsecured and secured creditors, and in a world that relies heavily on secured international finance, the *Principles* underline the importance of states having a comprehensive system of priorities and effective registration systems. Additionally, the *Principles* link to cross-border insolvency issues by stressing the importance of recognition of kindred proceedings and co-operation between courts. The *Principles* were elaborated by a study of the design of bankruptcy laws produced by the World Bank in 2001.[94]

The educative role of the World Bank is mirrored to an extent by the private enterprise work of the International Insolvency Institute. No work recording the efforts of those involved in globalising insolvency law would be complete without paying tribute to the work of this organisation. The Institute, whose membership consists of leading insolvency judges, practitioners and academics, is dedicated to the advancement of studies in international insolvency. It provides a forum in which insolvency professionals can meet and discuss matters of concern. Its practical importance may be demonstrated by the production of comparative studies, in the dissemination of information concerning cross-border Protocols and running conferences. Its website provides ready access to materials from around the world.[95]

The Institute has links with the international professional body co-ordinating the work of insolvency practitioners, including those who have experience of appointments as foreign representatives in cross-border proceedings–INSOL International. Among the contributions of this organisation to the creation of a globalised insolvency law is the *Statement of Principles* for a global approach to multi-creditor workouts, drafted by the INSOL Lender's Group. The significance of this *Statement of Principles* is its focus on the attitude and actions of major bank lenders whose support is essential in multi-bank rescues of financially troubled enterprises. The *Statement of Principles* endorses a 'standstill' period in an international insolvency so that information about the debtor and an evaluation of the

---

[94] S Claessens et al, 'Resolution of Financial Distress–An International Perspective on the Design of Bankruptcy Laws' World Bank: Working Paper 2001.
[95] The website is http://www.iiiglobal.org/.

rescue plan can be communicated to supporting banks. The chances of a successful turnaround are enhanced by workout creditors adopting a period of voluntary restraint in relation to possible default claims. Central to the success of any creditor organised recovery is the co-ordination of support and this is enjoined by Principle 4. While it is noteworthy that major international lending institutions have agreed to this INSOL inspired document, it should be stressed that this is an entirely voluntary code and there is nothing to prevent creditors breaking rank should a major insolvency threaten their security or solvency.

CONCLUSION

Cross-border insolvencies have increasingly dominated news headlines, and the problems of achieving resolution of the issues that they raise are manifold. With the enactment of the EU Regulation there is now in force at least one regional binding measure designed to achieve co-ordination in multi-state insolvencies, and through the consequences of the recognition system established by the Regulation, to develop a universal conflict of laws system operational throughout the European Union. We have indicated in this chapter the strengths of the Regulation and the potential flashpoints in which the objectives of the Regulation could become undermined.

The UNCITRAL Model Law on Cross Border Insolvencies provides a looser response to the mechanics of recognition. Its success will depend on the willingness of states to adopt and operate conscientiously its terms in their systems of cross-border insolvency.

There is also a very large undercurrent of work in the field of international insolvency and creditor protection law and practice. The developmental work of the World Bank and the invaluable role of the International Insolvency Institute and INSOL International are creating a groundswell of information and goodwill necessary for legislatures, courts and actors in the insolvency systems to create a truly harmonised and congruent international insolvency system.

7

Global Transparency

PATRICK BIRKINSHAW

INTRODUCTION

G LOBAL TRANSPARENCY MUST address the position of transnational corporations (TNCs) which operate at the national, supranational and international levels. All major companies share to greater or lesser degrees global ambitions. There are 60,000 TNCs in the world today with 800,000 affiliates.[1] There are 300 or so Intergovernmental Organisations (IGOs) and about 40,000 Non Governmental Organisations (NGOs). The top twenty TNCs have sales of over US$1600 billion and employ over five million people. In a global commonwealth, TNCs are seen by many as Hobbes saw corporations in the Commonwealth: as 'lesser common-wealths in the bowels of a greater, like wormes in the entrayles of a natural man.'[2] Their capacity to avoid legal or fiscal regulation through their global operations is well known. TNCs may generate ethical problems through the unaccountability of economic and organisational power which rivals that of governments. As we shall see, global transparency has national, supranational and international implications and is intimately linked with access to information. This is the territory of freedom of information (FOI) laws. It will be argued that FOI laws have as much relevance to powerful 'private' corporations and organisations as they do to more traditional forms of public power. This chapter sets out the international context in which freedom of information will have to operate in order to bring necessary transparency to TNCs and IGOs.

---

[1] UNCTAD, 2001 World Investment Report 2001: *Promoting Linkages* New York, United Nations; H Anheier, M Glasius and M Kaldor (eds), *Global Civil Society 2001* (Oxford, Oxford University Press, 2001) cited in H Kovach, C Neligan and S Burall, *Power Without Accountability?* (One World Trust, 2002–03).

[2] T Hobbes, *Leviathan* ch 29 (ed CB Macpherson, Pelican Classics, 1979) 375.

THE ARGUMENT

FOI laws emerged as a result of serious imbalances in social/political relationships brought about by complex organisational opacity and the opportunities this presented for unchallengeable power to be used to abuse relationships. The classic paradigm is the state/citizen relationship where the public and private realms are clearly defined. More recent additions to FOI laws are beginning to realise the limitations of this form of analysis: the private sector is either assuming responsibilities for government through one process or another, or private commercial organisations are assuming a central role (have for many years assumed a central role) in exploitation of transnational and global markets. This latter (no less than the former) is invariably hinged on some form of state support/encouragement/partnership. The problem posed by such developments in the global sphere is how do we ensure FOI laws and policies in that sphere address contemporary structural complexities and power distortions? But a traditional attitude to the public/private divide was shown fairly recently in Australia where suggestions to reform the Australian FOI Act to allow access to private sector information were rejected by the Australian Law Reform Commission: 'Private sector bodies should not be under an obligation to disclose to any member of the public any document in their possession.' They are already subject to numerous laws including health and safety, consumer protection and one may add environmental protection.[3]

I am reliably informed that about fifty nation states now possess some form of FOI legislation. In addition, the EU in 2001 adopted an Access Regulation (1049/2001 under Art 255 EC) covering documents of the Council, Commission and European Parliament (EP)(together with their committees and agencies. Furthermore, the provisions apply to second and third pillar documents. In addition, the Charter of Fundamental Rights of the European Union has included a right of access to documents (built on and basically repeating the Access Regulation) as a Fundamental Right of the Union. The Working Group on the Charter has recommended that the Charter be incorporated within the EU Constitution and this has been taken up with the drafts of the Constitution published in February 2003 and thereafter, and which were approved by the heads of Member States in June 2004, but which still awaits ratification. I note that openness and access were not subjects consigned to Working Groups of Giscard d'Estaing's Convention. These concentrated on simplicity and single legal personality and the provisions on access emerging in the draft Constitution were rather anaemic and largely rephrased existing Treaty provisions, although the

---

[3] ALRC Review of Federal FOIA 1982 (1995) para 15(5). On changes to government structures and FOI see A Roberts, 'Structural Pluralism and the Right to Information' School of Policy Studies Working Paper No 15 (2001).

European Council is now included as a body whose documents will be under access laws. In the Council of Europe (CoE), the question of a treaty providing for access to official documents binding on the CoE's Member States has been discussed. This would build on the CoE Recommendation 2002 (2) on Access to Official Documents (http://www.justiceinitiative.org/db/resource2?res_id=102667).

The New Global Order

To some extent the battle for FOI at national level seems to be won and five years ago campaigners could confidently expect to move on to access to information at the global level. Transnational companies, international agreements between nation states, states or unions of states operating internationally, IGOs and NGOs were to become the target of access. But, there has been a reversal of practice and policy at state level–most dramatically and importantly within the US. I think this context has to be seen before we can explore the international dimension, not least because the US was so powerful in setting the original context towards openness throughout so many nation states and because its changes in practice are dominating new attitudes towards closure and secrecy.

The background is very much the government/private organisation interface and interdependibility. The most important developments include:

Attorney General's Memo of October 2001 to all Departmental and Agency Chiefs

This contains advice on a presumption of non-disclosure under FOIA: 'Any discretionary decision by your agency to disclose information protected under FOIA should be made only after full and deliberate consideration of the institutional, commercial, and personal privacy interests that could be implicated by disclosure of the information.' They will be defended by the US Department of Justice unless the department's decision lacks a 'sound legal basis.'

Patriot Act 2001

The Director of Central Intelligence may suspend the release of information under FOIA and there was to be no judicial review of the DCI's decisions–this provision was not successful.

Critical Infrastructure Information Security Act and Homeland Security Act (2002)

The implications of this legislation are massive. The US government is asking private organisations to share information about the nation's critical infrastructure assets. A President's Critical Infrastructure Protection Board was established shortly after September 11 2001, which in 2002 produced a 'clear roadmap to protect a part of its infrastructure so essential to our way of life.' (www.whitehouse.gov/pcibb) Part of the roadmap is an 'unprecedented partnership between federal government and private organisations' in which a voluntary sharing on information with the government has been requested. It is suggested that up to 90 per cent of the nation's infrastructure is controlled by private industry. Companies worry that such information may be released under FOIA. Federal government was concerned that without such information, the US may be more vulnerable to further terrorist attacks.[4]

Critical Infrastructure Information (CII) is therefore excluded from FOIA the details of which are to be finalised in regulations; criminal sanctions are imposed for unauthorised disclosures for CII under the latter (reminiscent of Official Secrecy laws in the UK); the provisions in this Act override state and local FOIA laws. CII includes: physical and cyber-based systems and services essential to national defence, government or economy of the US, including those systems essential for telecoms (including voice and data transmission and the internet), electrical power, gas and oil storage and transportation, banking and finance, water supply, emergency services (including medical fire and police) and the continuity of government operations. Think for a moment of the Bechtel corporation. In public private partnerships more information is required from the 'traditionally private functions' of energy and telecoms relating to risk assessment, risk prevention and security testing amongst other items. *Voluntary* sharing of information by the private sector companies will be protected under FOIA by the Homeland Security Act s 5(a)(1)(A). A provider has to mark information with an express statement. Just think about the Enron, Andersen and Worldcom scandals or police corruption. Enron filed a suit against the state of California when the state attempted to *subpoena* Enron's record of electricity sales. After the collapse, the Enron documents showed that the company had rigged electricity markets, created power shortages, raised prices and artificially boosted its own profits. Under s 724 Homeland Security Act, CII includes the identity of the provider. The legislation overrides agency rules specifically on rule-making, judicial case law on ex parte contacts–ie, access given to privileged parties only in law making–and disclosure under the Act does not waive Legal Professional Privilege or trade secret privilege. The effect is to reverse the presumption of disclosure in FOIA. Challenge could only be on a jurisdictional basis–this information is not Critical Infrastructure Information. Opponents argued vigorously that existing exemptions covered such

---

[4] J Summerill [2003] *The Federal Lawyer* 24. See further, GM Stevens, *Homeland Security Act 2002: Critical Infrastructure Information Act* (Congressional Research Service, 2003).

information adequately especially exemption one and four FOIA on trade secrets and commercial confidentiality.

Review of EO 12598

This is the executive order allowing exemption for national defence and foreign policy by presidential order. This is effectively executive law-making which does not have to be, indeed cannot be, approved by Congress.[5] Classification of information for security and international reasons rose by 18 per cent under President Bush in 2001; declassification of documents is more restricted than previously and there are reviews of declassified documents to reclassify them. If in doubt classify–I don't know if that is unprecedented but it is unusual.

What is interesting in all this is the role of leading political figures who featured in long past practices to embrace greater secrecy or who were formerly connected to companies subsequently embroiled by commercial scandals that have damaged financial confidence: Cheney, Rumsfeld and Henry Kissinger. The latter was involved in the review of security actions following September 11. He had to step down from the September 11 Commission enquiring into the events of September 11 when he refused to disclose his personal interests including fees of over US$5,000 paid to his business in the previous two years.

The tone has been set by September 11, but one cannot but fail to see the opportunist's initiative in this, not I believe unlike the UK Official Secrets Bill of 1911. Section 2–the catch-all provision–was drafted by the War Department/Ministry and was awaiting for a 'crisis' in order to present the Bill to Parliament! There is no doubt that these developments in the US will have a constraining influence on FOI policy worldwide. They have also been accompanied by global attempts to ensure that executive hostage taking and detention are immune from supervision by the US courts. In such a context, it appeared somewhat out of character for the President in Executive Order 13392 of 14 December 2005 to exhort agency improvement of disclosure of information under the FOIA.

The International Dimension

The international dimension here is seen in the role of NATO especially (but not exclusively) as concerns former communist countries and the security of information agreements that they have to sign. It is a NATO (US) requirement that all new NATO Member States and all aspirant EU members have to agree to the introduction of secrecy laws. For many, this is

---

[5] *Chadha v I&NS* 462 US 919 (1983).

reminiscent of former Soviet dictatorship. Poland as I understand the situation has strongly objected. The NATO 'Security of Information' policy, ie, the principles on which secrecy is maintained, is itself secret.[6] This will continue despite the very public spats concerning NATO's deliberations and preparation for hostilities against Iraq.

If one turns attention to the EU Access Regulation referred to above 'sensitive documents', ie, security/defence and NATO related, are *excluded* from access where the provider does not agree to release. Furthermore, they do not have to be registered by the EU institutions as existing. The provisions on classification of documents are in two extremely voluminous official documents and an inter-institutional agreement exists between the Council and European Parliament on access.[7] Make no mistake, this classification is exclusion and many are not alive to the way in which the provisions operated.

Less dramatically, the WTO has been accused of seeking to undermine the position of local authorities in the enforcement of environmental protection by the WTO's attempts to incorporate wealth opportunising and deregulatory measures in the GATT.

We have some domestic problems. There have been difficulties in gaining access to information about abuses of human rights of British citizens by the Iraqi regime in 1991 and the Parliamentary Ombudsman's investigation into a refusal to release information about inter-departmental correspondence concerning human rights in relation to the Ilisu dam project.[8] One should also note the complaint into the Home Office's refusal to publish *any* information about ministerial declarations of interests and the refusal to accept the Parliamentary Ombudsman's conclusions against the Home Office.[9] The action by the Home Office caused a frustrated ombudsman to seek removal from the ombudsman of the jurisdiction under the Code on Access which operated until January 2005. These are worrying developments and could be the harbinger of things to come in relation to access rights under the 2000 UK FOIA which have taken effect from 1 January 2005.

There are still considerable domestic problems which are setting global agendas. What is or has occurred globally?

---

[6] A Roberts, 'Entangling Alliances: NATO's Security of Information Policy and the Entrenchment of State Secrecy' (2003) 36 *Cornell Intl L J* 329. I am grateful to Al Roberts for information on this section. See also, A Roberts in *National Security and Open Government: Striking the Right Balance* (Campbell Public Affairs Institute, the Maxwell School of Syracuse University, 2003) 147 *et seq.*

[7] Council Decision 2001/264 OJ L101/1 (11.4.01); Commission Decision 201/844 OJ L317/1 (3.12.01) and an interinstitutional agreement between the Council and European Parliament on 'sharing' ie disclosing information: (2002) OJ C298/1 (20.11.02).

[8] Inv A 26/01.

[9] Inv A 28/01.

The International Legal Requirements

Those bodies which are international in dimension or which operate globally present particular difficulties from the perspective of FOI. On the international plane, we do of course face a much wider and immediately more sensitive context that a purely national one. This is after all the arena of prerogative and diplomacy as the British Prime Minister was quick to remind us before hostilities commenced against Iraq. This context in the UK is still imbued with a secretive Foreign and Commonwealth Office culture. There was an interesting example of this in attempts by the FCO to get a reform of the Data Protection Act 1998 in order to introduce a subject access exemption covering 'international relations.' Disclosure of colourful personal data on 'local politicians' would cause embarrassment if those politicians were allowed access to the data. There have been high profile instances of where that culture of secrecy has not always been effective to silence senior FCO advisers.

Despite these diplomatic sensitivities, there is a remarkably prescient UN Resolution of 1946 which states that 'Freedom of Information is a fundamental human right and is the touchstone for all freedoms to which the United Nations is consecrated.'[10] We had to wait almost sixty years before there was official confirmation of access to information as a human right, albeit in a draft EU Constitution, which awaits ratification after its rejection by France and the Netherlands. These provisions build on existing EU laws.

Supranational bodies are created as a result of agreement between national states and increasingly take the form of global and regional bodies. These include the UN, WTO and GATT,the World Bank at the global level, and the Council of Europe and other regional bodies. The most developed legally of the latter is the European Union.

In terms of states and international affairs–defence, national security and intelligence, and international and diplomatic relationships all require that information be given in confidence. The sensitivity of domestic (and foreign) courts in these areas is notorious.[11]

What is the position with global or transnational corporations and non-governmental organisations? In the former case the position of such companies operates along lines of commercial secrecy and non-sharing of information to secure competitive advantages. Traditionally such companies operate in those countries where impoverished conditions, non-unionised

---

[10] Resolution of the UN General Assembly 14 December 1946–(65th plenary meeting). I develop this theme in P Birkinshaw, 'Freedom of Information and Openness–Fundamental Human Rights?' [2006] 58 *Administrative Law Review* 177.

[11] *Rehman v Secretary of State* [2002] 1 All ER 122; see, however, *A and Ors v Secretary of State* [2005] 3 All ER 169 (HL) and *A (FC) et al v Secretary of State* [2005] UKHL 71 on executive detention and receipt of intelligence extracted by torture.

work forces and cheap labour attract inward investment and where legal duties to disclose information are undeveloped. Freedom of Information laws do not usually cover such bodies directly. Information which they have provided to governments may be requested, however, when it is held by government departments or agencies. Access laws invariably allow such bodies a right to challenge disclosure, and consultation rights. One should recall the reforms in the US outlined above which seek to exclude such information from FOI laws where it concerns critical infrastructure information. The UK FOI Act applies to private companies when they are basically providing a public service and which are designated by the Secretary of State.

In the case of NGOs, there are problems: do they represent international civil society or are they representative of 'dangerous shifts of power to unelected and special interest groups'? From the early years of the nineteenth century the role of interest groups in setting international agendas for the development of international law and standards was appreciated as being of strategic importance. Their role in reform was seen as being so important that governments could not be left to operate alone: one clear example is the role of the very effective British and Foreign Anti-Slavery Society from that period. Are contemporary NGOs simple additions to pluralistic debate in the public interest, or do they share in power arrangements for which they should be rendered accountable?

Sir Kenneth Keith has written that the 1899 Hague Peace Conference was the first step in the process of continuing multilateral diplomacy within an ever widening reach of subject matter.[12] It was not entirely unprecedented.[13] The conference was conducted on an egalitarian basis and the press were present and regularly briefed. In 1918, Woodrow Wilson spoke of 'open covenants of peace, openly arrived at, after which there shall be no private international undertakings of any kind but diplomacy shall proceed always frankly and in the public view.' The subject of such treaties would be the result of sensitive negotiation and policy formulation in the most delicate of areas where–as Versailles showed in 1919–there would be full protection for secrecy of negotiations.

In accordance with Article 102 of the Charter of the UN, treaties are to be published. There are, however, treaties that are classified. The US/Canada treaty concerning General Security of Information review of NATO's policy on secrecy classifications was classified and when requested under Canadian ATIA its existence was denied. This was subsequently accepted as a mistake and the treaty, the requester was informed, had been

---

[12] In J Beatson and Y Cripps (eds), *Freedom of Expression and Freedom of Information* (Oxford, Oxford University Press, 2000) ch 21.
[13] Geneva Conference for Protection of War Victims 1863.

sent for declassification. The same request sought details of Canada's position on NATO review of security of information policy. Only a two-page memo was found by the Department of Foreign Affairs and International Trade. Subsequently, it discovered 1900 pages of documents of such a review which were to be reviewed for possible release.[14]

Treaties which are not registered are not enforceable before UN organisations especially the International Court of Justice. Treaties cover war and peace, disarmament and arms control, nuclear technology, international trade, international commercial transactions, international communications, international spaces, the environment, torture, human rights and related matters, international crimes and an international criminal tribunal, labour conditions, other areas of international and economic and social co-operation and children.

Treaties may require signatories to disclose steps taken to implement their provisions either at the outset or as a recurring duty as in human rights and labour treaties. Treaties often include provision for inspection, reporting on disarmament (nb, the situation in Iraq), nuclear generation, monitoring of performance of the subject matter of the Treaty and access to information. NGOs very often contribute to the drafting of reports on implementation and participate before monitoring committees. This does not of course prevent disputes emerging about the specific contents of provisions on access as witnessed by the dispute brought before the international tribunal under the permanent court of arbitration investigating Ireland's complaint over secrecy of the MOX plutonium fuel plant's discharges at Sellafield, a move which arguably contravenes European law.[15] Treaties frequently contain provisions on information exchanges on subjects such as crime and taxation and the steps taken to implement agreements on human rights protection. Information on tariffs and restraints on trade are contained in trade agreements. Treaties may make provision for notification and details of environmental disasters and so on as under the provisions of the Rio Declaration (1992). The Århus Convention on Access to Environmental Information (implemented by regulations into UK law) provides not only for access rights, but for participation rights and rights to justice. The laws will apply to a broad range of private bodies operating on behalf of government. Treaties may also require access to assessments on activities prejudicial

---

[14] This example comes from Al Roberts; above n 6.

[15] In the *Opinion* of Advocate General, Poiares Maduro, delivered on 18 January 2006 Case C459/03 *Commission of the European Communities v Ireland* he proposed that the court declare that, by instituting dispute settlement proceedings against the United Kingdom under UN provisions concerning the MOX Plant located at Sellafield, Ireland has failed to fulfil its obligations under Arts 292 EC and 193 EA; and declare that, by instituting the said proceedings without previously consulting the Commission, Ireland has failed to fulfil its obligations under Arts 10 EC and 192 EA. The European Court of Justice upheld this opinion on 30 May 2006.

to other states' interests, eg, underground nuclear weapons testing. This was a subject before the International Court in 1995 when New Zealand wanted access to reports by France on the latter's tests in the Pacific.

Kofi Annan[16] called for 'a global partnership for information' in 1997–the information revolution left us no choice, he said. 'The great democratising power of information has given us all the chance to effect change and alleviate poverty in ways we cannot even imagine today. With information on our side, with knowledge for all, the path to poverty can be reversed. The Commonwealth Human Rights Project has indicated forcefully the importance of access to information in relation to humanitarian aid: following through the accounting details of what was supposed to have been given and what was actually given by way of aid. Access to such information has been seen as essential to disclose corruption and incompetence.[17]

'An informed citizenry is the greatest defender of freedom' said Annan 'an enlightened government is a democratising government.' He continues: 'The quantity and quality of available information is changing dramatically every day in every country in the world. Citizens are gaining greater and greater access to information, too. And perhaps most importantly, the spread of information is making accountability and transparency facts of life for any free government. The consent of the governed–the condition for any free society–must be an informed, enlightened consent. The challenge now, for us, is to make information available to all.'[18]

The UNESCO constitution had perceived that ignorance of each other's ways of life had commonly caused wars and their disastrous consequences. 'Wars' the constitution says, begin in the minds of men. And 'it is in the minds of men that the defences of peace must be constructed.' Daniel Moynihan spelt out how the American practice of governmental secrecy developed over international relationships in the last century 'blighted prudent policy-making.'[19] Secrecy became a losing proposition; it was for losers.' J Stiglitz made a similar point in *Right to Tell* when he argued that as adviser to the World Bank he found secrecy destructive of enterprise and economic growth. And yet secrecy is back on the front burner of the agenda.

In international obligations we can see efforts to enhance general conditions of life in relation to human rights and enhanced information on behaviour and treatment; information on accident prevention such as Chernobyl or troop movements. A 1952 convention covers the International Right of Correction of Information in relation to acts of

---

[16] Cited by Keith in Beatson and Cripps, above n 12, at 366.
[17] See *Financial Times (Fund Management)* 2 June 2003.
[18] Keith, above n 12, at 366.
[19] *Ibid.*

aggression where misleading or inaccurate reports are produced and addresses the absence of appropriate mechanisms to correct such reports. The convention attempts to provide a means for states to publish commensurate information on their attempts to correct misleading information.

The importance of information for the 'proper functioning of the international system' is evidenced by UN reports on Sebrenica and Rwanda–can one add Iraq–and the early warning capacity of the UN which to universal agreement needs to be improved. They were crucial in seeking to prevent genocide and mass slaughter.

Some deficiencies in human rights protection closer to home have been witnessed in relation to the EU. The Court of Human Rights has ruled that Article 10 ECHR (a free speech provision) does not provide for a right of access to information; Article 8 may provide access rights to protect private and family life.[20] A 2002 Recommendation No2 has provided for a new recommendation from the Committee of Ministers of the Council of Europe on access to officially held information.

The European Union

The provisions of the Treaty on European Union (TEU) that cover democracy, the rule of law and human rights protection are well known. Accession agreements all require an undertaking by new members to abide by democratic standards and the rule of law and to protect human rights, now presumably including access to information under Article 42 of the EU Charter of Fundamental Rights which replicates Article 255 EC (with modifications) and which under the draft constitution of the EU is to become an integral part of the EU Constitution (Part II, but access to documents is also contained in Parts I and III of the draft constitution). Several commentators have observed that the EU in fact is more exacting of its standards 'abroad' than at 'home'. There is no Human Rights Commission or Commissioner although in October 2004 the Commission commenced consultations on an EU Fundamental Rights Agency. Human rights have been an unhappy experience in the jurisprudence of the ECJ until comparatively recently and the tardiness of that court to accept access to information as a human right has been widely criticised. The CFI has been more adventurous, although judgments in 2004 and 2005 have displayed great sensitivity to the right of Member States to veto disclosure of their documents sent to the EU institutions.[21] In terms of external relations, Article 11 TEU defines one of the

---

[20] *Gaskin v UK* (1086) 12 EHRR 36; *Guerra v Italy* (1998) 4 BHRC 63, *and McGinley v UK* (1998) 27 EHRR 1. See p 139 above on attempts to obtain a CoE Treaty on FOI.
[21] Council Reg (EC) 1049/2001 EC Reg 4(5): *Sison v Council* Cases T-110/03, 150/03 and 405/03; *IFAW* Case T-168/02; *Scippacercola* Case T-187/03.

objectives of the Common Foreign and Security Policy as 'to develop and consolidate democracy and the rule of law, and respect for human rights and fundamental freedoms.' Article 177(2) EC on development cooperation states: 'Community policy in this area shall contribute to the general objective of developing and consolidating democracy and the rule of law, and to that of respecting human rights and fundamental freedoms.'

To take one example of such provisions, the Treaty relations between the Community and the African Caribbean and Pacific States (fourth amendment, November 1995—a new agreement entered into force on 1 April 2003) sets out the dignity of man provisions with gusto. The consequence of the detailed provisions is that 'the protection of human rights within the territory of the parties to the Lomé Convention becomes a matter of common concern. Human rights clauses are included (1999) in 'over fifty Community agreements.' In its Common Position of 25 May 1998 concerning Article 12 TEU and human rights, the rule of law, democratic principles and good governance in Africa 'freedom of information' is included among the basic democratic principles. Good governance includes 'transparent and accountable management of all of a country's resources for the purpose of equitable and sustainable development.'[22]

What of monitoring and the detail of practice? Alston notes for instance how access to country strategy papers and to national indicative programmes is 'highly restricted' despite their importance in establishing that human rights are taken into account seriously in policy making. Very little existed by way of evaluation or published information. Detailed statements are required to enhance the transparency of the cooperation process and the EU access regulation may help.[23] Moreover means of enforcing these human rights provisions within the Community are non-existent via the European Parliament, European Court of Justice, Court of Auditors and the EU Ombudsman. The European Parliament has passed resolutions in relation to the denial of freedom of speech for journalists in the Cameroon and written questions on, for example, Croatia and elsewhere. Annual reports' published criteria for choosing standards and published procedural rules for terminating agreements with third parties should be available.[24] Alston notes the budgetary constraints on human rights within the Community and the paucity of coverage it gets in public statements (1998) though the position is probably better now.[25]

Furthermore, action by the EU on human rights protection, and the International Criminal Court and bilateral EU/US agreement concerning

---

[22] 98/350 (CFSP) [1998] OJ L158/1.

[23] P Alston, M Bustelo and J Heenan(eds), *The EU and Human Rights* (Oxford, Oxford University Press, 1999) 38.

[24] *Ibid*, at 38–39.

[25] Alston, above n 23. See L Bartels, *Human Rights Conditionality in the EU's International Agreements* (Oxford, Oxford University Press, 2005).

impunity of US officials/military as well as EU requirements maintaining communications data for two years and so on, do not augur auspiciously for human rights' considerations.

There is also a growing European legal space which can be both beneficial and threatening: a German court has ordered non-disclosure of details–by an English newspaper–of former Chancellor Schroeder's allegedly unstable marriage in *England and the rest of the UK*. Breach will attract criminal sanctions. This represents the enforceability of foreign laws that are more restrictive than English law.[26] There is a problem about an absence of a level playing field in terms of access and privacy protection.

Secrecy in International Agreements

In relation to secrecy in international agreements, national security is often used to protect industrial secrets. The International Labour Convention draft on liability, based on another precedent, provides that under Article 15: '.... [the] State of origin shall cooperate in good faith with the other states concerned in providing as much information as can be provided under the circumstances.' Does this avoid the use of commercial reasons being misused to hold back information? Sir Kenneth Keith believes that there is an element of objectivity here but other models seem to acquiesce in the *ipse dixit* of the state seeking to withhold information. [27]

In GATT and related instruments:
'Nothing in this Agreement shall be construed
- (a) to require any contracting party to furnish any information the disclosure of which it considers contrary to its essential security interests; or
- (b) to prevent any contracting party taking any action which it considers necessary for the protection of its essential security interests
   - (i) relating to fissionable materials or the materials from which they are derived
   - (ii) relating to the traffic in arms, ammunition and implements of war [and materials relating to military establishments]
   - (iii) taken in time of war or other emergency in international relations; or
- (c) to prevent any contracting party from taking any action in pursuance of its obligations under the UN Charter for the maintenance of international peace and security.'[28]

---

[26] *The Guardian*, 17 and 20 January 2003.
[27] See Keith in J Beatson and Y Cripps (eds), *Freedom of Expression and Freedom of Information*, above n 12, ch 21.
[28] GATT Art XXI.

On questions of 'essential security interests' the authors of a study on this area suggest 'Any [WTO] panel dealing with such issues will have to defer to the government concerned in that regard.'[29]

Under the 1998 European Environmental Convention a power was included to withhold information on the ground that disclosure would adversely affect international relations, national defence or public security, subject to: 'The grounds for refusal shall be interpreted in a restrictive way, taking into account the public interest served by disclosure and taking into account whether the information requested relates to emissions into the environment' (Article 4(4)). The provisions implemented on access to environmental information in the UK are very broad, far more open than the UKFOIA (see below).

What is the position of information 'received in confidence'? The Chemical Weapons Convention for instance could not have been agreed unless the worldwide chemical industry had been assuaged about protection of confidential information relating to trade secrets. Information is only available to allow testing of compliance and then only to the relevant international body on a restricted basis. There are variables on this theme.

Voluntary Disclosure

One should note the position of the World Bank.[30] Its disclosure policy dates from 1993. A new policy was agreed in August 2001 with effect from January 2002. Requirements to disclose information on Environmental Impact Assessments predate that year. Environment Impact Assessments have to be disclosed in Washington DC and in the country affected prior to the board's consideration of the project. Sometimes disclosure has to take place prior to appraisal of the project. Failure to comply with this policy (known as 'OP 4.01') by Bank staff is a ground for complaint to the Inspection Panel. Loan agreements are treaties which are registered with the UN and are public documents once they are signed. The One World Trust has reported that 'However, conditions attached to lending are not always readily available despite this being a highly contentious issue among civil society groups.'[31] Conversely, transparency and openness are invariably World Bank requirements placed upon borrowing states.

The operations of the WTO, OECD, EU, NAFTA and so on are replete with the provision of guidelines and voluntary schemes. An interesting

---

[29] H Schloemann and S Ohloff (1999) 93 *AJIL* 424, 450. *Cf* Art 296 EC and secrecy of information concerning national security.

[30] On NGOs and FOI, see www.freedominfo.org/index.htm. I am grateful to Andrew Ecclestone for bringing my notice to this web site.

[31] H Kovach, C Neligan and S Burall, *Power without Accountability?*, above n 1, at 13.

example of a voluntary arrangement comes with the UN's Global Compact.[32] This is a voluntary arrangement whereby companies agree to reveal in reports their commitment to social responsibility. There were nine principles in existence and a tenth, on corruption, was added in June 2004. The tenth principle, derived from the UN Convention against Corruption[33] states: 'Businesses should work against corruption in all its forms, including extortion and bribery.' The other principles cover human rights, child labour, core labour standards on freedom of association, discrimination and environmental protection. Some see this as compromising of the UN; companies gain powerful legitimacy without actually changing practices significantly. Furthermore, it allows companies to influence the UN in regulatory activities and the UN traditionally is not seen as an advocate of pro market economics as are the WTO and World Bank. There are complaints about the absence of any enforcement mechanisms and the failure of the Compact to address injustices through inequality brought about by market liberalisation.

Others have written extensively about these matters and the negotiated agreements concerning access to health, social and environmental information.[34] The prevailing mood of security and secrecy stemming from the US is dramatically juxtaposed with the US government's criticism of unnecessary WTO secrecy less than a decade ago.[35] The Earth Summit in Johannesburg (Autumn 2002) saw the US attempt to block information provision to NGOs representing the impoverished in order to prevent litigation against multinationals and to stifle effective peaceful protest. Exxon has sought the assistance of the Department of Justice (US) (successfully) to argue that an action brought in federal US courts by the ILO was out of jurisdiction as an interference with the US government's foreign affairs responsibilities. It concerned extraction of gas in Sumatra against the protests of local residents who had not been consulted and who were rough handled by police hired by Exxon when they demonstrated. The OECD Convention against corruption by large companies (one would think North American and European but this was a worldwide survey) in developing countries was reported to have met with little success in meeting its objectives.[36] The 2002 UK budget contained provisions to remove tax breaks for

---

[32] McIntosh, Thomas, Leipziger and Coleman, *Living Corporate Citizenship* (FT Prentice Hall, 2003) ch 6.

[33] The United Nations Convention against Corruption entered into force on 14 December 2005. The Convention, adopted by the United Nations General Assembly in October 2003, has been signed by 140 countries and ratified by 38. It is the 'first legally binding global instrument designed to help Member States fight corruption in both the public and private sectors': http://www.unglobalcompact.org/NewsAndEvents/news_archives/2005_12_14.html.

[34] N Douglas Lewis, *Law and Governance* (Cavendish Publishing, 2001).

[35] *Financial Times*, 15 July 1998.

[36] *Financial Times*, 15 May 2002. For the UN Convention against Corruption, above n 33.

payment of foreign bribes by UK companies (s 68 Finance Act 2002). The Anti-Terrorism and Security Act 2001, the Proceeds of Crime Act 2002, both in the UK, and the US Patriot Act 2001 make companies legally responsible for detecting fraud or bribery by their clients or employees and companies may be prosecuted for acts of bribery committed abroad.

The International Federation of Accountants (IFA) has recommended a requirement of independent boards to oversee the accountancy profession but the IFA stopped short of recommending substantive changes to many practices: eg, restrictions of services rendered by accountants. Oversight of the accounting profession has now become a matter of primary interest for the European Commission. Member States of the EU are likely to be placed under increasing pressure to have formal regulatory mechanisms in place to oversee accounting standards and auditing of firms and to move away from professional self regulation. In the US, a US Public Company Accounting Oversight Board was established following the Enron and other scandals.

The US Sarbanes-Oxley Act 2002 has provided a variety of reforms after such scandals and Patricia Hewitt's announcement as Secretary of State for Trade that substantial reforms were not required for accountants in the UK was surprising. There would for instance be no mandatory rotation of accountants' firms every five years. There is likely to be an Accountancy Regulator. There will be use of best practice codes and not legislation. But legislation may cover disclosure of payments by companies made to auditing firms for audit and non-audit work. The reforms came in the Companies (Audit, Investigations and Community Enterprise) Act 2004 under which the Secretary of State has broader powers of delegation to the Financial Reporting Council. This is a private independent body funded by the accountancy profession and firms and government. At the global level, the International Standards Accounting Board in Europe and the Financial Accounting Standards Board in the US are jointly attempting to produce a single set of high quality, comprehensible and enforceable accounting standards that can be adopted worldwide.

Where Are We Getting To?

Should there be more reliance on national laws?–after all, many of the problems emerge from the global activities of US, UK and other European TN companies.

Corporate Management, Transparency and Accounting

Standard and Poor found that US companies lagged behind international counterparts in the amount of information they published in annual reports although overall, corporate disclosure in the US ranks highly. More disclosure, the report argued, assisted stock market evaluation.[37] A study of FTSE 250 companies by the Institute of Business Ethics found that companies that adopted ethical codes of conduct performed more highly on three out of four long-term financial measures.[38] Most UK companies argue they are under too heavy a burden in being forced to disclose information: health and safety, environmental and data protection for instance. Of 400 US companies studied, only seven earned more than six out of ten for disclosure in annual reports although many of those would have to file detailed accounting, financial and salary information in 'regulatory filings.' [www.standardandpoors.com]. When these are taken into account, the US companies rank on a par with UK companies–the highest ranking in the world. Reforms are in place in terms of accounting and regulation in the US (see above). President Bush has said that he will not rest until every 'corporate miscreant was in hand-cuffs.'[39] OECD Principles on Good Corporate Governance were promulgated in 1999.

The Higgs proposals on corporate governance in the UK are relevant–but Higgs noted that the Cadbury 'reforms' of 1992 had still not been implemented by 'many companies.' These proposals included up to half of the board being comprised of independent non-executive directors (not including the chairman), a chief executive should not normally become its chairman and an independent director should be appointed to champion the case of shareholders. The position is to be examined after two years by the Financial Reporting Council which oversees the company code, and which will assess the impact of the reforms. These measures fall far short of the steps required to democratise global players. Nevertheless, business has hit back. The Institute of Chartered Accountants said the proposals were far too 'prescriptive' and 'rule-based' (basic principles in the code increased by one but rules increased from over forty to over eighty) and that reforms should be deferred.[40] Another common complaint was that the proposals when implemented would lead to too much board division. The CBI and Institute of Directors were predictably hostile. Two highly influential critics–the President of the CBI and the Chairman of the Institute of Chartered Accountants–were included in the Financial Reporting Committee reviewing Higgs' proposals. By July 2003, it was reported that the final draft of the Higgs Combined Code on Corporate Governance had become far more 'flexible' and 'less prescriptive.'[41] The critics had been successful. Conversely, fifteen major financial institutions had supported Higgs' proposals.

---

[37] *Financial Times*, 16 October 2002.

[38] *Financial Times*, 3 and 13 April 2003.

[39] *Financial Times*, 14 April 2003. The irony of this statement in relation to members of his own administration has not been lost!

[40] *Financial Times*, 2 April 2003. The Code applies to UK companies with full listing on the London Stock Exchange for reporting years commencing on or after 1 November 2003.

[41] *Financial Times*, 19/20 July 2003. Companies were concerned about the 'undermining' of the role of company chairmen.

On voluntary disclosure of social and environmental information by UK companies, fifty of the country's largest companies reported for the first time in 2001–02 on environmental or social performance–there were sixteen new reporters in 2000–2001.[42] One hundred and three of the FTSE 250 had substantial environmental and/or social information reports most of them separate from annual reports; eighty-seven produced no more than short notes and the rest provided limited data with no detail. Investment trusts were not included. The movement comes as there is growing pressure for legislative reform in this area (see Århus below, p 157). It is also interesting to observe that only 36 of the 250 had their environmental and social reports independently verified.[43] In the UK, a report commissioned by the Institute of Directors on disclosure practices by its member companies was critical of such practices drawing the wrath of the IoD's head of policy. 'We paid for this and it's only right we should get something into the public domain that we are happy with!'[44] The report by the Institute for Public Policy Research felt there were limits to *voluntary* arrangements for disclosure. The Institute of Directors complained of the regulatory burden of existing legislative duties.

A voluntary scheme on transparency and access adopted by a British company and which relates to all information held by it (subject to exemptions) and on which the author has detailed experience is that which has been produced by NIREX UK Ltd. NIREX is the UK nuclear industry's adviser on nuclear waste disposal. Since 2000, NIREX has operated a voluntary code on access which includes an Independent Transparency Panel.[45] The Panel deals with complaints from those who are denied access to information requested under the code. The overwhelming majority of requests are accepted. Since the autumn of 2002, NIREX has taken steps to align its voluntary code with the UK FOIA 2000. It is remarkable testimony to what can be done if a genuine will for access is present. From 1 January 2005, Nirex became a body within the terms of the UK FOIA and Environmental Information Regulations.

Legal reforms are likely to come from the European Commission in relation to the provision of information to investors to encourage EU transnational investment. European traditions are seen as bureaucratic; the Anglo American tradition is seen as more directed to price sensitive information. In the EU, a Directive on corporate reporting (EC Directive 51/2003) will

---

[42] info@salterbaxter.com and info@ccontext.co.uk.

[43] *Financial Times*, 29 July 2003. Christian Aid claims that businesses too often invoke corporate social responsibility as a mask to hide their lobbying for anti human rights and anti-environmental protection laws: *Behind the Real Face of Corporate Social Responsibility* (Christian Aid, January 2004).

[44] *Financial Times*, 4 December 2002.

[45] NIREX *Transparency Policy* August 2002, (2nd edn, Didcot, UK). Article 19 found that in a study of five corporations, Nirex was the most transparent in its policies and practices: *Transparency and Corporate Accountability* (2002) a preliminary study.

impose a duty on listed companies to produce quarterly financial reports in line with common European practice in some Member States (see SI 1011/2005 and SI 2947/2004).

An interesting development has been the UK Directors' Remuneration Reporting Regulations– SI 1986/2002 (and see SI 2417/2 005 The Companies (Disclosure of Auditor Remuneration) Regulations 2005) which build on the requirements in the Companies Act 1985, the Stock Exchange Listing Rules and the Combined Code on Corporate Governance in seeking to achieve greater transparency in terms of salary deals including share options and so on. The regulations are prospective and concern the future remuneration policy of the company towards its directors. A remuneration committee is independent of the managing board. Shareholders may vote on the report at the AGM but this vote is only 'advisory'. It has no effect on directors' remuneration should the vote not approve the report. A report by Deloitte for the DTI in November 2004 stated that 'most FTSE 350 companies were complying with the regulations.'[46]

The One World Trust has published a report of the transparency and accountability of inter-governmental organisations, transnational corporations and international non-government organisations.[47] The report found NGOs to be the worst in provision of information practices and that access to agendas, draft reports for meetings and minutes of meetings–let alone public access to non-commercial confidential items–to be uniformly poor. The authors list the scoring levels of the above bodies that were studied and set out good practice for such bodies in accountability. These include:

Governance: member control–good practice

— Are all members represented on the governing body?
— Do all members have the power to add items to the agenda of governing body meetings?
— Do all members have the power to nominate, elect and dismiss individuals on the executive?
— Are there mechanisms in place to ensure equitable representation of all members on the executive (where executive is composed of member delegates)?
— Are amendments to the governing articles subject to at least a two-thirds majority?
— Does a majority of members (75 per cent or more) hold a majority of the votes?

---

[46] Deloitte, *Report on the Impact of the Directors' Remuneration Report Regs* (2004) para 2.1.
[47] See above, n 31.

Access to online information–good practice

— Is a description of the objectives, targets and activities available?
— Are evaluations of main activities available?
— Can the public identify all key members of the organisation–NB the
  report in the *Observer* (20 April 2003) that 2000 company directors
  had had their addresses withdrawn from the Companies Register
  because of personal security fears?
— Is there a public record of the number of votes each member holds?
— Is a meaningful description of key decision-making bodies available to
  the public?
— Are individuals on the executive body publicly identified?
— Are the agendas, draft papers and minutes of both governing and executive body meetings available to the public?
— Is there an information disclosure policy available which clearly identifies the types of documents the organisation does and does not dis-
  close, stating reasons for non-disclosure?
— Are annual reports publicly available and do they contain externally
  audited financial information?
— Is the above information available in the languages of the organisations' stakeholders?

*South African Promotion of Access to Information Act (PAIA) and its
Coverage of the Private Sector*

Before examining this Act in further detail, I should refer to the decision of
the South African High Court ordering the release by TNC pharmaceutical
companies in South Africa of information about their pricing policies. The
companies refused to reveal how much they charged retailers in South Africa
(who were blamed for huge mark-ups) and how those prices compared with
US/EU levels. This followed an action by 39 companies seeking to have a law
set aside allowing parallel importation of generic substitutes. International
patent law does provide a let-out for emergencies. In February 2003, WTO
negotiations on trade and related intellectual property rights (TRIPS) covering drug patents and price reductions for poor countries collapsed (to be
resumed in September 2003). The US companies were reluctant to release
their veto on lucrative patents. It was not overlooked that they had also contributed US$60 million to the Republican Party in the 2002 mid-term elec-
tions which saw the Republicans gain control of the Senate. The companies
lobbied the US government to restrict any concessions as tightly as possible.
The interlocutors were key policy advisers to President Bush. These TNCs
had a fear that any concessions would be exploited by Indian and Brazilian
cheap generic drug specialists to the TNCs maximum cost. In some circumstances there may be permission for compulsory licensing (CL) of cheaper

generic substitutes.[48] In South Korea, there has been widespread lobbying for cheaper drugs for leukaemia sufferers and CL. The US government put extreme pressure on the South Korean government to prevent this and the US companies wanted any decisions to be made by judicial bodies in South Korea where judges, it is claimed, are easily biddable.

The South African PAIA provides an individual right of access to information in private hands, where that information relates to the exercise or protection of rights. Secondly, the Act permits the state to exercise the right of access to information in private hands. 'The Act starts from the assumption any information in private hands with a demonstrable and sufficient connection to the exercise or protection of any rights legitimately belongs to the public domain. It does this by providing a right to request such information and placing a burden on a private entity to justify why the requested information should not be disclosed. It allows public bodies to exercise this right, effectively granting a wide and general power to the state to seek information from the private sector to protect rights or the public interest.'[49]

This fulfils a right under the South African Constitution in s 32(1)(b) which provides for a right to state and privately held information. According to s 9 (e) PAIA, the Act is intended to promote 'transparency, accountability and effective governance of all public and private bodies.' Section 9(c) states that the purpose of allowing public bodies power of exercising the right to such information is 'to give effect to the constitutional obligations of the state of promoting a human rights culture and social justice.' The right to private sector information is described as on a 'need to know' basis to protect rights belonging to individuals including human rights. It does not require the same degree of access to private bodies as to public bodies–it does not equiparate the state and private sector to that extent. It recognises a right where there is toxic pollution, medical danger discoverable from medical records held by a private medical practitioner and information about hazards caused by consumer products.[50] It does not involve public sector transparency in private bodies. Regard must be had to foreign and international jurisprudence in interpreting the South African Bill of Rights which AIA gives specific expression to.

Århus and implementation of Access to Environmental Information Regulations (UK)

Århus covers not only access to information, but participation in decision-making and access to justice. One should note the extended definition of

---

[48] See, 'Big Pharma's Tiny Gesture' *The Observer Supplement*, 21 March 2004.
[49] I Currie and J Klaaren, *The Promotion of Access to Information Act Commentary* (Siber Ink Benchmark Books, 2002) 19 *et seq.*
[50] Cass Sunstein (1999) 147 *U of Penn L Rev* 613 on obligations on private bodies in the US; A Roberts (2001) 51 *Uni of Toronto L J* 243.

public authority, for example, privatised water authorities and energy companies and general alignment with the UK FOIA, ie, a public interest override is present but also a ministerial veto, as in the UK FOIA. The consultation exercise and draft regulations in Autumn 2002 did not include the participation rights. The 'Commission considers that the exhortatory reference at the end of Article 7 to public participation in the preparation of policies is "soft law" and that it does not require any Community legislation.'[51] These will be dealt with under other implementing measures and in the UK the government believed existing provisions fulfilled all necessary requirements.[52] Provisions will have to address trans-boundary Environmental Impact Assessments and participation. The Directive was implemented into UK law by SI 2004/3391 and Scottish equivalent.

US FOIA and Recent Case Law has not all been Anti Access

Vice President Cheney's Energy Task Force was instructed by court order to hand over 7500 documents under a Federal Advisory Committee Act request. It is not clear whether this has now been overtaken by legislative changes.[53] The documents indicated the degree of lobbying by energy companies when the President was drawing up the 2001 energy plan. Many of these were donors to the Republican Party.[54] But a federal court threw out an attempt to obtain the identities of businessmen consulted by the White House in the formulation of energy policy. The case was brought by a Congressional investigatory body.[55] Elsewhere, the hitherto secret US Foreign Intelligence Surveillance Court has published a decision restricting use of intelligence information by prosecutors in a manner which undermined Fourth Amendment rights.[56] The 2005 Executive Order of President Bush was referred to above.

Export Credit Guarantees (ECGs)

Much of the UK ECG Department's work would be covered by commercial confidentiality. Throughout the world ECGs have been criticised for insensitivity to environmental and human rights considerations. The German

---

[51] COM (2000) 839, final (6.1.01).

[52] See EU Directive 2003/4/EC OJ L41/26 (14.2.03).

[53] The Supreme Court has subsequently ruled that the President and Vice President may successfully claim executive privilege to protect documents requested in litigation more easily than was previously thought to be the case: *Nixon v US* 418 US 683 (1974) distinguished as that case concerned a *criminal* and not a *civil* matter–*Cheney v US District Court for the District of Columbia* No 03-475 (24 June 24 2004). The Federal Advisory Committee Act has been narrowed considerably by litigation arising from these events: *In re Cheney et al* 406 F.3d 723 (2005).

[54] *Natural Resources Defense Council v Department of Energy* 191 F.Supp. 2d 41 (2002).

[55] *The Guardian*, 11 December 2002.

[56] L Strickland (2003)20 *Government Information Quarterly* 1.

analogous agency in particular has been singled out for critical attention which is buttressed by that country's privacy laws. In the UK, new guidelines speak of the ECGD supporting 'sustainable development' and human rights considerations. In 2001, the OECD export credit group produced a voluntary plan for environmental disclosures but Germany's practice was seen as the least transparent.[57]

A Level Playing Field

Reference has been made to the example of German privacy laws and stringent confidentiality laws (protecting a bank client's information) and their enforcement in other Member States. How do we enhance national approaches to FOIA? Germany has only recently introduced FOI laws at the federal level–Germany, with the UK, was one of the last of the developed democracies to introduce such laws. In some of what are effectively single party states it has been stated that FOI laws are in reality little more than press censorship laws. On the other hand some very good state practices may be seen. In France, a government decree has established the National Commission for National Debate which will examine projects regarding the construction of railways, motorways, nuclear power stations and sports infrastructures. The decree provides for the application for proposals by proponents, access to information about them and public debate where projects are designed by government, local authorities, public institutions or private persons listed in categories in Article 1.[58] Good examples exist in particular nations, but our target here is some form of consistency at the global level to embrace bodies operating globally.

Interest Group Representation

Leading on from this, a real problem is an absence of adequate enforcement mechanisms. Denying groups access to courts has become an enduring strategy. The South African litigation referred to above emerged after an interest group was allowed to intervene and which represented AIDS victims seeking affordable alternative medication and treatment to that provided by the TNC pharmaceuticals. In a domestic setting, *R (Kathro) v Rhonnda Cynon Taff CBC*[59] concerned the inability of third parties to challenge an award of a Public Private Partnership contract through the negotiated procedure under EC procurement rules. The contract was a *res inter alios acta* from the third parties' perspective, the court held.

---

[57] *Financial Times*, 31 May 2002.
[58] Decree 2002-1275 (22 October 2002): [2002] JORF 17545.
[59] [2002] Env LR 15.

CONCLUSION

Access laws and practices address the problem engendered by organisational opacity where that opacity and its assistance to structural power operate against the interests of groups and individuals who are weak through lack of resources, including information. The imbalance inevitably threatens self dignity, civil liberties and human rights. Openness and transparency have become totemic phrases in contemporary government—although their appearance in Giscard d'Estaing's draft EU constitution and the draft approved by the European Council in Dublin largely reformulate existing provisions in earlier treaties and pay lip service to 'participatory democracy and Union/civil society dialogues which are well under way.' They have, however, been elevated to *constitutional* measures. Nonetheless, this was not a topic that was suitable for the attention of one of the working groups reporting to Giscard d'Estaing. Indeed, he subsequently refused access to working papers of the *Praesidium*, which was responsible for vital aspects of drafting, when requested by a public interest group. The Commission has addressed some of these points in relation to better law-making and policy making in its follow-up to the White Paper on European Governance.[60]

The effect of September 11 has been to rekindle forces of secrecy, certainly in the US. This could have a blighting effect on tentative steps towards global transparency. I view the South African legislation with particular interest, doubting very much whether a similar development could take place in Zimbabwe or many other African, Asian or far eastern countries where TNCs predominantly operate. What chances are there of getting effective access and open meetings laws established as norms of international behaviour? The US will not accept data protection laws such as those required by the EC Directive because they are too unpopular with corporate America; they make do with self-regulatory devices—'safe harbours.' Even in our Data Protection Act we find opportunities to defeat openness and freedom of speech—the use of the Act and Directive to block access because of a named person on publicly held documents. This has been argued as a justified reason to deny public access by the Commission— I believe without proper legal foundation.[61] There is also the spectre of putting information technology law and copyright to use to attempt to prevent access.

Access to information that shapes our lives has become a human right; I have no doubt of that. It is no longer a matter of purely national concern. But how do we proceed at the international level? Is there scope for using

---

[60] COM 709, final (11.12.02).
[61] See European Data Protection Supervisor *Public Access to Documents and Data Protection* Background Paper Series No1 (July 2005).

South Africa's access statute as a model on which to attempt international agreement for national implementation? How realistic is this? Would it be too ethnocentric? The *raison d'etre* for access laws is widely accepted in the West and in the Antipodes. The qualification to that has been discussed. But what of vastly different cultures which are frequently driven by fundamental religious doctrine and even those that are not? What scope is there for international agreements on participation rights and access to courts or judicial or administrative remedies? Should any universal standards be in legal instruments or soft law requirements and conventions? A part of the problem identified in this paper concerns the non-binding nature of informational requirements in so many areas examined. How do we guarantee adequate enforcement mechanisms? Again, is it best to think primarily of national levels of enforcement? What areas, if any, will remain the province of international legal regimes?

In short, how do we ensure the general interest of the openness of the world community and not simply that of individual states, or as in the case of the European Union, confederations of states? This world community, or commonwealth, is heavily shaped by TNCs, NGOs and IGOs. It seemed in the recent past that growing trends to supranationalism and internationalism were encouraging greater access to information held by governments as they became subject to greater demands from supranational and international bodies to inform the publics they served on the basis of how they exercised shared power. In the process, claims to secrecy and immunity based on national sovereignty seemed increasingly to be compromised. But the last three years have brought home how supranational forces may well be influential in impeding greater access and openness: on the grounds of national security, trade secrets and commercial confidentiality. While no one can rightfully demand that greater openness should form the basis of a state-sponsored suicide pact, it should also be remembered that humanity has advanced under conditions of openness and knowledge, power-sharing and human empathy. It does not thrive in conditions of secrecy, ignorance, power distortion and abuse. FOI laws have their role to play in combating power distortions, whether brought about by the existence and operation of governments or by private corporations and organisations.

8

Ecological Modernisation and Environmental Regulation: Corporate Compliance and Accountability

JUANITA ELIAS AND ROBERT LEE

INTRODUCTION

IN THIS CHAPTER we wish to explore the changing face of environmental regulation of large corporations in the light of the influence of ecological modernisation approaches. Following a brief reflection on the term 'corporate governance' in terms of the internal and external regulation of companies, we seek to demonstrate that ecological modernisation thinking has influenced regulation away from command and control methods of regulation and towards incentives to find technological solutions to pollution. This involves not de-regulation, but re-regulation, and although it is signalled as a return to the market in an effort to support liberalisation, it involves significant interventions by government to produce the necessary climate for investment in technological change. However, these are of questionable efficiency and involve a decline in the direct control of the nation state upon business operating within its territory. We examine some consequences of this latter phenomenon not least in terms of the growing influence and declining accountability of multinational corporations (MNCs) as the nation state abandons policies of strong external control in favour of ill-devised incentives to environmental protection.

CORPORATE GOVERNANCE AND EXTERNAL REGULATION

In his assertion of the delivery of shareholder value as lying at the heart of corporate social responsibility, Milton Friedman[1] describes corporate governance as arising out of the responsibility,

[1] M Friedman, 'The Social Responsibility of Business is to Increase Profits' *New York Times Magazine*_13 September 1970, 32–36.

to conduct the business in accordance with (shareholder) desires, which generally will be to make as much money as possible while conforming to the basic rules of society, both those embodied in law and those embodied in ethical custom.

Later writers then argue the stakeholder theory case for engagement with a wider range of actors, though sometimes from the same instrumental standpoint of profit maximisation.[2] The importance for this chapter, however, is that even in this carefully limited view of corporate governance there is a recognition that regard has to be paid to the external as well as the internal governance of the company. In this chapter we wish to look at environmental regulation. This is an area traditionally within the external governance arena, but which, we shall argue, is increasingly a matter left to choices made by the company as an internal matter of corporate policy.

This confusion in the use of corporate governance to reflect both internal procedures and external regulation reflects a wider definitional uncertainty. Corporate governance has been criticised from the legal standpoint as 'ill-defined and consequently blurred at the edges' by Maw in the introduction to his book and he refers to a tension between two differences in the use of the term. One reflects a 'too narrow' shareholder value view, while the other demonstrates a wider concern with stakeholder groups generally and the 'reputation and standing of our nation and its economy.'[3]

This tension between narrower (and more internal) issues and wider questions of external accountability finds its way into descriptions of the enterprise at international institutional levels. Thus for the OECD (Organisation for Economic and Cooperative Developpment), corporate governance is about,

the distribution of rights and responsibilities among different participants in the corporation ... and spells out the rules and procedures for making decisions on corporate affairs.[4]

This contrasts with the World Bank view of corporate governance as 'promoting corporate fairness, transparency and accountability.'[5] The shareholder/stakeholder discourse with its differing emphases has been depicted

---

[2] ER Freeman, *Strategic Management: A Stakeholder Approach* (Boston, Pitman, 1984) and see T Donaldson and LE Preston, 'The Stakeholder Theory of the Corporation: Concepts, Evidence and Implications' (1995) 20 *Academy of Management Review* 65 for a categorisation of stakeholder theory into descriptive, instrumental and normative approaches.

[3] N Maw, P Lane, M Craig-Cooper, A Alsbury, *Maw on Corporate Governance* (Aldershot, Dartmouth, 1994) 1.

[4] Organisation for Economic Co-operation and Development, Ad Hoc Task Force on Corporate Governance, *OECD Principles of Corporate Governance* (OECD, Paris, 1999).

[5] Reported by J Plender 'Speak up for dialogue: The World Bank and the OECD Recognise that the Issue of Corporate Governance in Developing Countries needs more Consensus-building' *Financial Times*, 21 June 1999, 22.

as the juxtaposition between a utilitarian view on one hand, and a deontological approach on the other.[6] This seems problematic in that a utilitarian approach according to Mill would deliver 'the greatest happiness for the greatest number'[7] and not merely maximisation of gain for a few at the expense of others. Equally an adequate understanding of Kantian principles would deny any necessary conflict between acting in self-interest and acting according to moral principle. This is because, for Kant,[8] to act against moral principles is to act against one's self-interest, or to act in ignorance of where self-interest lies.

All of this is of direct relevance for this chapter on the environmental regulation of companies in which we consider ecological modernisation theory. Described more fully below, this suggests that acting in the interest of the environment may be within the self-interest of companies. That being so, the more traditional forms of external regulation of companies may be relaxed to give way to incentives and other mechanisms that encourage companies to act in enlightened self-interest. Thus the definitional problems of corporate governance can be informed by addressing problems of environmental regulation under the influence of ecological modernisation. However, the chapter goes on to address questions of corporate accountability under a regulatory framework influenced by the ecological modernisation model.

ENVIRONMENTAL REGULATION THROUGH
THE LENS OF ECOLOGICAL MODERNISATION

The Ecological Modernisation Idea

At the heart of the literature on ecological modernisation is the idea[9] that though industrial enterprise has undoubtedly given rise to environmental degradation, this is not an inevitable pattern, and moreover modernisation may give rise to technological change delivering not merely economic but environmental benefits. The literature is very much concerned with questions of environmental gains though similar claims are made increasingly, without the ecological modernisation label, in other areas such as the social

---

[6] BK Burton and CP Dunn, 'Stakeholder Interests and Community Groups: A New View' *International Association for Business and Society Annual Meetings* (1996).

[7] JS Mill, *Utilitarianism* 1863 (Oxford, Oxford University Press, 1998).

[8] I Kant, *Foundations of the Metaphysics of Morals* 1785 (Cambridge, Cambridge University Press, 1991).

[9] M Janicke, *State Failure: The Impotence of Politics in Industrial Society* (Cambridge, Polity, 1990) has described ecological modernisation as a strategy or a system of beliefs. For arguments that ecological modernisation remains indistinct in terms of wider theoretical development see F Buttel, 'Ecological Modernisation as Social Theory' (2000) 31 *Geoforum* 57.

sustainability agenda[10]. The origins of the ecological modernisation concept, alongside other notions strongly influential in environmental regulation, lie in environmental debates in Germany[11] and in particular responses to Green Party presentations of economic development and environmental protection in inevitable opposition.[12] Ecological modernisation in resolving this supposed conflict between growth and sustainability posits a win/win situation or a double dividend of economic growth and environmental protection.[13]

To some degree there is an obvious case of this kind to be made. In its nature, industrial waste represents cost. An essential premise of Dalton's atomic theory of matter is the law of conservation of mass, ie, the notion that total mass of the products will always be equal to the total mass of the reactants in any chemical reaction. Thus, the total mass of materials utilised by industry remains the same whatever the process. Those materials emitted or discarded in a manufacturing process constitute a loss, and only the failure to internalise the true costs of using the environment as a repository of such waste has disguised the true extent of this loss. Elimination of this loss, particularly in terms of minimising or preventing the waste arising, ought to represent a gain over earlier less efficient forms of industrialisation.[14] Empirical studies have sought to make this case in relation to the adoption of clean technologies. These include studies of the strategic management of industrial processes[15] (such as the use of flue gas scrubbers or heat recovery) and of broader approaches to redesigning processes (such as the elimination of volatile organic compounds in the wood and furniture industry).[16] Approaches based on strategic environmental management may hit problems of diminishing returns, but innovative structural change may eliminate environmental impacts while producing lower consumption of materials or improved productivity.

Ecological modernists have unashamedly sought to move environment up the agenda. The notion of environmental protection as an unwelcome obligation imposing unwarranted costs on industry stems, in their view, from

[10] Look, eg at the language of 'win-win' that has characterised writings and policy statements concerning the 'business-case' for Corporate Social Responsibility (CSR).

[11] MS Andersen and I Massa, 'Ecological Modernisation–Origins, Dilemmas and Future Directions' (2000) 2 *Journal of Environmental Policy and Planning* 337.

[12] A Mol and G Spaargaren, 'Ecological Modernisation Theory in Debate' (2000) 9 *Environmental Politics* 1.

[13] This is one of the storylines of ecological modernisation developed by M Hajer, *The Politics of Environmental Discourse: Ecological Modernisation and the Policy Process* (Oxford, Oxford University Press, 1995).

[14] *Ibid*, the second storyline.

[15] H Nishimura, *How to Conquer Air Pollution: A Japanese Experience* (Amsterdam, Elsevier, 1989).

[16] Andersen and Massa, 'Ecological Modernisation–Origins, Dilemmas and Future Directions', above n 11.

its low priority on the corporate agenda, and its depiction of something that addresses end-of-pipe problems. In contrast, anticipatory and preventative approaches integrated into the heart of the enterprise may deliver unforeseen benefits. Similarly at a policy level, it is said to be necessary to move away from a model in which regulation is seen as placing yet another additional burden on industry to an iterative process in which industry can advocate efficient solutions. This is seen as a move away from oppositional environmental politics, which may have produced bargains about permitted levels of environmental impacts but rarely generated innovative and efficient solutions to the problems of environmental pollution.[17]

Ecological Modernisation and Regulation

This places great faith in the modernisation agenda and in a continual technological progress that outstrips the environmental problems thrown up by industrialisation. Nonetheless, the discourse of ecological modernisation has proved persuasive and it is possible to track its influence within the European policy framework. To take the example of the UK, the development of 'integrated pollution control' (IPC)[18] strongly reflected ideas of ecological modernisation. Integration, in the form of embedding environmental concerns at the heart of all areas of government policy, is a recurrent theme in the literature. In the case of IPC, integration has a more limited meaning of tying in potential outputs into the environmental media under a single permit. In its later EU model, this is extended both in terms of the environmental impacts (such as noise) covered, and an examination of inputs (such as energy) governed by the permit. However, a major aim of the legislation is to prevent, minimise or render harmless emissions by the selection of the 'best practicable environmental option' (BPEO) and the adoption of 'best available techniques' (BAT) to the permitted process.

There are a number of ecological modernisation resonances here. Strategic environmental management techniques are required but only at the point at which the process offering the best practicable environmental option is adopted. Also, there is the apparent freedom of the operator to opt for technological innovation and defend the choice in terms of the success of these techniques in preventing environmental impacts. In practice it must be said that the workings of IPC look somewhat different to this model. As a regulatory process it is much more akin to command and control than to

---

[17] J Hertin and F Berkout, *Ecological Modernisation and EU Environmental Policy Integration* (SPRU Paper 72, Sussex, 2001).

[18] Under the Environmental Protection Act 1990, and see now the Pollution Prevention and Control Act 1998 transposing the requirements of the EU Directive on Industrial Pollution Prevention and Control (IPPC) REF.

voluntarism. Indeed the regulatory controls are said to be important in 'playing a role in persuading regulated companies to consider clean technologies.'[19] In fact, through guidance notes, the Environment Agency has often been prescriptive in terms of what it considers BAT, leaving little room for innovation.[20] Moreover, the attempts at integration under IPC have been thwarted initially by the lack of an integrated Agency,[21] and latterly by the difficulties in combining regulators in a single Agency.[22]

Since 1990 however a second generation of environmental controls has offered much greater endorsement of ecological modernisation by resort to so-called 'market mechanisms.' In fact these constitute Pigouvian type interventions in the market to address problems of the social costs attaching to pollution. Examples include taxes (such as landfill and aggregate taxes[23] and climate change levy)[24] and tradable instruments (such as 'producer responsibility notes'–PRNs–attaching to packaging waste[25] and emissions trading).[26] Notwithstanding the supposed 'win-win' formula, proponents of ecological modernisation strongly advocate this type of approach to provide a stimulus for change.[27] The regulatory task is seen here as removing barriers to take-up of clean technology and the promotion of innovation by

---

[19] J Murphy and A Gouldson, 'Environmental Policy and Industrial Innovation: Integrating Environment and Economy Through Ecological Modernisation' (2000) 31 *Geoforum* 33.

[20] Indeed Janicke suggests that both state and industry are complicit in the search for convenient standardised solutions to environmental problems–one event of Janicke's state failure. See now the development of European Guidance in the form of BREF notes: B Lange, 'From Boundary Drawing to Transitions: The Creation of Normativity under the EU Directive on Integrated Pollution Prevention and Control' (2002) 8 (2) *European L J* 246.

[21] Although the Environmental Protection Act 1990 introduced the concept of integrated pollution control the creation of an integrated Environment Agency took place in 1996, following the passage of the Environment Act 1995.

[22] The Select Committee on Environment, Transport and Regional Affairs, Sixth Report, *The Environment Agency* (HC 34-1, May 2000).

[23] The Landfill Tax was introduced by the Finance Act 1996, and the Landfill Tax Regulations 1996 (SI 1996/1527). As its name suggests the measure taxes the tonnage of waste going to landfill at a rate which rises year on year in an attempt to incentivise waste minimisation or alternative routes for waste such as re-use, recycling or recovery. In contrast, aggregate tax introduced by the Finance Act 2001 charges a tax on every ton of sand gravel or crushed rock extracted in the UK or in territorial waters.

[24] The levy is chargeable on the industrial and commercial supply of taxable supply of energy for lighting, heating and power by industrial, commercial, agricultural and public body consumers: See Part II Finance Act 2001.

[25] The Producer Responsibility Obligations (Packaging Waste) Regulations 1997 (1997/648) implement the EU Directive on Packaging and Packaging Waste (94/62/EEC) and intended broadly to double UK recycling and recovery rates in relation to packaging. Evidence of compliance ia largely through a system of proformas issued by accredited reprocessors known as Producer Responsibility Notes or PRNs. These are tradeable instruments so that businesses failing to meet targets can purchase PRNs from those exceeding targets.

[26] This is an experimental voluntary system of trading in emissions capacity–for a more detailed account of its operation see: S Sorrell, *Back to the Drawing Board? Implications of the EU Emissions Trading Directive for UK Climate Policy* (SPRU, Sussex, 2003).

[27] D Wallace, *Environmental Policy and Industrial Innovation: Strategies in Europe, the USA and Japan* (London, Earthscan, 1995).

business in line with its own programme of investment. To take one illustration, emissions trading began as a voluntary scheme, kick started by £215m of government money. Participant firms work within an agreed target for reduction in greenhouse gases. Those making the investment in greenhouse gas reduction can sell spare capacity to those delaying their investment and needing to buy in the short term. Clearly those making significant process changes delivering major emissions reductions as against targets set by historic working may realise a quick return on investment in this change. Indeed, given the public subsidy involved in the system, the potential for windfall profit has already been criticised.[28]

We wish to draw attention to three aspects of this new generation of regulatory controls. The first is that although the approaches are described in the language of de-regulation and the phrase 'market mechanisms' is often employed, in fact they involve re-regulation in the form of different sorts of interventions in the market. Quite how much of a double dividend a tax can deliver must depend both on the tax avoidance incentive to invest in, for example, energy reduction, and the size of the environmental benefits delivered on the back of the taxation levied.[29] So the policy adjustments are problematic, and they represent a new mode of regulation in which it is left to industry to respond to the intervention, rather than requiring the industry to comply with specific permit conditions. This re-regulation then eases state direction of business, and in Beck's description,[30] weakens rule-directed models of corporate governance in favour of processes for rule altering.

A second feature of this process is that these approaches begin to straddle jurisdictions. Thus, the UK emissions system is a precursor of an international system based on the Kyoto Treaty to be introduced shortly on an EU-wide basis.[31] Similarly, other features of the new generation of regulation share a common base in international or EU law (as with the Packaging Waste Directive) or are commonly-found policy instruments developed in particular jurisdictions before being adopted more widely (examples would

---

[28] Sorrell, *Back to the Drawing Board? Implications of the EU Emissions Trading Directive for UK Climate Policy*, above n 26, at 25.

[29] LH Goulder, *Environmental Taxation and the Double Dividend* (NBER Paper 4896, Cambridge Mass, 1994).

[30] U Beck, *Risk Society–Towards a New Modernity* (London, Sage, 1992); for an analysis of the relationship of the Risk Society thesis to ecological modernisation, see R Lee and E Stokes, 'Ecological Modernisation and the Precautionary Principle' in J Gunning and S Holm, *Ethics, Law and Society* (Aldershot, Ashgate, 2005) 103.

[31] See EU Greenhouse Gas Emission-Projections for Europe: European Environment Agency Technical Report No 77 (EEA, Copenhagen, 2003) and see Proposal for a Directive of the European Parliament and of the Council establishing a scheme for greenhouse gas emission allowance trading within the Community and amending Council Directive 96/61/EC 2001/0245(COD).

include landfill taxation or product take-back obligations). Inevitably wider policies of liberalisation leave limited scope for regulatory divergence, and ironically this is particularly true for the new generation of economic instruments.[32] States must be conscious therefore of competitive implications of economic regulation, and increasingly problems can arise between this type of regulation and other international rules (such as free movement of goods) serving the globalisation agenda. A good example of this is the European Commission's concerns that the incentives in the UK emissions trading scheme constituted a state aid under EU law.[33]

Finally, the shift to economic instruments may imply a different process of regulation for 'multinational companies' (MNC) and for 'small and medium enterprises' (SMEs). Noticeably, IPC applied only to the larger operators and effectively to some 2000 of the largest sites in the UK. Packaging waste targets have been met by the adoption of a system in which participation depended on turnover. This, like emissions trading, was a scheme promoted by companies in the name of 'producer responsibility' and in a new form of regulatory capture we see MNCs beginning to control the terms on which they are regulated. Expect more of the same in relation to integrated product policy measures on end of life vehicles or waste electrical and electronic goods. We wish to highlight this idea of regulatory capture, and in the following section of this chapter, we consider the implications of this process on the (regulatory) capacity of the state in an era of globalisation.

CORPORATE POWER AND THE CHALLENGE FOR NATIONAL REGULATION

Having rehearsed these features of environmental regulation under ecological modernisation, we wish to review how this new generation of (re-) regulation serves the nation state in the context of a growing global order. In particular it asks questions concerning: the influence of business to shape at the international level the background conditions for national regulation; the accountability of business operating under economic instruments that seek to influence rather than govern behaviour; and whether such regulation might allow the development of a corporate elite operating free from effective external control.

---

[32] L Westermark, *Integrate the Environmental Dimension–Visions in the Cardiff Process* (Stockholm, Euroest, Stockholm) points to the growing harmonisation of environmental charges and taxes in Europe.

[33] For the background see S Sorrell, *The Climate Confusion* (SPRU, Sussex, 2002) and see 'EU Emissions Trading Scheme–New Steps' 34 *Climate Change Initiative Newsletter* April 2003.

In this section of the chapter, we will focus on how the rise of multinationally organised firms over the course of the late twentieth century has posed certain challenges in terms of the ability of states to effectively regulate the activities of such businesses operating within their territories. Such an exploration is not possible without drawing upon the wider academic debates concerning the relationship between states and firms in the context of globalisation. (This is the context for understanding how and why states have embraced more hands-off forms of business regulation and understanding the intrinsic appeal of an ecological modernisation agenda that identifies itself as essentially 'non-regulatory' or market-oriented). Note, however, that despite the claim that MNC-led economic globalisation is accompanied (or indeed initiated) by processes of liberalisation (deregulation and privatisation), in fact as we have already shown these more hands-off, 'market oriented' systems of business regulation represent an ongoing commitment to the regulation of business[34].

Nonetheless, these new forms of business regulation involve the state moving away from direct forms of regulation to indirect forms, and pose problems for the emergence of an effective system of environmental regulation within the global economy promoted by MNCs. For example, unless there is room for the clear expression of choice through the market instruments developed within ecological modernisation frameworks, these may constitute a process that acts to privilege business interests over those of local populations. In effect, by taking a less interventionist approach to regulation—one that stresses incentives and voluntary self-restraint—states are creating a regulatory power vacuum which powerful multinational business interests can easily fill. It should be added that the MNCs are not subject through such regulation to the true discipline of the market via the definition and enforcement of property rights. For all the rhetoric of 'market instruments' to further environmental policy, the mechanisms concerned have little to do with bringing the efficiencies of the market to bear in any sense that Coase would understand.[35]

The Growth of the Global Corporation

Many studies of globalisation have placed considerable emphasis on the idea that nation states have become less able to regulate what goes on within their borders.[36] The rise of the MNC is central to an understanding

---

[34] BR Dijkstra, *The Political Economy of Environmental Policy: A Public Choice Approach to Market Instruments* (Northampton, Mass, Edward Elgar, 1999).

[35] R Coase, 'The Problem of Social Cost' (1960) 3 *Journal of Law and Economics* 1.

[36] JA Scholte, *Globalisation: A Critical Introduction* (Palgrave, MacMillan, 2000).

of this loss of state power, or at least autonomy, not least because in mainstream globalisation literature, the MNC is placed at the centre of the emergence of the global economy[37] with analysts pointing to the rapid growth of number of MNCs in the late twentieth century as well as the fact that, by the 1980s, FDI flows outstripped flows in international trade (and much of this international trade was itself controlled by the MNCs).[38] Indeed, in many of the accounts of globalisation that emerged in the 1990s, globalisation was simply equated with the rapid rise in FDI that occurred during that period.[39]

The presentation of the firm as an agent of (neo-liberal) globalisation has been further legitimated by the idea of the transnational or 'stateless' corporation. Hence, the firm is placed at the centre of the emergence of a global economy 'in which the stress is placed upon the erosion of national boundaries and the movement of economic activities across national boundaries.'[40] This significance attached to the MNC in the emergence of a global economy is often equated with discourses relating to the 'decline of the state' in an era of globalisation.[41] The MNC in particular is identified as a rival source of power and influence to the state, with states not only finding it increasingly difficult to regulate such transnational actors, but finding themselves increasingly subject to the dictates of these powerful economic players.[42] These kinds of arguments are often backed up with the presentation of tables and/or figures that compare the annual revenue of MNCs with country Gross Domestic Product (GDP). [43] One such table is reproduced below (table 1).

It is important to recognise however that such figures, while providing a useful overall picture, tell us in effect very little about the nature of corporate power. Large companies may well rival the economic might of many of the world's states, but what is the significance of this economic power? In terms of the subject of environmental regulation addressed in this chapter, it could be suggested that this economic power makes it increasingly difficult for states to regulate the large corporations operating within

---

[37] RJ Barnet and J Cavanagh, *Global Dreams: Imperial Corporations in the New World Order* (New York, Simon and Schuster, 1995) 59; D Julius, *Global Companies and Public Policy: The Growing Challenge of Foreign Direct Investment* (London, Pinter, 1990).

[38] J Stopford, cited in H-j Chang 'Globalization, Transnational Corporations and Economic Development: Can the developing countries pursue strategic industrial policy in a globalizing world?' in D Baker, G Epstein and R Pollin, *Globalization and Progressive Economic Policy* (Cambridge, Cambridge University Press, 1998) 98.

[39] S Ostry, 'The Domestic Domain: The New International Policy Arena' (1992) 1 *Transnational Corporations* 7.

[40] J Allen, 'Crossing Borders: Footloose Multinationals' in J Allen and C Hammnett (eds), *A Shrinking World?* (Oxford, Oxford University Press, 1995) 59.

[41] See, eg K Ohmae, *The Borderless World* (London, Harper Collins, 1994).

[42] S Strange, *States and Markets* (London, Pinter, 1998).

[43] See, eg CW Kegley and ER Witkopf, *World Politics: Trend and Transformation* (New York, St Martin's Press, 2001).

Table 1: Annual Revenue of Selected MNCs in US$ billions and Country Equivalents measured in GDP

Rank	Company	Revenue $ billions 1998	Country (Approximate GDP equivalent)
1	General Motors (US)	161.3	Denmark/Thailand
10	Toyota (Japan)	99.7	Portugal/Malaysia
20	Nissho Iwai (Japan)	67.7	New Zealand
30	AT&T (US)	53.5	Czech Republic
40	Mobil (US)	47.6	Algeria
50	Sears Roebuck	41.3	Bangladesh
60	NEC (Japan)	37.2	United Arab Emirates
70	Suez Lyonnaise des Eaux	34.8	Romania
80	HypoVereinsbank (Germany)	31.8	Morocco
90	Tomen (Japan)	30.9	Kuwait
100	Motorola (US)	29.4	Kuwait
150	Walt Disney (US)	22.9	Belarus
200	Japan Postal Service (Japan)	18.8	Tunisia
250	Albertson's (US)	16.0	Sri Lanka
300	Taisei (Japan)	13.8	Lebanon
350	Goodyear Tyre & Rubber (US)	12.6	Oman
400	Fuji Photo Film (Japan)	11.2	El Salvador
450	CSX (US)	9.9	Bulgaria
500	Northrop Grumman (US)	8.9	Zimbabwe

Source: UNRISD, Visible Hands: Taking Responsibility for Social Development, UNRISD, January 2000 http://www.unrisd.org/unrisd/website/document.nsf/ (httpPublications)/ FE9C9439D82B525480256B670065EFA1?OpenDocument [accessed 13 August 2002] 77

their territories (hence, as we have described above, certain forms of regulation that apply only at the big-business level). Of course, part of the problem of regulation is the very fact that MNCs are multinational. The ease with which firms are able to move goods and capital between territories is part of the reason for their ability to often escape (or at least negotiate around the process of) regulation. This applies not only to environmental regulation, but to other interventions such as the regulation of employment contracts. Furthermore, states may find themselves constrained in exercising freedom of choice in particular situations involving unequal power relations. Thus, the presence and actions of powerful multinational corporations may constrain a sovereign nation and its government in policy choices. Hence:

> The global strategies of individual MNEs play an ever more crucial role in economic development, in shaping the world economy and in significantly influencing the direction, content and outcome of public policy choices.[44]

---

[44] S Razeen, *States and Firms: Multinational Enterprises in Institutional Competition* (London, Routledge, 1995) 2.

In this sense, states are viewed as trying to attract FDI because it is an essential source of capital in trying to bring about economic development in a globally competitive era. Thus, states will tailor their economic, social or environmental policy and regulatory decisions in order to suit the demands of international business. In effect, therefore, the idea is that the deregulatory policies associated with laissez-faire economic liberalism are designed to attract FDI. Thus, MNCs can be viewed as playing a role in the declining significance of traditional forms of state interventionism.

The State and 'Re-regulation'

By emphasising the role of state-led policies of deregulation as part of the story of the global spread of MNCs, we are arguing effectively that (economic) globalisation is as much a state-led strategy as it is a market one. The globalisation of the world economy would not have been so dramatic without the emergence of government policies that sought to positively welcome investment from MNCs. Since the 1980s, policies of liberalisation have enhanced the access that MNCs have to overseas markets. These policies included moves toward privatisation of publicly owned enterprises and services and deregulation (the easing of rules and restrictions on companies). Although MNCs are often credited as the key agents of economic globalisation–it is notable that the widening 'global reach' of the MNC in today's political economy is a reflection of state policies toward FDI.[45] Certain popular globalisation texts have taken up this theme of the declining significance of state-interventionism and the rise in corporate power as an outcome of this process.[46]

However, a more nuanced analysis of this process leads one to the conclusion that the process of economic globalisation was not so much driven by the rise of MNCs, but was political in its origins, reflecting the important role of the state in the establishment of a global market economy (ie, that the market economy did not emerge spontaneously, or naturally, in the way that more liberal influenced economic theory might have us believe).[47]

---

[45] In addition to the liberalisation of economies in order to create a regime more favourable to FDI, the same period also witnessed the (State-led) deregulation of financial markets. These changes to the rules governing financial flows, have led to the emergence of a global financial market and the growth of massively powerful, multinationally organised, banking corporations. Indeed in the EU legal framework, free movement of capital is seen as a fundamental freedom underpinning the single market.

[46] See, eg E Luttwak, *Turbo Capitalism: Winners and Losers in the Global Economy* (London, Orion Business Books, 1999).

[47] See, eg RJ Barry Jones, 'Globalisation in Perpective' in RD Germain (ed), *Globalisation and its Critics: Perspectives from Political Economy*, (Basingstoke, MacMillan, 2000); S Strange, *Casino Capitalism* (Oxford, Basil Blackwell, 1986); R Stubbs and GRD Underhill, 'Global Issues in Historical Perspective' in R Stubbs and GRD Underhill (eds), *Political Economy and the Changing Global Order* (Basingstoke, MacMillan, 1994); PG Cerny, *The Changing Architecture of Politics: Structure, Agency and the Future of the State* (London, Sage 1990).

This position takes as an important starting point the work of Karl Polanyi, who in his book *The Great Transformation*, charted the rise of the market economy in the nineteenth century arguing that '[t]he road to the free market was opened and kept open by an enormous increase in continuous, centrally organised and controlled interventionism[48].' Polanyi's emphasis on interventionism to support the functioning of a global market economy, is echoed in the kinds of regulatory practices we have already discussed. Although perceived as more market-friendly approaches to business regulation, there is a need for on-going intervention in the workings of the market-economy. Regulation, or re-regulation, is as much a feature of state-business relations in an era of globalisation as it was fifty years ago.

What has happened, as charted in this chapter, is that the nature of this regulation, and other forms of state interventionism in the economy has changed. While states have many incentives to open their economies to FDI, the picture is not a simple matter of deregulation; '[r]ather a complex process of deregulation, regulation and selective government intervention is evident[49].' More importantly, the competitive environment of the global economy in which states compete to attract FDI has rendered states less able to pursue welfare-oriented goals. Hence, in his book *The Changing Architecture of Politics,* Cerny recounts a shift from welfare states to so-called 'competition states.' These states are focused on maintaining their competitive position in the global economy or the 'hard decisions of industrial policy' within the context of 'the competitive rat race of the open world economy.'[50] To return to the comments made earlier in the chapter regarding the powerful nature of firms as political actors, the powerful influence of MNCs lies not so much in the fact of their economic size, but rather in the structural power that they have over policy-makers. In the context of economic globalisation then, firms are increasingly able to place constraints on governments and state policy-makers.[51]

The irony is, however, that the rise of the competition state as a response to the rise of the open (global) market, has actually led to new forms of state intervention–'for the state will be enmeshed in the promotion, support, and maintenance of an ever widening range of social and economic activities.'[52] Thus, we can see that the development of an approach to

---

[48] K Polanyi, *The Great Transformation: The Political and Economic Origins of Our Time* (Boston, Beacon Press, 1944).

[49] S McGuire, 'Firms and Governments in International Trade' in B Hocking and S McGuire (eds), *Trade Politics: International, Domestic and Regional Perspectives* (London, Routledge, 1999) 159.

[50] Cerny, *The Changing Architecture of Politics: Structure, Agency and the Future of the State*, above n 47, at 229.

[51] Strange, *States and Markets*, above n 42.

[52] Cerny, *The Changing Architecture of Politics: Structure, Agency and the Future of the State*, above n 47, at 230.

regulatory reform influenced by ecological modernisation regulation reflects the needs of states to maintain their competitive position and attract FDI within the context of an open market based global economic system. In a sense, the adoption of these forms of (re)regulation means that governments are seen to be doing something (ie, regulating), while at the same time are able to employ the rhetoric of the market. As noted earlier in this chapter, the link between the idea of ecological modernisation and the neo-liberal economic discourse that emphasises the role of 'market' mechanisms and the importance of de-regulation, constitutes a crucial source of the appeal of ecological modernisation to governments and policy-makers.

Others, however, have argued that new forms of environmental regulation are a reflection of the growing complexity of social relations and conflicts and institutions of governance (at both the global, regional and sub-national level) in an interdependent world.[53] In this sense the emphasis is on states responding to the uncertainties associated with economic as well as political globalisation (new and emerging forms of global governance). However, the development of approaches to regulation based upon ecological modernisation needs to be viewed as more than simply a technical policy solution in an increasingly uncertain world. We also need to think critically about the extent to which policy instruments such as landfill taxes or tradable targets can effectively bring big business to account for the role that they play in environmental degradation. The question needs to be asked: do EM influenced approaches to regulation effectively meet the call for accountability of big business?

Problems with this Form of Regulation

Although the re-design of regulatory structures noted in this chapter highlights the enduring importance of the state in the global economy, these new forms of regulation may actually do very little to deal with the privileged and powerful position of transnational business interests. One popular call for greater accountability of MNCs for example claimed that:

> The power these giant businesses wield is awesome: they have consolidated economic power in boardrooms remote from the communities where they are located; they are unaccountable to anyone other than those who make decisions for large institutional investors; they have also transmuted economic power into political power through institutions such as the World Trade Organisation, which limit the political autonomy of states in favour of the economic freedom of large companies. But are they using their power responsibly? And can they be held to account?[54]

---

[53] I Blühdorn, 'Local Capacity Building and Global Governance' (2001) 10, *Environmental Politics* vol 178.
[54] Reported by M Phillips, 'Business Power must be Checked' *The Observer* 8 July 2001.

Viewing corporations as political actors helps place emphasis on the way in which firms, as holders of significant economic resources, are able to use this economic might in order to bargain with states, or to encourage states down particular policy routes. Beck, for example, has discussed the way in which business could be viewed as part of the field of 'sub-politics'–powerful institutions that are increasingly involved in decision making but are not democratically elected or publicly accountable.[55] Therefore, what is of concern to us is that although new forms of regulation emerge and continue to be of importance to state-business relations, there is no concerted effort on the part of government to bring the power of big business to account. The ecological modernisation approach to business regulation, places emphasis on business as the driver of economic development, with the state taking a facilitatory role. In this respect, states remain preoccupied with attracting FDI and businesses are able to exert a far greater influence over the regulatory structures that are aimed at making business more accountable. As Sklair explains:

> [W]hile TNCs have always been political actors, the demands of the global economy require them to be political in a more systematic sense than previously... Historically, the relationship between the economic power and the political power of TNCs has been highly controversial. While the involvement of ITT in the bloody coup against President Allende's government in Chile in 1973 appears to be the exception rather than the rule in the second half of the twentieth century, there is a growing body of research to suggest that major corporations are currently using more subtle methods to achieve political objectives that will serve their economic interests[56]

It has been noted that business interests have exerted a massive influence over environmental policy at both the national and international level, a reflection of the way in which business promotes its input into environmental policy as 'rational' and 'scientific'.[57] The ecological modernisation agenda suits business because it endorses this role for business as experts best able to pursue technically rational solutions to public policy problems. Concerns have been raised concerning the effective capture of scientific knowledge by firms, for example, through corporate funding of research within universities.[58] The environmental think tank SustainAbility goes further, levelling criticism at the way in which business gains influence through

[55] Beck, *Risk Society–Towards a New Modernity*, above n 30 , at 186.

[56] L Sklair, 'Debate: Transnational Corporations: As Political Actors' (1998) 3 *New Political Economy* 284.

[57] S Eden, '"We Have the Facts"–how business claims legitimacy in the environmental debate' (1999) 31 *Environment and Planning A* 1295.

[58] G Muttit, *Degrees of Capture: Universities, the Oil Industry and Climate Change* (London, New Economics Foundation, Platform, Corporate Watch, 2003).

scientific committee membership, sponsored research, corporate philanthropy, and 'revolving door' appointments (when ex-civil servants are
recruited by industry to lobby their former departments).[59] At issue then is
the input of corporate-controlled 'epistemic communities'[60] of scientific
experts into debates on environmental regulation.[61]

Furthermore, we should also highlight the role of trade associations in
influencing government policy, often expressing a far more negative view of
sustainable development policies than their members since they do not have
to fear the reputational damage to their brand that such an anti-sustainable
development stance might produce.[62] Trade associations, therefore, can be
credited with creating a highly negative climate within which the promotion
of sustainability through government policy-making becomes increasingly
difficult. The trade association might talk about job losses or a loss of competitiveness, they will play a role in watering down international agreements at the level of national negotiations (eg, they may lobby for national
exemptions from certain standards) and they can offer industry expert advi-
sors when last minute changes to legislation are being made[63]. At a
European regional level, it has also been noted that firms plays an increasingly important and politically sophisticated role in the EU policy process,
developing strategic alliances that act to grant them access to European
level policy forums.[64]

The influence of trade associations acting in this way plays a crucial role
in the development of modern environmental regulation. As we have seen
this is based increasingly on incentives to meet goals, the setting of targets
that form the basis of tradable instruments or the fixing of tax thresholds.
It would be good to think that these targets are carefully devised to achieve
Pareto optimal outcomes. However, we know from the experience of so
many of these instruments that they are devised through protracted negotiation that to a large degree reflects what business is prepared to tolerate at
a point in time. A couple of examples may suffice to make this point. It is
widely accepted that the UK is in crisis in terms of all efforts to promote

---

[59] The Janus Programme, *Politics and Persuasion: corporate influence on sustainability
development policy* (London, SustainAbility/GPC, 2001).

[60] P Haas, 'Introduction: Epistemic Communities and International Policy Co-ordination'
(1992) 46 *International Organization* 1.

[61] P Newell and D Glover, *Business and Biotechnology: Regulation and the Politics of
Influence*, Paper prepared for the project Globalisation and the International Governance of
Modern   Biotechnology,   available   at   http://www.gapresearch.org/governance/
PNDGDRAFTBusinessFIELDpapIIv3.pdf [accessed 10.10.03].

[62] The Janus Programme, *Politics and Persuasion: corporate influence on sustainability
development policy*, above n 59.

[63] *Ibid.*

[64] D Coen, 'The Evolution of the Large Firm as a Political Actor in the European Union'
(1997) 4 *Journal of European Public Policy* 91.

alternatives to the landfilling of waste. Taxation seems to have had little apparent influence on this trend or indeed on levels of waste, which continue to rise in all sectors. This is because the level of taxation and the rate of its increase at £1 per annum is grossly insufficient to act as a deterrent.[65] But the taxation rate is fixed not at what might be needed to influence waste generation and disposal, but by the political question of what is acceptable to those industrial and commercial enterprises that generate 84 per cent of all waste arising.[66] This might not matter so much if the revenues from landfill tax where then redeployed to fund ambitious programmes of research and development in waste minimisation, but the assumption is that the introduction of environment taxes must be revenue neutral, with funds reverting back to the general revenue.

A second example can be taken from the attempts to develop a market in PRNs to support initiatives to recycle packaging waste. Here targets were set at an interim level following protracted negotiations with industry. The MNCs most closely affected by the EU Directive in this area were highly proactive at the time of transposition of the Directive seeking to promote the industry sponsored 'producer responsibility' scheme rather than more traditional forms of regulation. The PRN system was meant to promote compliance by allowing trading where there were shortfalls in compliance as against the target set. But prices of PRNs have remained ludicrously low. This is because the underpinning targets themselves were set too low in the negotiating process. A knock-on effect of this was that 'lower than expected levels of investment have been directed at increasing collection and reprocessing capacity, and developing end-use markets, in order to meet the 2001 targets.'[67] Targets have been changed subsequently and their toughening led to some slight increase in demand, but the market remained generally flat. Yet despite the ease with which industry met the targets, no increase in target was announced in 2003.[68] Targets rose in 2004, but the danger is that the low level of both volume and prices of PRNs will lead to a decline in recycling infrastructure, which would take some time to reverse even if targets were heightened.

---

[65] I Brisson, 'How Can Economic Forces be Harnessed to Help Control Waste?' (2002) *Fiscal Instruments for Waste Management Conference–ESRC Transdisciplinary Seminar Series* (Cardiff, Brass, 26 September 2002), and P Kellett 'Implementing the Landfill Directive Through the PPC in England and Wales' in J Boswall and R Lee, *Ethics Economics and the Environment* (London, Cavendish Press, 2002).

[66] Department for Environment, Food and Rural Affairs, *E-Digest Statistics about Waste and Recycling* at www.defra.gov.uk/environment/statistics/waste/index.htm.

[67] Department of Environment, Transport and the Regions, *Consultation Paper on Recovery and Recycling Targets for Packaging Waste in 2001* (London, DETR, 2000) para 1.7.

[68] Ironically this was not the subject of public consultation because consultation is required only where targets are to be changed–see parliamentary question by Gregory Baker MP on 4 February 2003 (Hansard, HC col 166W).

The packaging example demonstrates that firms are much more likely to support forms of regulation in which the state takes less of an intervention-ist role. Indeed, they may be willing to take the lead in creation and intro-duction of this type of policy instrument. However, there are real questions of whether this will produce efficient forms of regulation and real concerns as to the extent to which regulation driven by ecological modernisation the-ory promote the interests of big business as a technically-rational sub-polit-ical elite group.

CONCLUSION

The influence of ecological modernisation has allowed environmental regu-lation to become much more of an internal matter for large corporations and has led to a decline of external enforcement of environmental perform-ance in the form of command and control measures. This is not necessarily a bad thing. There are notorious problems of the traditional regulatory model ranging, not just in terms of its cost and complexity, butin its propen-sity to regulatory capture and its drift to inconsistency of enforcement.[69] However, the move towards offering incentives to business to make choices about investment in technologies and safeguards for environmental protec-tion does carry with it a risk. This is that environmental protection is seen not to arise out of the external regulation of business as a 'rule embodied in law'[70] but becomes an internal governance matter. If the ecological dou-ble dividend is attainable then this need not matter for the shareholder interest and any environmental interest should merge. However, the very presence of targets, taxes and incentives suggests that the gains of ecologi-cal modernisation are not readily obvious to industry, and that environmen-tal performance will be sidelined as an optional governance issue rather than a strict legal requirement.

If there is (as we believe possible, though by no means inevitable) the potential double dividend of economic benefit through environmental pro-tection then one might expect that business would pursue such opportunity without too great a need for regulatory intervention. Where this is not the case, it might be necessary to seek to educate or to promote the ecological modernisation case. In the final analysis it might be necessary to correct assumptions as to the lack of responsibility for the external costs of pollu-tion by, for example, clear liability rules. But the influence of ecological

---

[69] EW Orts and K Deketelaere, *Environmental Contracts: Comparative Approaches to Regulatory Innovation in the United States and Europe* (New York, Kluwer Law International, 2000) and more generally R Baldwin and M Cave, *Understanding Regulation* (Oxford, Oxford University Press, 1999).

[70] Friedman, 'The Social Responsibility of Business is to Increase Profits', above n 1.

modernisation thinking appears to have given way to a new generation of regulation in which broad targets are set and mechanisms are largely left to business. There is no objection to this in principle, for as we have tried to explain, markets are constructed rather than appearing by magic, so that one might expect legal change as a vital component of the activity. But what appears to be happening is that there are negotiated settlements with bigger business concerning the nature of these targets and incentives. As a result these bear little relationship to the underpinning markets that they supposedly influence.

This appears to be a drive towards the positioning of the state as pursuing a liberalised model of deregulation, enabling it to appear more market oriented (and hence more attractive to foreign investors). At the same time, these more market-oriented forms of regulation are more open to greater corporate influence. This move is taking place not merely in the UK but across wider institutional settings such as the EU. At an international level, we can also trace the significance of regulatory approaches influenced by ecological modernisation—for example in the case of Kyoto emissions trading, or the persistent emphasis on voluntarism as embodied in the UN's Global Compact. Cutler claims that these legal frameworks provide 'a normative framework generated by a transnational elite, a mercatocracy, that comprises corporate and government actors whose interests are associated more generally with the transnational expansion of capitalism.'[71]

If more formal processes of environmental law, such as criminal enforcement, are to be replaced by systems that move corporations to determine choices promoting the gains posited by ecological modernisation, careful consideration needs to be given to the type of instruments necessary. The supposed 'market instruments' pursued so far seem to have more to do with incentives to MNCs to subscribe to the instruments themselves than towards clear environmental gains. Negotiated targets and taxes are substituted for the clear allocation of rights and responsibilities (or liabilities) that might truly direct a market based approach. In short, rather than calling corporations into account for their environmental performance, modern policy instruments tend to suggest an increasing deficit in corporate accountability. This suggests also a strong indication that regulatory control in this area is slipping from the grasp of the nation state, in line with the economic power base of global corporations.

---

[71] AC Cutler, 'Locating "Authority" in the Global Political Economy' (1999) 43 *International Studies Quarterly* 67.

9

Legislating for Responsible Corporate Behaviour: Domestic Law Approaches to an International Issue

RORY SULLIVAN

ABSTRACT

T HE SO-CALLED PHENOMENON of globalisation has placed the issue of corporate responsibility for environmental, social and economic protection at the centre of public policy debates. These debates have, however, been characterised by argument and counter-argument on the roles and responsibilities of companies. While there is a growing consensus that companies do have responsibilities beyond profit, the extent of these responsibilities remains in question.

Two distinct questions need to be addressed. The first is how is responsible behaviour to be assured? The evidence is that neither international law nor corporate self-regulation, at present, provide the necessary guarantees regarding corporate performance. This then raises the question of whether domestic regulatory approaches can provide these guarantees? The chapter identifies possible domestic law and policy options for assuring corporate performance, including mandatory reporting, director liability regimes, removing the barriers to foreign direct liability, and harnessing the economic power of governments. The chapter concludes that such approaches offer, in the absence of an effective international law regime, practical solutions to the issue of the lack of corporate accountability. However, the political and business opposition to such measures represent substantial hurdles that need to be overcome.

INTRODUCTION

Transnational corporations (TNCs) have been heavily criticised for their impacts on human rights and the environment, in particular when operating in 'less-developed' countries.[1] These criticisms have been exacerbated by the limitations in the international legal mechanisms for ensuring that TNCs meet certain standards of performance. Given these concerns, this chapter considers whether (and how) the legislative powers available in the 'northern' or 'developed' countries can be harnessed to ensure the performance of organisations when operating outside their home country (or country of incorporation).

The intention is to provide an overview of the various regulatory approaches (including self-regulation) that can be used and to discuss the viability, feasibility and effectiveness of the different approaches. While the paper builds on the author's experience with the UK Corporate (Social and Environmental) Responsibility Bill 2002, the Australian Corporate Code of Conduct Bill 2000 and the recent initiatives (Green and White papers) of the European Commission in relation to corporate social responsibility, the intention is not to provide a country-specific analysis, but rather to provide a broad policy analysis of options and to sketch out key themes and issues (eg, potential barriers, pressures for regulation) that impact on the debate.

The chapter is divided as follows:

— An overview of the manner in which international law applies to companies
— An assessment of the potential contribution of self-regulation
— Domestic law approaches
— Discussion/conclusions.

The Limitations of International Law

The concerns about the social and environmental impacts of companies have been exacerbated by the apparent limitations in the international legal framework for ensuring the performance of companies. That is, the key issue is less that TNCs engage in gross violations of human rights or serious environmental damage (although these are clearly of great concern) than that TNCs, by and large, escape international legal scrutiny. International human rights law is based on the principle of state responsibility, and international law looks first to states to enforce its rules.[2] Even

---

[1] See, generally G Evans, J Goodman and N Lansbury (eds), *Moving Mountains* (Sydney, Australia, Otford Press, 2001); J Madeley, *Big Business, Poor Peoples* (London, Zed Books, 1999); M Dobbin, *The Myth of the Good Corporate Citizen* (Toronto, Stoddart, 1998); B Balanya, A Doherty, O Hoedeman, A Ma'anit and E Wesselius, *Europe Inc* (London, Pluto Press, 2000); G Monbiot, *Captive State: The Corporate Takeover of Britain* (London, Macmillan, 2000); D Korten, *When Corporations Rule the World* (London, Earthscan, 1995).

[2] International Council on Human Rights Policy, *Beyond Voluntarism: Human Rights and the Developing International Legal Obligations of Companies* (Geneva, International Council on Human Rights Policy, 2002); C Jochnick, 'Confronting the Impunity of Non-State Actors: New Fields for the Promotion of Human Rights' 21 *Human Rights Quarterly* 56–79; M Addo (ed), *Human Rights Standards and the Responsibility of Transnational Corporations* (London, Kluwer Law International, 1999).

where international agreements are incorporated into domestic legislation, this is of limited value if these are not accompanied by appropriate mechanisms to ensure compliance such as powers to monitor performance, inspect facilities and operations, gather information, take cases or impose penalties. This is the situation in many less-developed countries, where the pressures for investment or development have led to the weakening or waiving of legal protections for human rights or the environment, and appropriate mechanisms for ensuring the performance of TNCs are often not available within these countries.[3] Furthermore, the strong opposition of TNCs means that an international law regime explicitly regulating their activities is unlikely to become a reality.[4]

IS SELF-REGULATION THE SOLUTION?

Companies have seen self-regulation as a means of effectively responding to stakeholder (eg, suppliers, investors, customers, the public and shareholders) expectations that social and environmental issues will be effectively managed while also providing benefits such as facilitating partnerships between companies, public authorities and other stakeholders and improved financial performance.[5] Despite the strong business support for self-regulation, a number of issues have been raised in virtually every major evaluation of the effectiveness of self-regulatory regimes.[6] These are (1) the specific targets that are set and whether these targets will be met, (2) the capture of public policy, and (3) free-riders.

The targets specified in self-regulatory regimes are commonly suspected of being less stringent than those that would have been established in traditional regulatory regimes. However, this argument is difficult to prove as there is no guarantee that the targets in command and control approaches would necessarily be more stringent. It has been argued that the self-regulatory regimes that have achieved the most substantial outcomes are those that have come closest to establishing an effective system of sanctions

---

[3] C Jochnick, 'Confronting the Impunity of Non-State Actors: New Fields for the Promotion of Human Rights', above n 2; Evans et al, *Moving Mountains*, above n 1; J Richter, *Holding Corporations Accountable* (London, Zed Books, 2001); J Gamble and C Ku, 'International Law–New Actors and New Technologies: Centre Stage for NGOs?' 31 (2000) *Law & Policy in International Business* 221–62; M Addo, *Human Rights Standards and the Responsibility of Transnational Corporations*, above n 2, at 11.

[4] K Rodman, '"Think Globally, Punish Locally": Nonstate Actors, Multinational Corporations, and Human Rights Sanctions', (1988) 12 *Ethics and International Affairs* 19–42.

[5] P Bansal and K Roth, 'Why Companies Go Green: A Model of Ecological Responsiveness' (2000) 43 (4) *Academy of Management Journal* 717–36; J Blumberg, A Korsvold and G Blum, *Environmental Performance and Shareholder Value* (Geneva, Switzerland, World Business Council for Sustainable Development, 2000).

[6] R Sullivan, 'Enron: One Step Forward or Two Steps Back for Effective Self-Regulation?' (2002) 8 *Journal of Corporate Citizenship* 91–104.

or have offered the greatest rewards.[7] In the context of the present discussion, in particular in less developed countries, it is clear that governments are unlikely to have the necessary tools to compel corporate performance. While there is evidence that voluntary approaches can be effective at meeting their defined goals,[8] the fact that targets are achieved may simply reflect the limitations in the targets that are set (ie, the targets may simply represent business as usual outcomes).

A primary (although, frequently, unstated) objective of many self-regulatory regimes is to reduce the involvement of government in business decision-making processes. Business has been suspected of using self-regulation to capture environmental policy, through using such programmes to avoid or forestall regulation. For example, the fact that a self-regulatory regime is in place is often used to argue that regulation is not required or, if regulation is seen as necessary, that the targets specified in the voluntary approach represent acceptable targets for industry.[9] If business succeeds (ie, if regulation is avoided or if the preferred targets are adopted), policy is said to have been 'captured' by business. While capture is relatively easy to describe in qualitative terms, it can be very difficult to assess in practice. In the context of the present discussion, the capture of public policy is evidenced by the difficulties in establishing a binding legal regime on companies. For example, one (perhaps cynical) interpretation of the outcomes of the 2002 World Summit on Sustainable Development (Rio+10) held in Johannesburg could be that TNCs succeeded in capturing the debate over regulation, through arguing that voluntary approaches and partnerships were the preferred means of ensuring the business contribution to poverty alleviation and sustainable development.

Even though individual organisations may benefit from a self-regulatory regime, organisations that do not participate ('free-riders') may also benefit. The main forms of free-riding are (1) where all parties agree to the terms and conditions of the self-regulatory regime but some merely feign compliance, and (2) where part of the relevant industry simply refuses to sign on to the scheme.[10] The ability to control free-riders depends on factors such as the ability to detect non-compliance, the ability to punish or sanction

---

[7] S Krarup and S Ramesohl, *Implementation and Efficiency* (Copenhagen, Denmark, AKF Institute of Local Government Studies, 2000) 57

[8] N Gunningham, and J Rees, 'Industry Self-Regulation: An Institutional Perspective' (1997) 19(4) *Law & Policy* 363–414, at 406; OECD, *Voluntary Approaches for Environmental Policy: An Assessment* (Paris, OECD, 1999); S Krarup and S Ramesohl, above n 7, at 34–36.

[9] OECD, *Voluntary Approaches for Environmental Policy: An Assessment*, above n 8, at 25; J Maxwell, T Lyon, and S Hackett, 'Self-Regulation and Social Welfare: The Political Economy of Corporate Environmentalism' (2000) 43 *The Journal of Law and Economics* 583–617, at 583.

[10] N Gunningham, and J Rees, 'Industry Self-Regulation: An Institutional Perspective', above n 8, at 393.

non-compliant behaviour, and the presence of market or other pressures to ensure that organisations comply. Free-riders present a specific issue in the context of corporate accountability as the issues that are of concern (eg, major environmental damage, gross violations of human rights) are widely seen as 'unacceptable'. That is, self-regulation does not provide the necessary degree of dependability regarding the performance of companies.[11]

DOMESTIC LAW AND POLICY APPROACHES

While international law does not effectively regulate TNCs, this does not mean that practical measures cannot be taken at the domestic level to ensure the performance of TNCs. The first part of the equation is the measures taken to ensure the performance of TNCs within a specific country. This relates to the legislative framework within which companies operate and the measures (eg, enforcement and sanctioning processes) implemented to ensure compliance (or a defined standard of performance). The second part, which is the subject of this chapter, is the potential for the 'home countries' (or countries of incorporation) of TNCs to adopt measures to ensure the performance of TNCs when operating outside their home country. The following potential approaches are considered, namely:

— Mandatory social and environmental policy disclosure
— Mandatory social and environmental reporting
— Making directors and managers personally liable for the actions of their organisations
— Foreign direct liability, and
— Economic or other incentives.

Mandatory Social and Environmental Policy Disclosure

For 'Western' companies, formal policy commitments to specific actions or values are widely seen as the key starting point for developing organisational commitment to these values or actions.[12] Policies are statements of the organisation's goals and performance requirements and provide an overall framework and direction for the organisation's activities. A starting point for corporate accountability would be to require all corporations to disclose their policy regarding social responsibility, human rights and environmental

---

[11] For a discussion of self-regulation in the context of the mining industry, see R Sullivan and P Frankental, 'Corporate Citizenship and the Mining Industry: Defining and Implementing Human Rights Norms' (2002) 7 *Journal of Corporate Citizenship* 79–91.

[12] R Sullivan and H Wyndham, *Effective Environmental Management: Principles and Case Studies* (Sydney, Australia, Allen & Unwin, 2001) 25–32.

performance. For example, the London Stock Exchange requires that all listed companies create systems to identify, evaluate and manage their risks relating to environmental, reputation and social probity issues, and to make a statement on risk management in their annual reports. Internationally, many companies have already published their policies on issues such as human rights, environment and social performance. The advantages of making policy disclosure a mandatory requirement are that it formalises good practice in this area, it requires companies and senior managers to explicitly consider and define corporate attitudes to social and environmental issues, and it represents the first step in creating accountabilities within organisations for their social and environmental performance.

Mandatory Social and Environmental Reporting

Access to information is widely recognised as an essential prerequisite for effective community and stakeholder input into business decisions on social and environmental issues. The provision of more information to the public provides a basis for performance measurement and dialogue, increases the pressure on companies to ensure their performance and helps improve business decision-making processes on social and environmental issues. However, mandatory reporting requirements suffer from a lack of dependability (ie, there is no guarantee that information alone will lead to improved social and environmental performance) and the right to information does not translate into a right to act (eg, requirements to report information may be accompanied by protections that mean that facilities cannot be sued on the basis of information that they disclose). Furthermore, while environmental reporting is reasonably well-developed with broad agreement on key performance measures and data quality issues, many of the techniques for social reporting are still being developed. However, this should not be used as an argument against creating mandatory reporting requirements on social issues as it is likely that mandatory reporting requirements would create the impetus for these performance measures and techniques to be developed. The starting point could be to require companies to report on their performance against regulatory requirements and to report those environmental, human rights or other issues that represent a significant or material liability.

Make Directors and Managers Personally Liable for the Actions of their Organisations

Recognising the difficulties in directly ensuring the performance of TNCs (or corporate entities), it may be possible to target the directors and managers of TNCs. Specifically, national governments could impose requirements on their citizens, in their roles as directors or managers, to ensure the performance of their organisations. A potential model is provided by the principle of 'due diligence' (or related terms such as 'duty of care'). Due diligence is a well-established and tested principle of health and safety and environmental legislation in countries such as the UK, Australia and Canada. While a range of definitions for due diligence have been proposed, much of the writing refers to the decision in *R v Bata Industries*[13] in Canada. While the focus of *R v Bata Industries* was on environmental due diligence, the principles can be readily extended to social and human rights performance. In the decision, Ormston J specified a number of factors that could be used to evaluate the merits of an individual director's reliance on the due diligence defence. These were (1) did the director establish a pollution prevention system or ensure that such a system was in place, (2) did the pollution prevention system comply with industry norms, (3) did the director ensure that corporate officers report on the performance of the system to the board, and that any non-compliances were reported in a timely manner, (4) was the director personally familiar with industry norms, and (5) did the director immediately and personally react on becoming aware that the system had failed?

Such legislation could be built on the rights and obligations of citizens that are defined in constitutions and other relevant legislation (eg, the rights and responsibilities of citizens when overseas). However, care is required with the development of due diligence legislation. First of all, there is community resentment towards organisations that fail to react responsibly to the recognised harmful or risky nature of their operations and simply punishing individuals within the organisation is unlikely to be seen as sufficient sanction and may even be interpreted as 'scapegoating' an individual in order to hide corporate misconduct. The second is that, in most organisations, compliance responsibility is delegated downwards. The consequence is that it may actually be a relatively low level manager or operator who has the ultimate responsibility within the organisation, and prosecuting this individual may not be an appropriate or effective use of a regulatory body's powers.

Business interests have tended to oppose criminal sanctions (or the use of criminal law), arguing that criminal sanctions are blunt instruments, inefficient and impose extraordinary evidentiary burdens on the prosecutor for painfully small results. While these arguments have some validity, it is important to recognise that creating criminal offences can have a critical role in creating a strong enforcement system through creating a general deterrent effect and helping to promote voluntary compliance.

A number of practical design issues also need to be considered. The first is what is the subject of such a regime? In broad terms, such a regime should

---

[13] *R v Bata Industries Ltd* (No 2) (1992) 70 CCC (3rd) 394.

apply to gross abuses of the environment or human rights. That is, criminal law should only be used in situations where there is major harm or the potential for major harm. The second is what are the penalties? In broad terms, these should reflect those provisions that are provided under corporate legislation (eg, tax law) and could include financial penalties and/or custodial sentences, as well as other penalties (eg, community service, prohibition on guilty parties taking other directorships). The third is that, even where serious environmental or social impacts have occurred, suitable defences should be provided to ensure that unfair or unreasonable expectations are not imposed on corporate officers. These defences could be similar to those defences that are available in common law systems (ie, that the corporation acted without the constructive knowledge of the person, the person was not in a position to influence the actions of the corporation or, if the person was in a position of influence, the person took reasonable precautions and exercised 'due diligence' to avoid the contravention).

This chapter is not advocating a draconian or highly restrictive interpretation of due diligence. However, the basic premise underpinning such an approach is that managers and directors should be prepared, in return for the rewards that accrue as a result of their positions, to accept responsibility for the impacts of their organisations on human rights and the environment. Along with the rights to citizenship come responsibilities but, for far too long, the responsibilities have been seen as secondary to the rights that have been awarded. Of course, individuals have a choice in that they can choose to take the citizenship of another country. In such situations, it could be argued that these individuals have thereby forfeited the rights to reclaim their citizenship at a later date.

Foreign Direct Liability

One of the particular issues with ensuring corporate accountability is that those affected by corporate activities face many practical barriers to taking cases. These are not only the legal and political barriers (eg, the difficulties of taking cases in the country of incorporation, the difficulties in obtaining financial support for such cases, the political and diplomatic opposition to such cases), but the common situation where parent companies distance themselves from legally independent subsidiaries (or other legal structures such as joint venture partnerships). This is of particular importance when looking at the activities and operations of TNCs in less-developed countries. While the concept of foreign direct liability has been tested (ie, where cases for harm have been brought in the home country or other suitable jurisdiction), to date, the evidentiary thresholds that have been applied have been extremely high and the cases have struggled to demonstrate the unavailability of a suitable legal forum in the court where the harm was caused.[14] Those cases that have seemed likely to establish precedents regarding corporate liability have been settled out of court. That is, while litigation has provided, in some cases, recompense or compensation for affected parties, the cases have been less satisfactory from the perspective of establishing a formal legal framework for ensuring TNC accountability or, at least, the award of compensation when harm is caused. It is, therefore, recommended that national governments move to address the key barriers to pursuing TNCs for compensation in their country of incorporation. Specific measures that should be considered are, (1) ending the legal fiction that each company in a corporate group is to be treated as a separate entity (which is often used by companies as a means of limiting their liability), (2) provide access to a recognised court or forum for disputes or claims, (3) ensure that the potential for full, adequate and effective compensation is available, (4) allow for injunctions to be granted and upheld if there is the potential for serious environmental harm or gross violations of human rights, (5) provide the courts with effective enforcement powers to ensure that decisions are implemented.

Economic or other Incentives

Much of the debate around TNCs has assumed that the ability of government to control corporate activity is limited. While the barriers to regulation may prove insurmountable, at least in the short term, it is also important to recognise that governments have significant financial influence, as a contractor and purchaser of goods and services provided by the private sector, and through supporting the private sector through export credit insurance and other financial guarantees.[15] This financial power provides governments with powerful levers for encouraging responsible behaviour. Governments should insist on responsible corporate behaviour as a precondition for access to government funds (in the form of contracts, funds, etc) and through the introduction of conditions relating to environmental, social and human rights performance into all contracts and other financial agreements with companies. In addition, governments should ensure that there are processes for assessing performance, for the withdrawal of contracts in the event of non-conformance and, more proactively, that companies with a good record are given credit for this. To ensure the credibility of these

---

[14] For a useful overview, see H Ward, 'Governing Multinationals: The Role of Foreign Direct Liability, RIIA Briefing Paper No 18, February 2001' (London, The Royal Institute of International Affairs).

[15] See, eg the discussion in C McCrudden, 'International Economic Law and the Pursuit of Human Rights: A Framework for Discussion of the Legality of "Selective Purchasing" Laws under the WTO Government Procurement Agreement' (1999) *Journal of International Economic Law* 3–48.

requirements (ie, so they are not just seen as 'paper' requirements), governments should not only commit to the inclusion of such requirements in contracts, but to publicly explaining how performance is to be assessed and to public reporting on performance assessments and on the actions taken in he event of non-compliances being identified.

It has been argued that introducing these requirements into public contracts is inappropriate or may lead to indiscipline or lack of rigour in decision-making. To an extent this argument is justified given that many of the necessary metrics for assessing social and environmental performance are still being developed. Equally, it is pertinent to note that many private sector organisations already have such evaluation processes developed and implemented (eg, many require their suppliers and contractors to have systems of environmental management in place, to meet certain quality and labour requirements, to report on their social and environmental performance). It is also pertinent to note that such criteria can be seen as a part of the overall specification for carrying out government work, ie, that organisations need to meet the general deliverables required while also meeting certain human rights, environmental or social standards.

WHAT ACTIONS HAVE GOVERNMENTS TAKEN?

The UK as an Example

To date, the response from 'Northern' governments has been to sidestep most of the issues around corporate accountability, with the majority refusing to take responsibility for the overseas actions of their companies.[16] The actions taken by the UK government (which has seen itself as a leader in this area) are illustrative of the more general issue.

Perhaps the most substantial change to the UK regulatory framework has been the amendment of the Pensions Act 1995 to require pension funds to disclose the extent to which they take social, ethical and environmental issues into account when investing money (a measure which has a similar effect to the mandatory disclosure of an organisation's social and environmental policy). It has been argued that this has had an important influence in focusing interest in the financial sector and in companies on the importance of these issues.[17] However, it is difficult to tell how this has influenced the actual performance of companies, or whether it has created strong incentives for companies to explicitly

[16] J Woodroffe, 'Regulating Multinational Corporations in a World of Nation States' in M Addo (ed), (1999), *Human Rights Standards and the Responsibility of Transnational Corporations* (London, Kluwer Law International, 1999) 131–42.

[17] Department of Trade and Industry, *Business and Society: Corporate Social Responsibility Report 2002* (London, HMSO, 2002a).

address their social or environmental issues. For example, just fourteen of the listed UK companies have explicit policy commitments to human rights (from the Business & Human Rights Resource Centre, http://www.business-humanrights.org, reviewed on 15 October 2002) and less than one third of the top-350 listed companies produce an annual environmental report.

On the question of mandatory reporting, the current White Paper on Company Law is extremely weak.[18] At present, under UK legislation, there are no formal requirements for companies to report on the social, environmental or economic dimensions of their activities. The White Paper proposes (under the 'Operating and Financial Review (OFR)' requirements) to leave the scope of such reporting to the discretion of the directors, where the focus is on 'material environmental issues.'[19] That is, the intention appears to be that companies will only report on such issues when they are material (or significant) to the company's financial performance. The consequence is that issues that are significant (eg, major environmental impacts, human rights violations) need not be reported unless these present a significant financial risk.

Internationally, the UK government has supported initiatives such as the OECD Guidelines for Multinational Enterprises, the UN Global Compact and the Voluntary Principles on Security and Human Rights. These are all voluntary initiatives. While the various government initiatives are important, they do not substantially alter the context within which UK business operates overseas. That is, the UK government has not moved towards supporting an internationally binding regulatory regime for companies, nor has it sought to extend domestic legislation to apply to UK companies operating overseas.

Emerging Pressures for Regulation

One of the interesting features of the debates around corporate accountability has been the growing number of efforts to introduce regulation to ensure the performance of domestic companies when operating overseas. These have included:

— The European Parliament Resolution on Standards for European Enterprises Operating in Developing Countries and the recent Green and White papers on corporate social responsibility
— The McKinney Bill in the United States

---

[18] Department of Trade and Industry, *Modernising Company Law White Paper. Presented to Parliament by the Secretary of State for Trade and Industry, July 2002* (London, TSO, 2002b).
[19] *Ibid*, at 38.

— The Australian Democrats Corporate Code of Conduct Bill 2000: The Bill was the subject of a parliamentary inquiry.[20] One of the primary motivations for introducing the Bill was the record of the Australian mining industry (in particular, the controversy surrounding BHP's Ok Tedi mine in Papua New Guinea). While the Parliamentary Inquiry into the Bill recommended that the Bill not be adopted, both of the major opposition parties in tabled dissenting reports on the conclusions of the Inquiry

— The UK Corporate (Social and Environmental) Responsibility Bill 2002 which was introduced by Labour MP Linda Perham and which was supported by a coalition (the CORE Coalition) of NGOs including Amnesty International (UK), Save the Children (UK), Friends of the Earth, CAFOD and New Economics Foundation. The key elements of the legislation were that (1) companies must produce and publish reports on their social, environmental and economic impacts, (2) companies must consult their stakeholders on company activities and impacts, (3) directors of companies are required to consider the environmental, social and economic impacts of their operations and must take the interests of all stakeholders into account when making decisions on these aspects, (4) directors must take all reasonable steps to minimise any negative social, environmental or economic effects of their operations, and (5) stakeholders will be able to require companies and directors to meet these obligations.

While the specific details differed, the various proposals all related to the regulation of companies operating overseas (ie, outside the company's home country or country of incorporation), included provisions relating to issues such as human rights, environment, labour and occupational health and safety, required some form of reporting and included independent monitoring and, where necessary, sanctioning of companies. The public policy debate surrounding each has followed a similar pattern with NGOs supporting the legislation and companies strongly opposing the legislation (on the grounds that legislation is a blunt instrument that cannot possibly account for the range of situations that companies need to address and that regulation is inefficient). While the debates were 'won' by industry (ie, the Bills were defeated or, in the case of the EU Resolutions, the final wording emphasised voluntary approaches rather than regulation), what they have done is address many of the technical arguments that were advanced about the manner in which such legislation could work. For example, the Parliamentary Inquiry into the Australian

---

[20] Parliamentary Joint Statutory Committee on Corporations and Securities (2001), *Report on the Corporate Code of Conduct Bill 2000* (Canberra, Parliament of the Commonwealth of Australia, 2001).

Code of Conduct Bill considered the issue of extraterritoriality in some detail, including an assessment of the constitutional, statute and case law provisions that related to this issue.[21] The Inquiry identified a number of pieces of Australian legislation with extraterritorial application (relating to issues such as bribery, child sex tourism and pollution of the marine environment).

Barriers to Home State Regulation

Efforts by home states to regulate or ensure the performance of TNCs are likely to encounter a number of practical barriers. The first barrier is that such regulation may be seen as interference in the territorial sovereignty of another state (which conflicts with the principle of state responsibility that underpins international human rights and environmental law). However, there are a number of grounds on which the home state can regulate the activities of a TNC that is operating beyond the territory of that state.[22] States can regulate the conduct of their nationals (and this can include 'corporate nationals') abroad (as proposed above), so long as they are not required to breach the laws of the state in which they are operating, and there is also a growing recognition that regulation can be applied to issues that are in the general interests of the international community (eg, those human rights that have attained the status of customary international law). The second barrier is the procedural limitations in domestic legal systems that can inhibit actions against TNCs for their activities outside the territory of the state in which the proceedings are brought. For example, TNCs may argue *forum non conviens* (ie, that there is some other forum where the case may be tried more suitably). Such arguments tend to be procedural and do not necessarily provide an indication of substantive willingness on the part of the home country to hold the parent company to account.[23] The third is that there is strong political and business opposition to regulation. The arguments used to include the financial costs imposed on business (ie, the risk of competitive disadvantage), the risk that companies will be driven offshore or will move to incorporate in other jurisdictions, the potential damage to the home country's foreign relations, the potential

---

[21] *Ibid*, at 13–26.

[22] R McCorquodale, 'Human Rights and Global Business' in S Bottomley, and D Kinley, (eds), *Commercial Law and Human Rights* (Aldeshot, Ashgate Publishing, 2002) 89–114; T Waelde, 'Legal Boundaries for Extraterritorial Ambitions' in J Mitchell (ed), *Companies in a World of Conflict* (London, Earthscan/Royal Institute of International Affairs, 1998) 114–92.

[23] R Meeran, 'The Unveiling of Transnational Corporations: A Direct Approach' in M Addo (ed), *Human Rights Standards and the Responsibility of Transnational Corporations* (London, Kluwer Law International, 1999) 161–70.

conflicts with other international law regimes (in particular, those relating to trade and investment.[24] However, none of these barriers are insurmountable and there is no inherent reason why suitable 'technical' solutions cannot be found to each of these issues.

CONCLUSIONS

This chapter is not intended to argue for the creation of unwieldy legal structures that hamper the ability of TNCs to work outside their home country or to limit their ability to take advantage of the many opportunities offered by globalisation. Rather, it has been written as a response to some of the clear limitations in the existing regulatory framework for ensuring the performance of TNCs. The proposed requirements on mandatory policy disclosure and mandatory social and environmental reporting create a framework for enabling corporate performance to be discussed and assessed, while the due diligence and foreign direct liability approaches are intended to provide mechanisms for ensuring corporate performance.

Of course the legal issues and implications are complicated, and such proposals are likely to be strongly opposed. However, the issue may be expressed in a very stark manner as follows: TNCs have been granted significant rights and powers but the present legal framework does not provide adequate mechanisms for ensuring their performance. The approaches proposed in this chapter are intended to redress this balance, at least in part. It is recognised that the measures proposed in this chapter represent 'second best solutions.' Yet, the absence of the ideal solution of a legally binding international convention, that sets reasonable standards of performance for all companies, and that is enforceable (both by states and by citizens), means that it is incumbent on national governments to take effective action to ensure that companies are accountable for their actions.

[24] C McCrudden, 'International Economic Law and the Pursuit of Human Rights: A Framework for Discussion of the Legality of "Selective Purchasing" Laws under the WTO Government Procurement Agreement', above n 15.

10

Self-Regulation of Transnational Corporations: Neither Meaningless in Law Nor Voluntary

CAROLA GLINSKI

INTRODUCTION

FOREIGN DIRECT INVESTMENT in developing countries is seen as an important tool for their economic development. Much investment takes place in countries whose labour, environmental and safety standards are low, be it due to legislation or lack of enforcement. Many of these countries do not avail of appropriate regulation of industrial processes and of adequate control mechanisms. Spectacular accidents but also continuous exploitation and pollution of people and the environment have brought this issue on the international agenda. Nevertheless, these aspects of foreign direct investment in developing countries have remained largely unregulated until now. International conventions have not yet been adopted, and the regulative power of those countries where the parent companies are situated is limited, due to the international law principle of sovereignty.[1] At the same time, public interest in transnational corporations meeting adequate standards when investing in developing countries is great in industrialised countries and on the increase in developing countries.

Below and besides direct regulation of foreign direct investment, legislators and politics at all levels have developed political concepts aiming at improving production patterns abroad. The main areas are corporate social responsibility and environmental legislation. Thereby, self-regulation by (transnational) corporations has been identified as an important mechanism to improve corporation-wide compliance with reasonable standards. Most

---

[1] See K Böttger, *Die Umweltpflichtigkeit von Auslandsinvestitionen im Völkerrecht* (Baden-Baden, Nomos, 2002).

initiatives operate through incentives to transnational corporations to improve their reputation and therefore their market performance. Indeed, industry has found such instruments a useful marketing tool. Another aspect of these initiates, however, is the strengthening of the transnational corporations' responsibility for the conduct of all their subsidiaries.

As a matter of fact, the number of private self-regulatory instruments is constantly increasing. Besides those initiated by national or supranational institutions, others have been negotiated with non-governmental organisations (NGOs) or trade unions, or they have been unilaterally adopted by single enterprises, groups of enterprises or by business associations. They come in various forms and include codes of conduct, guidelines, or management handbooks. In some of these instruments, transnational corporations promise, in more or less specific wording, to follow certain social and environmental goals, and to take measures accordingly. In others, they simply organise the operation of their various enterprises or aspects of their operation, such as the safety or environmental management, internally.

According to the long-standing opinion of the vast majority of authors, such self-regulatory instruments create moral obligations at best but have no legal effect whatsoever. This chapter revisits this belief, discussing two grounds for legal effects of private self-regulation in private law. In its first part, the chapter shows that non-compliance with a company's promises may have legal consequences in the law of unfair competition and in contract law. In its second part, it develops a model under which transnational corporations are held liable for damage caused by their subsidiaries in developing countries if they fail to organise their structures adequately by using self-regulatory instruments. The article concludes that private self-regulation is legally binding, and that it is even required by law in industries with high potential for causing pollution and damage.

PUBLIC STATEMENTS AND CONSUMER CONFIDENCE[2]

Introduction

A number of self-regulative instruments address the public. The most prominent examples are labels that relate to the social and environmental conditions of the production of goods. These aspects form part of the

---

[2] For a more detailed analysis, see C Glinski, 'Bindungswirkung produktionsbezogener Selbstverpflichtungen im Kauf- und Werberecht' in G Winter (ed), *Die Umweltverantwortung multinationaler Unternehmen* (Baden-Baden, Nomos, 2005) 87.

requirements set up by EC law on environmental labelling,[3] and they are in the focus of a number of labels that are awarded by NGOs, trade unions etc,[4] such as the 'TransFair'[5] or 'Rugmark'[6] labels, the 'Flower Label'[7] or the seal of the 'Forest Stewardship Council'[8] However, enterprises also use their internet presentations, brochures, and even special reports on their social and environmental conduct in order to communicate their commitment to certain environmental standards. Or, they refer to a code of conduct dealing with environmental behaviour[9] or to their adherence to an official programme, such as the UN Global Compact initiative.[10]

All these measures have been designed to build consumer confidence, or in a broader sense, public trust in the enterprise, and this is indeed the function that, for example, EC environmental policy assigns to them. In particular, the Sixth Community Environment Action Programme aims at improving environmentally sound production by promoting more sustainable consumption patterns within the EC but also abroad in connection with foreign direct investment and trade,[11] and so does the Green Paper on Integrated Pollution Control.[12] With the Regulation on eco-labelling[13] and Regulation (EC) No 761/2001 allowing voluntary participation by organisations in a Community eco-management and audit scheme (EMAS),[14] these thoughts have made their way into EC secondary legislation. More recently, the EC has turned its eye directly to the performance of multinational enterprises. And again, in its Communication on Corporate Social Responsibility, the EC Commission stresses the role of codes of conduct, reporting requirements and labels.[15]

---

[3] See the recitals and Art 1 of Reg (EC) No 880/92 of 23 March 1992 on a Community eco-label award scheme, OJ L99 of 14 November 1992, 1, and the recitals and Arts 1 and 3 of Reg (EC) No 1980/2000 of 17 July 2000 on a revised Community eco-label award scheme, OJ L237 of 21 September 2000, 1.

[4] For an overview, see www.label-online.de.

[5] A label that supports farmers in developing countries by guaranteeing a purchase price above world market level, and by establishing long-term business relationships.

[6] A label for the carpet industry that guarantees, among others, that no children under 14 are employed, that lawful salaries are paid, and that 1% of the import price is donated to social programmes in developing countries.

[7] A label on flowers that have been grown maintaining certain social and environmental standards.

[8] A label on tropical lumber and related products from sustainable foresting.

[9] See, eg the webpage of ALTANA Chemie, http://www.altanachemie.com/deutsch/ uw_responsible.cfm, that expresses respect for the principles of the Responsible Care programme of the chemical industry.

[10] See, eg the webpage of BASF AG at http://www.basf.de.

[11] Decision No 1600/2002/EC of 22 July 2002 laying down the Sixth Community Environment Action Programme, OJ 2002 L242 of 10 September 2002, 1, at 2, 5, 13–14.

[12] COM (2001) 68 final, at 20.

[13] See above, n 3.

[14] OJ 2001 L114 of 24 April 2001, 1.

[15] COM (2002) 347 final at 14.

It should be noted that, at EC level, environmental law and private law do not act separately from each other. Instead, Article 6 EC contains a horizontal environmental clause according to which environmental protection requirements must be integrated into the definition and implementation of all EC policies and activities. While the precise scope of this clause is being discussed controversially,[16] Article 6 EC is recognised to be a rule for interpreting all primary and secondary EC law. Thus, it applies to all internal market law, including EC consumer law, where the wording of relevant provisions is open to interpretation.

Confidence and Law

To varying extent, all legal orders recognise that building confidence has some relevance in law.[17] Where, in a business context,[18] one party attracts confidence by another party, the other party must be protected by law. The key element consists of a (self-)binding behaviour that makes the impression of being serious and that create legitimate expectations of others.[19] Typical examples for such statements are codes of conduct and social and environmental reports[20] but also advertising. Sociological research into self-regulatory instruments has revealed that they all use the language of promises.[21] The only crux, in particular with advertising messages, can lie in their vagueness. However, even from vague statements or promises one can extract a minimum content.[22]

Another issue is that codes of conduct sometimes explicitly declare that they are not binding, and there appears to be wide belief that promises in codes of conduct can be invalidated in such a way.[23] However, declarations on the non-binding character of a statement are inconsistent with the trust the statement aims to build otherwise. Thus, they can only destroy the

---

[16] See, eg N Dhondt, *Integration of Environmental Protection into other EC Policies* (Europa Law Publ, Groningen, 2003) 144 ff, 180. See also, C Glinski and P Rott, 'Umweltfreundliches und ethisches Konsumverhalten im harmonisierten Kaufrecht' [2003] *Europäische Zeitschrift für Wirtschaftsrecht* 649, at 654.

[17] For English law, one may refer, eg, to the case law on promissory estoppel. See J Adams and R Brownsword, *Understanding Contract Law* (London, Sweet & Maxwell, 2004) 82 ff.

[18] This may be different in a social context. See R Fehlmann, *Vertrauenshaftung–Vertrauen als alleinige Haftungsgrundlage* (St Gallen, 2002) 179 f.

[19] See J Köndgen, *Selbstbindung ohne Vertrag* (Tübingen, Mohr, 1981) 10, 175.

[20] See J Ewert, *Wettbewerbsrechtliche Beurteilung von Umweltwerbung ohne Produktqualitätsbezug nach deutschem Recht und europäischem Gemeinschaftsrecht* (Berlin, Duncker und Humblot, 1999) 83.

[21] See M Herberg, 'Codes of Conduct und kommunikative Vernunft' (2001) 22 *Zeitschrift für Rechtssoziologie* 25.

[22] See J Köndgen, *Selbstbindung ohne Vertrag*, above n 19, at 301 f.

[23] See, eg W Gerhardt, 'Die Haftungsfreizeichnung innerhalb des gesetzlichen Schuldverhältnisses' [1970] *Juristen-Zeitung* 535, at 537 f.

addressee's trust if they are as visible and as prominent as the trust-building features of advertising. In contrast, small print is not capable of countering the overall impression of advertising,[24] and the same is true for a declaration of the non-binding character at the very end of a long code of conduct.[25]

If consumers shall be given incentives for ethical purchasing, and if EC private law is supposed to be consistent with EC environmental law, then the only logical consequence is that consumers must be afforded legal protection of their confidence in the environmental and social performance of producers.[26] This is particularly true where recognition by official authorities, such as the UN Global Compact logo, increases public trust further.[27] Discrepancy in expertise and knowledge between the producer and the consumer makes the consumer more dependent from the producer's information so that his trust in the producer's statements deserves even more protection.[28] Besides, their consumption patterns are the only way in which consumers can take influence on production patterns in developing countries.[29]

Advertising law has always protected consumers from misleading public statements, and the 1999 EC Consumer Sales Directive has improved their legal position further.

Advertising Law

Misleading advertising has been regulated at EC level since 1984 when Directive 84/450/EEC was adopted.[30] Although this Directive has only aimed at establishing a minimum standard for advertising, its interaction with Articles 28 and 30 EC has led to significant harmonisation of the law of misleading advertising throughout the EC.[31] It covers the protection of

[24] See J Köndgen, *Selbstbindung ohne Vertrag*, above n 19, at 184.

[25] See also German case law on environmental advertising, eg, Bundesgerichtshof (1989) *Wettbewerb in Recht und Praxis* 163; Bundesgerichtshof (1991) *Wettbewerb in Recht und Praxis* 159. For more details, see C Glinski, 'Bindungswirkung produktionsbezogener Selbstverpflichtungen im Kauf- und Werberecht', above n 2, at 198.

[26] See, eg T Wilhelmsson, 'Contribution to a Green Sales Law' in T Wilhelmsson, *Twelve Essays on Consumer Law and Policy* (Helsinki, Publications of the Department of Private Law, University of Helsinki, 1996) 267, at 278.

[27] See J Köndgen, *Selbstbindung ohne Vertrag*, above n 19, at 233.

[28] See J Ewert, *Wettbewerbsrechtliche Beurteilung von Umweltwerbung ohne Produktqualitätsbezug nach deutschem Recht und europäischem Gemeinschaftsrecht*, above n 20, at 121; I Roth, *Umweltbezogene Unternehmenskommunikation im deutschen und europäischen Wettbewerbsrecht* (Frankfurt a.M., Lang, 2000) 2.

[29] See T Wilhelmsson, 'Contribution to a Green Sales Law', above n 26, at 284 f.

[30] Directive 84/450/EEC relating to the approximation of the laws, regulations and administrative provisions of the Member States concerning misleading advertising, OJ 1984 L250 of 19 September 1984, 17. This Directive was implemented in the UK by the Control of Misleading Advertising Regulations 1988, SI 1988 No 915.

[31] See, eg W.-H. Roth, 'Zur Tragweite der Harmonisierung im Recht des unlauteren Wettbewerbs' in U Immenga, W Möschel and D Reuter, *Festschrift für Ernst-Joachim Mestmäcker* (Baden-Baden, Nomos, 1996) 725, at 726 ff.

consumers as well as of traders, to whom advertising is addressed, obviously with different standards of understanding expected.[32] The recent proposal for a new Directive on unfair commercial practices[33] would even harmonise the protection of consumers from misleading advertising totally.

Advertising

Advertising comprises all measures that aim at increasing one's own or a third person's sales. Clearly, all the above-mentioned public statements do constitute 'advertising' in the terms of Article 3 of the Directive. When determining whether advertising is misleading, account shall be taken, according to Article 3 (a) and (c), among others, to the method of manufacture and to the nature, attributes and rights of the advertiser. This ensures that advertising with clean production, and also advertising with the 'clean' image of a company, must not be misleading.[34] Publicised codes of conduct or guidelines with social or environmental content usually express the specific engagement and also competence of a trader in this field, for example, with respect to the responsible use of resources, to clean production, or to waste management, that is not restricted to the production of a specific type of good but extends to all goods produced by this company. Also, social or environmental reports qualify as advertising.[35] Even industry-wide codes of conduct may constitute advertising if a certain industry competes with another industry as, for example, the oil industry competes with the natural gas industry. Consequently, the proposal for a new Directive explicitly mentions groups of traders as addressees of advertising law, Article 2 (i).

The new notion of 'commercial practices' is defined in Article 2 (e) of the proposal as 'any act, omission, course of conduct or representation, commercial communication including advertising and marketing, by a trader, directly connected with the promotion, sale or supply of a product to consumers.' This definition appears to be narrower than the definition of

---

[32] See ECJ, Case C-112/99 *Toshiba Europe GmbH v Katun Germany GmbH* [2001] ECR I-7945, at 52. German courts, however, held that even traders do not have much experience with the environmental characteristics of goods. See, eg OLG Köln, (1988) *Gewerblicher Rechtsschutz und Urheberrecht* 630, at 631.

[33] Proposal for a Directive of the European Parliament and of the Council concerning unfair business-to-consumer commercial practices in the Internal Market and amending Directives 84/450/EEC, 97/7/EC and 98/27/EC (the Unfair Commercial Practices Directive), COM (2003) 356 final.

[34] For details, see J Ewert, *Wettbewerbsrechtliche Beurteilung von Umweltwerbung ohne Produktqualitätsbezug nach deutschem Recht und europäischem Gemeinschaftsrecht*, above n 20, at 26; G Federhoff-Rink, *Umweltschutz und Wettbewerbsrecht* (Heidelberg, Verlag Recht und Wirtschaft, 1994) 84 ff; EB Zabel, *Die wettbewerbsrechtliche Zulässigkeit produktunabhängiger Image-Werbung* (Konstanz, Hartung-Gorre, 1998) 20 ff.

[35] See also the US American case of *Marc Kasky v Nike, inc, et al*, 2 Cal. Daily Op. Serv. 3790.

advertising in Directive 84/450/EEC since it excludes measures that are merely indirectly connected with the promotion, sale or supply of a product to consumers.[36] This latter restriction, however, does not apply where a connection is made between issues of social responsibility or morals and the marketed product.[37] Due to this connection, codes of conduct, guidelines and reports that aim at improving the image of traders should continue to come under EC law on misleading advertising and should therefore be regarded as 'commercial practices.' Certainly, this interpretation would be preferable with a view to the horizontal environmental clause of Article 6 EC.[38]

Misleading Advertising

If self-regulatory instruments deceive or are likely to deceive consumers and, by reason of their deceptive nature, are likely to affect their economic behaviour, they constitute misleading advertising. The standard is set by the average consumer who the ECJ describes as being reasonably well informed and reasonably observant and circumspect.[39] This very definition shall now be codified in Article 2 (b) of the proposed Unfair Commercial Practices Directive. German courts have already created a body of case law on environmental advertising. For example, longer texts, such as environmental codes of conduct or environmental reports have to be informative and true.[40] Of course, a product that is described as being environmentally sound must not be below average in this respect.[41] Negative aspects that are not mentioned must not nullify the mentioned positive aspects.[42] The same rules apply to traders that hold themselves out as being environmentally friendly.[43] Particularly high requirements apply to traders in dirty industries, such as extraction industries.[44] Also, the use of environmental labels

---

[36] What this exactly means is rather unclear, see H Köhler and T Lettl, 'Das geltende europäische Lauterkeitsrecht, der Vorschlag für eine EG-Richtlinie über unlautere Geschäftspraktiken und die UWG-Reform' [2003] *Wettbewerb in Recht und Praxis* 1019, at 1034.

[37] See the explanations to the proposal, n 33, at no 39 and 68.

[38] For more details, see C Glinski, 'Bindungswirkung produktionsbezogener Selbstverpflichtungen im Kauf- und Werberecht', above n 2, at 193.

[39] See, eg Case C-112/99, *Toshiba Europe GmbH v Katun Germany GmbH* [2001] ECR I-7945, at 52; Case C-44/01, *Pippig Augenoptik GmbH & Co. KG v. Hartlauer Handelsgesellschaft mbH* [2003] ECR I-3095, at 55.

[40] See G Federhoff-Rink, *Umweltschutz und Wettbewerbsrecht*, above n 34, at 249.

[41] See I Roth, *Umweltbezogene Unternehmenskommunikation im deutschen und europäischen Wettbewerbsrecht*, above n 28, at 241. The OLG Düsseldorf (1988) *Gewerblicher Rechtsschutz und Urheberrecht* 55, at 59, has required a significant improvement of the environmental characteristics compared with competing products.

[42] See I Roth, *Umweltbezogene Unternehmenskommunikation im deutschen und europäischen Wettbewerbsrecht*, above n 28, at 242 f.

[43] *Ibid*, at 248.

[44] See G Federhoff-Rink, *Umweltschutz und Wettbewerbsrecht*, above n 34, at 85. See also the very restrictive decision of the OLG Düsseldorf, above n 41.

necessitates a high level of transparency since labels make the impression of being somehow official. Thus, it must be clear what features make a product environmentally sound, and who has verified these features and allowed the use of the label.[45] This latter requirement is also explicitly included in Annex I of the proposed Unfair Commercial Practices Directive. In this respect, the mentioning of internal environmental guidelines that are not publicly accessible is particularly problematic.

Codes of conduct have received a great deal of attention in the new proposal. On the one hand, they shall enable industries to design standards of good commercial practice.[46] On the other, non-compliance with standards that traders have subscribed to is an unfair commercial practice under Article 6 (2)(b) of the Proposal.[47] Thus, it should become easier in the future to sanction traders that do not keep their promises.

Advertising Law and Freedom of Speech

In many jurisdictions, advertising enjoys the protection of the fundamental right to freedom of speech. This is true for the US,[48] and also for Germany.[49] Thus, bans on advertising, for example, for certain groups, are highly problematic. However, constitutional law does not allow advertising with untrue or deceptive statements.[50]

Remedies

Under Article 4 of Directive 84/450/EEC, Member States shall make effective remedies available, which does not include, according to the EC Commission, individual rights for consumers. Instead, the Commission lays its focus on enforcement of advertising law by public bodies.[51] The proposed Unfair Commercial Practices Directive will not call for individual

---

[45] See Bundesgerichtshof (1989) 105 *Rechtsprechung des Bundesgerichtshofs in Zivilsachen* 277. See also T Wölwer, *Zur Zulässigkeit der Werbung mit Umweltslogans und Umweltzeichen im deutschen und amerikanischen Recht* (Frankfurt a.M., Peter Lang, 1999) 108 ff.

[46] See Art 10 of the proposal, above n 33. See also A Wiebe, 'Die "guten Sitten" im Wettbewerb–eine europäische Regelungsaufgabe?' [2002] *Wettbewerb in Recht und Praxis* 283, at 288, 290 ff; A Beater, 'Europäisches Recht gegen unlauteren Wettbewerb–Ansatzpunkte, Grundlagen, Entwicklung, Erforderlichkeit' [2003] *Zeitschrift für Europäisches Privatrecht* 11, at 49 f.

[47] The same applies to commitments that traders have made to authorities, Art 6 (2)(c) of the Proposal, above n 33.

[48] See *Bigelow v Virginia* (1975) 421 U.S. 809, 825, 95 S.Ct. 2222, 44 L.Ed.2nd 600.

[49] See, eg Bundesverfassungsgericht (2001) *Gewerblicher Rechtsschutz und Urheberrecht* 170, at 172.

[50] See *Marc Kasky v Nike, inc, et al*, 2 Cal. Daily Op. Serv. 3790.

[51] See especially the Green Paper on European Union Consumer Protection, COM (2001) 531 final, at 11 ff.

remedies either.[52] Consumer associations could claim injunctions under Injunction Directive 98/27/EC as implemented in the Member States. In contrast, environmental associations usually do not have legal standing for such claims.[53] Thus, on the remedies side, advertising law may prove to be of limited effectiveness unless traders that use misleading advertising are liable for damages. For example, Germany is about to introduce the consumer associations right to claim restitutional damages that would, however, have to be paid to the state.[54]

Sales Law

Individual remedies of consumers, or of purchasers in general, for non-compliance of producers with their own public statements on production patterns, made in codes of conducts and other self-regulatory instruments, may stem from the Consumer Sales Directive 1999/44/EC.[55]

Directive 1999/44/EC protects the consumer in the case of the sale of goods that are not in conformity with the contract, Article 2 (1). The notion of conformity is further concretised in Article 2 (2). According to Article 2 (2)(d), it includes conformity with public statements on the specific characteristics made about them by the seller, the producer or his representative, particularly in advertising or on labelling. Thus, in principle codes of conduct and other public statements are capable of describing the conformity of a product with a sales contract. In fact, one of the very modern features of EC consumer sales law is to acknowledge that the producer's statements, especially those made in advertising, may have a far greater effect on the purchasing decision of consumers than the immediate contact between the seller and the consumer.[56] For many national sales laws, this constitutes a novelty.[57]

---

[52] Germany offers some weak individual remedy in misleading advertising law but intends to abolish this. See, eg F Weiler, 'Ein lauterkeitsrechtliches Vertragslösungsrecht des Verbrauchers?' [2003] *Zeitschrift für Rechtspolitik* 423.

[53] See the failed attempt by Greenpeace, OLG Hamburg (1993) *Neue Juristische Wochenschrift* 1867.

[54] See, eg A Stadler and H-W Micklitz, 'Der Reformvorschlag der UWG-Novelle für eine Verbandsklage auf Gewinnabschöpfung' [2003] *Wettbewerb in Recht und Praxis* 559 ff.

[55] For a more extensive analysis, see C Glinski and P Rott, 'Umweltfreundliches und ethisches Konsumverhalten im harmonisierten Kaufrecht', above n 16.

[56] See, eg D Staudenmayer, 'The Directive on the Sale of Consumer Goods and Associated Guarantees–a Milestone in the European Consumer and Private Law' [2000] *European Review of Private Law* 547, at 551. This element does not form part of Art 35 CISG that has otherwise served as a model for Art 2 of Directive 1999/44/EC. See S Grundmann, 'Verbraucherrecht, Unternehmensrecht, Privatrecht–warum sind sich UN-Kaufrecht und EU-Kaufrechts-Richtlinie so ähnlich?' [2002] 202 *Archiv für civilistische Praxis* 40, at 47.

[57] For German sales law see, eg S Jorden, *Verbrauchergarantien* (VVF, München, 2001) 153 ff. For England, see D Oughton and C Willet, 'Quality Regulation in European Private Law' (2002) 25 *Journal of Consumer Policy* 299, at 311; R Bradgate and C Twigg-Flesner, 'Expanding the Boundaries of Liability for Quality Defects' (2002) 25 *Journal of Consumer Policy* 345, at 346 ff. For Scotland, see M Hogg, 'Scottish law and the European Consumer

The trader is liable for the producer's statements because he also benefits from the advertising.[58]

The concept of conformity does not only extend to product-related characteristics of the goods in question, such as their toxicity, but to the circumstances under which they were produced.[59] In particular, the value that is accorded by some consumers to the social and environmental effects of the production is capable of constituting a conformity requirement. One example is a recent case decided by the Higher Regional Court of Munich, under Article 35 (1) CISG that had served as a model for Article 2 (1) of the Directive. Barley had been sold as being in conformity with Regulation (EEC) No 2092/91 on organic production of agricultural products.[60] This Regulation does not relate to specific product standards, but to a specific form of production at farm level. Of course, consumers may hope that products produced in such a way are of higher quality. However, they may also wish to support environmental protection and the conservation of the countryside. Therefore, products that have been produced organically are usually more expensive than their industrially produced equivalents. This could not be proven by the trader since relevant documents were missing. Therefore, the Court held that the products were not in conformity with the contract.[61] In conclusion, the conditions of production will always be relevant for the conformity with the contract if they form part of the consumer's legitimate expectations. Especially where a purchase price of the ethically produced goods is equal to goods produced otherwise, the specific production patterns may be decisive for the purchase. The only reservation to be made is that public statements must relate to the 'specific characteristics' of a good. The emphasis is on the term 'specific'. This means that public statements must relate to facts that can be proven,[62] which is usually the

---

Sales Directive' [2001] *European Review of Private Law* 337, at 345. It merely formed part of the modern Scandinavian and Dutch sales laws, see T Wilhelmsson, 'Contribution to a Green Sales Law', above n 26, at 276; A Schwartze, *Europäische Sachmangelhaftung beim Warenkauf* (Mohr, Tübingen, 2000) 99.

[58] See, eg H Beale and G Howells, 'EC Harmonisation of Consumer Sales Law–A Missed Opportunity?' (1997) 12 *Journal of Contract Law* 20, at 30. The only exception of practical relevance is if the trader shows by the time of conclusion of the contract the statement had been corrected, Art 2 (4) of the Directive.

[59] See D Staudenmayer, 'The Directive on the Sale of Consumer Goods and Associated Guarantees–a Milestone in the European Consumer and Private Law', above n 56, at 551.

[60] Council Reg (EEC) No 2092/91 on organic production of agricultural products and indications referring thereto on agricultural products and foodstuffs, OJ 1991 L198 of 22 July 1991, 1.

[61] OLG München (2003) *Neue Juristische Wochenschrif –Rechtsprechungs-Report* 849. In another case, the LG Ellwangen (2003) *Neue Juristische Wochenschrift* 517 held that a Volkswagen car that was advertised as produced in the EC, whereas it had been produced in South Africa, was not in conformity with the contract.

[62] Whereby a fact content can usually be extracted from any statement on social or environmental performance, see above, n 22.

case with labelling or codes of conduct but not necessarily with advertising spots that relate goods to a certain lifestyle etc.[63]

This interpretation of the conformity test offers the consumer the opportunity to enforce promises that are related to the circumstances of the production. This can be of particular relevance if it comes to mass protests against specific producers that have been identified to act against their public statements, such as the anti-Nike movement. Furthermore, consumer associations may sue for injunctions,[64] stopping sellers sellinggoods that are not in conformity with the producers' public statements without correcting these statements.

LIABILITY OF PARENT COMPANIES[65]

Introduction

The liability of parent companies for damages caused by their subsidiaries in developing countries is back to the political agenda as well. After a confrontational approach, in particular by UN institutions in the 1980s, to the industry's conduct in developing countries, most international organisations had stepped back and favoured voluntary commitments. Prominent examples are the OECD Guidelines for Multinational Enterprises,[66] Kofi Annan's Global Compact,[67] the EC Commission's Communication on Corporate Social Responsibility[68] and similar national initiatives.[69] These initiatives have in common that they address transnational corporations to keep standards related to the protection of human rights, social rights and

---

[63] For details, see C Glinski and P Rott, 'Umweltfreundliches und ethisches Konsumverhalten im harmonisierten Kaufrecht', above n 16, at 653. See also D Staudenmayer, 'The Directive on the Sale of Consumer Goods and Associated Guarantees–a Milestone in the European Consumer and Private Law', above n 56, at 552; S Grundmann and CM Bianca, *EU-Kaufrechts-Richtlinie* (Schmidt, Köln 2001) Art 2, at 37.

[64] Under Directive 98/27/EC on injunctions for the protection of the consumers' interests, OJ 1998 L166 (11. 6.98) 51, as implemented in the national legal systems.

[65] For a more detailed analysis, see C Glinski, 'Haftungsrelevanz konzernweiter Selbstregulierung bei Direktinvestitionen in Entwicklungsländern', in G Winter (ed), *Die Umweltverantwortung multinationaler Unternehman* (Baden-Baden, Nomos, 2005) 231.

[66] On their version of 2000 see S Tully, 'The 2000 Review of the OECD Guidelines for Multinational Enterprises' (2001) 50 *International and Comparative Law Quarterly* 394.

[67] Available at http://www.unglobalcompact.org. For critical comments see, eg A Zumach, 'Der "strategische Handel" des Generalsekretärs–Ernüchternde Erfahrungen mit dem Globalen Pakt von Davos' (2002) 50 *Vereinte Nationen* 1.

[68] COM (2002) 347 final.

[69] See the French Décret no 2002-221 du 20 février 2002 pris pour l'application de l'article L. 225-102-1 du code de commerce et modifiant le décret no 67-236 du 23 mars 1967 sur les sociétés commerciales, J.O. no 44 of 21 February 2002, 3360, or the English Corporate Responsibility Bill, Bill 145 of 2002.

the environment. Thereby, they focus on self-regulation that is, at best, accompanied by reporting obligations.[70]

However, most recent initiatives go further. The UN has tabled 'Norms on the Responsibility of Transnational Corporations and other Business Enterprises with Regard to Human Rights'[71] ('Norms'), and NGOs representatives call for a 'Corporate Accountability Convention'.[72] Besides the transnational corporations' respect for human rights, social rights and environmental standards as formed by international law, both initiatives demand the introductionof the transnational corporations' liability for damages, sanctions for violations, and the victims' access to justice.[73] In contrast to the voluntary approaches, they aim at a binding mechanism that shall be based on self-regulation by transnational corporations. All these initiatives address transnational corporations as a whole and thus treat them as entities, disregarding their legal separation in different legal units.[74] For example, the 'Norms' define 'transnational corporations' as economic entities operating in more than one country or a cluster of economic entities operating in two or more countries–whatever their legal form, whether in their home country or country of activity, and whether taken individually or collectively.[75] Central control by the parent company is apparently not essential.[76]

Reasons for demands for direct liability of the whole transnational corporation, and in particular its parent company, are manifold. The UN Sub-Commission argues with global trends which have increased the influence

---

[70] See, eg EC Commission's Communication on Corporate Social Responsibility, COM (2002) 347 final, 14.

[71] UN document E/CN.4/Sub.2/2003/12/Rev.2 (2003).

[72] For details, see H Ward, 'Towards a New Convention on Corporate Accountability? Some Lessons from the Thor Chemicals and Cape PLC Cases' (2001) *Yearbook of International Environmental Law* 105, at 136 ff.

[73] For an account, see P Muchlinski, 'Human Rights, Social Responsibility and the Regulation of International Business: The Development of International Standards by Intergovernmental Organisations' (2003) 3 *Non-State Actors and International Law* 123, at 135 ff; K Nowrot, 'Die UN-Norms on the Responsibility of Transnational Corporations and Other Business Enterprises with Regard to Human Rights–Gelungener Beitrag zur transnationalen Rechtsverwirklichung oder das Ende des Global Compact?' in C Tietje, G Kraft and R Sethe (eds), (2003) 21 *Beiträge zum Transnationalen Wirtschaftsrecht*; CF Hillemanns, 'UN Norms on the Responsibilities of Transnational Corporations and Other Business Enterprises with regard to Human Rights' (2003) 4 *German Law Journal* 1065 ff.

[74] See the 'Norms', above n 71, at 20.

[75] 'Norms', at para 20. The 'Norms' also cover 'other business enterprises' which extends the scope to domestic enterprises that have trade relations with partners abroad. For details, see P Muchlinski, 'Human Rights, Social Responsibility and the Regulation of International Business: The Development of International Standards by Intergovernmental Organisations', above n 73, at 136 f.; K Nowrot, 'Die UN-Norms on the Responsibility of Transnational Corporations and Other Business Enterprises with Regard to Human Rights–Gelungener Beitrag zur transnationalen Rechtsverwirklichung oder das Ende des Global Compact?' above n 73, at 19 f.

[76] See also, K Nowrot, above n 73, at 19.

of transnational corporations and other business enterprises on the economies of most countries and in international economic relations, but also their capacity to cause harmful impacts on the human rights and lives of individuals through their core business practices and operations.[77]

One should be aware of the fact that the principle of legal separation between legal persons and their owners was developed in order to protect natural persons, and to offer them a legal framework for investment without risk for their personal property. The model was then transposed to legal entities owning other legal persons, one argument being that the breakdown of one company should not affect the whole corporation. Whether not this argument holds valid with regard to transnational corporations is discussed controversially.[78] The German chemical industry, for example, did not use this separation in earlier years.[79]

In a global economy, the separate treatment of legal persons offers ample opportunity for abuse, in particular, where subsidiaries are established in countries with low company law standards. Consequently, some of these subsidiaries do not have the capital available for adequate health, safety and environmental management, and they may not be able to pay compensation if it comes to damages. Also, subsidiaries may simply be dissolved as happened with Thor Chemicals in the Republic of South Africa.[80]

But even beyond the problem of abuse, it appears legitimate that those who initiate the dangerous activities and who benefit from them are held responsible for damages. More precisely, those who are in control of production patterns that cause damage should be held responsible in accordance with the polluter pays principle.

In this context, it is important to note that corporations from industrialised countries export plants or technologies into developing countries with an entirely different socio-economic background. Local staff may not be sufficiently educated or experienced to deal with the related dangers appropriately,[81] and local people may not be aware of the risks. Thus, difficulties are foreseeable, and the exporting parent company with

---

[77] See the Preamble of the 'Norms', above n 71.

[78] For doubts, see P Muchlinski, 'Corporations in International Litigation: Problems of Jurisdiction and the United Kingdom Asbestos Cases' (2001) 50 *International and Comparative Law Quarterly* 1, at 16, against L Bergkamp and W-Q Pak, 'Piercing the Corporate Veil: Shareholder Liability for Corporate Torts' (2001) 8 *Maastricht Journal of European and Comparative Law* 163, at 181.

[79] See P Hommelhoff, 'Gesellschaftsformen als Organisationselemente im Konzernaufbau' in E-J Mestmäcker and P Behrens (eds), *Das Gesellschaftsrecht der Konzerne im internationalen Vergleich* (Baden-Baden, Nomos, 1991) 91, at 94.

[80] See H Ward, 'Towards a New Convention on Corporate Accountability? Some Lessons from the Thor Chemicals and Cape PLC Cases', above n 72, at 121, 127.

[81] As, eg in the Thor Chemicals case, see H Ward, 'Towards a New Convention on Corporate Accountability? Some Lessons from the Thor Chemicals and Cape PLC Cases', above n 72, at 117.

its superior expertise must take responsibility for safe production, regardless of whether the subsidiary is a separate legal entity or not. Indeed, empirical research into the German chemicals industry has found that parent companies actually do regulate their subsidiaries conduct, at least in the field of safety and environmental management. Not only do they publish guidelines; in high-risk industries such as the chemicals industry, they also issue detailed handbooks on proper procedure, and they avail of central control units that sends auditors to the subsidiaries in order to control compliance and to introduce improvements.[82]

Finally, access to justice may point at the parent company's liability, as the claims of Ecuadorians and South Africans against Texaco,[83] Thor Chemicals and Cape Industries, Ltd.[84] respectively demonstrate. With regard to enforcement, it seems natural to sue the parent company at its place of business. Moreover, the developing country's legal system may not offer legal aid, or instruments such as class actions, or multi-party actions.

Two areas of law could be utilised in order to allow claims for compensation of damages: the law of corporations, and tort law, or special environmental liability laws.

Jurisdiction

While jurisdiction for such claims is not an issue in civil law countries, courts in common law countries have regularly applied the *forum non conveniens* doctrine in order to bar claims brought by victims from developing countries where subsidiaries were established and had caused damage. Prominent examples are the *Bhopal*[85] and *Texaco*[86] cases where US American courts have denied having jurisdiction. In recent years, Australian and English courts have relaxed their position with a view to granting access to justice to claimants from developing countries.[87] In the *Unocal*

---

[82] See M Herberg, 'Codes of Conduct und kommunikative Vernunft', above n 21, at 38 ff.

[83] See S MacLeod, 'Maria Aguinda v Texaco Inc: Defining the Limits of Liability for Human Rights Violations Resulting from Environmental Degradation' [1999] *Contemporary Issues in Law* 188 ff.

[84] See H Ward, 'Towards a New Convention on Corporate Accountability? Some Lessons from the Thor Chemicals and Cape PLC Cases', above n 72, at 120, 130.

[85] *In Re Union Carbide Corporation Gas Plant Disaster at Bhopal, India*, 1984, 634 F. Supp. 842 (S.D. N.Y. 1986).

[86] See S MacLeod, 'Maria Aguinda v Texaco Inc: Defining the Limits of Liability for Human Rights Violations Resulting from Environmental Degradation', above n 83.

[87] See the decision by the Victorian Supreme Court in *Dagi and others v BHP*, cited by P Prince, 'Bhopal, Bougainville and Ok Tedi: Why Australia's *Forum Non Conveniens* Approach is Better' (1998) 47 *International and Comparative Law Quarterly* 573, at 593 ff. Concerning the decisions by the House of Lords in the Thor Chemicals and Cape Industries cases, see P Muchlinski, 'Corporations in International Litigation: Problems of Jurisdiction and the United Kingdom Asbestos Cases', above n 78, at 11 ff; H Ward, 'Towards a New Convention on Corporate Accountability? Some Lessons from the Thor Chemicals and Cape PLC Cases', above n 72, at 129.

case, the US have recently extended their jurisdiction under the Alien Tort Claims Act that allows claims for damages from human rights violations.[88] However, with a view to environmental damages, jurisdiction under the Alien Tort Claims Act can only applies to immense pollution that amounts to a human rights violation. Thus, US law still falls short of providing access to justice as required by the 'Norms', and the situation in other common law jurisdictions is also unsatisfactory since the *forum non conveniens* test always puts the claimants at risk of being denied jurisdiction.

Of course, victims of environmental damages can bring claims in their domestic courts and then try to have them recognised and enforced in the parent company's state. However, all legal systems know an *ordre public* reservation, and there are limits to such recognition and enforcement. For example, in *Deltec*, the New York Supreme Court refused to recognise a decision by the Argentinean Supreme Court that had held a US American parent company liable for damages caused by a subsidiary in Argentina.[89]

Law of Corporations

The law of corporations, in its current state, is rather unhelpful to claimants in developing countries that try to sue the subsidiaries' parent companies. This is because it follows the principle of legal separation of parent company and its subsidiaries. Rare exceptions focus on the protection of the subsidiary, whilet the relationship to third parties is only a reflex of the protection of the subsidiary. In contrast, the law of corporations does not have any mechanism available to base the parent company's liability on regulation of the subsidiaries' safety and environmental conduct through codes of conducts or other means.

The rules of conflicts of law generally point at the subsidiary's law so that the law of the developing country in question applies.[90] Nevertheless, the law of the parent company is of utmost importance since it bars overly generous rules on the liability of parent companies for their subsidiaries' conduct if this is against the *ordre public* of the parent company's country.[91]

Current law of Corporations

Generally speaking, three models can be distinguished: (1) the English and US American model where parent companies are merely liable for their

---

[88] See A Seibert-Fohr, 'Die Deliktshaftung von Unternehmen für die Beteiligung an im Ausland begangenen Völkerrechtsverletzungen' (2003) 63 *Zeitschrift für ausländisches öffentliches Recht und Rechtsvergleichung* 195 ff.

[89] See P Muchlinski, *Multinational Enterprises and the Law* (Oxford, Blackwell, 1995) 332.

[90] See KA Hofstetter, *Sachgerechte Haftungsregeln für internationale Konzerne* (Tübingen, Mohr, 1996) 162, with further references.

[91] Above, n 65.

subsidiaries' obligations in cases of blatant abuse of the allocation of activities to other legal entities, (2) the entity model where a parent company and
their subsidiaries are regarded as one legal entity once they form an economic entity, and (3) a mixed model such as the one followed in Germany.
In addition to this, English law offers a speciality in that a parent company
can be director of a subsidiary and therefore come under the rules on director's liability.

(1) Abuse Model

Under the abuse model, 'piercing of the corporate veil' is justified where the
subsidiary is a mere shell or instrument for the parent company's activities
and where the legal separation is illegitimate or fraudulent.[92] One example
is where a subsidiary is grossly undercapitalised. With a view to environmental damage, the parent company will only be liable if the subsidiary has
been undercapitalised and misused in order to externalise environmental
damages that were likely to occur from risky activities. One such case was
the oil spill caused by the sinking of the Amoco Cadiz where the parent
company had total control and the subsidiary was totally undercapitalised.[93] Self-regulatory instruments of transnational corporations have no
role to play in such a model.

(2) Entity Model

Under the opposite entity model, joint and several liability would be
imposed on the parent company and its subsidiary where the parent company controls the subsidiary and both form an economic entity.[94] In the
1970s, the EC Commission had intended to introduce this model with an
EC Directive on corporations[95] that was, however, never adopted. While
the entity model would appear to come close to the ideas of the 'Norms',
no current statutory law of corporations seems to follow it. Centralised

---

[92] For an overview of US American law, see KA Hofstetter, 'The Ecological Liability of
Corporate Groups: Comparing US and European Trends' in G Teubner, L Farmer and D
Murphy (eds), *Environmental Law and Ecological Responsibility* (Chichester, Wiley, 1994) 99
ff; C Alting, 'Piercing the Corporate Veil in American and German law–Liability of Individuals
and Entities: A Comparative View' (1995) 2 *Tulsa Journal of Comparative and International
Law* 187 ff; M Landwehr, *Die Durchgriffshaftung in konzernverbundenen Gesellschaften*
(Frankfurt a.M., Lang, 2002). For English law, see the landmark decision of *Salomon v
Salomon* [1897] AC 22, and *Adams & Others v Cape Industries Plc and Another* [1990] Ch
433. See also, E-M Schuberth, *Konzernrelevante Regelungen im britischen Recht* (München,
CH Beck, 1997) 178 ff.
[93] *In re Matter of Oil Spill by the Amoco Cadiz off the Coast of France on Mar 16, 1978,*
954 F.2d 1279, 1303 (7th Cir. 1992). See also JE Antunes, 'Neue Wege im
Konzernhaftungsrecht–Nochmals: Der "Amoco Cadiz"-Fall' in UH Schneider et al, *Festschrift
für Marcus Lutter zum 70. Geburtstag* (Köln, Otto Schmidt, 2000) 995, at 1000 f.
[94] See G Teubner, 'Unitas Multiplex–Das Konzernrecht in der neuen Dezentralität der
Unternehmensgruppen' [1991] *Zeitschrift für das gesamte Gesellschaftsrecht* 189, at 200 ff.
[95] See W Schilling, 'Bemerkungen zum Europäischen Konzernrecht' [1978] *Zeitschrift für
das gesamte Gesellschaftsrecht* 415 ff.

environmental management, for example, in the form of a code of conduct, guidelines or other instruments might support evidence for control over subsidiaries but would not be an essential element of such control.[96]

(3) German Law as a Mixed Model

German law of corporations is regarded as being modern, and its basic ideas have served as a model for more recent statutes, such as the Brazilian law of corporations.[97] In principle, it follows the model of separate legal entities with their own respective responsibilities. The subsidiary has its own legitimate interests, and the parent company has the fiduciary duty to respect these interests. This rule applies whenever the subsidiary is dependent on the parent company, which is usually the case if the parent company owns the majority of shares. However, even ownership of 25 per cent of the shares can suffice in combination with other means of control.[98] While such other means can be economic or legal control, control over the corporation-wide safety and environmental management will not be decisive.

If the company fails to respect these duties it is liable to compensate the subsidiary for related and identifiable losses that have not been made good until the end of the year.[99] Creditors can claim compensation from the parent company if they cannot obtain compensation from the subsidiary. However, there is one important prerequisite to the parent company's liability: The parent company is only liable if it has taken or omitted a measure that a responsible director of the subsidiary would not have taken or omitted.[100] With a view to environmental management, this means that a parent company will only be liable if it has forced some irresponsible conduct onto the subsidiary. In this system, self-regulatory instruments are of very little relevance.

(4) Parent Company as the Subsidiary's Director

English law provides for the speciality that a parent company can be the subsidiary's director,[101] and it can also act as a '*de facto* director' or a 'shadow director' if it has not been formally appointed director.[102] Under s

---

[96] See also JE Antunes, 'Neue Wege im Konzernhaftungsrecht–Nochmals: Der "Amoco Cadiz"-Fall', above n 93, at 1002.

[97] See GW Rothmann, 'Die Behandlung des Konzerns als gesellschaftsrechtliches Sonderproblem in Brasilien' in E-J Mestmäcker and P Behrens (eds), *Das Gesellschaftsrecht der Konzerne im internationalen Vergleich* (Baden-Baden, Nomos, 1991) 217, at 226.

[98] See K Eschenbruch, *Konzernhaftung: Haftung der Unternehmen und der Manager* (Düsseldorf, Werner, 1996) 150 ff.

[99] On the violation of duties related to environmental management see I Ossenbühl, *Umweltgefährdungshaftung im Konzern* (Berlin, Duncker & Humblot, 1999) 186 ff.

[100] For details, see K Eschenbruch, *Konzernhaftung: Haftung der Unternehmen und der Manager*, above n 98, at 246 f, 251, 261 ff.

[101] This rule, however, has come under pressure, see the White Paper, *Modernising Company Law*, Command Paper Cm 5553, July 2002, at 31.

[102] For an overview of European company laws see H Fleischer, 'Juristische Personen als Organmitglieder im Europäischen Gesellschaftsrecht' [2004] *Recht der Internationalen Wirtschaft* 16.

251 of the Insolvency Act, 'shadow director' means a person in accordance with whose directions or instructions the directors of the company are accustomed to act. *'De facto* director' means a person who acts openly as a director without having been formally appointed.

The degree of intervention that is necessary to be a shadow director is unclear but it appears to be lower than the degree of control required by German law of corporations.[103] Influence on day-to-day business might be sufficient. Whether or not active influence on the safety management or the environmental management makes a parent company shadow director would probably depend on the circumstances of the individual case. It appears possible in dangerous industries such as the extracting industry or the chemicals industry where safety and environmental management gain high importance.

In such a case, the director's duties are imposed on the parent company, and the liability of the latter can stem from insolvency law but potentially also from breach of the director's fiduciary duties. The details are subject to much discussion.[104] The crucial issue, however, is similar to German law. The rules on director's liability protect the subsidiary's interest, not the interests of third parties. Thus, if the subsidiary's board agrees with an intervention by the parent company, no liability occurs.[105] Merely in the wake of insolvency, the creditors' interests come into play,[106] a situation that is largely unrelated to environmental damages. The only imaginable situation would be where the parent company's intervention causes predictable environmental damage that inevitably leads to the subsidiary's insolvency.

(5) Conclusion

In conclusion, law of corporations in its current state is largely unsuited to deal with third parties' damages that are caused by unethical or dirty production patterns.[107] Even in those legal systems that recognise that parent companies should be liable for inappropriate influence on their subsidiaries activities, the focus lies entirely on the protection of the subsidiary.

Proposals for a Sectored Model

Because of this failure of the law of corporations, it was proposed not to look at the influence of a parent company on its subsidiary as a whole but on the allocation of responsibilities within the corporation, which can vary

---

[103] See E-M Schuberth, above n 92, at 195.

[104] For an overview, see J Schneider, 'Die Haftung der Muttergesellschaft als Organ der Tochtergesellschaft nach deutschem und englischem Recht' (2003) 102 *Zeitschrift für vergleichende Rechtswissenschaften* 387, 408 ff.

[105] See E-M Schuberth, above n 92, at 118 ff.

[106] See E-M Schuberth, above n 92, at 206 ff.

[107] See also JE Antunes, 'Neue Wege im Konzernhaftungsrecht–Nochmals: Der "Amoco Cadiz"-Fall', above n 93, at 1005 f.

from sector to sector. The parent company would be liable for damages caused in sectors that lie in its responsibility. Whether or not the parent company is in breach of duties vis-à-vis its subsidiary would be irrelevant.[108] Such a view would certainly reflect the reality of modern transnational corporations better.[109]

In a sectored model, centralised health, safety and environmental management through corporation-wide codes of conduct, guidelines or handbooks would give important evidence on the allocation of responsibility to the parent company. Control by auditors of the parent company would complete the picture.

Tort Law and Environmental Liability Law

After the unsatisfactory experience with law of corporations, tort law has been recently used to pursue claims against parent companies of subsidiaries that have caused environmental damage. Claims under tort law, or environmental liability law, are generally independent from the barriers built by the law of corporations.[110]

In environmental damage cases, the geographical aspect is so strong that the rules on conflicts will usually point at the law of the state where the damage has occurred.[111] However, rules on tort law, or at least their basic considerations, are similar worldwide, and modern environmental liability law statutes from industrialised countries may serve as model for respective legislation in developing countries.

Liability for Detrimental Influence on the Production Process

If the parent company takes influence on the production process, for example, by giving instructions or by issuing environmental management

---

[108] See G Teubner, 'Die "Politik des Gesetzes" im Recht der Konzernhaftung' in JF Baur et al (eds), *Festschrift für Ernst Steindorff zum 70. Geburtstag am 13. März 1990* (Berlin, de Gruyter, 1990) 261, at 275 ff; 'Unitas Multiplex–Das Konzernrecht in der neuen Dezentralität der Unternehmensgruppen', above n 94, at 207 ff. See also JE Antunes, 'Neue Wege im Konzernhaftungsrecht–Nochmals: Der "Amoco Cadiz"-Fall', above n 93, at 1006 ff.

[109] JE Antunes, 'Neue Wege im Konzernhaftungsrecht–Nochmals: Der "Amoco Cadiz"-Fall', above n 93, at 1006 ff, also regards the decision by the State Court of Illinois in the Amoco Cadiz case as an example for such a sectored model. This, however, may be doubted since the court had already named the subsidiary an instrument of the parent company before addressing specific issues such as the safety and the maintenance of the ships.

[110] For English law, see *Williams v Natural Life Health Foods Ltd* [1998] 1 WLR 830, with a critical comment by R Grantham and C Rickett, 'Directors' "Tortious" Liability: Contract, Tort or Company Law?' (1999) 62 *MLR* 133. For German law, see P Hommelhoff, 'Produkthaftung im Konzern' [1990] *Zeitschrift für Wirtschaftsrecht* 761.

[111] See, eg Arts 3 and 7 of the EC Commission's proposal for a Regulation on the law applicable to non-contractual obligations ('Rome II'), COM (2003) 427 final, at 21 f.

handbooks and the subsidiary causes damage while following these instructions, the parent company is liable if the procedures followed were below the standard of a reasonable operator.[112] This result should be obvious in all legal orders. The parent company should also be liable if it restricts the subsidiary's funds for environmental management unduly.

Liability for Responsibility for the Environmental Management

(1) Tort Law

In *Cape Industries* and *Thor Chemicals*, the claimants sued under the tort of negligence.[113] For example, in *Cape Industries* they claimed that the parent company was in breach of its duty of care towards the employees and the neighbours of the plant that was run by its South African subsidiary. They argued that the parent company acted negligently by establishing a company and a plant in South Africa and not taking care of its proper safety and environmental management afterwards. Unfortunately, the defendants settled the claims once the English courts had decided to have jurisdiction for the cases so that no case law is available.[114]

In the *Amoco Cadiz* case, the State Court of Illinois found that the oil spill was caused negligently by the parent company that had been responsible for the safety and the maintenance of the ship.[115] Thus, the reason for the parent company's liability was the allocation of responsibility for this element of the operation of the subsidiary. The same rule should apply under German tort law.[116] Apart from actual influence on the production patterns, the appearance is of some relevance. If a parent company makes the impression of controlling production patterns, this may cause a duty of care. In this context, publicised instruments of self-regulation that imply control over the subsidiaries' safety and environmental performance can play an important role.

(2) Environmental Liability Law

Environmental liability statutes usually establish a strict liability system for environmental damage that is meant to compensate the specific dangers from certain industries. The focus on compensation for damage from environmental pollution makes them independent from the values of the laws on corporations.[117]

---

[112] See, eg HP Westermann, 'Umwelthaftung im Konzern' (1991) 155 *Zeitschrift für das gesamte Handelsrecht* 223, at 239 f.

[113] See P Muchlinski, 'Corporations in International Litigation: Problems of Jurisdiction and the United Kingdom Asbestos Cases', above n 78, at 3 f.

[114] For details, see H Ward, 'Towards a New Convention on Corporate Accountability? Some Lessons from the Thor Chemicals and Cape PLC Cases', above n 72, at 113 ff.

[115] See JE Antunes, 'Neue Wege im Konzernhaftungsrecht–Nochmals: Der "Amoco Cadiz"-Fall', above n 93, at 1007.

[116] See P Hommelhoff, 'Produkthaftung im Konzern', above n 110, at 764, on tort law rules for product liability.

[117] One rare exception is the German Soil Protection Act, see, eg H-J Müggenborg, 'Die "bodenschutzrechtliche Konzernhaftung" nach § 4 III 4 Fall 1 BbodSchG' [2001] *Neue Zeitschrift für Verwaltungsrecht* 1114.

Typically, environmental liability laws establish the liability of the operator. This is true for the US American Comprehensive Environmental Response, Compensation and Liability Act (CERCLA),[118] for the German Environmental Liability Act,[119] and also for the yet to be adopted EC Environmental Liability Directive.[120] Under CERCLA, courts have adopted a wide interpretation of the notion of 'operator' that included companies that had the control over or participated in the actual running of the plant. Some courts even regarded those who had the opportunity to control as operators.[121] Under German law, the operator is the one who exercises the decisive influence on the operation of the plant, ie, the one who has the legal and factual power to make the necessary decisions on the operation and the who benefits economically from the operation.[122] Thus, the operator is the one who controls the risks that stem from the plant and who is therefore able to avoid damages.[123] This is also meant to serve as an incentive for investment into safety management.[124] Hence, determination of the subsidiary's environmental management, for example, by technical guidelines, is a strong indicator for the parent company being the real operator.[125] The same is true for centralised environmental units that control the environmental conduct of the whole corporation.[126]

Finally, the EC Environmental Liability Directive will define 'operator' as any person who operates *or controls* the occupational activity or, where this is provided for in national legislation, to whom decisive economic power over the technical functioning of such an activity has been delegated. This

---

[118] 42 U.S.C. Par. 9601-9675 (1991). For details, see U Vettori, *Haftung für Ökoschäden im Recht der USA* (Bern, Lang, 1996) 100 ff.

[119] BGBl. 1990 I, 2634.

[120] See EC document IP/04/246.

[121] For details, see U Vettori, *Haftung für Ökoschäden im Recht der USA*, above n 118, at 103 ff; F Ochsenfeld, *Direkthaftung von Konzernobergesellschaften in den USA: die Rechtsprechung zum Altlasten-Superfund als Modell für das deutsche Konzernhaftungsrecht?* (Berlin, Duncker und Humblot, 1998) 46 ff; M Landwehr, *Die Durchgriffshaftung in konzernverbundenen Gesellschaften*, above n 92, at 113 ff. However, in *United States v Bestfoods*, 118 S.Ct. 1876 (1998), the US Supreme Court took a more restrictive view and held that only those who have actively caused the pollution is the 'operator'.

[122] See Verwaltungsgericht Mannheim (1988) *Neue Zeitschrift für Verwaltungsrecht* 562.

[123] See UH Schneider, 'Die Überlagerung des Konzernrechts durch öffentlich-rechtliche Strukturnormen und Organisationspflichten' (1996) *Zeitschrift für das gesamte Gesellschaftsrecht* 225, at 239; P Salje, *Umwelthaftungsgesetz* (München, CH Beck, 1993) 48; A Hucke and H Schröder, 'Umwelthaftung von Konzernen' [1998] *Der Betrieb* 2205, at 2206; C-P Martens, 'Environmental Liability of Parent Companies' [2003] *European Environmental Law Review* 135, at 139.

[124] See G Teubner, 'Die "Politik des Gesetzes" im Recht der Konzernhaftung', above n 108, at 265 ff.

[125] See HP Westermann, 'Umwelthaftung im Konzern', above n 112, at 240; UH Schneider, 'Die Überlagerung des Konzernrechts durch öffentlich-rechtliche Strukturnormen und Organisationspflichten', above n 123, at 239 f.

[126] See K Schmidt, 'Haftungsrisiken für Umweltschutz und technische Sicherheit im gegliederten Unternehmen–Gesellschafts- und konzernrechtliche Betrachtungen' (1993) 26 *Umwelt- und Technikrecht* 69, at 84.

definition is broader than the one in Article 2 No 9 of the original proposal by the EC Commission[127] in including the person who *controls* the activity. This is understood to encompass parent companies.[128] In fact, in its explanatory memorandum on the original proposal, the EC Commission had expressly named the goal of preventing circumvention of liability through the law of corporations.[129]

Once a parent company is the 'operator' of a plant, it is liable for environmental damage caused from the operation of the plant irrespective of whether it was responsible for the individual malfunction. Overall, it is apparent that a parent company that takes active influence on the operation of the subsidiary's plant may be held liable as the operator of the plant even if the law of corporation would not recognise such liability. Self-regulatory instruments can play an important role in providing evidence of control over the subsidiary's environmental conduct.

Liability for Lack of Corporation-wide Health, Safety and Eenvironmental Management

All the approaches discussed so far have one thing in common: They do not hold a parent company liable that simply leaves the responsibility to a subsidiary that is not capable of dealing with risks appropriately, be it for lack of financial resources or for lack of technical knowledge and experience, whereas the parent company avails of the necessary know-how and financial means. This is the situation that regularly arises in transnational corporations that include subsidiaries in developing countries.

The next step would therefore be to recognise the parent company's duty to organise the corporation in such a way that damage can best be avoided. A parallel can be drawn to product liability law. While in product liability law potentially dangerous products are put into circulation, here dangerous technologies are exported. Product liability law holds the producer liable for damages since he is the one who is responsible for the design of the product and who is best suited to instruct users and to monitor the functioning of the product in practice.[130] In a transnational corporation, the parent company that designs a product that is then produced by subsidiaries worldwide will be liable for damages. Transposed to production processes, this would mean that the parent company that develops technology and makes it available to a subsidiary in a developing country has to

---

[127] COM (2002) 17 final.
[128] See C Leifer, 'Der Richtlinienentwurf zur Umwelthaftung: Internationaler Kontext, Entstehung und öffentlich-rechtliche Dimension' [2003] *Natur und Recht* 598, at 604. See also the similar considerations by AG Kokott, Case C-1/03 *Ministère Public v Paul van de Walle and others* [2004] ECRI-7613, at 53, on the notion of 'holder of waste.'
[129] COM (2002) 17 final at 5.
[130] See P Hommelhoff, 'Produkthaftung im Konzern', above n 110, at 763 ff.

take responsibility for its proper functioning and use. This includes the duty to instruct and educate the users, ie, the employees of the subsidiaries, on safety and environmental issues. The parent company would also have to monitor the functioning and use of the technology in practice, and to take into account the lower level of education of employees in developing countries as well as climatic differences etc. In case of problems, the parent company would have to take action, for example, by taking over certain functions or by introducing additional safety elements. In fact, this is exactly what the German chemical industry is already doing.[131] However, it would mean that they do not do it voluntarily but in fulfilling their legal duties under tort law. It is safe to say that some of the duties can only be fulfilled by the skilled and experienced personnel of the parent company that has developed a certain technology.

In conclusion, this would mean that parent companies of transnational corporations are obliged to introduce a corporation-wide safety and environmental management system that allocates responsibilities where they can best be exercised. Otherwise they are liable for damage that occurs from insufficient management and control. If however a reasonable structure has been established, and a subsidiary's employee still causes damage, the parent company is not liable, but only the subsidiary or the employee in question. Usually, the burden of proof for such a structure would lie with the parent company.[132] Self-regulatory instruments would become an important tool for establishing a corporation-wide safety and environmental management system. The relevant standards for a reasonable system can be developed from interplay of practical experience and normative requirements. Tort law would then serve as an incentive to introduce environmentally friendly corporate structures and production schemes.[133] Whether or not such adequate management systems are already in place cannot be decided at this stage. The practice of the German chemicals industry to use a worldwide system of codes of conduct, guidelines, handbooks and auditing schemes appears to be rather progressive. Certainly, management systems such as ISO 9000 and ISO 14000 do not reach an adequate standard since they firstly merely apply to individual enterprises and secondly are far too unsophisticated for the necessities of safety and environmental management.[134]

---

[131] See M Herberg, 'Codes of Conduct und kommunikative Vernunft', above n 21, at 39.

[132] See G Brüggemeier, 'Enterprise Liability for Environmental Damage: German and European Law' in G Teubner, L Farmer and D Murphy (eds), *Environmental Law and Ecological Responsibility*, above n 92, at 75, 90 ff, for the organisation of enterprises.

[133] See G Brüggemeier, 'Enterprise Liability for Environmental Damage: German and European Law', above n 131, at 91 f; KA Hofstetter, 'The Ecological Liability of Corporate Groups: Comparing US and European Trends', above n 92, at 109.

[134] See R Krut and H Gleckman, *ISO 14001–A Missed Opportunity for Sustainable Global Industrial Development* (London, Earthscan, 1998); A Matusche-Beckmann, *Das Organisationsverschulden* (Tübingen, Mohr, 2001) 332 ff.

Only such a duty to organise a transnational corporation adequately does justice to demands that transnational corporations should guarantee not only their own compliance with human rights, social standards and environmental standards, bu compliance of all their subsidiaries. Thus, the recent international initiatives could help forming transnational rules of economic law that supersede, in the long run, traditional law of corporations, with its separation of responsibilities, and that make parent companies from industrialised countries responsible for the world-wide protection of human rights, social standards and environmental standards.

CONCLUSION

Many aspects of economic globalisation, such as the obligation of corporations to respect human right and social and environmental standards in foreign direct investment in developing countries, have remained largely unregulated by international law or domestic public law until now. Instead, a variety of political initiatives aiming at improving production patterns abroad have been developed. They are all based (at least to a certain extent) on private self-regulatory instruments.

Private self-regulation by transnational corporations is not merely morally desirable but it is relevant in law, namely in private law. Private law provides for instruments to achieve the political goals expressed in the mentioned initiatives. Confidence in public statements is protected by advertising law and sales law. While advertising law prevents abuse of self-regulatory instruments to mislead consumers, contract law serves their enforcement. However, self-regulation also plays an important role in tort law. It constitutes responsibility for the operation, for example, of plants in developing countries but may even be required where the parent company avails of superior know-how and financial means. If a reasonable structure has been established, the parent company is exempted from liability. Otherwise, it is liable for damage that occurs due to insufficient safety, health or environmental management. Through this interplay of private law and developing international law of transnational corporations, transnational economic law can emerge that is capable of overcoming the traditional principle of legal separation and of making transnational corporations responsible for the worldwide protection of human rights, social rights and the environment.

11

The IMF and its Relation to Private Banks: Risk Free Banking?

JANET DINE

INTRODUCTION

MANY CONTRIBUTORS TO the 'globalisation' debate call for imposition of regulation on multinational companies. Alternatively, multinationals are urged to abide by codes of conduct imposing corporate social responsibility. However, much of the literature has ignored the biggest and richest companies of them all. Attention focuses on companies which produce tangible items which end up with a consumer. This lends an extra veil of invisibility to the operations of giant banks. Thus, their activities have frequently been left off the globalisation agenda. However, there is evidence to show that they are making money from poor countries with the assistance (whether voluntary or involuntary) of the International Monetary Fund. (IMF).There is evidence to show that banks are lending large sums on short-term contracts to developing countries. Where the currency of such countries is in crisis the IMF will pour in money to support the country concerned, enabling the banks to be repaid as they refuse to roll over the loan contracts. This has a profound effect on development possibilities, has largely gone unnoticed in the debate on corporate social responsibility and may be seen as a 'market failure.' Where the economists identify market failure the usual response is to regulate, but the complexities of regulation on the international stage and in the light of the IMF's persistent policy of opening up financial markets poses a difficult legal challenge.

THE FINANCIAL POLICY OF THE IMF

The International Monetary Fund (IMF) has largely (rightly) been vilified for the conditionality policies which it pursues—demanding severe cutbacks in social services in return for its loans—rather than for its financial policies.

Recently, however, the financial policies behind its activities have been questioned, as also has the effect that its structural adjustment policies and their successors have had on the poorest within creditor nations. Stiglitz writes:

> The IMF is pursuing not just the objectives set out in its original mandate of enhancing global stability and ensuring that there are funds for countries facing a threat of recession to pursue expansionary policies. It is also pursuing the interests of the financial community . . . Simplistic free market ideology provided the curtain behind which the real business of the 'new' mandate could be transacted. The change in mandate and objectives, while it may have been quiet, was hardly subtle: from serving global *economic* interests to serving the interests of global *finance*.[1] Capital market liberalisation may not have contributed to global economic stability, but it did open up vast new markets for Wall Street.[2]

This reassessment of the IMF turns partly on the 'bail-out' policies it has pursued. The allegation is that loans to risky areas are encouraged and underpriced because it is known that the IMF will support the country's currency when a crisis threatens.

The allegation that the IMF is in the service of international finance essentially flows from the insistence by the IMF on liberalisation, in particular capital account liberalisation.[3] The intended result of this is to permit capital flows to take place freely across the world. However, while this may be good for the financial community, it is not necessarily good for developing countries because:

> [T]he cocktail of free capital flows, floating exchange rates, domestic financial liberalisation in G3 countries, and unregulated innovations in financial instruments and institutions such as derivatives and hedge funds has dramatically increased financial instability after the collapse of the Gold- Dollar standard.[4]

This analysis is based on Keynes' beauty contest analysis, referring to a game in the UK tabloid press in the 1930s in which readers were asked to assess from pictures which women would be judged as the most beautiful by the entire readership:

> [I]n other words, readers would not win by giving their own opinion about the women's beauty, not even by assessing what others' personal opinions would be,

---

[1] Italics in original.

[2] J Stiglitz, *Globalisation and its Discontents* (London, Allen Lane, 2002) 206–07.

[3] Capital account liberalisation prevents countries from imposing controls on the amount of currency entering and leaving the country. This is intended to increase the quantity of capital flow (preferably) into a country but it may have the opposite effect of facilitating flow out of the country.

[4] J Eatwell and L Taylor, *Global Finance at Risk* (New York, The New Press, 2000) cited in Oxfam, *Global Finance*, 26.

but by guessing what people would, on average, believe average opinion to be. In financial markets, a trader will not bid a price according to what he or she believes an asset's fundamental value to be, but according to what he or she assesses average opinion to be about average opinion of the asset's value. The beauty contest analogy helps understand why market participants tend to engage in 'momentous trading' (ie, herd behaviour) and why market valuations are subject to sudden shifts in 'market sentiment.'[5]

Much research has been concerned to assess whether, in the long term, the opening of capital markets has been good for growth. However, the results of these studies conflict and no certain conclusions can be drawn. Individual benefits of capital liberalisation also have corresponding negative effects. What does seem to be clear is that the interaction between the IMF and the provision of private finance from banks operates to increase inequality of income both within and between nations and has a disproportionate impact on the poor. The mechanisms are as follows:

— An insistence on capital account liberalisation by the IMF
— A consequent increase in the provision of foreign finance often on a short-term basis and at rates poorly assessed for risk increased volatility due to 'hot money' flowing freely in and out of the country
— The loss of control over fiscal policy by states
— Crises caused by poor domestic policies, speculators and 'herd' behaviour
— The IMF bailout response causing the repayment of the wealthy and poor future risk assessment
— The imposition of conditionality and the removal of many public services.

Liberalisation

The embrace by developing countries of liberalisation of capital markets and the acceptance of 'pushed' incoming capital flows is difficult to understand without an understanding of the central role that the IMF plays in credit rating. It has the power to alter the domestic policies of states simply by a suggestion that they will alter the credit rating of a country, thus making credit of any sort either impossible to obtain or very expensive. While a country might prefer limited credit controls, it is unlikely to wish to be cut off entirely from access to credit. The naked power of the IMF to impose liberalisation against the wishes of developing countries derives from its power to cut off any source of finance. Why then does the IMF insist on capital market liberalisation?

[5] Oxfam, *Global Finance*, 26.

Why Liberalisation? Overall Assessment of Benefits and Disadvantages

Stiglitz claims that the push for liberalisation was driven by arguments that it would enhance economic stability by diversification of sources of funding and increase efficiency by dismantling 'inefficient' capital controls and by a belief in the ultimate efficiency of markets and the inefficiency of government controls on market activities.[6] These arguments he finds false on the grounds that it is clear that liberalisation decreases global stability, that capital controls used properly can prevent 'hot money' flowing rapidly into a country at boom times and leaving it in times of recession and that sensible government intervention in markets can protect fragile local industries until they are ready to compete globally.[7] Oxfam identifies a further disadvantage of capital flows, 'the interest payments and profit repatriation that can represent an unsustainable drain on a country's resources.'[8] Although discussed in a different context, the increase in avoidance or evasion of taxes is also identified by Oxfam as a mechanism which costs developing countries US$15 billion a year.[9] Although correlation between lower tax rates and capital liberalisation cannot be shown,[10] 'capital account liberalisation is probably correlated with the administrative capacity to collect taxes on capital, which is hard to control for in econometric regressions' and 'international tax evasion would simply be impossible under strict international control of capital flows.'[11]

The World Bank agrees that capital inflows can have a negative effect by creating increased volatility, but argue that there are three potential benefits: they permit the financing of trade deficits allowing countries to invest more than they save and thus accumulate capital faster; they permit the import of technology which is essential to build a productive capacity; and they may improve the working of the financial sector.[12] Support for liberalisation is based on the belief that the benefits outweigh the effect of the increase in volatility. Do the benefits outweigh the disadvantages, contrary to Stiglitz's view? A wide-ranging literature review by Oxfam of the studies that attempt to measure the long-term effect of capital flows on investment concludes that:

> The empirical studies summarised in this section leave the reader with a sense of confusion. In the past decades, capital account liberalisation may have, on average, had an independent and causal positive effect on growth—or maybe not. . . The

---

[6] Stiglitz, *Globalisation and its Discontents*, above n 2, at 100–02.

[7] See also J Williamson, 'Costs and Benefits of Financial Globalisation' in G Underhill and X Zhang, *International Financial Governance under Stress: Global Structures versus National Imperatives* (Cambridge, Cambridge University Press, 2003).

[8] Oxfam, *Global Finance*, 38.

[9] Oxfam, 'Tax Havens: Releasing the Hidden Billions for Poverty Eradication' (Oxford, Oxfam Policy Papers, 2000).

[10] Oxfam, *Global Finance*, 35.

[11] *Ibid.*

[12] World Bank, *Global Development Finance 2001* (Washington, World Bank, 2001).

lack of robust correlation between capital inflows and growth, together with the weak correlation between capital account liberalisation and capital inflows, sheds some doubt about the causality of the relationship between capital account liberalisation and growth.[13]

There are two factors here, capital flows and capital account liberalisation. The studies show that there is no *causal* proof that capital flows increase growth and further no strong evidence that capital account liberalisation increases capital flows. Many of the attempts to measure effects identify correlation rather than causation and are therefore suspect, as relevant variables affecting growth may be omitted. Choice of country may also be significant as other studies indicate that 'success breeds success' and capital is attracted to already booming economies. The only clear result is that a 'one-size fits all' policy is most unlikely to work as the effect of capital flows is critically dependent on individual factors within the country concerned including an adequate 'absorptive capacity'. In particular it may be that 'a certain threshold of development needs to be reached before liberalisation becomes beneficial.'[14]

Benefits and Disadvantages of Liberalisation: Detailed Assessment

If the overall effect of both capital flows and liberalisation of those flows is in doubt, it may be useful to consider the benefits and disadvantages studied individually. It will be remembered that the first benefit identified by the World Bank was the increase in investment causing capital accumulation. The World Bank shows that an increase in private capital inflows equal to one per cent of GDP has increased domestic investment by an average of 0.72 per cent of GDP in the south over the past three decades.[15] However, this trend significantly weakened in the 1990s compared with the 1970s and 1980s[16] due to the rise of merger and acquisitions following privatisation programmes and the significant outflows of capital occurring at the same time.[17] While it is clear that increases in investment occur, they do so

---

[13] Oxfam, *Global Finance*, 42.

[14] Oxfam, *Global Finance*, 41, citing five recent (2001) papers: G Bekaert, H Campbell and C Lundblad, 'Does Financial Liberalisation Spur Growth?' (Cambridge, National Bureau of Economic Research, Working Paper 8245, 2001); S Edwards, 'Capital Mobility and Economic Performance: Are Emerging Economies Different?' (Cambridge, National Bureau of Economic Research, Working Paper 8076, 2001); C Arteta, B Eichengreen and C Wyplotz, 'When does Capital Account Liberalisation Help more than it Hurts?' (Cambridge, National Bureau of Economic Research, Working Paper 8414, 2001); D Quinn, C Inclan and A Maria Toyoda, 'How and Where Capital Account Liberalisation Leads to Economic Growth', paper presented at the 2001 American Political Science Review, 30 August 2001.

[15] World Bank, *Global Development Finance 2001* (Washington, World Bank, 2001).

[16] World Bank, *Global Development Finance*, Fig 3.3.

[17] Oxfam, *Global Finance*, 43. Mergers and acquisitions consist of the transfer of ownership of existing capital and thus may be contrasted with 'greenfield' foreign direct investment which involves creation of physical capital.

differently in different countries. The reasons are unclear although the World Bank finds some evidence that 'absorptive capacity' of Foreign Direct Investment (FDI) increases with better education and that the impact of short-term debt on investment increases with political stability.[18] In a study of nearly one hundred countries, Rodrik found no correlation between open capital accounts and long-term economic performance once the other determinants of growth are controlled for.[19] Stiglitz contends that instability has a negative effect on economic growth.[20] Studies by Quinn, Klein and Olivei appear to find a positive and statistically significant association between international financial openness and long-term financial growth.[21] Williamson asks 'Are these findings in conflict or is it possible to reconcile them? . . . The first three studies [that found no impact] use a variable which measures whether the capital account was open or closed, whereas Quinnand Olivei sought to construct a measure of the *degree* to which the capital account was open . . . Now most countries liberalised FDI relatively early on, and most also liberalised long-term before short-term capital. . . we have strong reasons for believing that liberalisation of FDI, portfolio equity and other long-term capital should be beneficial for growth; it is what is usually the last stage–of opening up to unlimited flows of short-term money–that is problematic.'[22] Williamson concludes therefore that the studies thus show that opening to long-term capital is helpful whereas exposure to short-term capital mobility is harmful. Further, the Quinn, Klein and Olivei studies included developed countries, whereas the Rodrik and Stiglitz studies focused on developing countries.

The second benefit identified by the World Bank is the import of technology by FDI. In summary, the ability of countries to benefit from FDI in this or other ways is country- and industry-specific. It appears to depend on a country's 'absorptive' capacity, which grows strongly with better education. The poorest countries have the least absorptive capacity and are most likely to suffer the social and environmental dangers which come with FDI.

The third identified benefit is improvement in the capacity and efficiency of domestic financial systems. The World Bank states that:

> Greater financial sector development is expected with faster economic growth, and larger international capital flows are associated with improvements in financial sector depth and liquidity. However, an inflow of foreign capital does not, in

---

[18] World Bank, *Global Development Finance*, cited Oxfam, *Global Finance*, 44.

[19] D Rodrik 'Who Needs Capital Account Convertibility?' in 1998 Princeton Essays in International Finance 55–86.

[20] J Stiglitz, 'Capital Market Liberalisation, Economic Growth and Instability' (2000) 28(6) *World Development* 1075–86.

[21] D Quinn, 'The Correlates of Change in International Financial Regulation' (1997) 91(3) *American Political Science Review* 531–51; M Klein and G Olivei, 'Capital Account Liberalisation: Financial Depth and Economic Growth' Working Paper 7384, National Bureau of Economic Research 1999, Cambridge, Mass.

[22] Williamson, 'Costs and Benefits', above n 7, at 48.

itself guarantee improvements in the financial sector. The short-term consequences may well be unfavourable, given the volatility of capital flows, which can have negative implications for output and employment.[23]

This less than glowing endorsement is greeted with some further doubts by Oxfam. Accepting the link between financial sector development and growth in most cases, Oxfam cites Durham whose study shows that:

[T]he relationship between stock market development and growth does not hold with samples including only low-income countries and that interacting stock market development with the level of GDP produces very significant results, suggesting that promoting financial development through stock markets is not a very good idea in low-income countries.[24]

Further, while a correlation between capital inflows and financial development is accepted, the World Bank recognises that this also only holds good for middle-income countries.[25] Oxfam believes that even where correlation can be shown, 'the direction of causality is again problematic, as global capital is likely to flow into countries with well-developed financial markets.'

The link between inflows and growth depends on the ability of financial systems to improve the allocation of capital across industries, but there are many reasons why this link may break down, not least the absence of strong regulatory frameworks and the consequent rise of criminal activity on stock markets.[26] Thus:

There is good evidence that financial development improves the allocation of capital across industries and enterprises, and hence boosts economy-wide productivity and growth. However, the evidence supporting the view that openness to foreign capital increases financial development is much weaker. To the contrary, there are reasons to believe that capital account liberalisation can worsen the allocation of resources in low and middle-income countries, including thee lack of adequate financial supervision, the existence of price distortions, or the narrowness of capital markets. Macroeconomic instability can also harm the allocation of financial resources.

Volatility

What about the disadvantages? The major disadvantage identified by most, with the notable exception of the IMF, is the increase in volatility. For

---

[23] World Bank, *Global Development Finance* 70, cited Oxfam, *Global Finance* 48.

[24] Oxfam, *Global Finance* 48, citing J Durham, 'Econometrics of the Effects of Stock Market Development on Growth and Private Investment in Lower Income Countries' (Oxford, Queen Elizabeth House Working Papers 53).

[25] World Bank, *Global Development Finance*.

[26] Oxfam, *Global Finance* 49.

Oxfam, '[t]he questions are whether the effect is transitory or permanent and, in the latter case, whether it outweighs the positive impacts of capital inflows on growth.'[27] While studies can be found to support both optimistic (no long-term effects) and pessimistic (permanent effects) views,[28] many are intent on an aggregate analysis. The World Bank makes the point that financial crises have a disproportionate effect on the poor due to their impact on health, schooling and nutrition and that this is often not regained by a simple improvement in growth.[29] The inequality impact should not be lost sight of in considering overall growth rates. Eatwell and Taylor put forward a hypothesis that linked lower growth rates across the world since the late 1970s and the increased volatility which emerged following the collapse of the Gold-Dollar exchange Standard system in 1971.[30] In other words, increased liberalisation inducing volatility is hurting worldwide. They argue that:

—Flexible exchange rates are prone to major misalignments in the medium term. It is hard or impossible to hedge currency exposures in the medium term and enterprises' investment decisions can be misguided, which harms growth. Short-term exchange rates fluctuations can be hedged, but at a cost

—Volatile exchange rates feed the volatility of interest rates

—The volatility of both exchange rates and interest rates increases long-term real interest rates . . . debtors must pay higher risk premia to cover the increased likelihood of financial crisis, financial crisis contagion, or mere over or undershooting of exchange rates. This happens not only in the South, but also in the North (eg, Scandinavia, Japan and the European currency zone in the late 1980s and early 1990s)

—High and volatile interest rates reduce investment and hurt enterprises, particularly firms with high debt ratios and small companies that do not have easy access to credit. This results in high rates of corporate bankruptcies, which dampens economic growth. High default rates on corporate bonds justify high long-term interest rates, generating a vicious cycle.[31]

While not accepting this thesis completely and citing other factors which might be of significance such as the oil shocks of 1974 and 1979, the end of Europe's 'catch-up' potential vis-a-vis the United States in the 1970s, the

---

[27] Oxfam, *Global Finance* 50.

[28] For an analysis of a range of studies, see Oxfam, *Global Finance*, ch 11.

[29] World Bank, *Global Economic Prospects* (Washington, World Bank 1999) 48.

[30] J Eatwell and L Taylor, *Global Finance at Risk* (New York, The New Press, 2000).

[31] As summarised in Oxfam, *Global Finance* 51. See also D Sacks and P Thiel, 'The IMF's Big Wealth Transfer' in I McQuillan and P Montgomery (eds), *The International Monetary Fund* (Stanford, California, Hoover Institution Press, 1999) 32–33.

slowing of technological progress in the 1970s and social conflicts and unrest in the south. While conceding that much research still needs to be done, Oxfam writes:

> Eatwell and Taylor's thesis should concentrate the minds of researchers and policy-makers who consider reforming the global financial architecture. It implies that global finance has decreased long-term growth in both South and North.[32]

It also means that comparative studies of individual nations do not provide the best research methodology, since,

> At best, further research along the cross-country methodology might robustly establish that capital account liberalisation is good for growth given the post Bretton Woods global financial architecture, for example because attempting to control capital movements when major financial centers let them move freely may prove counter-productive.[33]

Even if this hypothetical study established such a correlation it could only mean that liberalisation is a 'second best' solution. In order to improve growth, the global financial architecture needs to control fluctuations between the major currencies.

Causes of Financial Crisis

While domestic policies have a large part to play in countries' financial crises, many studies now show that two other factors have great significance. One is the role of speculators and the second is, '"crony capitalism" at the global level, in the form of IMF bailing out Wall Street.'[34] Opportunities for speculators increase every time markets are opened, as do opportunities for the most powerful multinational banks. Underhill and Zhang point out that 'more than seventy financial and monetary crises of different proportions and characteristics have occurred in both developed and developing countries over the past two decades.'[35] They see as 'A common background to these developments . . . the intensifying process of global financial liberalisation and integration . . . As financial crises have become more frequent and more severe over the past two decades, this has raised the question of whether the growing frequency and severity of crises correlate with the emergence of this liberal and transnational financial order.'[36]

---

[32] Oxfam, *Global Finance* 55; B Johnson and B Schaefer, 'Why the IMF is Ineffective' in I McQuillan and P. Montgomery (eds), *The International Monetary Fund*, above n 31, at 56.
[33] Oxfam, *Global Finance* 55.
[34] Oxfam, *Global Finance*, 28.
[35] G Underhill and X Zhang, *International Financial Governance under Stress*, above n 7, at 1.
[36] *Ibid.*

Economists now identify three types of currency crisis which may afflict either developing or developed countries, but have a particularly devastating effect on the poor when they occur in developing countries.[37] First generation crises,

> such as the Mexican crisis of 1982, involve excessive budget deficits yielding unsustainable current account deficits, depletion of reserves and eventually devaluation. The culprit here is thus clearly the national government.[38]

Second generation crises involve a government beset by temporary macroeconomic difficulties which may be responded to in two different ways, either by maintaining fixed interest rates and incurring short-term losses of output and employment or by devaluation and decreasing interest rates:

> Both solutions may make sense depending on the government's overall development strategy and priorities. But financial markets may bet on one response . . . Speculation then forces the government to increase rates higher than otherwise necessary, which increases the cost of maintaining fixed exchange rates. Eventually the government is led to devalue against its will–generating profits for the successful speculators. In such a scenario the government is the victim and speculators the villains.[39]

Let us not forget two things here. First, it is very difficult to distinguish between 'speculation' and 'hedging' and it may well be that banks, as the most powerful financial institutions, are involved in both. Secondly, we also need to remember the analysis of increased financial volatility which cited both the invention of the speculators' tools of derivatives and the freedom of finance to flow across the world, the latter being an article of faith for the 'Washington consensus.'

Third generation crises involve twin banking and financial crises:

> They were initially attributed to poor financial regulation and supervision as well as poor monetary policy, thereby putting the blame back on national governments and their 'crony capitalist' clientele. . . It is now recognised that third generation crises are more complex, and may also include multiple equilibria effects, originate from abroad due to contagion effects or involve 'crony capitalism' at the global level, in the form of IMF bailing out Wall Street.[40]

The 'bail-out effect' will be examined below as the IMF policies and the response of the banking sector will be examined in chronological order

---

[37] P Krugman, 'Currency Crises' in M Feldstein (ed), *International Capital Flows* (Chicago, University of Chicago Press, 1999).

[38] Oxfam, *Global Finance* 28.

[39] Oxfam, *Global Finance* 28.

[40] Oxfam, *Global Finance* 28; L Uchitelle, 'A Bad Side of Bailouts: Some go Unpenalised' in I McQuillan and P Montgomery (eds), *The International Monetary Fund*, above n 31.

from liberalisation to crisis to imposition of Structural Adjustment. Here it is important to note the multi-factorial cause of 'third generation' crises which include the macroeconomic policies of G3 countries. Reinhart and Reinhart link currency crises to the volatility of G3 exchange rates.[41] Other studies show links to dollar interest increases.[42] However, analysing the East Asia crisis, Stiglitz writes:

> [I]n retrospect, it became clear that the IMF policies not only exacerbated the downturns , but were partially responsible for the onset: excessively rapid financial and capital market liberalisation was probably the single most important cause of the crisis, though mistaken policies on the part of the countries themselves played a role as well.[43]

The most significant of those policies is the liberalisation of capital flows.

The Role of Private Banks

Given the advent of liberalisation, how do banks operate within it? The first impact of liberalisation of capital flows on poorer countries is often the overshadowing or disappearance of local banks, which may well be displaced by the multinational giants. Of course, this has the advantage of capital stability; absent a regulatory outrage, it is most unlikely that the bank will default. 'The advantages are clear: the increased competition can lead to improved services. The greater financial strength of the foreign banks can enhance stability.'[44] However, as we shall see, the inflow of money into the developing country is at the choice of the northern institution looking for a good return, and this may leave out the small businesses looking for small loans which take a considerable amount of administration on the part of the bank. Further, the temptation from the foreign bank's perspective is to reduce risk by opting for short-term loans that greatly increase the volatility factor. What is clear is that expansion of credit follows liberalisation.

A further consequence of liberalisation is that investment is 'pushed' into developing countries by the search for new investment markets. This 'push' effect is stronger than the 'pull' from the south driven by genuine desire or need for capital.[45] Studies show that there are significant correlations

---

[41] Reinhart and Reinhart, 'What Hursts Most?' Paper presented at the National Bureau for Economic Research Conference Preventing Currency Crises in Emerging Markets, Monterey, 20-31March 2001.

[42] J Frankel and N Roubini, 'The Role of Industrial Policies in Emerging Market Crises' (Cambridge, US, National Bureau of Economic Research Working Paper 8634, 2000).

[43] Stiglitz, *Globalisation and its Discontents*, above n 2, at 91.

[44] *Ibid*, at 69.

[45] Oxfam, *Global Finance* 13.

between money flows from north to south and periods of easing of US monetary policy:

> The effect is striking for bank lending. Periods of monetary easing usually correspond to the bottom of the business cycle, and banks have two reasons to expand their foreign lending activity: domestic interest rates are low and creditworthy domestic lending operations are few.[46]

The terms of these loans, as well as their duration, have been criticised as being heavily influenced by IMF behaviour at times of financial crisis. In several significant instances the IMF has reacted to a crisis by pushing in large amounts of money to stabilise the exchange rate. Critics argue that this has two major effects. First, knowledge that it will happen creates a 'moral hazard' in the setting of the terms of loans, and risk is not estimated in the absence of the understanding that this will happen, so the risk to foreign investors is significantly lower. Secondly, when the crisis in fact occurs the money pushed in enables foreign investors and very rich locals to remove the greater part of their money.

The terms of the loans are also driven by the foreign banks rather than by the government of the receiving country. Eatwell shows how countries lose control over fiscal policies on the opening of markets. Long-term interest rates are affected by market sentiment. Because long-term bond yields are simply the market's understanding of what will happen to short-term interest rates plus a risk premium and maturity calculation, if the market (ie, the banks) believe that attempts by a central bank to lower short-term rates is unlikely to succeed, long-term interest rates will remain high to the benefit of creditors.[47] However, if the central bank increases short-term interest rates, the markets see this as an appropriate move to pre-empt inflation above the long-term yields forecast, economic activity slows, inflation is kept low and real long-term interest rates remain high, to the benefit of creditors.[48] This low, or no risk, banking bears more heavily on small economies. As Oxfam observes,

> the sheer size of large economies protects them from the most severe forms of capital flight simply because the capital has nowhere else to go: if all European investors wanted to move their wealth to the United States, they would simply not find enough profitable investment opportunities. The South is much more vulnerable to sudden and steep capital flight which greatly reduces the scope for expansionary monetary policy.[49]

---

[46] Oxfam, *Global Finance* 13, citing in particular Reinhart and Reinhart, 'What Hurts Most?', above n 41.

[47] J Eatwell, 'International Capital Liberalisation: The Impact on World Development' (New York, Center for Economic Policy Analysis Working Paper Series III, 8).

[48] *Ibid.*

[49] Oxfam, *Global Finance* 58.

The fear of volatility keeps interest rates high–to the benefit of investors. The ability of governments to conduct expansionary policies at a time of recession is also weakened by market reactions to growing budget deficits and higher inflation. In both situations banks will quickly demand higher yields, slowing economic activity. The IMF prescriptions for high interest rates and balanced budgets support Stiglitz's claim that the IMF works primarily in the interests of the international financial community rather than in the interests of developing countries, and the claim here that between them the IMF and the international banks have invented risk-free banking.

Underwriting the Banks

The insistence on reserve building by the IMF and by national governments which fear volatility also fuels the net flow of resources from south to north:

> A substantial part of south-north capital outflows consists of the purchase of foreign exchange reserves by central banks aiming at cushioning the domestic economy from sudden capital flow reversals. This practice is thus equivalent to an insurance policy purchased by national governments to protect national and global investors.[50]

This effect together with other factors means that very often the cost of FDI is actually higher than its benefits.

The emphasis on market forces by the IMF has not rendered it free from criticism for distorting the market, both by the terms of its loans and the 'moral hazard' effect of its rescue operations:

> IMF loans, then, actually offered extraordinarily generous rebates of about 10% below market rates. On the $117 billion lent to East Asia under IMF auspices thus far, the region is saving about $12 billion a year in interest payments. Over three years, South Korea, Thailand and Indonesia will have received a direct wealth transfer of at least $35 billion, mostly from US and Western European taxpayers.
>
> But this $35 billion figure actually understates the true scale of the transfer. Investors priced South Korea's debt at a yield of 14.5 per cent only because there was a good chance the IMF would come in sooner or later and rescue them. Absent the market-distorting activities of the IMF, the risk premium on this sovereign debt would have been even greater.
>
> More specifically, much of the $35 billion will amount to a wealth transfer from middle-class Westerners to East Asian Governments, Banks, and their rich

---

[50] Oxfam, *Global Finance* 61.

equity owners and from there to wealthy Western and Japanese investors who risked capital in foolish ways (or perhaps not so foolish since there was a good chance they would be bailed out in the end). The whole series of transactions amounts to a remarkably regressive tax.[51]

Response to Crises

Analysing the East Asia crises, Stiglitz notes that the IMF's response was to provide:

> [H]uge amounts of money (the total bailout packages, including support from G-7 countries was $95 billion) so that the countries could sustain the exchange rate. It thought that if the market believed that there was enough money in the coffers, there would be no point in attacking the currency, and thus 'confidence' would be restored. The money served another function: it enabled the countries to provide dollars to the firms that had borrowed from Western bankers to repay the loans. It was thus, in part, a bailout to the international banks as much as it was a bailout to the country; the lenders did not have to face the full consequences of having made bad loans. And in country after country in which the IMF money was used to sustain the exchange rate temporarily at an unsustainable level, there was another consequence: rich people inside the country took advantage of the opportunity to convert their money into dollars at the favourable exchange rate and whisk it abroad.[52]

Finally, the loans from either the IMF or World Bank come, not only at a financial price, but at the cost of agreement to 'structural reforms.' While the IMF denies absolutely that it has any role in political matters, many have argued the contrary case. Stiglitz puts the matter succinctly[53]:

> The IMF took rather an imperialistic view . . . since almost any structural issue could affect the overall performance of the economy, and hence the government's budget or the trade deficit, it viewed almost everything as falling within its domain.

Loans came with a 'structural adjustment' plan (SAP) attached. Both IMF and World Bank claim that the imposition of conditions for loans 'conditionality' are designed by the countries themselves, usually include measures to 'foster greater efficiency in government spending' and come with advice on how best to design social safety nets' since '[a]djustment programs

---

[51] D Sacks and P Thiel, 'The IMF's Big Wealth Transfer' in I McQuillan and P Montgomery (eds), *The International Monetary Fund*, above n 31, at 32(33).

[52] Stiglitz, *Globalisation and its Discontents*, above n 2, at 95 and see L Uchitelle, 'A Bad Side of Bailouts: Some go Unpenalized' in I McQuillan and P Montgomery (eds), *The International Monetary Fund*, above n 31, at 28–29.

[53] Stiglitz, *Globalisation and its Discontents*, above n 2, at 14.

typically have an impact on income distribution, employment and social services.'[54]   However, many have questioned the effectiveness of such provision.

Loans and Growth

As we have seen, the inflow of FDI's effect on growth is by no means a simple matter to assess. Do loans from IMF achieve macroeconomic objectives and/or encourage growth? Again the measurement methodologies are problematic since it is impossible to observe the country in question as it would have been without the assistance. However a review of studies undertaken by the IMF itself in 1990 concluded that:

> [A] summary of the results obtained by the various studies that have evaluated the effects of fund-supported adjustment programs on the principal macroeconomic objectives . . . yield three conclusions. First, there is frequently an improvement in the balance of payments and the current account, although a number of studies show no effects of programs. Second, inflation is generally not affected by programs. Finally, the effects on the growth rate are uncertain, with the studies showing an improvement or no change being balanced by those indicating a deterioration in the first year of a program.[55]

Other studies are more forthright:

> In addition to weakening much of the world economy generally, IMF lending has hurt less-developed countries specifically. For example, a review of IMF loan recipients indicates that most are no better off economically today (measured in per capita wealth) than they were before receiving those loans. In fact, many are poorer: Forty-eight of the eighty-nine less-developed countries that received IMF money between 1965 and 1995 are no better off economically than they were before: thirty-two of these forty-eight countries are poorer than before: and fourteen of these thirty-two countries have economies that are at least 15 percent smaller than they were before their first IMF loan.[56]

These studies are all problematic since the number of variables that need to be considered are enormous, from the fluctuation of commodity prices to the change in WTO rules and other conditions of trade. Nevertheless, it is far from clear that the IMF loans, despite conditionality, achieve either macroeconomic objectives or encourage growth.

---

[54] IMF, 'Conditionality: Fostering Sustained Policy Implementation' in I McQuillan and P Montgomery (eds), *The International Monetary Fund*, above n 31, at 68–71.

[55] M Khan, ''The Macroeconomic Effects of Fund-Supported Adjustment Programs' in I McQuillan and P Montgomery (eds), *The International Monetary Fund*, above n 31, at 51.

[56] B Johnson and B Schaefer, 'Why the IMF is Ineffective' in I McQuillan and P Montgomery (eds), *The International Monetary Fund*, above n 31, at 56.

What Effect on Inequality?

The effects of financial volatility on inequality stem from multiple factors. While since by definition the poor have few assets, fluctuations in the value of assets will not directly affect them. However, the loss to governments is huge: 'The severest crises have cost governments between 20 per cent and 50 per cent of GDP with a cumulated fiscal cost of US$662 billion in 1995.'[57] Essentially, this is the cost incurred by defence of currency and represents an 'astounding transfer from taxpayers and users of public services to banks' depositors, creditors and shareholders.'[58] These figures relate to currency defence. Other effects are:

— Increased government debt
— Decrease of government revenue
— Lower credit worthiness causing increased interest rates.

All of these make governments poorer and less able to provide services, even before 'conditionality' bites demanding decreases in government spending. Moreover, taxes in developing countries tend to be regressive so increased taxation will bite into the income of the poor disproportionately.[59] UNCTAD show that in Latin America in the 1980s and 1990s and in Asia in the 1990s, even after a two-year recovery period wages remained lower and unemployment higher than before the respective financial crises.[60] Diwan argues that labour has been the 'shock absorber' of financial crises, allowing firms to recover profitability after crises, and moreover, since labour shares of GDP remain low after a crisis that, 'terms of trade and financial shocks induce an initial decline of the labor share, which fails to be offset by subsequent corrections because industrial relations are permanently transformed.'[61] For 32 developing countries this effect amounts to a loss to labour of US$27billion a year on average, two-thirds of which will be a permanent loss.[62]

Further drivers of inequality are:

— Unskilled labour loses out to skilled labour
— Small firms may experience credit rationing as a result of capital account liberalisation since large loans are administratively more efficient

---

[57] Oxfam, *Global Finance* 35.

[58] *Ibid.*

[59] *Ibid.*

[60] UNCTAD, *Trade and Development Report 2000: Global Economic Growth and Imbalances* (UN, Geneva, 2000).

[61] I Diwan, *Labor Shares and Financial Crises* (Washington, World Bank, 1999), cited Oxfam, *Global Finance* 34.

[62] *Ibid.*

— Small farmers and firms are more vulnerable to exchange rate fluctuations which they cannot hedge
— Tax evasion can only be carried out by the wealthy at the expense of governments; and
— Only the wealthy have access to sophisticated hedging mechanisms.

Oxfam concludes:

Worldwide financial instability generates massive transfers of income and wealth from the general public in the South, including the poor, to the rich in both South and North. ...[T]hree redistribution channels together account for a transfer of an order of magnitude that exceeds the benefits of capital inflows derived from spurred growth: falling labor shares of GDP, the fiscal cost of banking crises, and tax evasion. Although the part of these transfers born by the poor themselves is unknown, it is likely to be high. Taxes tend to be regressive or at least not very progressive in developing countries, and fiscal deficits are often reduced by cutting spending which harms the poor.[63]

The situation is, as Underhill and Zhang point out, that liberalisation of financial markets is often discussed without any understanding of the likely effects on social policy, and 'the difficulties which the transformation of financial market structures might present for the achievement of major policy commitments of democratically elected governments are given little attention.'[64] The consequences for the poor are dire.

---

[63] Oxfam, *Global Finance* 77.
[64] G Underhill and X Zhang, *International Financial Governance under Stress*, above n 7.

12

Towards an Acquisition of Human Rights by way of Business Practices

AURORA VOICULESCU

> Virtue is its own reward.
> (Italian proverb)

> These are the days of miracle and wonder
> This is the long distance call
> The way the camera follows us in slo-mo
> The way we look to us all
> The way we look to a distant constellation
> That's dying in a corner of the sky
> These are the days of miracle and wonder
> [...]
> (Paul Simon – 'The Boy in the Bubble' from the *Graceland* Song Album)

INTRODUCTION

IN THE NICOMACHEAN Ethics, Aristotle recommends that citizens take pleasure in virtue, and particularly in civic virtue, understood as a standard of righteous behaviour in relation to one's involvement in society. Aristotle also holds that citizens must know about these virtues before they can hope to better the community in which they live. We all have some intuitive idea of how we can exercise, as citizens, this type of virtue: voting might be an example of such an action, organising a campaign or volunteering for charity work, or for anything else that society might benefit from but it cannot impose upon us. Applying this theory to our 'fellow citizens,' the corporations, might appear as slightly more challenging. However, we find that more and more corporations and other business entities appear today to volunteer for a great number of things, not least for protecting and promoting human rights. This chapter will be looking into the role of voluntary codes of conduct for transnational corporations as a way of enhancing the realisation of human rights and human development, and as a way of exercising civic virtue in a global society. In this sense, the chapter highlights the main corporate social responsibility documents which have constituted the backdrop against which corporate voluntarism has proliferated, particularly in the form of voluntary codes of conduct. Next, it identifies some of the main points of tension between the international human rights discourse and the notion of voluntary corporate action. In the last part of the chapter, we look into the potential revealed by the latest developments in the international approach to human rights and corporate action to resolve some of these tensions.

CORPORATIONS AS GLOBAL GOVERNANCE PARTNERS

Global governance is 'the new black' of international affairs. Until about twenty, or even ten years ago, the main concern related to international development was how to accelerate foreign direct investment by freeing up trade and investment regimes. Very little consideration was given at the time to the impact those dimensions of development would have upon the environment, social relations or human rights. In other words, there was not much reflection on those rights we now tend to associate with *human development*.[1]

Being the new buzz expression, the notion of global governance is a very imprecise one, with a multitude of facets. Governance in itself can be said to be the sum of the many ways in which social actors (individuals and institutions) manage their affairs. It is seen as a continuing process; through it, conflicting or simply diverse interests are being accommodated, usually by generating some kind of co-operation between the different (competing) social actors.

The concept of *global* governance has taken on these characteristics and applied them to an ever more complex scale and agenda.[2] In this global dimension, the concept relates to the sum of (collective) rules, procedures and programmes intended to promote certain objectives related to the arena of world affairs. The way in which this promotion takes place is, generally, by shaping the global social actors' expectations, practices and interactions.[3]

The social actors partaking in the global governance processes are governmental as well as non-governmental bodies, civil society movements,

---

[1] J Braithwaite and P Drahos, *Global Business Regulation* (Cambridge, Cambridge University Press, 2000); R Francis, *Ethics and Corporate Governance* (Sydney, UNSW Press, 2000).

[2] CN Murphy, R Wilkinson and S Hughes, *Global Governance: Critical Perspectives* (London, Routledge, Taylor and Francis Books, 2002).

[3] JA Scholte, *Globalisation: A Critical Introduction* (London, Palgrave, 2000) 46; J Drake, *Defining ICT Global Governance*, Memo for the Social Science Research Council's Research Network on IT and Governance: (http://www.ssrc.org/programs/itic/publications/knowledge_report/memos/billdrake.pdf, accessed December 2004).

business organisations, international financial institutions or any other social bodies which might be seen as being or representing a social stakeholder related to a certain process or objective. Some definitions of the global governance concept would, for instance, include among the social actors the global mass media, or the major religions with potential impact on the development of certain issues.[4] From the list of stakeholders in the global governance processes, transnational corporations (TNCs) acquire a particular importance. This happens both through the TNCs' pervasive presence in a variety of processes more or less directly related to the globalisation of the market economy, and because of their economic power, which often surpassed the one of many of their host countries.[5]

In this context, with TNCs becoming major contributors to the process of global governance, rights—human, social, environmental—have become an intrinsic part of the global governance agenda; ie, an intrinsic part of the long list of problems the international community has to deal with by working together. The reason why human rights have expanded from the national and international agendas into the global governance agenda relates first of all, to their crucial value for human development. Second, human rights have become a global governance rather than just a national/international issue because of the rapid development of the global market economy.[6] This phenomenon has put those dimensions of human development protected by the human rights under considerable strain.[7] To quote Campbell:

> Human rights have come to represent the moral dimension of globalisation: the affirmation of universal standards to which we can look for guidance for the humanisation of capitalism, the revitalisation of democratic control and the protection of the values that give meaning and importance to human life. More particularly, in their affirmation of the equal worth and supreme value of every human being, human rights set the parameters and goals for any legitimate human organisations. It therefore seems appropriate to see human rights as a source of ideas for determining the normative ordering of global capitalism and its governmental structures.[8]

---

[4] D Kellner, *Globalisation and the Postmodern Turn*, UCLA:http://www.gseis.ucla.edu/courses/ed253a/dk/GLOBPM.htm.

[5] M McIntosh, D Leipziger, K Jones, G Coleman, *Corporate Citizenship* (London, FT/Pitman, 1998); RE Freeman, *Strategic Management: A Stakeholder Approach* (Boston, Pitman, 1984).

[6] Justice Michael Kirby, 'Human Rights: An Agenda for the Future' in B Galligan and C Sampford (eds), *Rethinking Human Rights* (Sydney, Federation Press, 1997); KJ Arrow, 'Social Responsibility and Economic Efficiency' (1973) 21 *Public Policy* 303; AK Sen, 'The Moral Standing of the Market' (1985) 2 *Social Philosophy and Policy* 1.

[7] United Nations Development Programme 'UNDP Poverty Report 2000: Overcoming Human Poverty', at: http://www.undp.org/povertyreport; J Elkington, *Cannibals with Forks: The Triple Bottom Line of 21st Century Business* (New Society Publishers, 1998).

[8] T Campbell, 'Moral Dimension of Human Rights' in T Campbell and S Miller (eds), *Human Rights and the Moral Responsibilities of Corporate and Public Sector Organisations* (The Hague, Kluwer Academic Publishers, 2004) 11.

It was said earlier that global governance implies co-operation between the different social actors with competing interests. In this co-operative approach an important role is taken by, as well as conferred upon the business organisation, and in particular upon the transnational corporation. Given the private, rather than public, nature of the corporate legal persona, this somewhat institutionalised role bestowed upon TNCs and other business enterprises is to some extent controversial.[9] However, as it has been repeatedly argued, especially in the past decade, this role can be seen as a spontaneous result of the changes in the nature and location of power in the global social sphere. This assertion is not meant, generally, to supplant the primary responsibility for the realisation of human rights which rests with the state. It is rather an acknowledgement of the new pressures put upon the process of realisation of these rights and, also, of the fact that the Universal Declaration of Human Rights is addressed not only to governments, but to all other 'organs of society.'[10] In the process of promoting and protecting human rights, TNCs, as organs of society, acquire a new, social or ethical dimension of their corporate responsibility. This situation is true especially with respect to those corporations which already are active players on the global market and in the arena of international political affairs. In the context of globalised free-market practices, business is now expected, even called upon, to act more responsibly in relation to social, labour, environmental and human rights issues and to engage in what one could call virtuous civic activities.

It is estimated that transnational corporations' influence can sometimes be more far reaching than any political intra-governmental initiative. Based on this (partially anecdotal) assumption, in the past decade, the list of corporate social responsibilities (CSR) has become wider, more complex and comprehensive. While, for instance, the initial attempts at CSR in the early 1970s referred to these responsibilities in the most general terms, or focused on those rights more directly linked to the production process (such as labour rights, health and safety, or later the environmental rights), it is quite common now to acknowledge in the CSR debate the human rights corporate responsibilities through a complex list of concrete rights, (some better defined than others). For instance, civil and political rights, long term argued to be the exclusive domain of the state, are now put on the corporate agenda alongside economic, social and cultural rights.[11] So are the 'third generation' rights of collective solidarity, such as the right to development or the right of

---

[9] Amnesty International, *Business and Human* Rights: http://www.amnestyusa.org/business/index.do; P Alston, *Non-State Actors and Human Rights (Collected Courses of the Academy of European Law)* (Oxford, Oxford University Press, 2005).

[10] *Universal Declaration of Human Rights*, G.A. res. 217A (III), UN Doc A/810 at 71 (1948), Preamble. See also P Zumbansen, 'The Conundrum of Corporate Social Responsibility: Reflections on the changing Nature of Firms and States' (2006) *CLPE Research Paper* No 01–3.

[11] O Schachter, 'The Erosion of State Authority and its Implications for Equitable Development' in F Weiss, E Denters and P De Waart (eds), *International Economic Law with a Human Face* (The Hague, Kluwer Law International, 1998) 31–44.

indigenous people.[12] Associated with the human rights agenda, through the impact certain business practices can have on local communities and generally on the less developed countries, other substantive issues (which go beyond the conventional human rights agenda) have also been added to the list. Such issues refer to fair business practices, marketing and advertising practices, as well as to the safety and quality of goods and services.[13]

All these issues have made it on the global governance agenda and, implicitly, on the business agenda, proposing business as an active social agent and collaborator in the global governance processes. However, the active role played by the business organisations in the complex process of global governance is a mixed blessing. Regulating corporations, and especially TNCs, in matters regarding human rights, proves to be difficult, both at the domestic and the international level. Such regulation would need to address the substance of the rights to be covered, the implementation and monitoring that would secure the credibility of any normative system, and last but not least, it would have to address the issues of the participating stakeholders in the defining of such a system of organisational responsibility. The options exercised so far have been, predominantly, a combination of legally non-binding 'soft law' mechanisms such as ethical investment schemes, social labelling, codes of conduct generated by corporations as well as codes of conduct originating in international organisations initiatives. In this context, many have praised the virtues of voluntarism, of giving business organisations the chance to become good citizens. The present proliferation of voluntary codes of conduct is a mirror of this trend which presents business entities as virtuous citizens, or tries to teach them how to become one.[14]

The voluntary codes of conduct, together with other types of private initiatives, emerged as attempts to harness the forces of global markets in order to address the needs of the broader community as well as those of the corporate entities and shareholders. The codes came about as by-products of simultaneous, yet separate, processes of globalisation of both the market economy and the human rights discourses. The promotion of human rights values through codes of conduct is one of the many ways in which various stakeholders in the social arena attempt to instil in some markets a missing ethical dimension, while in others to keep at bay dreaded legally- binding regulatory intervention.[15]

---

[12] WH Meyer, *Human Rights and International Political Economy in Third World Nations: Multinational Corprations, Foreign Aid, and Repression* (Westport, CT, Praeger, 1998).

[13] Amnesty International, *Business and Human Rights*: http://www.amnestyusa.org/business/index.do.

[14] T Donaldson, 'Moral Minimums for Multinationals' (1989) 3 *Ethics and International Affairs* 163–182; D Vogel, *The Market for Virtue: The Potential and Limits of Corporate Social Responsibility* (Washington DC, Brookings Institutions Press, 2005) 4ff.

[15] JM Diller, 'A Social Conscience in the Global Market? Labour Dimensions of Codes of Conduct, Social Labelling and Investors Initiatives' (1999) 138 *International Labour Review* 2; J Makower, *Beyond the Bottom Line* (New York, Simon and Schuster, 1994); G Teubner, 'Foreword: Legal Regimes of Global Non-state Actors' in G Teubner (ed), *Global Law Without a State* (Dartmouth, Aldershot, 1997) xiii-xvii.

The codes of conduct adopted by the TNCs are non-legal regulatory arrangements that aim to shape the corporate behaviour in the market-place by establishing benchmarks for both individual and organisational behaviour. They add a new dimension to the 'corporate charter,'[16] attempting to consolidate into the ethos of the TNCs a set of values and principles which, although not economic or financial in character, are seen as paramount in mitigating conflicting social interests. Generally speaking, such codes are hoped to encourage organisations to conduct business in ways which would benefit both themselves and the communities in which they operate. Such instruments are usually initiated in response to NGO campaigns, consumer or competitive pressures, to real or perceived threat of new legislation, regulation or trade sanctions, or a combination of these factors.

Being generated under this type of pressures, and if it stays unconnected to any other external and independent normative system, a code of conduct may well remain dependent upon these external and often difficult to mobilise pressures.[17] This makes the voluntary codes of conduct a contra-diction in terms, both with respect to the idea of civic virtue and with respect to the concept of 'voluntarism'; both these notions pre-supposing the relative absence of externally defining pressures.

SETTING THE SCENE FOR CORPORATE VOLUNTARISM: THE IGO INITIATIVES

Questioning the authenticity—in the Aristotelian sense—of the CSR as social virtue, would be one way of approaching these issues.[18] However, a more directly constructive way is to identify the points of tension where the nexus between human rights and corporate voluntarism might be questioned. Signs of the tensions existing in the discourse of voluntary human rights obligations of the business entities can be observed not only in the lack of significant impact of the codes,[19] but in the way in which the discourse of

[16] PA French, 'The Corporation as a Moral Person' in L May and S Hoffmann (eds), *Collective Responsibility: Five Decades of Debate in Theoretical and Applied Ethics* (Savage Md, Rowman & Littlefield Publishers, Inc, 1991) 133–51.

[17] C Forcese, *Commerce with Conscience? Human Rights and Corporate Codes of Conduct* (Montreal, International Centre for Human Rights and Democratic Development, 1997); J Murray, 'Corporate Codes of Conduct and Labour Standards' in R Kyloh (ed), *Mastering the Challenges of Globalization: Towards a Trade Union Agenda* (ILO, 1998) 45–115.

[18] RC Solomon, 'Aristotle, Ethics and Business Organizations' (2004) 25 *Organization Studies*, 1021–43.

[19] JM Diller, 'A Social Conscience in the Global Market? Labour Dimensions of Codes of Conduct, Social Labelling and Investors Initiatives', above n 15, at 17 ; J Murray, 'Corporate Codes of Conduct and Labour Standards', above n 17, at 110ff; C Forcese, *Commerce with Conscience? Human Rights and Corporate Codes of Conduct*, above n 17.

CSR is evolving in spheres beyond the voluntary codes, such as the IGOs generated documents.[20]

In order to understand the regulatory gap in which the voluntary codes emerged and proliferated, and to be able to grasp the tensions still existing between the voluntary nature of this type of mechanism and the essence of the human rights discourse, it is useful to look outside the voluntary codes, and especially to the CSR parameters offered by inter-governmental documents.

It was mentioned earlier that human rights obligations spelt out in the Universal Declaration of Human Rights addressed not only governments, but business enterprises as 'organs of society.' However, traditional views on human rights obligations still distinguish between public and private actors. The state is seen as the main entity responsible for implementing programmes to reduce poverty, to promote human development, and generally to protect and promote human rights. This once widely accepted dichotomy between state and non-state agencies is now increasingly being perceived as blurred.[21] Private actors, whose rights are established and enforced by state action, may now be deemed liable for violations of economic, social and cultural rights as well as often being seen as responsible, in conjunction with the state, for the implementation of policies that would enhance the realisation of these rights.

Of all the private actors taken into the partnership for addressing complex issues of human rights, TNCs are some of the most controversial. This is because of the reluctance of the less developed countries' governments to regulate TNCs and thus forfeit their chances for direct investment and, on the other hand, the unwillingness of the 'TNC exporting'—developed—countries to impose social responsibility on the corporations they send abroad.[22] The pressures from the different stakeholders for some kind of framework of human rights responsibility for corporations turned initially towards various intergovernmental settings. The most important of such initiatives took place in the 1970s, mainly via UN, ILO and OECD initiatives. The CSR parameters set initially through some of these initiatives reveal the ground on which the seeds of corporate voluntarism were sown, while the latest developments of

[20] O Schachter, 'The Erosion of State Authority and its Implications for Equitable Development', above n 11, at 41–42; FG Snyder, 'Governing Globalisation' in MB Likosky (ed), *Transnational Legal Processes* (Cambridge, Butterworths, 2002).

[21] O Schachter, 'The Erosion of State Authority and its Implications for Equitable Development', above n 11, at 31ff; G Teubner, '"Global Bukowina": Legal Pluralism in the World Society' in G Teubner (ed), *Global Law Without a State*, above n 15, at 3–28.

[22] R Gilpin, *The Political Economy of International Relations* (Princeton, Princeton University Press, 1987); W Greider, *One World, Ready or Not: The Manic Logic of Global Capitalism* (New York, Simon and Schuster, 1997); J Robinson, *Multinationals and Political Control* (Aldershot, Gower, 1983); J-Ph Robé, 'Multinational Enterprises: The Constitution of a Pluralistic Legal Order' in G Teubner (ed), *Global Law Without a State*, above n 15, at 45–77; O Schachter, 'The Erosion of State Authority and its Implications for Equitable Development', above n 11, at 31ff.

the same or similar initiatives allow us to have a glimpse of things to come in the field of voluntary codes of conduct.

As part of the process of globalisation of market economy, in the past three decades the activities of the TNCs in the less developed countries have multiplied considerably, mostly via direct investments. Capital mobility has increased considerably and, given the declining costs in transport and communications, TNCs have become 'footloose', acquiring an increased flexibility in choosing their bases. This situation gave TNCs an enormous bargaining power against the states and trade unions.[23] At the same time, some of the most immediate drawbacks of the TNCs' activities have started to emerge: environmental devastation, poor or non-existent labour standards, discrimination and child labour, to name only a few aspects.[24] Alongside these emerged increased pressures from various stakeholders for the activities of TNCs to be better regulated.

One of the first UN systematic attempts at regulating transnational corporations was the UN Centre for Transnational Corporations' initiative towards a code of conduct for TNCs (Draft Code).[25] The discussions around the Draft Code began in 1977 and were abandoned in 1992 without having reached an agreed enforceable treaty. This initiative was an attempt to make corporations assume responsibility for the complexity of their impact on the host countries, and not only for their bottom line results. In order to achieve these goals, UNCTC had the task of identifying the rights and responsibilities of both TNCs and of the countries in which they operated, systematising those findings and expressing them in a regulatory format which could then be uniformly and universally applied. The potential outcome of this initiative was a mutual supportiveness between the main stakeholders. A basis for co-operation was proposed, not between the TNCs' countries of origin and the TNCs' host countries, rather between the TNCs themselves and their host countries.

The proposed system was meant to empower TNCs, although not to the same extent as the later voluntary systems would do it.[26] If adopted and implemented, the Code would have had a significant impact upon the way in which the TNCs operated in their host countries. On the one hand, it would have confirmed the TNCs role as an important social actor collaborating in global governance policies. On the other hand, it would have created a basis for more clearly defined social responsibilities of TNCs in their host countries, especially in those countries where the law would not offer

[23] K Ohmae, *The Borderless World: Power and Strategy in the Interlinked Economy* (New York, Harperbusiness, 1990).

[24] N Klein, *No Logo* (London, Flamingo, 2000); G Monbiot, *Captive State: The Corporate Takeover of Britain* (London, Palgrave, 2000).

[25] *United Nations Code of Conduct on Transnational Corporations* (UNCTC, 1986).

[26] P Muchlinski, *Multinational Enterprises and the Law* (Oxford, Blackwell, 1995) 593–96.

the minimum desired social protection. Disclosure requirements, for instance, would have forced TNCs to provide information on issues from human rights to health and safety records of their employees, in countries where there are no such legal protections, as well as provide details of any prohibitions, restrictions and other regulatory measures imposed on their products in any other country. These provisions would have created the ground for the development of those rights related to work but also to health and environment.[27]

During the negotiations on the Draft Code, it was acknowledged that the TNCs were both part of the problem and of the solution regarding the negative impacts of the process of market globalisation.[28] However, in spite of some progress, difficult disagreements brought the negotiations to a halt, and in 1992 the UNCTC abandoned the Code. One of the major stumbling blocks (apart from the North–South tensions, which politicised even more the issues), was the issue related to the Code's position within the international law system and the United Nations' role in administering the Code. In other words, any hint, even in the 'softest' possible way, of an enforceable character of the Code and of a credible monitoring system was strongly opposed. Another message sent by the negotiations of the substantive elements of the Draft Code, a message which we will find reflected in the debate on the voluntary codes of conduct, was that consensus is difficult to achieve when dealing with a treaty that is too broad, and that obscure and imprecise language can only hamper achievement of the articulated goals.

Given that the first port of call for any TNC contribution to addressing the side effects of the process of free-market globalisation was in the areas of labour rights, one other international agency through which the negotiations between the need for regulation and the corporate preference for voluntarism took place was the International Labour Organisation (ILO). During the 1960s and 1970s the less developed countries (LDCs) increased their pressure on the international community for a legally binding code for the TNCs. At the ILO level, this pressure, however, could not countervail the very strong opposition from the employers' representatives, who favoured a voluntary code.

The result of this debate was the Tripartite Declaration of Principles Concerning Multinational Enterprises and Social Policy (the Declaration) adopted in 1977.[29] The Declaration stated the traditional link made between trade and development by emphasising the fact that the TNCs—or, in the language of the Declaration, the multinational enterprises (MNEs)—through

---

[27] UN CTC Reporter No 22, Autumn 1986 at: http://unctc.unctad.org/ data/ctcrep22a.pdf).
[28] *Ibid*, at 2 and also at 7–9.
[29] ILO, *Tripartite Declaration of Principles Concerning Multinational Enterprises and Social Policy (1977)* 17 ILM 422.

international direct investment, can bring substantial benefit to both home and host countries by contributing to a more efficient utilisation of capital, technology and labour. In engaging MNEs in the process of promoting human development, the Declaration went even further than restating this traditional, yet often contested, link. The Declaration recognised an even deeper correlation between the activity of the MNEs and human development by anticipating MNEs' potential to make an active contribution to the promotion of economic and social welfare, to the improvement of living standards and the satisfaction of basic needs, to the creation of employment opportunities, and to the enjoyment of basic human rights throughout the world.

The title of this ILO document, however, reveals two potential weaknesses. First of all, the word 'tripartite' reveals that the process through which this document came to life was a selective tool, considering only certain stakeholders: the governments of Member States of the ILO, the employers' organisations and the workers' organisations. Secondly, an even more important aspect of the nature of this document is revealed by the word 'declaration'. The Declaration only invites governments, the employers' and workers' organisations concerned and the MNEs operating in their territory, to observe the principles embodied in this document. The Declaration establishes as its aim 'to encourage the positive contribution which multinational enterprises can make to economic and social progress and to minimize and resolve the difficulties to which their various operations may give rise.'[30] In order to achieve this aim, it sets out principles in the areas of employment, training, conditions of work and life, as well as industrial relations, but the observance of these principles by the governments, employers' and workers' organizations and MNEs is set, yet again, on a voluntary basis.[31]

The Declaration, therefore, is not legally binding. It does not offer an easily available mechanism which can be used to redress a misuse of power by the MNEs, even when such a misuse breaches the Declaration itself. This aspect is considered by many as an important limitation of the potential of the Declaration to bring about any significant change in the ethos of the global market, by making it work more directly and foremost for the development of the weakest parts of the global society.

The fact that the Declaration initially did not provide for any follow-up machinery which would at least monitor the compliance with its principles, was (partially) rectified in 1980 by the ILO Governing Body which established a Committee on Multinational Enterprises. The basic functions of the Committee are to receive periodic reports on the implementation of the Declaration, reports which take the format of questionnaires sent to union and business organisations via the national governments; to conduct periodic

---

[30] *Ibid*, para 2.
[31] *Ibid*, para 7.

studies on labour issues related to the MNEs' activity; and to interpret the standards and principles contained in the Declaration. None of these functions, however, amount to an effective and comprehensive enforcement mechanism.

Another limitation is that the Declaration offers a rather conservative depiction of the MNEs engagement in global governance, in the sense that it does not require MNEs to engage in socially responsible activities over and above what is required by law in their host countries.

While there has been some progress regarding the supervision of compliance from the 1977 ILO Tripartite Declaration to the present,[32] the mechanisms instituted by the ILO remain a rather 'soft' tool.[33] However, through its well-established and coherent system of negotiated conventions, the ILO represents a source of inspiration and substance to be incorporated in other potential documents, such as voluntary codes of conduct adopted by TNCs. In this sense, it should be noted that the Secretary-General's declaration on the Global Compact refers to the ILO conventions as an authoritative source for labour standards which should be upheld by the TNCs.[34]

Similar—externally generated—attempts to 'teach' corporate citizens civic virtues and to involve them as partners in the civic duty of global governance have been made by other organisations. Just as the ILO document, these codes have taken the format of recommendations. Amongst the most used of such documents are the OECD Guidelines for Multinational Enterprises,[35] the Sweatshop and Clean Clothes Codes, the 'football codes' FIFA code and the Sialkot code.[36] Of all these CSR initiatives, the OECD Guidelines are probably the best known, given their inter-governmental origin and their broader applicability (as opposed to those codes designed for a particular industry).

The OECD Guidelines came as an attachment to a 1976 OECD document, The Declaration on International Investment and Multinational Enterprises.[37] In this format, the Guidelines are a legally non-binding instrument which only recommends multinational enterprises and OECD Member States to observe certain rules of conduct in the course of their economic activities in a host country. The observance of the Guidelines is, yet again, voluntary. Although in cases such as the OECD Guidelines, the codes have been agreed upon by a number of sovereign governments, this process has never reached to change a code's status from recommendation into international law

---

[32] P Alston, 'Labour Rights as Human Rights: The Not So Happy State of the Art' in P Alston (ed), *Labour Rights as Human Rights* (Oxford, Oxford University Press, 2005) 1–61.

[33] F Maupain, 'Is the ILO Effective in Upholding Labour Rights?: Reflections on the Myanmar Experience' in P Alston (ed), *Labour Rights as Human Rights, ibid*, 85–143.

[34] UN, 'A Compact for the New Century', at:
http://www.unglobalcompact.org/gc/unweb.nsf/webprintview/thenine.htm.

[35] OECD (1976) 'OECD Guidelines for Multinational Enterprises' 15 ILM 967–79.

[36] Clean Clothes Campaign, 'Codes of Conduct for Transnational Corporations: An Overview' at: http://www.cleanclothes.org/codes/overview.htm.

[37] OECD (1976) 'OECD Guidelines for Multinational Enterprises', 15 ILM 967–79.

norm. Given the strong opposition coming mainly from the corporate quarters, these institutional codes, therefore, have never reached to have a legally binding effect on the corporations or governments of those states who have adopted the code. The only obligations arising from them have therefore been moral, in the realm of the praxis of civic virtues, rather than capable of enforcement through use of external sanctions.

Moreover, up until 2000, the Guidelines gave absolute priority to national laws. Such priority of jurisdiction, often encountered in CSR documents, means that the obligations established can only supplement but never contradict obligations stemming from the national laws of the host states.[38] This bias towards the domestic law fuelled, rightly or wrongly, the demand for codes which would go (or would appear to go), further than this largely ineffective international document in protecting and promoting human rights and human development.

Ironically, the success of the corporate lobby in influencing the shaping of these international instruments, and in keeping the CSR in the vaguest possible terms, or devoid of any meaningful implementation teeth, backfired. Although some of these documents made some progress in defining CSR, they failed to capture the stakeholders' imagination and inspire trust. Documents such as the ILO Declaration or the OECD Guidelines could do nothing to address the roots of the corporate scandals related to human rights in the US arms industry or in the apparel and sports industries. These documents, as formulated in the 1970s, represented a fertile ground for the proliferation in the following two decades of both re-active and (after learning the rules of the 'CSR game'), pro-active voluntary codes of conduct. In this context, corporations looked upon internally generated codes of business ethics as a way of promoting self-regulation which would fend off consumer and investor criticism yet keep at bay government intervention and legally enforceable regulatory actions. These two corporate interests led very fast to an institutionalisation of business ethics programmes, taking a variety of forms, yet largely dominated by voluntary codes of conduct.[39]

THE VOLUNTARY CODES OF CONDUCT AND HUMAN RIGHTS NEXUS

In the past decade the voluntary codes of conduct have been the object of both business and academic attention abundantly in the past decade.[40] As

---

[38] Clean Clothes Campaign, 'Codes of Conduct for Transnational Corporations: An Overview', above n 36.

[39] J Murray, 'Corporate Codes of Conduct and Labour Standards', above n 17, at 47ff.

[40] A Wawryk, 'Regulating Transnational Corporations Through Corporate Codes of Conduct' in J Fynas and S Pegg (eds), *Transnational Corporations and Human Rights* (Basingstoke, Palgrave Macmillan, 2003) 54; JM Diller, 'A Social Conscience in the Global Market? Labour Dimensions of Codes of Conduct, Social Labelling and Investors Initiatives',

in the case of any other regulatory instrument which would try to negotiate between competing interests (or, to put it more generally, between competing social discourses), the voluntary codes of conduct have revealed a series of tensions. Some of the points of tension of these codes are of a particular importance with respect to human rights, especially in the context of the corporate partnership in the global governance processes.[41] These points of tension relate mainly to the fact that human rights, as a socially constructed concept, sits in an uncomfortable and controversial position on the platform of corporate voluntarism as form of social action. This uncomfortable position relates to a couple of basic questions which stem from the social importance assigned to the human rights discourse: Who is selecting the human rights values to be championed by the corporate citizens? Who is defining those human rights values? What gives those values consistency, and thus aspirational value towards a socially defined notion of justice?

Human rights have been recognised in many voluntary codes as an important dimension of corporate social responsibility. However, more often than not, the corporate codes avoid using the human rights concepts in a precise and focused manner.[42] Consequently, it becomes very difficult to know (even by those from within the corporation with sufficient good will to abide by the values included in the codes) what those human rights at particular risk from the activities of a particular corporation are, and indeed what human rights are at all. The reason for this ambiguity is somewhat due to the same tendency which has left the externally generated standards (such as UN, ILO, OECD) half way on the road to effective regulation: the desire to keep the business ethics in the realm of voluntary action. A way of securing this voluntary dimension is not only by keeping the CSR outside the realm of externally enforceable regulation, but by keeping the CSR in the realm of ambiguous boundaries.[43] One way of doing this

---

above n 15, at 17; C Forcese, *Commerce with Conscience? Human Rights and Corporate Codes of Conduct*, above n 17; J Murray, 'Corporate Codes of Conduct and Labour Standards', above n 17, at 45–115.

[41] S Joseph, 'An Overview of the Human Rights Accountability of Multinational Enterprises' in M Kamminga and S Zia-Zarifi (eds), *Liability of Multinational Corporations under International Law* (The Hague, Kluwer Law International, 2000) 75ff; Amnesty International UK Business Group, *Human Rights Guidelines for Companies* (London, Amnesty International, 1998); JG Fynam and S Pegg (eds), *Transnational Corporations and Human Rights.*

[42] M Page and LF Spira, 'Ethical Codes, Independence and the Conservation of Ambiguity' (2005) 14 *Business Ethics: A European Review* 306–08; Clean Clothes Campaign, 'Codes of Conduct for Transnational Corporations: An Overview'; J Murray, 'Corporate Codes of Conduct and Labour Standards', above n 17.; HW Baade, *Codes of Conduct for MNEs: An Introductory Survey* in N Horn, *Legal Problems of Codes of Conduct for MNEs* (Antwerp, 1980) 441.

[43] K Webb and A Morrison, 'The Law and Voluntary Codes: Examining the "Tangled Web"' in K Webb (ed), *Voluntary Codes: Private Governance, the Public Interest and Innovation* (Ottawa, Carleton University Research Unit for Innovation, Science and the Environment, 2002) 94; D Kinley and J Tadaki, 'From Talk to Walk: The Emergence of Human Rights Responsibilities for Corporations at International Law' (2004) 44 *Virginia Journal of International Law* 957.

is to avoid the reference to the more exact terminology and definitions used in international human rights law. Referring directly to these definitions, it is feared, would create the danger of contamination with the legal discourse and, potentially, could generate new liabilities, both outside and inside the law.

This vagueness in the human rights provisions included in the voluntary codes is related also to another important issue regarding the CSR instruments: the selection of participants involved in the drafting of the codes. While the content of the corporate codes of conduct comes more easily under scrutiny, companies are seldom questioned as to who participates in the drafting of their codes. While, for instance, the top human resource executives are most likely to be consulted in the drafting of a voluntary code of conduct, or even with employee representatives,[44] very few companies consult with organisations specialised in monitoring the implementation of human rights at the national or international level.[45] The BP, for instance, has adopted this latter approach regarding the human rights impact of the Baku-Tbilisi-Ceyhan (BTC) pipeline project. However, this approach has been adopted only after serious concerns have siphoned out into the public domain. Moreover, the project is still in question both with respect to the domestic law of the countries of operation and with respect to international human rights standards.[46]

The lack of involvement of specialised human rights organisations in the writing of the codes questions the issue of what exactly is incorporated in the codes. If the defining of the human rights concepts remains either unaddressed (as we mentioned above) or is left to the interpretation of the corporation's senior executives, the question is what guarantees the substance of the standards incorporated in the code of conduct? And, placing the issue in the wider picture, what guarantees the consistency of the thus internalised human rights?

Similar concerns are raised with respect to the monitoring of the voluntary codes in general and especially with respect to the human rights clauses. The general issue regarding voluntary codes of conduct is that often the codes do not include any, or hardly any, monitoring mechanism.[47] In the

---

[44] Clean Clothes Campaign, 'Codes of Conduct for Transnational Corporations: An Overview'; ILO, *Corporate Codes of Conduct*: http://www.itcilo.it/english/actrav/telearn/global/ilo/code/main.htm at 7.

[45] Danish Institute for Human Rights, Human Rights and Business Project, *Human Rights Compliance Assessment*: http://www.humanrightsbusiness.org/020_project_publications.htm, 2004.

[46] Amnesty International, *Human Rights on the Line: The Baku-Tbilisi-Ceyhan Pipeline Project*: www.amnesty.org.uk/business, May 2003.

[47] World Bank Group, *Implementation Mechanisms for Codes of Conduct*. Study prepared for the CSR Practice Foreign Investment Advisory Service Investment Climate Department: http://www.ifc.org/ifcext/economics.nsf/AttachmentsByTitle/Implementation+mechanisms/$FILE/Implementation+mechanisms.pdf, November 2004; Clean Clothes Campaign, *Codes, Monitoring and Verification*: http://www.cleanclothes.org/codes/monitoring.htm; US Labor

KPMG survey of 251 Canadian companies in 1996, for instance, it was revealed that just over 40 per cent of the participant companies in that survey had a senior-level manager whose role specifically included the implementation, monitoring, or assurance of the ethics programme.[48] Thus, a first concern would be that in almost 60 per cent of the cases, the human rights standards or any other standards included in the voluntary code are not monitored.

The other more specific issue, however, is that the substance and consistency of human rights principles and standards are frequently left to well-intended but often inexperienced (human rights wise) human resources managers. Although the number of companies that use an outside auditor is on the increase,[49] only a limited number of companies make use of such an assurance mechanism, and even fewer companies take such an auditor from among the human rights specialised NGOs. A survey of the existing US codes of conduct undertaken in the late 1990s revealed, for instance, that most monitoring conducted by US corporations primarily covers quality control issues, usually with relatively little interaction between monitors on the one hand, and workers and the local community on the other. More importantly, the survey also revealed that in most cases, monitors have a technical background in production and quality control and are relatively untrained with regard to the implementation of the different social standards included in the codes they are monitoring.[50]

Moreover, in a global market economy where the connection between the brand company and the production outlet is often very loose and non-hierarchical, the monitoring is often left to the buying agents.[51] This procedure avoids the financial and logistical burden of monitoring, as well as the public accountability risk. At the same time, it also removes the corporation from the direct line of control in implementing its CSR policies. The Children's Rights Division at Human Rights Watch, for instance, has campaigned repeatedly for a more effective monitoring and implementation of children's rights by both governments and businesses.[52] In spite of this,

Department, *The Apparel Industry and Codes of Conduct: A Solution to the International Child Labor Problem?* Child Labour Report 2005: http://www.dol.gov/ILAB/media/reports/iclp/apparel/main.htm.

[48] KPMG, Business Ethics Survey Report: http://www.itcilo.it/english/actrav/telearn/global/ilo/code/1997kpmg.htm; ILO, *Corporate Codes of Conduct*: http://www.itcilo.it/english/actrav/telearn/global/ilo/code/main.htm.

[49] ILO, *Corporate Codes of Conduct*: http://www.itcilo.it/english/actrav/telearn/global/ilo/code/main.htm.

[50] US Labor Department, *The Apparel Industry and Codes of Conduct: A Solution to the International Child Labor Problem?* Child Labour Report 2005: http://www.dol.gov/ILAB/media/reports/iclp/apparel/main.htm.

[51] ILO, *Corporate Codes of Conduct*: http://www.itcilo.it/english/actrav/telearn/global/ilo/code/main.htm.

[52] Human Rights Watch, *Human Rights Watch Comments on the UN Special Session on Children Draft Provisional Outcome Document 'A World Fit for Children'*: http://www.hrw.org/press/2001/09/childstate.htm.

monitoring the implementation of child labour provisions of various codes of conduct remains very challenging, both because of the lack of use of expert monitoring mechanisms and because of the nature of the global mechanisms of production.

Generally, the closer the relationship between an importer and the actual producer of the imported items, the greater the ability of the importing company (usually a transnational company originating in a developed country) to influence substandard human rights practices in the production process (usually based in a developing country), including the prohibition of child labour. However, these days there can often be up to five steps between the producer and the final buyer, with layers and layers of buying agents, contractors and sub-contractors. This layering of the production chain reduces significantly the ability of the retailer company to influence significantly labour practices abroad.[53] Often, such companies include in their codes of conduct a statement of principles regarding various human rights values (such as the protection of children against abusive labour practices or non-discrimination in the work place, etc), and then they rely on unmonitored self-certification processes throughout the production chain. Only a very small proportion of the TNCs using a code of conduct have volunteered so far for stringent and comprehensive monitoring mechanisms.[54]

Another area where the voluntarism of the corporate codes can be perceived as being at odds with the importance assigned to the human rights values imported in those codes, concerns the enforcement provisions present or, more correctly, absent from these codes. Most corporate codes of conduct include no enforcement provisions and are not specific regarding enforcement measures.[55] If the issue is addressed at all, it is usually covered by vague statements such as in the Boeing code, which states that 'violations of the company standards of conduct are cause for appropriate corrective action.'[56] Very few corporations go as far as in the Halliburton code, which states clearly disciplinary measures for non-compliance with the code, ranging from counselling to demotion, reduction in salary or even termination of employment. Moreover, the Halliburton code acknowledges the importance of the chains of command and responsibility when specifying that

---

[53] World Bank Group, *Implementation Mechanisms for Codes of Conduct.* Study prepared for the CSR Practice Foreign Investment Advisory Service Investment Climate Department: http://www.ifc.org/ifcext/economics.nsf/AttachmentsByTitle/Implementation+mechanisms/$FILE/Implementation+mechanisms.pdf, November 2004, at 35–36.

[54] United Nations Research Institute for Social Development (UNRISD), *Corporate Social Responsibility and Development: Towards a New Agenda?*: http://www.unrisd.org/publications, (November 2003 36-7.

[55] ILO, *Corporate Codes of Conduct*: http://www.itcilo.it/english/actrav/telearn/global/ilo/code/main.htm.

[56] Boeing Ethics and Business Conduct Programme, 3(D): http://www.boeing.com/companyoffices/aboutus/ethics/pro3.pdf.

persons subject to such disciplinary measures will be not only the direct violators of the code, but the persons who condoned the violation or failed to use reasonable care in detecting a violation.[57]

While such positions are laudable, it is still important to bear in mind that without specialised input in the definition of the standards included in the codes, the ones who shape those standards remain largely the corporations. We return, therefore, to the question of what the special status of the corporation is in the global governance processes, so that it is allowed not only to collaborate in the process of defining those standards but actually to define them. It is important to acknowledge the incentive which TNCs can bring in their supply chain for compliance with human rights standards. However, it is just as important that those standards are in keeping with the internationally-established human rights norms, and that they are monitored and enforced independently and authoritatively. Could this be done via voluntary codes of conduct as they are predominantly tabled at the moment? Maybe; however, so far, no voluntary authoritative mechanism has proved acceptable to the main, if not all, stakeholders.[58] This brings us to a new phase in the process of defining the concept of corporate responsibility, a process in which we witness a symbolic (if not substantial, for the time being), erosion of voluntary approach to human rights as a dimension of CSR.

CORPORATE VOLUNTARISM: *QUO VADIS?*

Where does one go from here? As mentioned earlier, occasionally, there are corporate codes of conduct which include relatively credible mechanisms of monitoring and implementation. This path taken by some TNCs and other business enterprises erodes the absolute voluntary character of the codes themselves. An even stronger evidence of this erosion of the reliance on voluntarism is reflected through the way mechanisms other than the corporate-generated codes are evolving.

One such way in which the dilution of the voluntary approach to human rights is attempted consists in designating certain authoritative international human rights documents that the corporate citizens would have to comply with, whether those documents have been incorporated formally into the corporate charter or not. One such step was taken within the ILO in 1998 through the adoption of the ILO Declaration on Fundamental

---

[57] Halliburton Code of Business Conduct: http://www.halliburton.com/about/business_conduct.jsp.

[58] T Campbell, 'Global Justice, Human Rights and Multinational Corporations' (2004) 5 *Australian Journal of Professional and Applied Ethics* 53–70; G Wood, G Svensson, J Singh, E Carasco and M Callaghan, 'Implementing the Ethos of Corporate Codes of Ethics: Australia, Canada and Sweden' 13 *Business Ethics: A European Review* 389.

Principles and Rights at Work.[59] Addressing the need for socially responsible actions on the part of corporations, this document represents an important symbolic step toward a more consistent body of CSR by setting itself up as the foundation upon which individual corporate social policies must be built. The Declaration was adopted by the International Labour Conference in June 1998, two decades after the ILO Tripartite Declaration, and it emphasises the particular importance of a set of ILO Conventions, namely: the conventions referring to freedom of association and the effective recognition of the rights to collective bargaining; the elimination of all forms of forced or compulsory labour; the effective abolition of child labour; and the elimination of discrimination in respect of employment and occupation.

The very important aspect which makes this document a step towards the regulatory consolidation of at least certain dimensions of the CSR, and especially of the voluntary codes of conduct as CSR mechanisms, is the fact that the Declaration states that all Members, *even if they have not ratified the Conventions in question*, have an obligation arising from their very membership in the ILO, to respect, promote and realise, in good faith and in accordance with the Constitution, the principles concerning the fundamental rights which are the subject of those conventions.[60] Given that the ILO membership involves a partnership between the government and the most representative organisations of employers and workers, this declaration acquires a particular importance for the way in which corporations assimilate the rights protected through those Conventions into their agenda.

Of course, this attempt to impress the ILO Conventions upon the CSR policies does not make the 1998 ILO Declaration a perfect tool for corporate social action. Other dimensions of the voluntarism imbued in the concept of CSR are still to be contended with. While, for instance, there has been some progress regarding the supervision of compliance from the 1977 ILO Tripartite Declaration to the 1998 Declaration,[61] it is still not a real enforcement mechanism. However, the 1998 Declaration represents a step forward towards a tighter definition of the rights to be included in the corporate social policies and corporate codes of conduct.

Similarly important changes have taken place regarding the OECD Guidelines. Since being adopted in 1976, the Guidelines have been updated

[59] ILO *'Declaration on Fundamental Principles and Rights at Work'*, International Labour Organisation, Geneva 1998: http://www.ilo.org/punlic/english/standards/decl/declaration/tindex.htm.

[60] ILO *'Declaration on Fundamental Principles and Rights at Work'* para 2, International Labour Organisation, Geneva 1998, at: http://www.ilo.org/punlic/english/standards/decl/declaration/tindex.htm.

[61] The 1998 ILO Declaration generated a Committee of Experts on the Application of Conventions and Recommendations, who give their opinion on the application of the ratified Conventions and provide guidance on how to apply the set standards in specific circumstances. ILO Declaration, 1998, Annex, para 2.

periodically. None of the updates, however, has been more thoroughgoing than the latest, the OECD Guidelines Review 2000.[62] As mentioned earlier, the original (1976) Guidelines focused on the MNEs compliance with the national law and practice of the host country. The revised (2000) Guidelines now place the emphasis on MNEs' obligations in relation to a range of international standards. The profile of international law is now much higher than in the original Guidelines, with explicit references to a number of international instruments such as the 1948 Universal Declaration of Human Rights, and the 1998 ILO Declaration. Moreover, the revised Guidelines now use the regulatory technique of directly specifying a number of standards to be met, requesting MNEs to engage in conduct consistent with all of the core labour standards of the ILO 1998 Declaration. While the new OECD revised Guidelines remain largely a non-regulatory instrument, they go one step further away from the realm of voluntary CSR standards.

Since the aim of the OECD Guidelines is to offer exactly what it says in the title, ie, a set of guidelines to both governments and corporations as to the standards of corporate responsibility to be followed, the fact that these guidelines have become more precise by referring to important human rights and labour standards documents is of great significance.[63] For those corporations in search of a CSR tool, the Guidelines constitute yet another opportunity, to give more substance to their social policies by referring to transnational documents such as the OECD Guidelines and the ILO 1998 Declaration.

Using this type of document as point of reference has been endorsed in particular by the UN Secretary General Kofi Annan's Global Compact initiative in 1999. This initiative was taken in an attempt to build up the attractiveness of CSR. The values and principles proposed in the Global Compact are not necessarily new: human rights, labour standards and environmental protection, each of them with its specific impact on human development.[64] Regarding human rights, the Global Compact requires corporations to support and respect the protection of the recognised international human rights within their own sphere of influence and to make sure that they are not complicit in human rights abuses. The Global Compact, however, took a different attitude towards voluntarism than the other transnational CSR initiatives and, rather than proposing ways to address

[62] OECD, *Guidelines for Multinational Enterprises: Decision of the Council* (OECD, June 2000) at: http://www.oecd.org/daf/investment/guidelines/decision.htm; J Murray, 'Corporate Codes of Conduct and Labour Standards', above n 17, at 261.

[63] P Muchlinski, 'Human Rights and Multinationals: Is there a problem?' (2001) 77 *International Affairs* 31.

[64] UN, 'Secretary-General Proposes Global Compact on Human Rights, Labour, Environment, in Address to World Economic Forum in Davos' (UN Press Release, 1 February 1999 [SG/SM/6881]) at: http://www.unglobalcompact.org.

the weaknesses of the corporate voluntarism identified earlier, it chose to encourage it, thereby legitimising voluntarism and self-regulation as major tools for addressing the human rights and global market issues.[65] In this context, voluntary codes of conduct become, yet again, confirmed as tools in addressing human development in those parts of the world where governments cannot protect their own citizens against the market failures and the side-effects of the process of globalisation. However, the apparent loose attitude towards enforcement and monitoring professed through the Global Compact should be put in context; and the context, part of which is represented by the international CSR documents, seems to be moving slowly towards a hardening of the corporate social responsibilities.

While the UN Global Compact represents a rather novel approach to CSR, an approach based exclusively on the idea of partnership between the UN and business,[66] the problematic relationship between human rights and voluntarism in the corporate action context hasn't remained totally unaddressed at the UN level. After years of consultations and negotiations, in August 2003, the Sub-Commission on the Protection and Promotion of Human Rights within the UN Commission on Human Rights, adopted the 'Norms on the Responsibilities of Transnational Corporations and other Business Enterprises with Regard to Human Rights' ('the Norms').[67]

Unlike the Global Compact, the UN Norms address directly all the tension points referred to above when discussing the voluntary dimension of the corporate codes of conduct: the substance of the human rights to be included in a CSR document; the enforcement and the monitoring mechanisms; and also, the issue of the stakeholders' involvement.[68]

First of all, the UN Norms link CSR to a very comprehensive list of rights: civil and political human rights, socio-economic and cultural rights, 'third generation' rights referring to human development as well as to community rights. The UN Norms also refer to specific issues formally outside the human rights agenda, yet with a deep impact on communities in the context of global market economy, such as marketing and advertising practices, as well as safety and quality of goods and services.[69] The way in which the UN Norms generate this list of human rights is by referring to a comprehensive list of international documents which offer the substance of

---

[65] Amnesty International, *Amnesty International and the United Nations Global Compact*: http://web.amnesty.org/pages/ec-globalcompact-eng.

[66] UN, *Guidelines: Cooperation Between the United Nations and the Business Community* (UN, 13 July 2000 at: http://www.unglobalcompact.org).

[67] UNHCHR, *Norms on the responsibilities of transnational corporations and other business enterprises with regard to human rights* (UN Doc E/CN.4/Sub.2/2003/12/Rev2, 26 August 2003).

[68] S Deva, 'UN's Human Rights Norms for Transnational Corporations and Other Business Enterprises : An Imperfect Step in the Right Direction ?' (2004) 10 *ILSA Journal of International Comparative Law* 496.

[69] UN Norms, Parts A–G.

each particular right.[70] By doing this, the UN Norms specify the human rights obligations for TNCs and any other business enterprise. These obligations referred to in the Norms are expressed in terms of 'shall', giving the signal of a moral, if not yet legal, imperative. Moreover, international human rights law appear in the UN Norms to be given authoritative precedence over the domestic law of a TNC's host country.[71] As to the prospect that the Norms would become something more than just 'soft law,' the document establishes a dynamic relation with the CSR concept; while resting upon international human rights law, it also forecasts that the Norms 'will contribute to *the making and development of international law*' which will address the corporate responsibilities and obligations.[72]

The specificity regarding the human rights placed on the corporate agenda via the UN Norms is expected to affect the corporate codes of conduct by offering the codes a firm point of reference which will fill in some of the regulatory gaps and offer more substance to corporate documents. This expectation that the UN Norms will end up being used for grafting the corporate social policies, ie, their codes of conduct, is confirmed by the discussions of the UN Working Group on the UN Draft Norms and the Commentary on the Norms which took place prior to their adoption.[73]

Moreover, the Norms require that each corporation 'shall adopt, disseminate and implement *internal rules of operation* in compliance with the Norms.'[74] This process is most likely to happen via the adoption of, or re-designing of already existing codes of conduct. However, when informed by the UN Norms, these codes will have lost that dimension of voluntarism which was given by the non-specificity of the codes with regard to the human rights values they are purporting to protect and promote. This loss occurs because of the increase in specificity of the UN Norms which, while in themselves staying in the realm of generality, refer expressly to authoritative sets of standards established via recognised international documents.

Internally generated, yet externally inspired, codes are not presented in the UN Norms as the only way to promote and protect human rights in the context of corporate action. The weaknesses of voluntarism in the context of corporate human rights action are acknowledged in the UN Norms through the recognition of the role of the state and the importance of regulation. In this sense, moving on from the past two decades of corporate voluntary actions in the human rights sphere, the Norms affirm that states

---

[70] UN Norms, Preamble and General Obligations.

[71] UN Norms, Part A: Respect for National Sovereignty and Human Rights, [10] and also [4].

[72] UN Norms, Preamble (emphasis added).

[73] UN Working Group 2002 on the Draft Norms on the responsibilities of transnational corporations and other business enterprises with regard to human rights. Report (UN Doc. E/CN.4/Sub.2/2002/13 15 August 2002) and Draft Commentary (UN Doc.E/CN.4/Sub.2/2003/WG.2/WP.1).

[74] UN Norms, Part H: General Provisions of Implementation (emphasis added).

'should establish and reinforce the necessary *legal and administrative framework*' for ensuring that the Norms and other relevant national and international laws are implemented by transnational corporations and other business enterprises.[75] In other words, the UN Norms break the taboo-like attitude to CSR regulation and look beyond voluntarism, asserting the need for a firmer legal basis for the protection and promotion of human rights.[76]

Apart from bringing specificity in the human rights standards, specificity which could potentially be imported and built into the corporate codes and policies, the UN Norms also address the very important issue of implementation of the prescribed human rights by the corporations. Not only do the Norms stipulate the imperative of adopting, disseminating and implementing internal rules of operation in compliance with the Norms (ie, externally inspired codes of conduct), they require that the business entities shall apply and incorporate these Norms in their contracts or other arrangements and dealings with contractors, subcontractors, suppliers, licensees, distributors, or natural or other legal persons that enter into any agreement with them.[77] Therefore, according to the UN Norms, a TNC's social responsibility for human rights protection and implementation is likely to cover its whole chain of production and distribution, regardless of the number of steps this chain might consist of. Adopting codes of conduct and implementing them within the narrow circle of production, will not be sufficient anymore in demonstrating an effective and comprehensive human rights policy.

Moreover, in order to stimulate implementation, the UN Norms demand that, through their CSR documents and policies, corporations *shall* provide prompt, effective and adequate reparation to those persons, entities and communities that have been adversely affected by failures to comply with the Norms.[78] This type of provision was very seldom, if at all, used during the two decades of corporate voluntary codes of conduct.

No implementation mechanism would be complete without a transparent and independent monitoring system and the UN Norms make provisions for such a system. Within this system, of course, TNCs and other business organisations are required to conduct periodic evaluations concerning the impact of their own activities on human rights. The UN Norms, however, go further by demanding that transnational corporations and other business enterprises shall be subject to periodic monitoring and verification of their compliance with the Norms, both by the United Nations and by 'other

---

[75] UN Norms, Part H: General Provisions of Implementation, [15] (emphasis added).

[76] C Hillemanns, 'UN Norms on the Responsibilities of Transnational Corporations and Other Business Enterprises with Regard to Human Rights' (2003) *4 German Law Journal* 1068; S Deva, 'UN's Human Rights Norms for Transnational Corporations and Other Business Enterprises: An Imperfect Step in the Right Direction ?' above n 68 at 498–99.

[77] UN Norms, Part H: General Provisions of Implementation .

[78] UN Norms, Part H: General Provisions of Implementation, [18].

international and national mechanisms already in existence *or yet to be created.'*[79] The UN Norms also demand that the monitoring system shall take into account input from stakeholders, including from non-governmental organisations.[80] Following the development of the CSR policies so far, it is conceivable that this type of complex and comprehensive monitoring system will acquire in time a significant presence in the monitoring of the (increasingly less voluntary) corporate codes of conduct.

From the analysis of the documents generated at three important levels of the transnational discourse of corporate responsibility (ILO, OECD and the UN), one can perceive that, in less than a decade, potentially significant progress has been made in acknowledging and dealing with the points of tension between the imperative nature of the human rights discourse and the corporate voluntarism. A striving for tighter definitions and authoritative specificity, for comprehensiveness and effectiveness, reveal, at least in some quarters, an aspiration for CSR structures and processes where corporate voluntarism is carefully managed through externally induced human rights standards and substance; in other words, where self-regulation is gradually converted into interactive regulation.

CONCLUSIONS

In the present format, the process of acquisition of human rights via business practices is riddled with tensions. Many of these tensions are rooted at the confluence between the human rights discourse and the notion of corporate voluntary social action. Due to the important, some would say privileged position occupied by the TNCs and other business organisations in the world, this type of acquisition of human rights is expected to continue to play a role in the global governance processes. However, as it could be inferred from the changes taking place in the CSR discourse, changes reflected in the development of international CSR initiatives, the process of acquisition of human rights via business practices is likely to develop new features.

Up until the mid 1990s, the voluntary codes of conduct–while being instrumental in putting certain human rights on the corporate agenda–have played a role mainly in fending off responsibility. In the past years though, there have been indications that, if the acquisition of human rights via business practices is to continue and improve, this is likely to happen on very different terms. The latest changes in the ILO, OECD and UN CSR documents give a good indication as to what those terms could be. Three important documents–the 1998 ILO Declaration, the revised OECD Guidelines

---

[79] UN Norms, Part H: General Provisions of Implementation, [16] (emphasis added).
[80] *Ibid.*

and especially the UN Norms–address the points of tension between voluntarism and human rights. The type of corporate human rights responsibility promoted by these documents is firmly anchored in the substance of international human rights documents and it addresses the very important issues of implementation, monitoring and stakeholders participation. In other words, they strive to fill in the gaps of the voluntary mechanisms brought about mainly through the corporate codes of conduct.

Of course, one cannot ignore the fact that these documents, including the UN Norms, are legally non-binding, part of the 'soft law' concretising the CSR. However, it is well documented that the boundary between 'soft law' and 'hard law' can shift, and what today appears as 'soft' regulation, tomorrow might be instrumental in a 'hard law' application. Such applications have already been developed tentatively, via the use of domestic tort law or consumer protection regulation. From this perspective, and taking into account their historical evolution over the past three decades, the voluntary codes of conduct fulfil a useful role, if only one of confirming that pure voluntarism in the human rights domain creates insuperable tensions. In so doing, the voluntary codes facilitate the furthering of the CSR debate.

Human rights, therefore, might still be acquired in the future, in the less developed parts of the world, through the business practices of the TNCs. However, it is hoped that this kind of social influence of the TNCs will progressively take place according to corporate responsibilities which have been decided, not exclusively through processes internal to the TNC, but rather through social debate and stakeholder participation, and which are based on independent mechanisms of implementation and monitoring. It is at this stage (and this stage only), when the defining elements of a CSR system have been established openly and democratically, that the TNCs, as stakeholders in the global governance processes, will be able to legitimately use their corporate power and aggregate creativity in order to generate their own social practice of human rights compliance, thus contributing to the development of a corporate human rights jurisprudence.